PROFESSOR RICHARD B. LILLICH (1933-1996)
Photograph courtesy of University of Virginia School of Law

INTERNATIONAL LAW STUDIES

VOLUME 77

# INTERNATIONAL LAW STUDIES

Volume 77

Lillich on the Forcible Protection of Nationals Abroad

In Memory of Professor Richard B. Lillich

Thomas C. Wingfield
James E. Meyen
*Editors*

Naval War College
Newport, Rhode Island
2002

Library of Congress Cataloging-in-Publication Data

Lillich, Richard B.
Lillich on the forcible protection of nationals abroad : in memory of professor Richard B. Lillich / Thomas C. Wingfield, James E. Meyen, editors.
    p. cm.--(International law studies ; v. 77)
   Includes index.
   ISBN 1-884733-23-9 (alk. paper)
   1. Intervention (International law) 2. Diplomatic protection. I. Wingfield, Thomas C. II. Meyen, James E. III. Title. IV. Series.

JX1295 .U4 vol. 77
[KZ6368]
341.5'84--dc21

                                         2002011813

# Contents

## Lillich on the Forcible Protection of Nationals Abroad

FOREWORD. . . . . . . . . . . . . . . . . . . . . . . . . . . . . . . . . . . . . . . . . . . . . . . . . . xi
INTRODUCTION . . . . . . . . . . . . . . . . . . . . . . . . . . . . . . . . . . . . . . . . . . . . . xiii
PREFACE . . . . . . . . . . . . . . . . . . . . . . . . . . . . . . . . . . . . . . . . . . . . . . . . . . . xv

RICHARD B. LILLICH (1933–1996): A TRIBUTE
Professor Robert F. Turner . . . . . . . . . . . . . . . . . . . . . . . . . . . . . . . . . . . . . xix

Author's Note . . . . . . . . . . . . . . . . . . . . . . . . . . . . . . . . . . . . . . . . . . . . . . xxvii

I. The Classical Publicists . . . . . . . . . . . . . . . . . . . . . . . . . . . . . . . . . . . . 1
    A.    Grotius . . . . . . . . . . . . . . . . . . . . . . . . . . . . . . . . . . . . . . . . . . . . 1
    B.    Wolff . . . . . . . . . . . . . . . . . . . . . . . . . . . . . . . . . . . . . . . . . . . . . 3
    C.    Vattel . . . . . . . . . . . . . . . . . . . . . . . . . . . . . . . . . . . . . . . . . . . . . 3

II. The Traditional Writers on International Law . . . . . . . . . . . . . . . . . . . . . . . 7
    A.    Phillimore . . . . . . . . . . . . . . . . . . . . . . . . . . . . . . . . . . . . . . . . . 7
    B.    Bluntschli . . . . . . . . . . . . . . . . . . . . . . . . . . . . . . . . . . . . . . . . . 8
    C.    Bonfils . . . . . . . . . . . . . . . . . . . . . . . . . . . . . . . . . . . . . . . . . . . 10
    D.    Pradier-Fodere . . . . . . . . . . . . . . . . . . . . . . . . . . . . . . . . . . . . . 11
    E.    Westlake . . . . . . . . . . . . . . . . . . . . . . . . . . . . . . . . . . . . . . . . . 11
    F.    Oppenheim . . . . . . . . . . . . . . . . . . . . . . . . . . . . . . . . . . . . . . . 12
    G.    Moore . . . . . . . . . . . . . . . . . . . . . . . . . . . . . . . . . . . . . . . . . . . 12
    H.    Stockton . . . . . . . . . . . . . . . . . . . . . . . . . . . . . . . . . . . . . . . . . 12
    I.    Clark . . . . . . . . . . . . . . . . . . . . . . . . . . . . . . . . . . . . . . . . . . . 13

|     |                                                              |     |
| --- | ------------------------------------------------------------ | --- |
| J.  | Hodges                                                       | 13  |
| K.  | Borchard                                                     | 14  |
| L.  | Fauchille                                                    | 15  |
| M.  | Hyde                                                         | 16  |
| N.  | Winfield                                                     | 16  |
| O.  | Offutt                                                       | 17  |
| P.  | Dunn                                                         | 18  |
| Q.  | Hindmarsh                                                    | 18  |
| R.  | Accioly                                                      | 19  |

III. State Practice During the Pre-United Nations Period............25
    A. French Blockade of Argentina. 1838–1840.................25
    B. Great Britain, Spain and France in Mexico. 1861..........26
    C. Great Britain and Abyssinia. 1867–1868..................27
    D. Great Britain in Honduras. 1873........................29
    E. Great Britain and France in Egypt. 1876–1879............29
    F. France and Portugal. 1893–1894........................30
    G. Boxer Rebellion, China. 1900..........................31
    H. Franco-Turkish Conflict. 1901.........................32
    I. Great Britain, Germany and Italy in Venezuela. 1902.....33
    J. Italian Invasion of Corfu. 1923........................33
    K. French Bombardment of Damascus. 1925.................34
    L. Japan and China. 1931–1932...........................35
    M. Germany in Czechoslovakia. 1938......................36

IV. Contemporary Case Studies of United States Forcible Protection of Nationals Abroad..............................................41
    A. Lebanon. 1958.......................................42
    B. The Congo. 1964....................................49
    C. The Dominican Republic. 1965........................57
    D. Iran. 1980..........................................64

V. Contemporary Case Studies of Non-United States Forcible Protection of Nationals Abroad..............................................97
    A. Suez Crisis. 1956....................................98
    B. Belgium in the Congo. 1960..........................98
    C. France in Mauritania. 1977...........................99
    D. France and Belgium in Zaire. 1978...................100
    E. France in Mauritania. 1978..........................101

|   |   |   |
|---|---|---|
| F. | France in Chad. 1978. | 101 |
| G. | France in Chad. 1979. | 103 |
| H. | France in Mauritania. 1979. | 103 |
| I. | France in Gabon. 1990. | 103 |
| J. | France and Belgium in Rwanda. 1990. | 104 |
| K. | France in Chad. 1990. | 105 |
| L. | France and Belgium in Zaire. 1991. | 105 |
| M. | France and Belgium in Zaire. 1993. | 106 |
| N. | Multinational Evacuation Operation in Rwanda. 1994. | 107 |
| O. | France in the Central African Republic. 1996. | 108 |

Appendix I:
    A Chronological List of Cases Involving the Landing of United States Forces to Protect the Lives and Property of Nationals Abroad Prior to World War II. . . . . . . . . . . . . . . . . . . . . . . . . . . . . . . . . . . . . . . . . . 115

Appendix II:
    A History of United States Navy Regulations Governing the Use of Force to Protect the Lives and Property of Nationals Abroad . . . . . 185

Conclusion. . . . . . . . . . . . . . . . . . . . . . . . . . . . . . . . . . . . . . . . . . . . . . . . . . 229

Index . . . . . . . . . . . . . . . . . . . . . . . . . . . . . . . . . . . . . . . . . . . . . . . . . . . . . . 259

# Foreword

The International Studies "Blue Book" series was initiated by the Naval War College in 1901 to publish essays, treatises, and articles that contribute to the broader understanding of international law. With this, the seventy-seventh volume of the historic series, we honor the late Professor Richard B. Lillich by publishing his final book, a long-awaited volume on the use of force in the protection of nationals abroad.

Professor Lillich is part of the Naval War College family. He held the Charles H. Stockton Chair of International Law from 1968-1969, and continued to support the Naval War College after his tenure. He was the co-editor of Volumes 61 and 62 of the Blue Book series: *Readings in International Law from the Naval War College Review 1947-1977, vols. 1 & 2.* As the Stockton Professor, he would engage his colleagues in discussions of the proper use of the U.S. Navy and Marine Corps in one of their most enduring missions, ensuring the safety of U.S. citizens overseas. This volume experienced a long gestation since then, with years of meticulous research and thoughtful analysis culminating in a manuscript shortly before Professor Lillich's untimely death in 1996. His conclusions, while not necessarily official positions of the United States Government, are firmly supported by exhaustive historical research and clearly presented case studies, and are an invaluable contribution to the field.

On behalf of the Secretary of the Navy, the Chief of Naval Operations, and the Commandant of the Marine Corps, I extend to the family, friends and colleagues of Professor Lillich, our gratitude for this, his final service to his country.

RODNEY P. REMPT
Rear Admiral, U.S. Navy
President, Naval War College

# Introduction

The Charles H. Stockton Chair of International Law was established at the Naval War College in 1951. Over the past half-century, the Stockton Chair has been held by many esteemed professors of international law. Professor Richard B. Lillich was one such Chairholder. Volume 77 of the International Law Studies (the "Blue Book") series, *Lillich on the Forcible Protection of Nationals Abroad*, memorializes Professor Lillich and his work. The commentary and case studies he wrote clearly show that foreign intervention to protect one's citizens has always been a relevant and dynamic part of international law, and will continue to be so.

This volume was made possible only through the efforts of its principal editor, Lieutenant Commander Thomas Wingfield, U.S. Navy Reserve. Tom was in the right place at the right time at the Naval War College while serving his annual active duty stint as a reservist. He shepherded the process of turning rough notes, documents and papers into a published book. Working closely with Tom as the co-editor was Lieutenant Colonel James Meyen, USMC, of our International Law Department.

Funding for this book was made possible by Dean Alberto Coll, Center for Naval Warfare Studies of the Naval War College. His leadership and support are key to the Blue Book Series. Invaluable contributions were also made by retired Professor Emeritus Jack Grunawalt and Captain Ralph Thomas, JAGC, USN, (Ret.), who volunteered many hours of their personal time in reviewing manuscripts and offering advice. Further assistance was provided by the rest of the staff of the International Law Department.

Volume 77 will serve as a standard reference work of case studies in this area, continuing the solid, scholarly tradition of the "Blue Books." The series is published by the Naval War College and distributed throughout the world to academic institutions, libraries, and both U.S. and international military commands.

                                          DENNIS MANDSAGER
                                          Professor of Law
                                          Chairman, International Law Department

# Preface

*"It was only one life. What is one life in the affairs of a state?"*

Benito Mussolini, after running down a child in his automobile (as reported by General Smedley Butler, 1931)[1]

Richard Bonnet Lillich—lawyer, professor, human rights expert and advocate—spent his life answering that question. The results of his life's work have proven very troubling for the Mussolinis of the world, in that no one has done more to chart the limits to which a State may go in protecting its citizens.

This particular work, Professor Lillich's last, had an unusually long gestation. As early as 1980, he wrote in the introduction to another volume in this series, *Readings in International Law from the Naval War College Review 1947-1977, vol. 2: The Use of Force, Human Rights, and General International Legal Issues*: "[t]his Introduction is not the place to discuss the Entebbe Raid in detail. Interested readers will find it considered at some length in my forthcoming monograph in the "Blue Book" series—*Forcible Self-Help to Protect Nationals Abroad*."[2] As Professor Lillich continued writing through the 1980s and into the 1990s,[3] he kept this manuscript close at hand, continually revising and updating the text to reflect each new example of State practice. With his untimely death in 1996, his colleagues gathered the largely complete but uncompiled work, and set about preparing it for its long-awaited publication.

It was my honor to be entrusted with overseeing this task during the last two years. Long a student of Professor Lillich's work (if, sadly, not the Professor himself), I had already published two articles based on his work in this area.[4] The first begins with a statement of why Professor Lillich's work in this particular area mattered so much:

[P]erhaps the best criterion for discriminating tyrannies from democracies is the sincere, proven emphasis placed upon the value of a single human life. The forcible protection of nationals abroad, when undertaken for non-pretextual reasons, is the clearest expression of that distinction in state practice. The academic challenge in evaluating such uses of force is to distinguish such protection from other legitimate uses of force, and then to distinguish the uses from other, illegitimate uses of force.[5]

In this volume, Professor Lillich rose to this challenge, and set the standard for future scholars to match. It was decided against including additional case studies covering the post-1996 period to "update" his work. Their academic value did not justify making the text not purely Lillich. Without them, every word, except for the Conclusion, is Professor Lillich's, which is more appropriate for a memorial volume such as this one. To say more about the text which follows is unnecessary, as its scope, depth, and clarity speak for themselves. There is also no need to say more about Professor Lillich himself, because Professor Robert Turner, also of the University of Virginia, has written movingly about his lost friend and colleague in the personal memoriam which follows.

Editing a Blue Book is as far from a solo undertaking as any could be. I wish to thank first Professor Michael N. Schmitt, now of the George C. Marshall European Center for Security Studies, for introducing me to the world of the Naval War College, allowing me to assist him in the editing of an earlier Blue Book, and advocating to the College's Oceans Law and Policy Department (now the International Law Department (ILD)) that I be given a crack at this project. Mike is one of the finest men I know, and to the extent that any of us can approach the level of his intellect, passion, humor, and thoughtfulness, we do so only asymptotically. The College was indeed lucky to have him, as the George Marshall Center is lucky now.

I would also like thank Commander Dean Markussen, USNR, who, in a burst of academic insight, set this chain of events in motion by dispatching me to the College for a two-week period of active duty training as a reservist. Great thanks are also due to the faculty of ILD—particularly Professor Emeritus Jack Grunawalt, his successor, Professor Dennis Mandsager; Captain Ralph Thomas, JAGC, USN (Ret.), his successor, Colonel Frederic Borch, USA; and Lieutenant Colonel James Duncan, USMC, and *his* successor, Lieutenant Colonel James Meyen, USMC, for accepting me into the ILD family and providing all the support and guidance an editor could need. Their faith in this project, and in me, is greatly appreciated.

Professor Robert Turner, author of this text's true introduction, is deserving of special praise. Given his already hectic schedule of writing, teaching, and speaking—made all the more demanding in wake of the recent attacks on our nation—he could have declined this writing project with a clear conscience. However, drawing on his limitless reserves of energy, he made time to honor his friend with the thoughtful tribute which follows. Bob Turner is living proof of Professor Lillich's talent for friendship.

No acknowledgments would be complete without thanking the people who actually undertook the steps to physically produce a hardcover book. First is LtCol Jim Meyen, my official co-editor and whom I mentioned above, for taking the finished manuscript through the process of publication in Newport. The sheer number of steps in such a task—from word processing to proofreading, from indexing to printing—make their coordination a challenging, time-consuming, and sometimes frustrating task. For handling the entire project with grace under pressure, Jim is to be sincerely complimented. An enormous debt is also owed to Captain Donald C. Hill, USNR, who spent a two-week training period, and a considerable amount of his own time, in organizing Professor Lillich's manuscript. The book's current organization is a result of Captain Hill's vision, and it is no overstatement to say that the project could not have moved forward without his dedication and patient work. Ms Patricia Goodrich, of the Naval War College Press, is also to be commended for her professional editorial assistance; as is the technically adept staff in the Publications Office, who made this volume a reality. Last, but certainly not least, is Lieutenant David Poff, USNR, who put considerable time and effort into updating Professor Lillich's work for publication. His contribution, completed after his recall to active duty in the current hostilities, may be seen throughout this text.

Finally, I would like to thank my friends and colleagues at Aegis Research Corporation, Georgetown University Law Center, and the University of Virginia School of Law for their patience, understanding, and support. Working and studying with such fine people is one of life's greatest rewards, and one that I now know was enjoyed just as deeply by Professor Richard Bonnet Lillich.

THOMAS C. WINGFIELD
Counsel and Principal National
Security Policy Analyst
Aegis Research Corporation

# NOTES

1. Benito Mussolini, *quoted by* Gen. Smedley Butler, *reprinted in* THE POCKET BOOK OF QUOTATIONS 379 (Henry Davidoff ed., 1952).

2. READINGS IN INTERNATIONAL LAW FROM THE NAVAL WAR COLLEGE REVIEW 1947-1977 (V. 2), THE USE OF FORCE, HUMAN RIGHTS AND GENERAL INTERNATIONAL LEGAL ISSUES (NAV. WAR C. INT'L L. STUD., v. 62, Richard B. Lillich & John Norton Moore eds. 1980), at xi.

3. For the most complete listing of Professor Lillich's writings, *see* Samuel Pyeatt Menefee, *A Tribute to Richard B. Lillich: a Bibliography of the Legal Publications of Professor Richard B. Lillich (1933-1996)*, 38 VA. J. INT'L L. 85 (1997).

4. *See* Thomas C. Wingfield, *Forcible Protection of Nationals Abroad*, 104 DICK. L. REV. 439 (2000) [hereinafter FORCIBLE PROTECTION], and Thomas C. Wingfield, *Lillich on Interstellar Law: U.S. Naval Regulations,* Star Trek, *and the Use of Force in Space*, 46 S. D. L. REV. 72 (2001) [hereinafter INTERSTELLAR LAW].

5. *See* Wingfield, *Forcible Protection, supra* note 4, at 439.

# RICHARD B. LILLICH (1933-1996):

# A Tribute

### Robert F. Turner

Richard Bonnot Lillich was born in Amherst, Ohio, on January 22, 1933. After undergraduate training at Oberlin College, he earned his LL.B. at Cornell and went on to earn his LL.M. and S.J.D. (academic law doctorate) at New York University. He served ten years on the faculty of Syracuse University, where he was Director of International Legal Studies. During 1968-69, he held the prestigious Charles H. Stockton Chair of International Law at the U.S. Naval War College. He then joined the faculty of the University of Virginia School of Law, where he served as the Howard W. Smith Professor of Law until his untimely death twenty-seven years later, from a heart attack at the age of sixty-three.

To that, one might add his Ford Foundation and Guggenheim Fellowships in London; service as Thomas Jefferson Visiting Fellow at Downing College, Cambridge; other fellowships at Oxford and the Max Planck Institute in Heidelberg; and assorted short-term teaching assignments at Indiana, Georgia, St. Louis, and Florida State—where at the time of his death he also served part-time as the Edward Ball Eminent Professor of International Law.

We can't forget his leadership positions: a dozen years on the Executive Council of the American Society of International Law, twenty-six years on the Editorial Board of the *American Journal of International Law*, founding member of The Procedural Aspects of International Law (PAIL) Institute, founder of the Washington, DC-based International Human Rights Law Group; just to mention some of the highlights. He was also a prolific writer, co-editing the nation's first law school casebook on human rights law among his more than forty books, sixty chapters in books edited by others, and more than one hundred published articles.

Then there was his role as valued adviser to the Office of the Legal Adviser at the State Department and to numerous non-governmental organizations in the United States and around the globe. As an advocate, he was often called upon by the United States Government and by numerous private clients to argue before international tribunals.

These are the data that inevitably make their way into *New York Times* obituaries, and they are important. They tell us that Professor Richard Lillich was a man of remarkable professional accomplishment and ability. But they don't capture the full measure of the man whose early experiences as an adopted child may have contributed to the loyalty and friendship he displayed to colleagues as an adult. In a tribute that appeared in the *American Journal of International Law*, University of Iowa Law School Professor Burns Weston recalled approaching Professor Lillich about sharing some materials he had collected for an unwritten study of the British Foreign Compensation Commission:

> [H]e not only said yes, but invited me to Syracuse where he was then teaching, provided me free room and board at home with his family, found me a quiet office, gave me all his research cards and notes to examine, and authorized me to Xerox whatever I needed, asking only that I put things back in the order that I found them. And I barely knew him! Richard Lillich always defied the conventional wisdom of jealously guarding one's hard-won unpublished research. He was uniquely generous and trusting in a profession not known for its deference to could-be rivals.

I first met Dick Lillich while a student in his first seminar on international human rights at the University of Virginia School of Law. The assigned text—*International Human Rights: Problems of Law and Policy*, the casebook he had just co-authored with Judge Frank C. Newman—did not arrive from Little-Brown until several weeks into the term.

I enrolled in that seminar with some trepidation. Even then, Dick had established a well-deserved reputation as one of the nation's foremost authorities on both international claims and human rights law. But he had also been a vocal opponent of U.S. involvement in Vietnam, and my involvement on the other side of that debate was no secret. Never one to withdraw from a good argument, I anticipated that our different perspectives would surface and I was unsure of the potential effect on my grade point average.

I was right about one thing. Not only in his human rights seminar, but in two other courses I later took from him, our divergent points of view surfaced—repeatedly. He was outraged over human rights abuses in South Korea, and I responded that cutting aid could play into the hands of the regime in Pyongyang, whose human rights record was incomparably worse across the board. In retrospect, perhaps we were just describing opposite ends of the same elephant. While it seemed to me that we disagreed about everything of significance, I knew even then that we were both deeply committed to the cause of human rights and human dignity.

When the time came to pick topics for our research papers, I informed the Director of the International Human Rights Law Group, who was assisting Dick in the seminar, that I was leaning towards doing a comparative piece on human rights in the two Koreas. She cautioned me that might be a mistake in view of Professor Lillich's strong views on the topic. I guess my passions were a bit intense, too, as I wrote instead about human rights in the two Vietnams. Given my views on the issue, I can only imagine the impact it had on poor Dick Lillich's blood pressure.

I knew Dick would get the last shot in our duel, and when grades arrived I was hoping for an "A-" and convinced that if he gave me below a "B" it would reflect his political biases. To my shock, in that seminar and the two subsequent courses I took from him, Dick gave me "A"s. At the time, Virginia was on a strict 3.0 curve, and to give an "A" required a professor to award another student a "C" or to downgrade several papers to balance off the 4.0. "A"s were thus uncommon. I honestly don't think I *earned* three "A"s from Dick Lillich, and my only explanation for his behavior is his strong sense of professional honor. He wanted there to be no question that he was not penalizing me for our strong disagreements in class. When I applied for admission to the graduate law program, Dick served on the admissions committee that decided to waive the LL.M. requirement and admit me directly into the S.J.D. program, even though I still think he viewed us as being at opposite ends of the political spectrum on key issues.

After several years working in Washington, I returned to Virginia in 1987, and as an additional duty volunteered to teach the introductory international law course in the Department of Government and Foreign Affairs until they could fill that faculty vacancy. When it came time to discuss international human rights, I asked Dick if he would come over as a guest lecturer—neither of us realizing that I had scheduled him for Wednesday of Thanksgiving week. He accepted, and year after year he returned on the same day to share his vast knowledge of international human rights law with a couple of hundred undergraduates. He never received a penny for his efforts, and twice he brought his young daughter with him so they could head off on the brief vacation he had delayed to do me a favor.

We talked a lot over the years, until I departed in 1994 for Newport to occupy the Stockton Chair that Dick had held twenty-five years earlier. We also took part in several conferences where I could hear his views as a colleague. The more I listened to him, the fewer points of disagreement I could find. His knowledge of the law was superb. As the present volume reflects, he shared my strong belief in the importance of using original sources, of understanding the historical development of legal rules through the writings of people like Grotius and Vattel, and the importance of careful research. The values he expressed as I grew older were largely my own. And on issue after issue, our bottom-line conclusions were fully in accord.

To this day, I do not pretend to know what happened. Perhaps the change was within me, and as I matured over the years my own views moved gradually towards where Dick had always been. Perhaps the end of the Cold War removed some filters that had influenced our vision during that controversy. Perhaps Dick changed. I don't know, but, in the end, my perception of him gradually changed. The man who at first appeared to be an exceptionally able teacher who was wrong on the issues but honorable and fair almost to a fault, had become a cherished friend and colleague—a world-class scholar—whose policy preferences on more and more issues I strongly shared.

Dick Lillich was perhaps best known for his work on international claims and State responsibility. I thought of him as a "Liberal" and on occasion, in the early days, a man of the "Left." But, in retrospect, he did not champion radical positions in either of these fields. Dick believed that it was important for States to be held responsible for their conduct, irrespective of any perceived injustices in their past, and he believed that when they took the property of others they had a duty to pay fair compensation.

Few issues have more divided international lawyers than that of unilateral intervention by one State in the territory of another for the purpose of protecting nationals. Once again, Dick Lillich rejected the "anti-imperialist" orthodoxy of the Left, arguing that when one State violated the clear rights of foreign nationals and endangered their safety, in the absence of an effective multinational remedy the victim State had a legal right to use necessary and proportional force to safeguard its nationals. This was clearly the majority view of the pre-Charter era, and I share Dick's view that the doctrine survived Article 2(4). Whether one reasons that an intervention limited to protecting the safety of one's own nationals is not a use of force against the territorial integrity or political independence of the host State, or argues that the rights set forth in 2(4) are predicated upon the host State abiding by its own duties not to threaten or use force improperly and are qualified by the right of self-defense, the outcome is the same.

Dick also did groundbreaking work on the issue of humanitarian intervention. He understood that human dignity and human freedom are of fundamental importance, and that people needed to be protected against at least the most flagrant abuses of internationally recognized human rights norms. Ideally, this should be done by a united world community under the leadership and direction of the United Nations Security Council. But Dick understood that the Security Council could be blocked from acting by the negative votes of any of five Permanent Members. And when the United Nations was unwilling or unable to act, Dick understood that individual States—or, preferably, multinational coalitions—had a right and duty to act to prevent the most egregious violations of human rights.

Another dear friend, Professor R. J. Rummel, has in recent years called attention to the problem he defines as "democide"—the slaughter of human beings outside of war by their own governments. I first learned of this theory in 1987 while serving as the first President of the congressionally-created United States Institute of Peace. Part of our statutory mandate was to make grants to institutions and scholars to do research and write books; and when I first read Rudy Rummel's initial proposal I could not believe his thesis. Surely, if he was right, we would have known this before now. But as I examined his preliminary work and contemplated his thesis over time, I became persuaded that he was correct and was delighted when our Board of Directors voted to support his research. Quite properly, he was nominated for the Nobel Peace Prize for his groundbreaking scholarship on Democide and the Democratic Peace.

Rudy Rummel has argued—very persuasively, in my view—that during the Twentieth Century, at least three times as many people were killed by their own governments unrelated to war than were killed in every war across the globe during the same period. This includes Stalin's purges of class enemies, Mao's land reform and other campaigns to kill class enemies, Hitler's Holocaust, Pol Pot's butchery of an estimated two million Cambodians, and assorted lesser crimes. And very importantly, Rummel has shown that there is a tremendous inverse correlation between democide and democratic governance. The mega-murderers are all totalitarian tyrants.

Arguably the two most important developments in international law during the Twentieth Century were the outlawing of aggressive war through the Kellogg-Briand Treaty and UN Charter, and the recognition in the Charter and subsequent instruments that sovereign States have a duty to protect certain human rights of both their own nationals and aliens who are under their control. In both categories, the primary violators have been the world's totalitarian regimes—whether from "Left" or "Right."

The world's leading scholars of international law are very much divided on whether it is permissible for any State, or any group of States in the absence of Security Council authorization, to use lethal force inside the territory of another State to protect human rights—even if the alternative is massive genocide. This debate is much like the dispute over the scope of the right of self-defense under Article 51 of the Charter, and for much the same reason. The scholars who oppose "humanitarian intervention" do so not because they favor genocide, but because they fear that if left unconstrained sovereign States will use the excuse of such intervention to justify aggression. Thus, in August 1990, Saddam Hussein could easily have pointed out human rights shortcomings in Kuwait to excuse his desire to take control of that country. For similar reasons, they want to narrow the right of States to use lethal force in "self-defense" because they recall that when Hitler went into Poland, and Kim Il Sung invaded South Korea, both told the world they had been attacked first.

One can acknowledge and even share these concerns and yet still recognize that States must be able to defend themselves when attacked—even when the attack is masked by the use of paramilitary forces and accompanied by propaganda designed to mislead the world. Ultimately, the world community can usually ascertain the facts and pass judgment upon the resort to lethal force. And, similarly, the world should be able to tell between genuine humanitarian intervention and the use of that doctrine as a façade to mask aggression.

At its core, the theory that there can be no lawful exercise of humanitarian intervention places international law on the wrong side. Its primary purpose is to promote peace and justice. If it holds that the world community must sit back in silence if another Hitler surfaces and begins slaughtering millions of innocent people because of their race, religion, or similar factors, then international law has become part of the problem and must be changed. For no set of rules that preordains such a result deserves the respect of civilized men or women. Dick Lillich understood this.

I am honored to be able to write a few words in tribute to this great man—a friend and colleague who, in retrospect, was throughout our years of friendship also a cherished mentor. I commend the Naval War College for its decision to bring out this important volume even after the untimely death of its author. Like so many other volumes in this extraordinary series, it will be a valuable tool for legal scholars for generations to come. Finally, I am deeply indebted to my friend Tom Wingfield, who agreed to undertake the important task of completing this manuscript when it became apparent to everyone that my own schedule would preclude my doing so.

Dick Lillich was a remarkable man to whom all who cherish the rule of law are indebted. His untimely death by heart attack on August 3, 1996, left the world poorer for the loss. But those of us who knew and admired him can take solace in the knowledge that his scholarship and ideas will live on both through the work of his former students and in the remarkable body of professional literature he has left behind. This will presumably be his final publication, and it reflects the exceptional talents that helped make Dick Lillich such a remarkable scholar and human being. As with all of us who have had the distinction to hold the Charles H. Stockton Chair of International Law at the Naval War College, Dick cherished that association. I am confident that he would be delighted to know that the commitment he made more than three decades ago to write a Blue Book has been satisfied. I am all the more certain that this fine work will be welcomed by scholars around the globe.

*Charlottesville, Virginia*
*November 21, 2001*

# Author's Note

The development and implementation of the State's *right of forcible protection*, is the primary focus of this document.

As with many international law norms, the juridical origins of a State's right to protect the lives and property of its nationals abroad may be traced to the views of the early, classical publicists. Their writings routinely included a State's right of *diplomatic* protection of its nationals abroad. The validity of a State's right of forcible protection of its nationals abroad necessarily grew out of the practical aspects of the right of diplomatic protection of a State's nationals. Although often addressing the subject indirectly, the classical publicists had a significant impact upon the development of the State's right of forcible protection of its citizens abroad.

To the contributions of the classical writers, the later traditional writers on international law added descriptions of the evolving practice of States intervening to protect their nationals transiting or living in other States. One group of writers, including Phillimore, Bluntschli and Westlake, viewed the right of protection as limited primarily to the use of diplomatic measures. Recognizing the justifications offered by the classical writers, as well as the developing State practices, a second group of writers, including Bonfils, Pradier-Fodere, Oppenheim and Fauchille, asserted an established principle justifying forcible measures of protection as well. A third group of writers, primarily from the United States, including Moore, Stockton, Clark, Hodges, Borchard, Hyde and Offutt, also recognized the then established principle of using forcible measures, supplementing their theoretical reasoning with extensive appendices detailing instances of such protection, primarily in the form of prior US practice.

A fourth group of traditional writers, including Dunn and Hindmarsh, with world crisis imminent, grudgingly admitted the existence of the principle of forcible protection, but made clear their disapproval of its exercise in an increasingly interdependent international community.

Following the summary of the classical and traditionalist historical views on the State's right of forcible protection of its nationals abroad prior to the signing of the United Nations Charter, the impact of post-World War II State practice will be discussed.

With the signing of the United Nations Charter and its broad prohibition of the use of force found in Article 2(4), the right of forcible, as opposed to diplomatic, protection entered a new phase as the provision seriously questions the concept of forcible protection of nationals abroad. However, the human experience in dealing with the practicalities of traversing a foreign State having different laws, socio-economic experience and political differences, will no doubt keep the issue of the State's protection of its representatives and nationals abroad, a very timely and dynamic topic for some time to come.

Richard B. Lillich

# Chapter I

## The Classical Publicists

To facilitate an understanding of the historical development of the concept of the *right of forcible protection*, the earliest publicists are denominated herein as the "classical" writers. This group, spanning the Seventeenth and Eighteenth Centuries include Grotius, Wolff and Vattel. During this historical period the European State system assumed a preeminent position in the world.

A. *Grotius*. Grotius, the "father of international law," developed two fundamental principles that have influenced much of the later thinking on the subject of the protection of the lives and property of nationals abroad.

First, he maintained that a sovereign's concern for his subjects must be paramount. "[T]he first and particularly necessary concern," argued Grotius, "is for subjects, either those who are subject to authority in a family, or those who are subject to a political authority."[1]

Second, Grotius contended that under the law of nations there existed a principle that "for what any civil society, or its head, ought to finish . . . by not fulfilling the law, for all this there are held and made liable all the corporeal or incorporeal possessions of those who are subject to such a society or its head."[2] Grotius viewed this latter principle, which countenanced collective responsibility, as pragmatic, the "outgrowth of a certain necessity, because otherwise a great license to cause injury would arise."[3]

As a corollary to this forerunner of State responsibility, Grotius considered at least two remedial measures open to the protecting sovereign: the "seizure of persons" and the "seizure of goods." As to the former, Grotius cited the practice of the ancient Greeks, in the form of Attican law which stated: "If anyone die by a violent death, for his sake, it shall be right for his relatives and next of kin to proceed to apprehend men, until either the penalty has been paid for the murder, or the murderers are given up."[4] Grotius extended this approach to justify a sovereign's resort to self-help to protect his subjects from potential injury, stating that "there is nothing in this that is repugnant to nature, and it is the practice not only of the Greeks, but of other nations also."[5]

Grotius also discussed briefly "the right of detention of citizens of another state in which a manifest wrong has been done to a national, in order to secure his recovery."[6] While admitting the existence of such a right, Grotius nevertheless rejected its utility. In this regard, he described the reasons advanced against the seizure of Ariston of Tyre by the Carthaginians. The principal argument was that if Ariston were seized "(th)e same thing will happen to Carthaginians both at Tyre and in the other commercial centers to which they go in large numbers."[7]

With reference to the "seizure of goods," Grotius' second remedial measure, he cited, without discussion, the "withernam" of the Saxons and Angles and the "letters of marque" authorized by the King of France.[8] Additionally, he pointed to Homer's description in the *Iliad* of Nestor's seizure of "the flocks and herds of the men of Elis in revenge for the horses stolen from his father."[9] Finally, Grotius recounted an instance from Roman history in which Aristodemus, the heir of the Tarquins, held Roman ships at Cumae as compensation for Tarquin property seized by the Romans.[10]

For Grotius, the sovereign's right to use self-help to protect his subjects was a far-reaching one, justifying resort to force. As he put it: "Seizure by violence may be understood to be warranted not only in case a judgment cannot be obtained against a criminal or a debtor within a reasonable time, but also if in a very clear case (for in a doubtful case the presumption is in favor of those who have been chosen by the state to render judgment) judgment has been rendered in a way manifestly contrary to law; for the authority of the judge has not the same force over foreigners as over subjects."[11]

However, such resort to force did not include the taking of life. According to the "law of love," "particularly for Christians, the life of a man ought to be of greater value than our property. . . ."[12]

Thus, although Grotius did not directly address the question of the protection of the lives and property of nationals abroad, he did adopt certain premises that influenced subsequent writers in the development of theoretical justifications for such protection. Subsequent to Grotius, the importance of the citizen to the sovereign, as well as the recognition of the right of a sovereign to protect a citizen, by force if necessary, became recurrent themes in the literature on this subject.

B. *Wolff.* Wolff, writing in the mid-Eighteenth Century, elaborated upon the duty of a nation to preserve itself, a topic that had also been considered earlier by Grotius. "Every nation is bound to preserve itself," wrote Wolff, "for the men who make a nation, when they have united into a state, are as individuals bound to the whole for promoting the common good, and the whole is bound to the individuals to provide for them those things which are required as a competency for life, for peace and security."[13] Thus, although Wolff did not expressly mention the protection of nationals abroad, it can be inferred that, to the extent that such protection was required "as a competency for life, for peace and security," he believed that a State was obliged to extend its protection to its nationals abroad.

Moreover, Wolff recognized as valid the use of force to enforce a State's rights.

"The right belongs to every nation to obtain its right against another nation by force, if the other is unwilling to allow that right. For the right belongs to every nation not to permit any other nation to take away its right, consequently also not to permit it not to allow that right. Therefore it is necessary, when one does not wish to allow a right, that the other compel it by force to allow it. Therefore the right belongs to the one nation against the other nation to obtain its right by force, if the other does not wish to allow it."[14]

Indeed, a State had the right to defend itself and its rights against another State[15] and to punish another State, by force, which had injured it.[16] Thus, the forcible protection of nationals abroad can be brought under either of these concepts, especially the latter, without much difficulty.

C. *Vattel.* The first writer to focus directly upon the protection of nationals abroad was Vattel. Amplifying Grotius' concern for the citizen, as well as his justification for a State's enforcement of its rights against another State, Vattel argued that:

> Whoever offends the State, injures its rights, disturbs its tranquillity, or does it a prejudice in any manner whatsoever, declares himself its enemy, and exposes himself to be justly punished for it. Whoever uses a citizen ill, indirectly offends the state, *which is bound to protect this citizen;* and the sovereign of the latter should avenge his wrongs, punish the aggressor, and, if possible, oblige him to make full reparation; since otherwise the citizen would not obtain the great end of the civil association, which is, safety.[17]

Thus, building upon the Grotian premise that a State has a right to protect its citizens, Vattel argued that forcible protection not only was justified, but that it was an obligation owed by States to their citizens.

To illustrate the breadth of the principle of protection, Vattel used several hypothetical and real examples. For instance, "[t]he sovereign who refuses to cause reparation to be made for the damage done by his subject, or to punish the offender, or, finally, to deliver him up, renders himself in some measure an accomplice in the injury, and becomes responsible for it."[18] Vattel cited the example of King Demetrius' imputed responsibility for the murder of a Roman ambassador by one of the King's subjects in this regard.[19] In that case, after King Demetrius delivered the guilty persons to Rome for appropriate punishment, the Roman Senate sent them back, "resolving to reserve to themselves the liberty of punishing that crime, by avenging it on the King himself, or on his dominions."[20] It is interesting to note that Vattel, although agreeing that the King ultimately was responsible for the acts of his subject, found the Senate's conduct unjust, as appropriate reparation had been offered by sending the guilty persons to Rome. Vattel's analysis of this incident, applicable to many of the instances of forcible protection described herein, was that the Senate's decision was "but a pretext to cover their ambitious enterprises."[21]

Another instance, described by Vattel, where forcible protection may be exercised is when a State "accustoms and authorizes its citizens indiscriminately to plunder and maltreat foreigners. . . ."[22] In the face of such a situation, "all nations have a right to enter into a league against such a people, to repress them, and to treat them as the common enemies of the human race."[23] As instances of this use of the principle of protection, Vattel cited the "guilt" of the nation of the Usbecks for the robberies its citizens had committed, as well as the hypothetical justification for a Christian confederacy against the Barbary States, "in order to destroy those haunts of pirates, with whom the love of plunder, or the fear of just punishment, is the only rule of peace and war."[24]

Vattel's seeming endorsement of a broad right of forcible protection was tempered somewhat by his concern with the concept of sovereignty. "We should not only refrain from usurping the territory of others," argued Vattel, "we should also respect and abstain from every act contrary to the rights of the sovereign. . . . We cannot, then, without doing an injury to a state, enter its territories with force and arms. . . . This would at once be a violation of the safety of the state, and a trespass on the rights of empire or supreme authority vested in the sovereign."[25] Thus, "[t]he prince . . . ought not to interfere in the causes of his subjects in foreign countries, and grant them his protection, *excepting in cases* where justice is refused, or palpable and evident injustice done, or rules and forms openly violated, or, finally, an odious distinction made, to the prejudice of his subjects, or of foreigners in general."[26]

Being the first of the classical international law writers to expressly discuss the protection of nationals abroad, Vattel's analysis is not particularly far-reaching. The right to protection that he initially developed is qualified by his later emphasis on the rights of the sovereign. The fact remains, however, that Vattel recognized a State's right (obligation) to forcibly protect its citizens abroad by avenging the wrongs done to them and punishing their aggressors, at least in cases of flagrant injustice.[27]

## NOTES

1. H. Grotius, De Juri Belli Ac Pacis Bk. II, Ch. XXV, at 578 (F. Kelsey trans. 1925).
2. Id., Bk. III, Ch. II, at 624.
3. Id.
4. H. Grotius, De Juri Belli Ac Pacis Bk. III, Ch. III, at 625 (F. Kelsey trans. 1925).
5. Id.
6. Id. at 626.
7. Id.
8. Id. at 626-27
9. Id. at 627
10. Id. at 628
11. Id. at 627
12. Id. at 628
13. C. Wolff, Jus Gentium 22 (J. Scott ed. 1934).
14. Id. at 138-39.
15. Id. at 139.
16. Id.
17. E. Vattel, The Law of Nations 161 (J. Chitty ed. 1883) (emphasis added).
18. Id. at 162.
19. Id. at 163.
20. Vattel, however, also offered justifications for forcible measures directed against culpable States in the hypothetical situations of the "robber-nation" of the Usbecks and the pirate-ridden Barbary States. See E. Vattel, The Law of Nations 163 (J. Chitty ed. 1883).
21. Id.
22. Id. at 163.
23. Id.
24. Id.
25. Id. at 169.
26. Id. at 165 (emphasis added).
27. Id.

# Chapter II

## The Traditional Writers on International Law

The classical writers were followed by the "traditional writers" on international law of the Nineteenth and early Twentieth Centuries, they include Phillimore, Bluntschli, Bonfils, Pradier-Fodere, Westlake, Oppenheim, Moore, Stockton, Clark, Hodges, Borchard, Fauchelle, Hyde, Winfield, Offutt, Dunn, Hindmarsh and Accioly.

These writers witnessed the developing State practices which provided an interesting counterpoint to the theoretical foundations developed by the earlier classical scholars.

A. *Phillimore*. Phillimore, an English publicist writing in 1854, buttressed the theoretical premises of the "classical" textwriters with the actual practice of States as it had developed by the mid-Nineteenth Century. The general conclusion he reached was that "[t]he state, to which the foreigner belongs, may interfere for his protection when he has received positive maltreatment, or when he has been denied ordinary justice in the foreign country."[1] However, Phillimore specified certain preconditions that must be met before such self-help could be undertaken. "[I]t behooves the interfering State to take the utmost care," he cautioned, first, that the commission of the wrong be clearly established; second, that the "denial of the local tribunals to decide the question at issue be no less clearly established."[2] In addition to citing Grotius, Phillimore supported his assertion with a reference to the reply of Great Britain to the King of Prussia in 1753, wherein it was maintained that a State may exercise protection only "in cases of violent injuries directed or supported by the State; and justice absolutely denied . . . by all the tribunals, and afterwards by the Prince."[3]

Phillimore also distinguished between domiciliary and transient nationals in foreign countries. The essence of the distinction was that, while a national of one State who becomes domiciled in another State accepts conditions in that State for what they are, the transient national does not. According to Phillimore, the domiciliary

> "must be held to have considered the habits of the people, the laws of the country, and their mode of administration, before he established therein his household gods [sic] and made it the principal seat of his fortunes. He cannot therefore expect, that every complaint, which he may be disposed to urge upon his native Government, with respect to these matters, will of necessity be considered as requiring national interposition."[4]

Phillimore devoted an entire chapter to the then topical aspect of the protection and collection of debts owed by one State to another State's nationals. Citing Vattel, Phillimore stated that "[t]he right of interference on the part of a State, for the purpose of enforcing the performance of justice to its citizens from a foreign State, stands upon an unquestionable foundation, when the foreign state has become itself the debtor of these citizens."[5]

Building upon this theoretical foundation, Phillimore invoked relevant State practice, exemplified by the famous Palmerston Circular of 1848.[6] This statement of policy by the British government recognized that it had the right to bring claims on behalf of British subjects who held public bonds and money securities of defaulting foreign States, but that the decision whether or not to assert such a claim was entirely within its discretion. "It is therefore simply a question of discretion with the British Government," wrote Palmerston, "whether [a] matter should or should not be taken up by diplomatic negotiation, and the decision of that question of discretion turns entirely upon British and domestic considerations."[7] The circular suggested that only in exceptional cases would the government's discretion be exercised in the subject's favor.

Phillimore, drawing upon the theoretical foundations of Grotius and Vattel, substantiated his assertions with examples from ongoing State practice. From his discussion, it would seem that Phillimore was contemplating primarily the diplomatic protection of nationals abroad. In any event, he considered that a principle of international law had developed, both in theory and in practice, which justified a State's protection of the lives, property and debts owed its nationals living abroad, perhaps even by the use of forcible measures.

B. *Bluntschli*. To Bluntschli, writing in 1874, the right of a State to protect its nationals abroad appeared unquestionable. Bluntschli wrote:

The state has the right and the duty to protect its nationals abroad by all the means authorized by international law:

a) When the foreign state has proceeded against them in violation of the principles of this law.

b) When ill treatment or injuries received by one of its nationals was not caused directly by the foreign state, but it did nothing to oppose such ill treatment or injuries.

Each state has the right to request reparation for the injustice, reimbursement for the injuries caused, and to demand, according to the circumstances, guarantees against the commission of similar acts.[8]

Bluntschli illustrated this principle with several examples, including a State's enslaving of another State's nationals, depriving them of their religion, destroying their goods, treating them with cruelty, violating treaties of commerce, and not respecting the law of nations governing the relations between States.[9] As an example of State practice in this regard, Bluntschli cited the British military expedition against the King of Abyssinia in 1867 who refused to free British nationals whom the king illegally held.[10] According to Bluntschli, this example involved an exercise of the right of forcible protection *par excellence*.

Bluntschli expanded his examination to the situation where the foreign State citizen, and not the State itself, commits the injurious act. In such a case, he argued, the allegedly injured person or persons first must seek a remedy in the courts of the State in which the injury occurred. However, if that State refuses or otherwise fails to render justice, the State of which the injured party is a national may intervene.[11]

At the same time, Bluntschli limited the principle of protection—at least non-forcible protection—to times where there was no internal strife or civil war in the foreign State.[12] His rationale for this position appears to be that a State should not be held responsible for acts over which it has no control, as is likely to be the case in such circumstances. As is apparent, this reasoning illustrates Bluntschli's assumption of the inseparability of the corollary principles of the right of diplomatic protection and State responsibility.

In support of this limitation upon the right of protection, Bluntschli cited several examples, including the *Don Pacifico* case in 1849; the notes of Prince Schwarzenberg on 24 April 1850 and Prince Nesselrode on 2 May 1850, to the effect that a State forced by revolution to take one of its cities controlled by insurgents should not be obliged to indemnify foreigners who by chance are injured in the process; the refusal of the United States to indemnify Spanish nationals injured in New Orleans in 1851; the U.S. Civil War; and the decision of the Great Powers in resolving the Greek-Turkish conflict on 15 January 1869.[13]

In contrast to Phillimore, Bluntschi made no reference to the "classical" writings of Grotius and Vattel. Instead, he merely stated that a right and duty of protection existed and cited several supporting examples. As can be seen from the above discussion, however, Bluntschli—like Phillimore—apparently viewed the right of protection as involving principally diplomatic, rather than forcible, measures.

C. *Bonfils.* Writing in 1894, the Frenchman Bonfils similarly recognized the right of a nation to protect its nationals abroad stating, "To recommend its nationals to the authorities of the country in which they have established their residence, to defend their interests in diplomatic notes, to demand reparation for the wrongs which they have suffered . . . is not to intervene; on the contrary, it is to recognize the sovereignty of the State addressed."[14]

Although the above formulation may appear to support only the principle of diplomatic protection, it is clear from Bonfils' description of State practice that his principal concern lay with forcible protection. As examples, Bonfils cited the French blockade of Argentine ports in 1838-1840,[15] as well as the initial stages of the combined action of England, Spain, and France against Mexico in 1861.[16] According to Bonfils, this latter example began as a joint effort to obtain reparation for damages to nationals of the three States and to ensure Mexico's compliance with its international agreements. When the effort turned into an attempt by Napoleon to install an empire under Maximilian of Austria, the character of the action changed from the protection of nationals to that of flagrant intervention.[17]

Turning to the question of the right to protect nationals who are creditors of foreign governments, Bonfils again relied on State practice, citing the Palmerston Circular.[18] He observed that "[i]n fact, the European Governments have intervened in favor of their nationals who had lent money to foreign governments, against weak states, incapable of resisting, but not against strong States. . . ."[19] As an example of such intervention, Bonfils cited the control exerted by France and Britain over Egypt in 1876 to protect the investments of their nationals.[20] Clearly, for Bonfils the right of forcible protection extended to both creditor and property rights of a State's nationals as well as the protection of their lives.

D. *Pradier-Fodere.* The Frenchman Pradier-Fodere, writing in 1885, described the right of forcible protection of nationals and their property abroad as rooted in the writings of the "classical" publicists, particularly Vattel. According to Pradier-Fodere, "[i]t is the duty of all states to protect their nationals in foreign countries by all means which international law authorizes."[21] Citing Vattel, he stated further that States possess "the right to obtain justice by force, if it cannot be done otherwise."[22]

Pradier-Fodere, however, recognized certain restrictions upon the exercise of the right of protection. Thus, a foreigner who had become domiciled in a State had less justification to call upon his government for protection than a transient foreigner.[23] In addition, he observed that in most cases protection was accomplished more effectively by diplomatic demands for compensation than by forcible self-help.[24] Nevertheless, he pointed to certain examples where resort to force or the threat thereof was justified as a protective measure. In this regard he cited the Anglo-French control of Egypt in 1876 to protect the interests of British and French creditors,[25] as well as the threatened Anglo-French intervention in the Ottoman Empire in 1859 to remodel its financial laws.[26]

E. *Westlake.* Westlake, an Englishman writing in 1904, offered an extensive discussion of the right to protect nationals abroad under the heading of "denial of justice." "If [foreign States] are wanting either to the judicial or to the administrative department," he argued, "the state to which a foreigner belongs has a claim to step in for his protection which often has this in common with political claims, that the justice which the foreign power demands for its subject is not measurable by definite rules."[27] In support of this somewhat amorphous proposition, Westlake cited Vattel,[28] the "general conscience of the peoples of European civilization,"[29] and several statements by officials of the U.S. government.[30] Westlake, like Bluntschli, recognized an important limitation on the right to protect nationals abroad. "During an insurrection," he stated,

> "the best will on the part of the state government, backed by the best laws, is often unable to prevent or to punish regrettable occurrences. In those circumstances it is not usual for a state to indemnify its own subjects, and foreigners can have no better claim than nationals in a matter not generally recognized as one for indemnity. . . ."[31]

Westlake also considered the right of protection in the case of contractual claims. Examining, first, U.S. practice in this regard, he noted the adoption of a cautious policy. Citing statements by Secretary of State Seward in 1866 and

Secretary of State Fish in 1870, Westlake concluded that U.S. nationals investing in foreign States had "assumed the risk" of such ventures, and that the U.S. government normally would not intervene on their behalf.[32] Here can be seen the developmemt of the concept that in financial matters, (contracts, debtor-creditor relationships) that States would not intervene with force on behalf of a national who had contracted with a foreign State or one of its citizens.

F. *Oppenheim.* Oppenheim, another Englishman writing in 1905, recognized the validity of the right of forcible protection. According to Oppenheim, "[b]y a universally recognized customary rule of the "Law of Nations" every State holds a right of protection over its citizens abroad. . . ."[33] In his view, this right was discretionary, not obligatory.[34] Oppenheim recognized several means by which the right might be enforced, including diplomatic notes, retortion and reprisals, and intervention or war where necessary.[35]

Oppenheim offered little guidance about which protective technique was appropriate in a particular case. Instead, he merely stated that "[e]verything depends upon the merits of the individual case and must be left to the discretion of the State concerned."[36] However, he did mention certain criteria that a State might consider in exercising its discretion, including "whether the wronged foreigner was only traveling through or had settled down in the country, whether his behavior has been provocative or not, how far the foreign Government identified itself with the acts of officials or subjects, and the like."[37]

G. *Moore.* Writing in 1905 on the subject of U.S. diplomacy, John Bassett Moore also addressed the question of whether forcible self-help could be used to protect nationals and their property abroad.[38] Underlying his discussion was the proposition that "[a]mong the rules of conduct prescribed for the United States by the statesmen who formulated its foreign policy, none was conceived to be more fundamental or more distinctively American than that which forbade intervention in the political affairs of other nations."[39] However, Moore maintained that "[t]he right of the government to intervene for the protection of its citizens in foreign lands and on the high seas never was doubted; nor was such action withheld in proper cases."[40] Moore supplemented this brief analysis with a careful description of a large number of instances of intervention for such protective purposes.[41]

H. *Stockton.* A brief discussion of the right of forcible protection of the lives and property of nationals abroad is afforded by the work of Charles H. Stockton, a U.S. naval officer and legal scholar writing in 1911. Departing from the traditional emphasis upon diplomatic pressures to protect nationals abroad, Stockton proposed that special measures be utilized in situations involving "weak states with unstable governments." In such situations, he argued, "it at times occurs that citizens abroad must be protected at once, not by diplomatic representation; there is not time for that, but by the employment of naval force."[42] Stockton invoked as authority for his position the appropriate Navy regulations governing the use of naval force.[43] Stockton also discussed briefly measures that might be justified in the case of another class of governments, the "semi-civilized or barbarous." In these situations, "intervention by force on behalf of citizens domiciled or sojourning there is a more common matter. In these countries the employment of naval forces is the principal means of such protection, added thereto at times by landing of military detachments."[44]

I. *Clark.* The right of a State to protect its nationals and their property abroad was spelled out in considerable detail by J. Reuben Clark, writing as Solicitor for the U.S. Department of State in 1912.[45] According to Clark, the existence of such a right often was obscured by the tendency that many international law writers exhibited to apply the same strictures to the protection of nationals abroad that they applied to political interventions.[46] When a State's motive in employing forcible self-help was simply "the protection of citizens or subjects... until the government concerned is willing or able itself to afford the protection,"[47] he believed it not subject to the same criticisms as a purely political intervention. From an analysis of the writings of the many authorities cited in his study,[48] Clark concluded that:

> There is considerable authority for the proposition that such interposition by one State in the internal affairs of another State for the purpose of affording adequate protection to its citizens resident in the other, as well as for the protection of the property of such citizens, is not only not improper, but, on the contrary, is based upon, is in accord with, and is the exercise of a right recognized by international law.[49]

The remainder of Clark's study comprises an extensive listing of instances in which the United States had acted in accordance with this right of forcible protection.

J. *Hodges.* Henry Hodges, a U.S. author writing in 1915, discussed the right of forcible protection under the rubric of "non-political intervention."[50] His justifiable rationales for such intervention consisted of the protection of citizens, the denial of justice and the protection of missionaries. All three of these categories include situations, which could fall within the principle of forcible protection.

Regarding his rationale for the protection of citizens, Hodges stated that "[w]hen order is neglected by, or is impossible for the foreign government, then the more advanced state has a right to intervene for the protection of the life and property of its citizens."[51] According to Hodges the measures a protecting State could take might involve, "the establishment and enforcement of some degree of law and order in that community."[52]

With reference to the "denial of justice" justification for intervention, Hodges adopted the view of Secretary of State Bayard, who had stated "[t]hat the State to which a foreigner belongs may intervene for his protection when he has been denied ordinary justice in a foreign country, and also in the case of a plain violation of the substance of natural justice is a proposition universally recognized."[53] In contrast to the protection of citizens justification, Hodges' discussion of denial of justice appears to be geared more to diplomatic than to forcible measures of protection.[54]

"Respecting the protection of missionaries," Hodges noted, "the United States shows about the same consideration as she does in respect to other classes of citizens resident abroad."[55] Thus, according to Hodges, "[t]he United States does not go so far in these matters as do some of the European states which undertake to assume a limited protectorship over Christian communities, especially in Turkey."[56] In addition, the examples cited by Hodges in this regard, such as the *Caroline* case and Pelew Islands dispute in 1893,[57] suggest that such protection under those facts is limited to diplomatic as opposed to forcible measures.[58]

K. *Borchard*. In discussing U.S. practice, Edwin Borchard observed in 1915 that "[t]he army or navy has frequently been used for the protection of citizens or their property in foreign countries in cases of emergency where the local government has failed, through inability or unwillingness, to afford adequate protection to the persons or property of the foreigners in question."[59] His analysis consisted primarily of a description of U.S. practice with a minimum of theoretical discussion. The closest he came to justifying such forcible protection under international law was to cite the Memorandum of J. Reuben Clark which stated that "when confined to the purpose of assuring the safety of citizens abroad, or exacting redress for a delinquent failure to afford local protection, the action must be considered not as a case of intervention, but as non-belligerent interposition."[60]

Borchard listed at least five purposes for which U.S. military personnel had been landed for "non-belligerent interposition" reasons: (1) the protection of U.S. citizens in "disturbed localities"; (2) the punishment of natives for injuries to U.S. citizens; (3) the suppression of local riots; (4) the collection of indemnities; and (5) the seizure of custom houses as security for the payment of claims.[61] He observed that most of these landings had occurred in Latin America as the result of the "hegemony of the United States on this continent and the force of the Monroe Doctrine. . . . "[62] Borchard indicated that such landings had not always been against the will of the local government; indeed, sometimes they actually had been carried out in response to an express invitation.[63]

As examples of "non-belligerent interposition" involving the use of force, Borchard cited the joint action of the United States and other nations in China in 1900 at the time of the Boxer Rebellion,[64] as well as the landing of American troops in Nicaragua in 1910.[65] He maintained, however, that such interventions were "by accident or unavoidable consequence. . . , rather than by principal design.[66] This statement however, seems to be more political than legal pronunciation.

Borchard concluded his analysis with an examination of whether congressional action was required to authorize the use of the armed forces for the protection of U.S. citizens abroad.[67] His conclusion was that such authorization was unnecessary given the then-predominant view that "the Executive has unlimited authority to use the armed forces of the United States for protective purposes abroad in any manner and on any occasion he considers expedient."[68] Thus, in contrast to most of the writers discussed previously, Borchard avoided any detailed justification of the right of protection under international law. Instead, he analyzed U.S. practice as it had developed and attempted to draw generalizations therefrom. What emerged was the view that forcible protection was justified, at least for certain "non-belligerent" objectives.

L. *Fauchille.* In a discussion of intervention and international law, the Frenchman Fauchille, writing in 1922, noted that the use of force to protect nationals abroad was a recognized exception to the established principle of international law condemning intervention. He noted that many writers thought it not intervention "to force a state, either by reprisals or the force of arms, to fulfill its international obligations or to compensate for an injustice or an insult. There is, then, according to these writers, coercion, violence, but not intervention."[69]

As an example of such use of force, Fauchille cited the combined action of Great Britain, Spain and France against Mexico in 1861 to obtain compensation for injuries to their nationals and to ensure the fulfillment by Mexico of contractual obligations vis-à-vis the respective governments.[70] In addition, Fauchille cited the combined action against the Chinese during the Boxer Rebellion in 1900 to protect the diplomatic representatives and nationals of the countries concerned,[71] as well as the 1902 blockade of Venezuela by Great Britain, Germany and Italy to obtain payment on behalf of their nationals who were victims of civil wars in Venezuela.[72] Thus the views of Fauchille represent a further recognition of the right of forcible protection at the levels of both theory and State practice.

M. *Hyde.* Recognition of the right of forcible protection is evident in the work of Charles Cheney Hyde, writing in 1922.[73] Starting from the premise that forcible intervention by one State in the affairs of another was illegal, Hyde recognized several exceptions, including self-defense and the protection of nationals.[74] With reference to the latter principle, Hyde wrote that "[i]f it can be shown . . . that . . . acts [of a foreign State] are immediately injurious to the nationals of a particular foreign State grounds for interference by it might be acknowledged."[75] It is interesting to note, however, that Hyde seemed to prefer collective, rather than individual, measures to accomplish such interference. "It is the mode of collective interference, through an established agency . . . which characterize[s] the existing tendency and afford[s] hope of the development of a sounder practice than has hitherto prevailed."[76] Hyde's principle of "collective interference" proved to be the cornerstone of present day United Nations and NATO actions throughout the world.

Hyde noted several instances in which U.S. military forces have engaged in such interference for the protection of nationals, notably the collective measures in the Boxer Rebellion in 1900,[77] the unilateral action of U.S. naval forces in the punishment of natives on Formosa in 1867,[78] and the landings of U.S. forces in Nicaragua and Honduras in 1910 and 1911.[79] A common element present in most of the cases noted by Hyde was that such landings were on "foreign territory which, in most instances, has been that of a country not familiar with European civilization, and not, at the time, recognized for all purposes as a member of the family of nations.[80] This comment suggests that, in Hyde's view, forcible protection was easier to justify in instances involving acts in States not adhering to the standards of conduct observed by the more "advanced" European States.

N. *Winfield.* In his discussion in 1924 of both valid and invalid grounds for intervention in international law, Winfield, an Englishman, rejected as unsound the use of nationality as a justification for intervention. He observed that such arguments tend to present themselves in two forms: "(i) Where the interveners are of a nationality identical with that of the party for whose benefit they intervene ... [and] (ii) Where the grievance is not that there exists such an identity as between the interveners and the party, but that it is lacking as between the latter and the State of which it forms a constituent part and from which it seeks violently to dissociate itself."[81]

As to the first, Winfield saw only a moral justification, as international practice did not recognize any legal justification. He cited the intervention of Victor Emmanuel II and Garibaldi in Sicily in 1860 in this regard.[82] As to the second, Winfield similarly saw no legal justification, citing two serious objections to its validity. The first was that, if admitted "war might be raised in every corner of the world in its vindication."[83] Second, Winfield argued, "[i]t is problematical whether a single one of the above interventions would ... benefit any of the assisted races, much more whether the remote and doubtful good to be derived from them would outweigh the evils of what must almost certainly prove a long and bloody struggle."[84]

Thus, while it is somewhat unclear whether the situations posited by Winfield exactly correlate with the right of protection situations discussed by other writers, his general conclusion as to the doctrine's invalidity certainly is in marked contrast to their views.

O. *Offutt.* In his study of instances in which the armed forces of the United States have been used for the protection of U.S. nationals and their property abroad, Milton Offutt, writing in 1928, offered a brief discussion of the international legal principles justifying such use of force. He began by noting the obvious, namely, that "[t]he right of a state to protect by force its citizens living in a foreign country when sudden disturbances in the foreign state threaten the safety of their lives and property, and when the government under whose jurisdiction they reside has shown itself unable or unwilling to afford them reasonable protection, is a question which has engaged the attention of most writers on international law."[85]

His analysis, like that of most previous writers,[86] concluded that, when viewed as "non-political" intervention, the use of force for the protection of nationals may be justified. Thus, Offutt observed that "[w]hen, however, the distinction between political and non-political intervention has been appreciated, some authorities have held that the use of force for the protection of its citizens abroad becomes not only a right but, in certain cases, a duty of a sovereign state; and that the state against which such force is used may not justly consider itself aggrieved."[87] In support of this assertion, he relied upon a number of the authorities discussed previously in this chapter, including Oppenheim, Bonfils, and Pradier-Fodere.[88]

*P. Dunn.* Frederick Dunn, writing in the decade preceding World War II, offered another perspective on the right of forcible protection.[89] Although the central focus of his work was on a State's right to protect its nationals abroad diplomatically, he did recognize the existence of a right to forcible protection in certain circumstances. "It is only occasionally," observed Dunn, "where aliens are placed in a situation of grave danger from which the normal methods of diplomacy cannot extricate them, or where diplomatic negotiation for some other reason is believed to be useless, that forceful intervention is apt to take place."[90]

Although there can be detected in Dunn's work an undercurrent of disapproval of this type of forcible self-help, he recognized its validity given the existing international legal and political context. According to Dunn, "[i]n the present stage of organization of the international community, the enforcement of legal obligations is still left in large measure to the individual states, i.e., to what is called 'self-help' (a situation that naturally favors the stronger as against the weaker states). Armed intervention is only one of various means of enforcement that have been developed."[91]

Thus, although the primary focus of Dunn's work was on the right to diplomatic protection, he recognized the existence of a right of forcible protection in cases where the former proved ineffective. It is important to note, however, that Dunn viewed this right not as an absolute one, but as one formed from the exigencies of the existing international legal and political system.

*Q. Hindmarsh.* Representative of the thought on forcible protection of nationals abroad in the decade preceding World War II are the observations of Hindmarsh writing in 1933.[92] His analysis was two-fold, the first step being a recognition of the frequent use of military and naval forces to accomplish such protection, and the second step being an exposition and critique of the international legal principles allegedly justifying such actions.

Hindmarsh recognized that "[t]he use of military or naval force against an offending state to compel recognition of alleged international obligations has been a frequent practice of powerful states."[93] As examples, he singled out as representative a number of instances of forcible protection by the United States, particularly those instances analyzed by Offutt.[94] In addition, however, Hindmarsh pointed to the actions of other powerful States of the day, including the Italian bombardment of the Greek island of Corfu in 1923[95] and the

Japanese occupation of Chinese territory in Manchuria in 1931.[96] Hindmarsh concluded his survey of State practice with the sound observation that "[only] in a very primitive stage of law can such self-help sanctions be tolerated. Their exercise permits the confusion of law and vengeance, evades impartial judgment, and retards the free development of an international legal system. The continuation of self-help in modern international law is as much an anachronism as private vengeance in the legal relations of individuals."[97]

Hindmarsh's analysis of the legal underpinnings of the right of protection was characterized by his rejection of precedent as a justification for the continued validity of the right of protection in the modern international political and legal system.

Measures of force short of war were constantly employed during the Nineteenth Century and were justified as reprisals. Thus, after a century of practice the validity of such measures became recognized as part of customary international law. States which employed reprisals defended them as necessary, ultimate sanctions, short of war, for the enforcement of international rights. Finally, the practice of reprisals received some support from vague theoretical concepts such as the rights of existence, self-defense, and independence. Thus custom, necessity, and fundamental right were appealed to in order to justify continued resort to State self-help in time of peace. Little thought was given by jurists to the possibility that new conditions of international life might render custom obsolete and devoid of practical justification, that new and more effective means of enforcing law might be found, and further, that fundamental rights are always conditional upon fundamental duties.[98]

Hindmarsh argued that such a rationale, while applicable to the Nineteenth Century system of independent political units, was no longer appropriate in a System increasingly characterized by interdependence rather than independence among States. Accordingly, in his view, the development of an international organization to settle disputes among States, rather than the Nineteenth Century principles of unilateral forcible self-help, would best serve modern international legal and political conditions.[99]

R. *Accioly.* Yet another pre-World War II view of the right of protection was that of the Brazilian jurist Accioly, writing in 1940.[100] Following a traditional exposition of the right of a State to protect its nationals abroad through diplomacy, Accioly proceeded to discuss a State's remedies when such diplomatic efforts fail. "Should the local authorities declare themselves powerless to grant the claimed protection or demonstrate their indifference to the claims, an international conflict may arise; and if there is shown the impossibility of an amicable solution to the dispute, the claimant State has the right of recourse to coercive measures."[101]

Thus, Accioly, on the eve of World War II, demonstrated the continued acceptance of the broad right to use forcible protection, not limited to situations wherein the lives and property of a State's nationals were immediately at risk.

As the preceding discussion reveals, the juridical underpinnings of international legal principles justifying the use of force to protect nationals and their property abroad are rooted in the writings of the "classical" writers on international law, given the many references to the views of Grotius relative to the importance of the citizen to the State and the right of one State to enforce its rights against another State, by force if necessary.[102]

Similarly, Wolff's thoughts, particularly with reference to the validity of the use of force to enforce a State's rights,[103] also have influenced many of the later writers on the subject of forcible protection.[104] Vattel's position on the State's obligation to protect its citizen, albeit limited by a concern for the rights of other States,[105] finds restatement in the views of subsequent writers on the protection of nationals abroad.[106]

From this cursory survey of some of the leading publicists, there can be seen the gradual development of a principle justifying the forcible protection of nationals and their property abroad. Nevertheless, by the outbreak of World War II the desirability of forcible protection was being questioned by a growing number of writers.

## NOTES

1. 2 R. Phillimore, International Law 24 (1854).
2. *Id.* at 25.
3. *Id.*
4. *Id.* at 26. See the similar views of Pradier-Fodere at note 21 *infra*.
5. *Id.*
6. 42 Brit. & For. State Papers 385 (1852).
7. *Id.*
8. J. M. Bluntschli, Le Droit International Codifie 223 (1874) (author's translation).
9. *Id.* at 223 n.1.
10. *Id.* See the discussion of this incident at page 27 *infra*.
11. *Id.*
12. *Id.* at 224.
13. *Id.* at 224 n.1.
14. H. Bonfils, Manuel de Droit International Public 159 (1894) (author's translation).
15. *Id.* at 158. See discussion of this incident at page 25 *infra*.
16. *Id.* See the discussion of this incident at page 26 *infra*.
17. *Id.* at 158-59.

18. *Id.* at 159. See note 6 *supra*.
19. *Id.*
20. *Id.* See the discussion of this incident at page 29 *infra*.
21. F. Pradier-Fodere, Traite de Droit International Public 614 (1885) (author's translation).
22. *Id.* at 615.
23. *Id.* at 619. See the similar views of Phillimore at note 1 *supra*.
24. *Id.* at 620.
25. *Id.* at 629-30. See the discussion of this incident at page 29 *infra*.
26. *Id.* at 630.
27. 1 J. Westlake, International Law 313 (1904).
28. *Id.* at 314.
29. *Id.*
30. *Id.* at 314-15.
31. *Id.* at 216. For the views of Bluntschli, *see* note 8 *supra*.
32. *Id.* at 317-18.
33. 1 L Oppenheim, International Law 374 (1905).
34. *Id.* at 374 n.3.
35. *Id.* at 375.
36. *Id.*
37. *Id.*
38. J.B. Moore, American Diplomacy (1905).
39. *Id.* at 131.
40. *Id.*
41. *Id.* at 132-67.
42. C. Stockton, A Manual of International Law for the Use of Naval Officers 143 (1911).
43. *Id.* at 139-41. For a more detailed discussion tracing the development of United States Navy Regulations authorizing the use of force to protect United States nationals abroad, *see* Appendix II *infra*. The regulations in force at the time Stockton published his book may be found at pages 210-12 *infra*.
44. *Id.* at 143. For a similar discussion justifying forcible protection in underdeveloped countries, citing the examples of the Boxer Rebellion and revolutionary disturbances in Latin America, see Root, The Basis of Protection to Citizens Residing Abroad, 4 Am. J. Int'l L. 517 (1910).
45. J. Clark, Right to Protect Citizens in Foreign Countries by Landing Forces (3d rev. ed. 1934) (quotes identical to 1912 edition).
46. *Id.* at 24.
47. *Id.* at 25.
48. Authorities relied upon by Clark include Bluntschli, Bonfils, Pradier-Fodere, Phillimore, Oppenheim and Westlake. See *id.* at 25-34.
49. *Id.* at 25.
50. H. Hodges, The Doctrine of Intervention 58 (1915).
51. *Id.* at 58-59.
52. *Id.* at 58.
53. *Id.* at 66.
54. *Id.* at 65-74.
55. *Id.* at 74 (emphasis deleted).
56. *Id.* at 74-75.

57. *Id.* at 78-80.
58. *Id.* at 75-80.
59. E. Borchard, The Diplomatic Protection of Citizens Abroad 448 (1915).
60. *Id. See* J. Clark, *supra* note 45, at 24.
61. E. Borchard, *supra* note 59, at 449.
62. *Id.* at 451.
63. *Id.* at 450.
64. *Id.* at 452. See the discussion of this incident at pages 31-32 and 141-42 *infra*.
65. *Id.* This incident is discussed in Appendix I, at page 149 *infra*.
66. *Id.*
67. *Id.*
68. *Id.*
69. 1 P. Fauchille, Traite de Droit International Public 582 (1922) (author's translation).
70. *Id.* See the discussion of this incident at page 26 *infra*.
71. *Id.* at 583. See the discussion of this incident at pages 31-32 and 141-42 *infra*.
72. *Id.* See the discussion of this incident at page 33 *infra*.
73. 1 C. Hyde, International Law Chiefly as Interpreted and Applied by the United States (1922).
74. *Id.* at 117.
75. *Id.* at 121.
76. *Id.* at 118.
77. *Id.* at 350-51. See the discussion of this incident at page pages 31-32 and 141-42 *infra*.
78. *Id.* at 352 n.1.
79. *Id.* at 352 n.2. This incident is discussed in Appendix I, at pages 149-50 *infra*.
80. *Id.* at 351-52.
81. Winfield, The Grounds of Intervention in International Law, 5 Brit. Y.B. Int'l L. 149, 160 (1924).
82. *Id.*
83. *Id.*
84. *Id.*
85. M. Offutt, The Protection of Intervention in International Law, 5 Brit. Y.B. Int'l L. 149, 160 (1924).
86. *Id.* at 160 n.2.
87. *Id.* at 2-3.
88. *Id.* at 3.
89. F. Dunn, The Protection of Nationals (1932).
90. *Id.* at 19.
91. *Id.*
92. A. Hindmarsh, Force in Peace: Force Short of War in International Relations (1933).
93. *Id.* at 75.
94. *Id.* at 75 n.1.
95. *Id.* at 79. See the discussion of this incident at pages 33-34 *infra*.
96. *Id.* at 80. See the discussion of this incident at pages 35-36 *infra*.
97. *Id.* at 82.
98. *Id.* at 85.
99. *Id.* at 107-08.
100. H. Accioly, Traite de Droit International (1940).
101. *Id.* at 289-90 (author's translation).

102. *See e.g.*, R. Phillimore, *supra* note 1, at 24; J.B. Moore, *supra* note 38, at 131; F. Dunn, *supra* note 89, at 46-48; and A. Hindmarsh, *supra* note 92, at 87 n.1.

103. Wolff, Jus Gentium 138-39 (J. Scott ed. 1934).

104. Although not cited directly, Wolff's justification for the use of force finds support in the works of Bonfils, Pradier-Fodere, and Oppenheim, among the authors discussed in this chapter.

105. E. Vattel, The Law of Nations 161 (J. Chitty ed. 1883).

106. *See e.g.*, F. Pradier-Fodere, *supra* note 21, at 615; 1 J. Westlake, *supra* note 27, at 314; J.B. Moore, *supra* note 38, at 131-32; F. Dunn, *supra* note 89, at 48-53; and A. Hindmarsh, *supra* note 92, at 87 n.1.

# Chapter III

## State Practice During the Pre-United Nations Period

The State practices reviewed in Chapter III provide the background against which many of the traditionalist writers based and justified their pronouncements of the era.

A. *French Blockade of Argentina. 1838-1840.*[1] Following the adoption of an extremely restrictive import and export tariff policy by the Argentine government in the 1830s, many European powers whose nationals were trading with Argentina grew quite concerned. Under Article IV of the Treaty of Amity, Commerce, and Navigation between Great Britain and the United Provinces of Rio de la Plata, signed at Buenos Aires on 2 February 1825, British merchants had been accorded most-favored-nation status.[2] In 1836, when a frustrated French diplomat trying to negotiate a similar agreement with the Argentine government threatened naval intervention to roll back stiff duties, as well as to remedy the alleged mistreatment and imprisonment of French nationals,[3] Argentina responded with an even more stringent tariff law. Thereupon, France suspended diplomatic relations and several years later sent a fleet under Admiral Leblanc to initiate a blockade of the capital, Buenos Aires. The blockade was lifted after two years pursuant to a Convention between France and Argentina that was signed on 29 October 1840.[4] While the specific claims of France with respect to the protection of her nationals went unmentioned, both States agreed to accord the nationals of each other most-favored-nation treatment in the future.

The French blockade had a severe impact on Argentina. Between the second half of 1837 and the second half of 1838, imports dropped in value from 19 to 4 million paper pesos. Indirectly, however, the blockade, together with an earlier blockade by Brazil in 1826 and a subsequent joint blockade by France and Great Britain in 1845, had a beneficial effect on the Argentine beef industry. When the slaughter of animals for export stopped, cattle herds increased greatly. Where there had been an estimated 3 to 4 million cattle in 1837, the heads increased to 10 to 12 million head by 1850.[5]

Although Bonfils cited this incident as illustrative of a doctrine permitting forcible protection,[6] from the perspective of France it appears that the blockade was merely a military measure with the political and economic objectives of advancing France's commercial interests in Argentina. Perhaps more importantly France was defending a "point of honor" by not submitting to the policies of the Argentine government. The claims of French nationals were of tertiary importance.[7]

B. *Great Britain, Spain and France in Mexico. 1861.*[8] During the internal conflict ongoing in Mexico in the late 1850s, foreign nationals were indiscriminately insulted, robbed, injured, and murdered. Moreover, various financial obligations owed foreign nationals by the Mexican government were not met. The three major States that had nationals injured and debts unpaid—Great Britain, Spain, and France—collectively agreed in the Convention of London, signed 31 October 1861,[9] to intervene in Mexico with forces of sufficient size to seize and occupy different fortresses and military positions on the coast of Mexico. Article II of the Convention specified that:

> The High Contracting Parties engage not to seek for themselves, through the employment of the coercive measures contemplated by the present convention, any acquisition of territory, nor any particular advantage, nor to exercise in the internal affairs of Mexico any influence tending to abridge the right of the Mexican nation freely to decide upon and establish the form of its government.[10]

The signatories of the Convention agreed that the expeditionary forces should consist of 6,000 Spaniards and 3,000 Frenchmen, with Great Britain contributing a naval division and a landing force of 700 Marines.

On 14 December 1861, the Spanish fleet sailed into the harbor of Vera Cruz and three days later disembarked troops that entered the city. The combined French and British expedition arrived at Vera Cruz on 7 January 1862, and at once began to disembark more troops.[11]

Subsequent conferences between the three Powers revealed growing dissension over the purpose of the intervention. France revealed intentions beyond the mere exaction of damages for wrongs done to its nationals, while Great Britain and Spain continued to adhere to Article II of the Convention of London. Nevertheless, negotiations were initiated with the Mexican government.[12] As the negotiations proceeded, however, the lack of consensus of the parties to the Convention emerged. France sent substantial reinforcements, allegedly to guard against any disaster to the French troops as they marched into the interior of the country. Additional disputes arose over France's introduction back into the country of exiled Mexicans who had supported the prior monarchy in opposition to the two ruling Constitutionalists.[13]

The final rupture occurred at a conference held between the three Powers on 9 April 1862. Great Britain and Spain declared that, if France did not disassociate herself from the exiled Mexicans and continued to support the exiles' determination not to take part in pending negotiations with the Mexican government, they would withdraw their troops from Mexico. When the French refused, the British and Spanish terminated their role in the intervention, lowering their flags at Vera Cruz at sunset on 24 April 1862. France then initiated an independent policy aimed at the installation of a French-controlled monarch under Archduke Ferdinand Maximilian of Austria.[14]

Both Bonfils and Fauchille cited this incident as an example of the permissible use of force by States to rectify injustices to their nationals.[15] It does not appear, however, that the intervening States ever justified their actions in such legal terms. Implicit in the Convention of London, though, was the notion that an intervention for such purposes was permissible if conducted within narrow limits. That is to say, forcible intervention to rectify wrongs was legitimate so long as it did not severely impair the sovereignty of the country against which the action was undertaken.[16]

C. *Great Britain and Abyssinia. 1867-1868.*[17] Following a period of civil war, Theodore (Kassa) became Emperor of Abyssinia on 7 February 1855. Two Englishmen, Walter Plowden, who later was named British Consul to Abyssinia, and John Bell, aided Theodore's rise to, and consolidation of, power. Both Plowden and Bell, however, were killed during an uprising against Theodore in 1860. After their deaths, the Emperor began to lose hold over his army resulting in his "killing and burning alive thousands in a desperate attempt to save face by his frightfulness."[18]

In November 1861, the British government, having scant information regarding the situation in Abyssinia, decided to send Captain C. Duncan Cameron as Plowden's successor.[19] Upon receiving Cameron in July 1862,[20] the Emperor told the British consul the persons that had murdered Plowden and Bell had been slain and that he intended to crush the Turks and the Egyptians.[21] In a letter to Queen Victoria, Theodore suggested the establishment of an Abyssinian Embassy in Great Britain.[22] When this letter, delayed in the mails, elicited no reply,[23] Theodore took it as an insult to himself and his nation, summarily imprisoning Cameron and certain other Englishmen.[24]

In May 1864, the British government sent Hormuzd Rassam, an assistant to Colonel W. L. Merewether, Political Resident at Aden, to obtain the release of Cameron and his fellow prisoners.[25] After many delays,[26] Rassam met with Theodore on 28 January 1866, and the latter announced the release of Cameron and his companions the following day.[27] In July 1866, however, the King again imprisoned Cameron, along with Rassam and 60 other Europeans, "on the pretext that . . . [the British] Government ha[d] an intention of sending troops to make war against him."[28]

The British government responded to Theodore's actions by sending a rescue expedition under Sir Robert Napier that arrived in Abyssinia in 1867.[29] Overcoming the rugged terrain, Napier's expedition finally encountered Theodore's army at Arogee on 10 April 1868. The British, possessing modern weapons with superior firepower, soon overwhelmed Theodore's forces and entered the fortress at Magdala on Easter Monday, 1868. Theodore committed suicide upon their entry.[30]

Although the Emperor's rivals urged Napier to settle the succession, Napier contented himself with the rescue of the prisoners and began his march back to the coast.[31] When Napier left Abyssinia, in May 1868, the country immediately plunged into civil war among rival chieftains.

Bluntschli cited this incident as illustrative of a "state's right and duty to protect its nationals abroad by all means authorized by international law,"[32] and in this case by the use of force. Great Britain, however, did not explicitly mention this international law argument in its ultimatum to Theodore. Instead, it advanced the broad rationale that

> [i]t is impossible for the Queen any longer to endure such conduct on the part of your Majesty, and Her Majesty has therefore given orders that a military force . . . should without delay enter your dominions, and obtain from you by force a concession which you have hitherto withheld from friendly representation.[33]

The clear import of this language, of course, is that Great Britain considered its decision to use force to be a legitimate alternative to "friendly representation" and/or diplomacy.

D. *Great Britain in Honduras. 1873.*[34] In the summer of 1873, Honduran forces under the command of a General Stracber seized the castle at Omoa, Honduras, imprisoned the British subjects resident there and destroyed most of their property. In August 1873, when the British Man-of-War *Niobe* arrived at Omoa, its Captain made several demands of General Stracber, including a $100,000 indemnity for the losses sustained by British subjects, the immediate surrender of the British subjects held prisoner and a 21-gun salute to the English flag.

General Stracber replied that the demands were unjust, as he had no money, was not responsible for the British subjects and that responsibility rest with the Honduran government. The captain of the *Niobe* thereupon reduced the indemnity portion of the demand to $50,000, giving General Stracber until 2 p.m. on 19 August to comply with it and the other two demands. If not satisfied, the Captain warned that the *Niobe* would bombard the castle. When a satisfactory response was not forthcoming, the bombardment began at 3:45 p.m., continuing until the following day when General Stracber, at last accepting the British demands, turned over the British prisoners and signed a document binding the Honduran government to pay all the losses claimed.

Clark listed this incident as an example of the use of force to protect nationals by States other than the United States.[35] Again, although Great Britain apparently offered no international law argument in support of its use of force, the circumstances of this incident illustrate the readiness with which a decision to employ force to protect British subjects abroad was reached, a readiness presumably buttressed by the belief that such an action was compatible with the norms of international law.

E. *Great Britain and France in Egypt. 1876-1879.*[36] Under the rule of Mohamed Said, Egypt in 1854 granted a concession to Ferdinand de Lesseps, a retired official of the French diplomatic service, for the construction of a ship canal across the Isthmus of Suez. The grant of the Suez Canal concession was the first episode in an era of extravagant development and foreign speculation in Egypt. Egyptian rulers, in their rush to encourage foreign merchants, who supplied them with short-term loans and acted as import and export agents for Egyptian government monopolies, greatly extended the freedom of Europeans from the processes of Egyptian civil and criminal law. The privileged position accorded them naturally acted as a powerful magnet to attract persons from all over Europe to Egypt. Between 1854 and 1874, the number of European nationals resident in Egypt increased from roughly 15,000 to 85,000. More important than the numerical increase, however, was that European interests—in many cases assisted by diplomatic intervention—acquired a virtual stranglehold on the economic life of the country.

Ismail, who succeeded Mohamed Said in 1863, sought simultaneously to modernize Egypt, to enrich his own extensive private estates and to establish an enlarged Egyptian Empire. He attempted to accomplish these goals with money borrowed from foreign merchants and through long-term loans contracted with foreign banking houses. However by 1875 Ismail's financial position had deteriorated so greatly that he asked the British government not only for assistance in managing the receipts and revenues of Egypt, but also for advice on all financial matters.

The British government sent, as an envoy to Egypt, the Paymaster-General, Stephen Cave. Cave's report recommended that a substantial loan be made to aid Egyptian finances. Following additional negotiations between Great Britain and France, which also had a large number of nationals who were creditors of Egypt, a joint proposal was presented to the Egyptian government, with an agreement being reached on 14 November 1875. Under the settlement a substantial portion of the Egyptian debt was liquidated and British and French nationals were appointed to a number of high financial posts within the Egyptian government. Pradier-Fodere cited this incident as a "very striking example of foreign intervention in the internal affairs of another state with a view to the protection of the nationals of the intervening powers."[37]

Although the example follows a discussion of the right to use force to protect nationals, it is clear that the actions of Great Britain and France involved only diplomatic, rather than forcible, measures. Bonfils also referred to this incident in his discussion of the protection of nationals abroad.[38] For him it illustrated the fact that "European Governments have intervened in favor of their nationals who had lent money to foreign governments, against weak states, incapable of resisting, but not against strong States. . . ."[39] Certainly this incident, although not illustrative of the principle of forcible protection, indicates once again that strong States were inclined to intervene with weaker ones, financially as well as forcibly, to protect the interests of their nationals.

F. *France and Portugal. 1893-1894.*[40] Pursuant to a decree of 9 November 1893, the Portuguese government declared the liquidation of the Portuguese Railway Company, many of whose creditors were foreigners, including numerous French citizens. Although the decree provided that a commission was to be formed to direct the disposition of the company's assets, only two of its nine members represented the interests of the foreign creditors. Coincidentally, the commission's decision, published on 5 January 1894, had the effect of favoring the Portuguese government and certain preferred creditors to the detriment of the foreign creditors.

Frustrated by this turn of events, the French creditors asked their government for assistance in obtaining a fair share of the company's assets. The French government promptly adopted their claims and vigorously complained to Portugal.[41] Indeed, France went so far as to threaten the use of force should the wronged creditors not be compensated satisfactorily.[42] The Portuguese government quickly acceded to the French demands and compensated the French creditors in a more equitable manner. Thus, although force actually was not employed in this instance, it certainly was contemplated by France as the ultimate means of obtaining redress for its creditors.

Bonfils referred to this incident as an example of the use by States of the threat of force to protect their nationals who were creditors of foreign governments.[43] He viewed this type of protection as peculiarly susceptible to unfortunate consequences in terms of popular resentment against foreigners and the straining of international relations.[44]

G. *Boxer Rebellion. China. 1900.*[45] The last decade of the Nineteenth Century was marked by violent anti-colonial agitation in China. Behind much of this turbulence was the Society of Harmonious Fists, or "Boxers." Although opposed to Christianity and Europeans, the Boxers' prime goal was to evict the Manchus from the Throne and end the Ching dynasty that seemed incapable of preserving the Chinese Empire intact. By 1899, however, the Boxers increasingly directed their attacks against the "foreign devils," who they believed were the real source of China's ills.

During the spring of 1900, attacks on foreigners in China, largely at the instigation of the Boxers, became increasingly frequent. By 9 June the threat to the foreign legations located in the capital, Peking, had become very real. News of such danger prompted the governments affected (primarily Great Britain, France, Russia, Germany, the United States, Japan, Italy, and Austria-Hungary) to direct their naval forces in the area of China to take any action deemed necessary to save the legations. Admiral Seymour, the commander of the British fleet, assembled an international force of about 2,000 men on 10 June to proceed to Peking to defend the legations. The force made extremely slow progress toward Peking, however, as the Boxers had destroyed the railway lines. On 15 June, when it had become apparent that the relief force could advance no further, the decision was made to fall back to the coast.

Meanwhile, the attacks on the legations in Peking had increased in intensity, with the German Minister having been killed. Upon hearing this news, the allied military forces attacked and captured Chinese government forts at Taku in order to establish a coastal beachhead. Next, in mid-July, they captured the city of Tientsin, where another group of foreigners was endangered. The latter part of July and early August were spent in building up an expeditionary force to rescue the legations. On 4 August, a relief column, numbering about 17,000 men, left Tientsin for Peking, arriving on 14 August, 1900.

The aftermath of the rescue included a number of punitive expeditions to areas with a reputation of anti-foreignism. The most noted of the punitive measures was the destruction of the city of Pao Ting Fu by a joint expedition of British, German, and French forces.[46] Moreover, a series of trials were held to punish persons responsible for the atrocities committed by the Boxers. Many executions and fines followed. Finally, on 1 February 1901, the Boxer Society was dissolved and membership in any "anti-foreign" society was declared to be a crime punishable by death. Later that same year, China agreed to pay a large indemnity and to prohibit the importation of arms for a period of two years.[47]

This incident was cited by Borchard,[48] Fauchille,[49] and Hyde[50] as an example of the forcible protection of nationals abroad. Probably the fact that China was viewed as semi-barbarous by most Western States, plus the exigencies of the moment, accounted most directly for this use of force, which the above commentators all regarded as permissible under international law.

H. *Franco-Turkish Conflict. 1901.*[51] During the last decade of the Nineteenth Century, several French creditors had difficulty with the Turkish government. Under a contract dated 7 November 1890, a French corporation agreed to construct docks in Constantinople. As soon as the docks were completed, however, the Turkish government seized them without compensating the French builders. Negotiations between the French and Turkish governments on the matter proved unsatisfactory to the French. In addition, substantial loans made to the Turkish government by two French banking concerns went unpaid. Finally, the Turkish government refused to honor a concession it made in 1894 to cede territory to a French group in return for destroying malaria-carrying mosquitos in an area of Turkey.

By 1901, it had become apparent to France that diplomatic measures alone were not going to resolve the claims. The French government therefore decided to employ forcible measures by seizing the customs house on the Turkish island of Mytilini and retaining the funds and goods contained therein until the Turkish government honored its commitments. A French fleet was sent to the Mediterranean which seized and occupied the customs house on 7 November 1901. Little force was involved in this action, since the governor of the island actually acquiesced in the occupation and sent the Turkish garrison to the island's interior to avoid any encounter with the French forces. The Turkish government promptly agreed to the French demands and the occupation soon ended.

Bonfils referred briefly to the Mytilini incident in his discussion of the forcible protection of nationals who are creditors of foreign governments. Noting the obvious, however, that such intervention "excites the resentment of the people against foreigners [and] complicates international relations."[52] Despite the effects of this incident, one of many, it illustrates that the use of force to protect nationals abroad and enforce creditor's rights in such situations was common at the turn of the century.

I. *Great Britain, Germany and Italy in Venezuela. 1902.* As the result of civil war in Venezuela from 1898 to 1900, British, German and Italian nationals sustained large amounts of property damage.[53] The strenuous protests by Great Britain and Germany yielding no results, on 13 November 1902, the countries agreed on joint action.[54] In the event that Venezuela failed to accede to their demands, they agreed to utilize coercive measures.[55]

On 2 December 1902, the diplomatic representatives of the British and German governments at Caracas presented an ultimatum to the Venezuelan government which made clear that in the event of an unsatisfactory response, forcible measures would be employed.[56] On 3 December, Italy asked to be allowed to join in the ultimatum against Venezuela as an ally of Great Britain and Germany, a request quickly granted.[57] The demands not having been met, on 10 December the three States imposed a blockade under which they seized or disabled four small Venezuelan ships.[58] Three days later the Venezuelan government, through the U.S. Embassy in London, requested arbitration of the claims in question, proposing certain conditions. The allies finally agreed to this method of settlement.[59]

Fauchille referred to this incident as an example of the justifiable use of force by a State to compel another State "to fulfill its international obligations or to compensate for an injustice or an insult."[60] However, it does not appear that the three States justified their use of force in legal terms at the time.[61]

J. *Italian Invasion of Corfu. 1923.*[62] The establishment of Albania following the Balkan Wars of 1912-1913 left the delimitation of its borders as one of the unresolved issues facing the Great Powers when World War I commenced in 1914. Following the war, with Albania's frontiers still unfixed and border disputes increasing, the British government proposed that a Conference of

Ambassadors fix the frontiers. On 9 November 1921, that conference decided to delimit the Albanian borders on the basis of lines drawn up before the war, with a special delimitation commission to mark the borders. The commission arrived in Albania on 7 March 1922. The relationship of the commission and its Italian President, General Enrico Tellini, to the Greek government and the Greek delegate attached to the commission, was extremely strained throughout. On 27 August 1923, General Tellini and his staff were murdered near the Greek-Albanian frontier, in Greek territory.

Mussolini, by then in control of Italy, instructed his ambassador in Athens to make "the most energetic protests" to the Greek government. Following several communications with the Ambassador, on 29 August Mussolini issued a series of demands to the Greek government. These demands included an apology by the highest Greek military authority, a funeral service in the Roman Catholic Cathedral in Athens to be attended by all the members of the Greek government, a criminal investigation to be completed within five days after the arrival of an Italian military attache, capital punishment for those persons responsible for the murders, an indemnity of 50 million Italian lire payable within five days; honor to be shown the Italian flag, and military honors to be paid to the corpses on the occasion of their transfer to an Italian vessel.

The following day the Greek government rejected the bulk of these demands, specifically, the investigation by the Greek authorities, capital punishment for the murderers, and the indemnity. Orders were issued immediately from Rome to Admiral Emilio Solari, commander of the Italian navy, "to proceed at once to the occupation of [the Greek island of] Corfu."[63] On 31 August, Italian naval units bombarded and occupied the island, an occupation lasting until 27 September 1923.

Hindmarsh cited this incident as an example of the practice of powerful States to employ military force against offending weaker States to compel recognition of alleged international obligations.[64] The incident, on its facts, involved a "point of honor" in the protection of nationals abroad, all that remained following their murder.

K. *French Bombardment of Damascus. 1925.*[65] The peace settlement following World War I included the division of parts of the Ottoman Empire into "mandates" of the League of Nations under the tutelage of the victorious allies. One such area was Syria, which was placed under French control until such time as it was deemed ready to take its place as an independent nation. French rule proved oppressive to the Syrian population, however, and the resulting discontent led to full-scale revolution in 1925.

Originating with the Druzes, a fiercely nationalistic sect living in the mountains southeast of Damascus, the revolt quickly gained momentum. By 18 October 1925, Damascus was severely threatened, the revolutionaries having entered and occupied a part of the city.

At this point the French authorities, "without notice or declaration of martial law, and without warning to foreign residents other than French,"[66] first evacuated French troops and then proceeded to bombard the city with artillery and aircraft. The bombardment, which continued for 24 hours and caused extensive damage, ceased only when the city officials agreed to pay an indemnity of £100,000 in gold and 3,000 rifles. The indemnity, in fact, never was paid. The bombardment so increased the resistance of the rebels that the revolt was not put down until 1927.

Bowett has cited this incident as a classic example of a reprisal, distinguishing it from the use of force to protect the lives and property of nationals abroad, which he characterizes as a permissible action of self-defense.[67] The justification offered by France at the time centered on the contention that the Druze rebellion was merely "banditry and brigandage," and hence any measures used to suppress it were merely police actions clearly within the exclusive jurisdiction of France, the legally constituted authority in Syria.[68] France cited no other principle of international law to support its actions. In fact, since no French nationals were being protected by the use of force, it seems apparent that France was merely re-establishing its control of the city in accordance with its mandate by the League of Nations.

L. *Japan and China. 1931-1932.*[69] On 18 September 1931, an explosion occurred on the Japanese-owned South Manchurian Railway in southern China. The Japanese argued that Chinese soldiers had caused the incident, a plausible (albeit actually untrue) claim because at the time there was serious friction between the Chinese and Japanese in the Japanese-leased territory along the railway zone. Additionally, the Chinese authorities' desired the reduction and/or elimination of Japanese interests in Manchuria. Within 24 hours after the explosion, Japanese forces occupied Mukden and several other important towns in South Manchuria.[70]

The Japanese army, which soon controlled all of Manchuria, proceeded to set up an "independent" State of Manchukuo with a former Emperor of China at its head. On 25 August 1932, the Japanese government recognized the State of Manchukuo and concluded a treaty of alliance with it. The Manchukuo government assumed control over the custom houses of its ports and thereby became self-sufficient. The League of Nations formed an investigatory body, named the "Lytton Commission," to investigate the situation. It issued a report on 1 October 1932, condemning the Japanese invasion as an illegal act of aggression in violation of the Covenant of the League of Nations.[71]

The Japanese government responded to these charges of aggression with several arguments,[72] one of which was that the purpose of the invasion was merely to protect Japanese nationals and treaty rights in China. To support this claim, the Japanese government asserted not only that such a use of self-defense was recognized as an accepted principle of customary international law, but also that it was not prohibited by the Kellogg-Briand Pact of 1928 that outlawed war as an instrument of national policy.[73]

Hindmarsh concluded that the Manchurian invasion illustrated the improper use of the forcible protection rationale by powerful States as a tool to achieve control over weaker States.[74] His characterization proved correct given Japan's subsequent resort to the "forcible protection" argument in the face of facts rather clearly indicating that its motives were essentially aggressive, and by Japan's subsequent actions leading up to, and during, World War II.

M. *Germany in Czechoslovakia. 1938.*[75] Coincident with the rise of Nazism in Germany in the 1930s was an intense nationalism on the part of the German ethnic community in the Sudetenland, an area of Czechoslovakia. Beginning in 1937, Germany's support for the "Sudeten Germans" became increasingly overt. In April 1938, at Berlin's urging, the German nationalist party in Czechoslovakia presented the Czech government with a number of demands, popularly known as the "Karlsbad Program," relating chiefly to autonomy for the Sudetenland. Following the Czech government's rejection of these demands, Germany began to escalate its propaganda attacks against Czechoslovakia for alleged mistreatment of its German ethnic minority.

During the next several months, intense negotiations were conducted between Germany and Czechoslovakia and the latter's allies, Britain and France. This diplomatic activity culminated in the Munich agreement of 30 September 1938. Czechoslovakia ceded the Sudetenland to Germany and the Western governments of Great Britain and France acknowledged that Czechoslovakia was both politically and economically within Germany's sphere of influence. Confronted by a strong neighbor and with weak allies, the Czech government and its armed forces had little alternative but to acquiesce in the German demands. German troops subsequently entered and occupied the Sudetenland on 1 October 1938, meeting no resistance.

The Munich crisis clearly illustrates the abuses to which the principle of forcible protection may be put.[76] Indeed, as Brownlie has argued, the crisis was one of several incidents that led to the drafting of Article 2(4) of the United Nations Charter—which purports to prevent States from using force for such purposes.[77]

## NOTES

1. An extensive discussion of the French blockade of Argentina may be found in J. Cady, Foreign Intervention in the Rio de la Plata: 1838-50, at 22-91 (1929). *See also* Y. Rennie, The Argentine Republic 54-55 (1945); H. Ferns, Britain and Argentina in the Nineteenth Century 241-80 (1960).

2. 3 L. Hertslet, Commercial Treaties 44, 45 (1841). Cady stated that this treaty placed British merchants "on a status of absolute equality with Argentine citizens in the matter of trading privileges, port and tonnage dues, etc." J. Cady, *supra* note 1, at 18.

3. According to Cady:

> [t]he specific claims . . . were neither numerous, important, nor particularly well founded. Two of them concerned instances of enforced service in the Argentine army. Another was the case of a French sutler in [the Argentine] army . . . who had been summarily imprisoned for six months for possession of property belonging to the Government. The most serious claim was that of the widow of a Swiss printer named Bacle, claiming French protection, who died at his home in January 1838, from illness contracted while serving a prison term for revolutionary intrigue. A fifth concerned an acknowledged claim of a French citizen named Despony, who had sustained, in the disorder of 1821, considerable damage to his business.

*Id.* at 26-27.

4. Convention Between France and Buenos Ayres for the Settlement of Differences, Oct. 29, 1840, 29 Brit. & For. State Papers 1089 (1840-1841).

5. Y. Rennie, *supra* note 1, at 55.

6. H. Bonfils, Manuel de Droit International Public 158 (1894).

7. "The particular merits of the claims were never . . . the primary subject of the dispute. . . . With a will for peace on either side, a settlement might easily have been arranged; in reality, it became a point of honor with each party not to surrender to the formal demands of the other." J. Cady, *supra* note 1, at 27.

8. A detailed discussion of this incident may be found in J. Musser, The Establishment of Maximilian's Empire in Mexico chs. 1-4 (1918).

9. Convention Between Great Britain, Spain and France Relative to Combined Operations Against Mexico, Oct. 31, 1861, 51 Brit. & For. State Papers 63 (1860-1861).

10. *Id.* at 64 (author's translation).

11. J. Musser, *supra* note 8, at 33.

12. The terms of the joint note were vague. Its apparent purpose was solely to open negotiations with Mexico. See 53 Brit. & For. State Papers 411-12 (1862-1863).

13. J. Musser, *supra* note 8, at 41.

14. *Id.*

15. *See* H. Bonfils, *supra* note 6, at 158; 1 P. Fauchille, Traite de Droit International Public 582 (1922). Both authors noted, however, that France's subsequent conduct constituted "flagrant intervention."

16. J. Musser, *supra* note 8, at 16.

17. A detailed description of the British intervention in Abyssinia may be found in F. Myatt, The March to Magdala: The Abyssinian War of 1868 (1970). *See also* A. Jones & E. Monroe, A History of Ethiopia 129-34 (1970); A. Moorehead, The Blue Nile 257 (1962).

18. A. Jones & E. Monroe, *supra* note 17, at 29.
19. See 53 Brit. & For. State Papers 51-54 (1852-63); 54 *id.* at 1153-55 (1863-64).
20. 55 *id.* at 1423 (1864-65). Cameron was delayed in reaching Gondar, where Theodore resided, when the Foreign Office ordered him to accompany the Duke of Saxe Coburg on an excursion into the northern frontier of Abyssinia.
21. 53 *id.* at 55.
22. *Id.* at 62-63.
23. Cameron, who was to deliver the letter, was stopped on his way to the coast by a rebel chief in Tigre. The stop delayed the transmission of the letter, which did not reach Great Britain until February 1863. 55 *id.* at 1424. Rather than responding to the letter, the British government, apparently uneasy about an alliance with Theodore in a crusade against Islam, chose a "course of masterly inactivity." See F. Myatt, *supra* note 17, at 38-39.
24. Cameron had returned to Gondar in July 1863. *Id.*
25. Rassam arrived at Massowah in August 1864, and dispatched two letters to Theodore requesting an audience with the Emperor in Gondar. *Id.* at 1425.
26. Theodore did not respond to Rassam until August 1865. The latter was further delayed when he was ordered to Egypt for instructions. *Id.*
27. 60 *id.* at 1036-37 (1869-70).
28. *Id.* at 1066. The Emperor apparently had heard that "a railroad had been laid down between Egypt and Kassala, for the purpose of transporting British, French and Turkish troops thereon, for the purpose of invading Abyssinia." *Id.* at 1067.
29. *Id.* at 1088.
30. A. Jones & E. Monroe, *supra* note 17, at 133-34.
31. The victorious troops plundered Magdala "in the best traditions of the British Army at the time." Apparently little of the loot remained in private hands, however, for the only practicable way out of the fortress was "in the hands of the provost, backed by a guard of the 33rd Regiment." F. Myatt, *supra* note 17, at 165. The loot was auctioned for a total of 5,000 British pounds, which was then distributed to the soldiers according to rank. A. Moorehead, *supra* note 30, at 272. Upon his departure from Magdala on 17 April 1868, Napier ordered the fortress to be mined with explosives; by the next morning it had burned to the ground. *Id.* at 271.
32. M. Bluntschli, Le Droit International Codifie 223 (1874) (author's translation). More recent scholars have criticized this use of force in view of the apparent lack of proportionality between the injuries suffered by the imprisoned Europeans and the substantial loss of life inflicted upon the Abyssinians by the British. See A. Moorehead, *supra* note 17, at 258, and Farer, Humanitarian Intervention: The View from Charlottesville, in Humanitarian Intervention and the United Nations 149 (R. Lillich ed. 1973). On this issue of proportionality, however, it should be kept in mind that mid-Nineteenth Century Ethiopia was not an area to which one could send a few troops to rescue imprisoned nationals. The distance and terrain probably justified the sending of a force the size of Napier's, if not all of its actions once it arrived in Ethiopia.
33. 60 Brit. & For. State Papers 1088 (1869-1870).
34. For a description of this incident, see Correspondence Respecting the Bombardment of the Fortress of Omoa, Honduras, by the British Man-of-War *Niobe,* the 19th and 20th of August, 1873, 67 *id.* 959-60 (1875-1876).
35. J. Clark, Right to Protect Citizens in Foreign Countries by Landing Forces 37 (3d rev. ed. 1934) (quotes identical to 1912 ed.).
36. A description of Egypt during this period may be found in J. Marlowe, Cromer in Egypt ch. 1 (1970).

37. F. Pradier-Fodere, Traite de Droit International Public 628-29 (1885) (author's translation).
38. H. Bonfils, *supra* note 6, at 159.
39. *Id.* (author's translation).
40. For a brief discussion of this incident, see Chronique des Faits Internationaux, 1 Rev. Gen. de Droit Int'l Pub. 291 (1894).
41. *Id.* at 294, citing the Statement of Foreign Minister Casimir-Perier of March 9, 1894.
42. *Id.*, citing the Letter of M. Edmon Villey of January 10, 1894.
43. H. Bonfils, *supra* note 6, at 159.
44. *Id.* at 160.
45. A detailed discussion of the Boxer Rebellion may be found in L. Giles, The Siege of the Peking Legations (L. Marchant ed. 1970). *See also* V. Purcell, The Boxer Uprising: A Background Study (1963) and the factual summaries of the U.S. role in the intervention contained in Appendix I, at pages 141-42.
46. W. Martin, The Siege in Peking 139-40 (1900).
47. Settlement of Matters Growing Out of the Boxer Uprising (Boxer Protocol), Sept. 7, 1901, 1 C. Bevans, Treaties and Other International Agreements of the United States of America 1776-1949, at 302 (1968).
48. E. Borchard, The Diplomatic Protection of Nationals Abroad 452 (1915).
49. 1 P. Fauchille, *supra* note 15, at 583.
50. 1 C. Hyde, International Law Chiefly as Interpreted and Applied by the United States 350-51 (1922).
51. A detailed analysis of this incident may be found in Moncharville, Le Coflit Franco-Turc de 1901, 9 Rev. Gen. de Droit Int'l Pub. 677 (1902). The facts found in the following two paragraphs of the text are taken therefrom.
52. H. Bonfils, *supra* note 6, at 160.
53. The British claims involved principally the destruction of British shipping and railway companies. *See* 95 Brit. & For. State Papers 1076-77 (1901-1902). The German claims involved injuries to German merchants and landowners through forced loans, the appropriation of supplies without payment, and the plundering of their houses and the devastation of their lands. *Id.* at 1120-21. The Italian claims involved personal injuries and damage to property occasioned by the Civil War, as well as many claims by bondholders. *See* The Venezuelan Arbitration Before the Hague Tribunal, 1903, at 848, 851 (1905) [hereinafter The Venezuelan Arbitration].
54. 95 Brit. & For. State Papers at 1083-84.
55. *Id.* at 1085.
56. *Id.* at 1100.
57. *Id.* at 1101.
58. *Id.* at 1110.
59. *Id.* at 1123-26.
60. 1 P. Fauchille, *supra* note 15, at 582 (author's translation).
61. The legal arguments that Great Britain, Germany, and Italy made at the subsequent arbitration of the dispute concerned the priority over other creditors in the claims process which the three States contended they deserved. *See* The Venezuelan Arbitration, *supra* note 53, at 759, 815, 857.
62. A detailed discussion of this incident may be found in J. Barros, The Corfu Incident of 1923: Mussolini and the League of Nations (1965). The facts found in the following two paragraphs of the text are taken therefrom.
63. *Id.* at 67.

64. A. Hindmarsh, Force in Peace: Force Short of War in International Relations 79-80 (1933).

65. For descriptions of this incident, see G. Haddad, Fifty Years of Modern Syria and Lebanon 75-78 (1950); S. Longrigg, Syria and Lebanon under French Mandate 157-62 (1958); Wright, The Bombardment of Damascus, 20 Am. J. Int'l L. 263 (1926).

66. S. Longrigg, *supra* note 65, at 159.

67. D. Bowett, Self-Defence in International Law 99 (1958).

68. Wright, *supra* note 65, at 265. Professor Wright disagreed with the French position and argued that international law should not countenance such a disproportionate use of force. Instead, he argued that a formal demand for discontinuance of the allegedly illegal acts should have been made and then, if such a demand had not been heeded, a monetary fine should have been imposed proportionate to the alleged crimes. *Id.* at 274.

69. For detailed discussing of this incident, see R. Storry, A History of Modern Japan 186-96 (1960), and I. Nish, A Short History of Japan 157-61 (1968). The facts found in the following two paragraphs of the text are taken from these accounts.

70. The explosion and subsequent invasion were part of a plan hatched by Japanese Army officers, apparently without orders from the military high command, and certainly not with the approval of the Japanese government, whose "weak diplomacy" Japanese military leaders had criticized. See R. Storry, *supra* note 69, at 186-87.

71. *See generally* Lauterpacht, "Resort to War" and the Interpretation of the Covenant during the Manchurian Dispute, 28 Am. J. Int'l L. 43 (1934).

72. These arguments are discussed in W. Willoughby, Japan's Case Examined 17-67 (1940).

73. Renunciation of War as an Instrument of National Policy (Kellogg-Briand Peace Pact or Pact of Paris), Aug. 27, 1928, 2 C. Bevans, Treaties and Other International Agreements of the United States of America 1776-1949, at 732 (1969).

74. A. Hindmarsh, *supra* note 64, at 81-82.

75. For detailed analyses of the events surrounding the Munich agreement, see J. Wheeler-Bennett, Munich: Prologue to Tragedy (1948), and V. Mastny, The Czechs Under Nazi Rule (1971).

76. *See* R. Falk, Legal Order in a Violent World 161 (1968):

> To vindicate intervention under certain circumstances [including the forcible protection of nationals abroad] raises some serious world order problems. Any authorization of intervention creates a manipulative nexus that can itself be used as a justification for an abusive intrusion upon the legitimate autonomy of another state. An intervening state may claim to protect human rights so as to hide its dominant motive which is remote from altruism. One need only recall that Hitler explained his invasions of Czechoslovakia and Poland by the need to rescue German minorities from aggression.

77. Brownlie, Thoughts on Kind-Hearted Gunmen, in Humanitarian Intervention and the United Nations, *supra* note 4, at 139, 143.

# Chapter IV

## Contemporary Case Studies of United States Forcible Protection of Nationals Abroad

As the views of the publicists and the evidence of State practice surveyed in the preceding chapters reveals, traditional international law has sanctioned a State's use of force to protect the lives and property of its nationals abroad. With the adoption in 1945 of the United Nations Charter, however, a new set of international norms governing the use of force emerged to challenge this traditional right. The impact of these norms and subsequent developments upon the right of forcible protection will be considered in the following chapter. The present chapter focuses instead upon those instances where the United States, in the post-Charter period, has claimed to act pursuant to such right.

Although occasionally invoked by France and other States during this period,[1] most prominently by Israel involving Entebbe, the main instances where the protection of nationals rationale has been used to justify forcible protection since 1945, involve the United States.

These case studies warrant extensive treatment not only because the political events surrounding many of the instances attracted great international attention. The legal debates they generated also shed considerable light on what one may characterize as a developing international consensus justifying the forcible protection of nationals abroad, on the grounds that it is a legitimate exercise of a State's inherent right of self-defense under Article 51 of the UN Charter.

The question then arises as to how one squares the tenets of Article 2(4), the broad prohibition of the use of force, with Article 51? Can the notion of self-defense of a State be properly extrapolated to extend protection by force to a national living or transiting abroad?

### A. Lebanon. 1958.

The spring of 1958 was a period of intense internal unrest for the small Middle East country of Lebanon. By midsummer, the convergence of internal, regional and international factors produced a situation where the United States deemed itself compelled to mount a medium-scale military intervention in Lebanon which lasted just over three months.

This brief treatment of the Lebanese crisis of 1958 will attempt to outline the most significant causative factors as well as the various legal explanations offered by the United States in support of its decision to intervene.[2] Particular emphasis will be given to the protection of nationals rationale, both as it influenced the initial decision to intervene and as it colored the subsequent justifications of this action.

Like many of the countries achieving independence during and after World War II, Lebanon was an artificially constructed State, in that historically it had no definite population or territory. An autonomous province of the Ottoman Empire until World War I, it originally consisted of the relatively small area surrounding Mount Lebanon on the Mediterranean coast. Under a Mandate from the League of Nations, granted in 1920, France transferred land from Syria to increase Lebanon to its present size. The population, always quite diverse, was and to this day remains bitterly divided along religious, ethnic and political lines. Officially, slightly more than one-half of the population is Christian, while several Muslim sects make up the remainder.[3] However, since the first and only official census was held in 1932, the continued validity of this breakdown is open to question.[4]

With the termination of the French Mandate in 1943, Lebanon became a sovereign State, its political foundation resting upon the "National Covenant," an "unwritten understanding, or gentlemen's agreement," between the Christian and Muslim segments of the population.[5] Under the National Covenant, the contending elements agreed that "(i) the Christians would not look to the West for 'protection,' (ii) the Muslims would not aspire for merger with the neighboring Arab States, (iii) Lebanon was to co-operate with all the Arab States but not to take sides in Arab disputes, and (iv) political and administrative offices would be equitably distributed among the recognized confessional groups."[6] Pursuant to the last requirement, the President was to be a Maronite

Christian, the Prime Minister a Sunni Muslim, and the President of the Parliament a Shi'a Muslim.[7]

Following an initial period of political instability, Camille Chamoun was elected President of Lebanon in 1952 as a reformist. For the next few years Lebanese politics were reasonably stable and the Lebanese economy grew quite prosperous.[8] By 1957, however, a number of factors began to appear that ultimately led to the crisis the following year. Internally, political opposition began to mount against Chamoun. The parliamentary elections saw the surprising defeat of many important opposition leaders. Rumors began to circulate that the President wanted to have the Constitution amended so that he might succeed himself. Charges of political corruption increasingly surfaced. The Muslims came to believe that they were being treated as "second class citizens" and demanded a larger role in the government. As the result of these internal political pressures, the opposition forces that had combined to form a "National Union Front" renewed their efforts to oust Chamoun as President.

Several regional developments during this period also contributed to the crisis in 1958. Relations with Lebanon's neighbor, Syria, became increasingly strained during the 1950s. The disagreement between the two Arab States stemmed primarily from Syria's adoption of socialist and nationalist policies in contrast to Lebanon's *laissez-faire* capitalism. In addition, the presence of large numbers of Syrian political refugees in Lebanon led to increased friction between the States.[9] Further, by 1957 Lebanon had adopted policies and positions varying from the ones held and taken by most other Arab States. During the Suez crisis, for instance, Lebanon, unlike the other Arab States, remained neutral and refused to sever diplomatic relations with France and Great Britain.[10] Increasingly, Lebanon seemed to be veering in a pro-Western direction, in contrast to the pan-Arab approach advocated by President Nasser of Egypt and by the leaders of Syria.[11]

These regional stresses produced conflicting reactions in Lebanon itself. The Christian population regarded Arab unity as a threat to its Christian identity. The Muslims, on the other hand, supported Arab nationalism as a means of bettering their position in Lebanese politics and society. As President Chamoun, through his public statements, increasingly became identified as an opponent of Arab unity, he accordingly lost what popularity he had retained with the Muslim population.[12]

The crisis in 1958 also was fueled by developments on the international level. By 1957 the United States and the Soviet Union, antagonists in the "Cold War," had begun to look for potential allies in the Middle East. The Soviet Union viewed Arab nationalism as a vehicle for gaining influence in the area, while the United States, through the Eisenhower Doctrine, sought to enlist Middle East nations in its efforts to block Soviet inroads into the area. The basic thrust of the Eisenhower Doctrine, which took the form of a Joint Resolution of Congress, was that the United States, upon the request of any State in the Middle East, would use its "armed forces to assist any such nation or group of such nations requesting assistance against armed aggression from any country controlled by international communism...."[13] The only State to accept this doctrine, as it turned out, was Lebanon.[14] President Chamoun's decision in this regard sparked severe criticism from his opponents on two grounds. First, they argued that Lebanon's acceptance of the doctrine violated the National Covenant's requirement that the State remain completely neutral. Second, they argued that it brought Lebanon's policies squarely into conflict with Egypt and Syria, countries which a large number of Lebanese supported. While one need not accept Garnet's over-generalized assertion that "the dissension stirred up by the proposed ideological alliance led directly to the civil war and American intervention a year later,"[15] it cannot be denied that President Chamoun's enthusiastic acceptance of the doctrine caused him more problems than it solved.

The above internal, regional and international factors combined to produce an extremely volatile political situation in Lebanon by the spring of 1958. Following the murder, on 8 May 1958, of Nasib il al-Matni, the editor of the leading opposition newspaper in Beirut, the anti-Chamoun leaders called a general strike and a wave of violence spread throughout the country.[16] Although pro-government and opposition forces soon were engaged in open warfare, the 6,000-man Lebanese army under General Chebab remained neutral.[17] To a large extent the army's neutrality prevented the civil strife from turning into a full-scale civil war.[18]

With the country in turmoil, President Chamoun on 21 May 1958, complained to the Arab League that Egypt and Syria, now comprising the United Arab Republic, were intervening in the internal affairs of Lebanon.[19] On the following day, 22 May 1958, Lebanon lodged a similar complaint before the United Nations Security Council.[20] Both complaints, in essence, alleged that the United Arab Republic was infiltrating men and arms into Lebanon, and that it was conducting an intense propaganda campaign aimed at the overthrow of the Lebanese government. When recourse to the Arab League proved fruitless, Lebanon, on 6 June 1958, pressed its case in the Security Council where Foreign Minister Charles Malik argued that:

> ... there has been, and there still is, massive, illegal and unprovoked intervention in the affairs of Lebanon by the United Arab Republic . . .;

. . . this intervention aims at undermining, and does in fact threaten, the independence of Lebanon . . . ; [and]

. . . the situation created by this intervention which threatens the independence of Lebanon is likely, if continued, to endanger the maintenance of international peace and security.[21]

After a bitter debate, during which the United Arab Republic denied these allegations,[22] the Security Council, on 11 June 1958, adopted a resolution establishing the United Nations Observation Group in Lebanon (UNOGIL), whose principal task was "to ensure that there is no illegal infiltration of personnel or supply of arms or other material across the Lebanese borders. . . ."[23] While UNOGIL's findings, according to an exhaustive survey of its operations, "indicated that the Lebanese government had exaggerated the degree of infiltration that might have been taking place . . ., the Group's observations could not be regarded as conclusive evidence of the degree and nature of infiltration since its failure to achieve anything more than a highly limited access to alleged infiltration routes prevented any thorough investigation of the Lebanese allegations."[24]

During this period, U.S. policy towards the Lebanese crisis remained officially "hands off." According to President Eisenhower, however, possible U.S. intervention was mooted as early as May 1958, when President Chamoun was informed that in such an eventuality "the mission of United States troops in Lebanon would be twofold: protection of the life and property of Americans, and assistance to the legal Lebanese government."[25] As a precautionary measure, the Department of State on 16 June 1958, advised U.S. citizens against travel in or through Lebanon except for "imperative reasons."[26] The protection of its nationals clearly was secondary as revealed by President Eisenhower's description of the atmosphere in which his 14 July 1958, meeting with Congressional leaders took place: "The time was rapidly approaching, I believed, when we had to move into the Middle East, and specifically into Lebanon, to stop the trend toward chaos. *An additional factor* in my deep concern was the presence in Lebanon of a relatively large number of American citizens whose lives might be endangered."[27]

The *coup d'etat* which took place in Iraq on 14 July 1958, triggered a rapid change in U.S. policy towards Lebanon. The leftist revolutionaries who took over the country murdered the Iraqi royal family and dragged their dismembered bodies through the streets of Baghdad. In addition, a number of Europeans, plus at least three U.S. citizens, also were murdered.[28] Fearful that the Iraqi coup was the forerunner of similar coups against other pro-Western countries in the area, President Eisenhower now readily acceded to President Chamoun's renewed request for military assistance. At about 3 P.M. on 15 July 1958, nearly 2,000 Marines in full battle gear waded ashore near Beirut. "In the unique spirit of the Lebanese civil war," recounts Kerr, "they were greeted at the water's edge by curious bathers and by soft drink vendors."[29] Although a near-incident occurred when the Marines moved down the highway toward Beirut,[30] skillful mediation by Ambassador Robert McClintock overcame this set-back. "The convoy proceeded into Beirut: a Lebanese army jeep in the lead, followed by the Ambassador's limousine flying both Lebanese and American flags and bearing both [General] Chehab and the Ambassador, followed finally by a contingent of American marines."[31] No shots were fired and no casualties were incurred.

On the same day that US troops landed in Lebanon, legal justifications for their use began flowing from Washington. Although White House decisionmakers evidently accorded the protection of nationals aspects of the problem a fairly low priority,[32] a press release issued in the President's name emphasized the plight of the 2,500 US citizens still in Lebanon, stating that the Marines had landed "to protect American lives and by their presence there to encourage the Lebanese government in defense of Lebanese sovereignty and integrity."[33] A contemporaneous Message to Congress paraphrased the above statement,[34] as did a subsequent radio and TV broadcast by the President that evening.[35] However, UN Ambassador Henry Cabot Lodge, addressing a hastily convened meeting of the Security Council, invoked protection of US nationals only as an ancillary argument.[36] Thereafter, the "protection of nationals" rationale justifying for US intervention was heard no more. Instead, the United States placed exclusive reliance upon the fact that the intervention had been pursuant to a request from the recognized government of Lebanon, and that it constituted an act of collective self-defense permitted under Article 51 of the United Nations Charter.[37]

By 25 July 1958, ten days after the initial landing, "the American forces ashore numbered at least 10,600 men—4000 Army, 6600 Marines—more than the entire Lebanese Army."[38] By 8 August 1958, the number had reached a peak of 14,357 troops—8,515 Army and 5,842 Marines—from which it soon started to recede.[39] The troops, deployed exclusively in the vicinity of Beirut,[40] engaged in routine patrols with their Lebanese counterparts.[41] Otherwise US troops saw no real action.[42] By all accounts their conduct was exemplary. Typical are the remarks of Qubain, who mentions:

. . . the great restraint which they displayed, which indeed [has] no parallel in modern times. In the first place, the main body of troops remained stationed outside Beirut. Only a very small number were assigned duty inside the city. Even these were restricted mainly to guard duty at such places as the harbor, American institutions, and certain areas where American citizens lived. Areas controlled by the opposition were completely out of bounds to troops whether on or off duty.[43] Second, at no time did Americans interfere in the internal conflict or give support to government forces against the opposition. American forces rigidly abstained from supporting one faction against another.[44]

Although occasionally the targets of snipers, the US forces held their own fire and inflicted no casualties upon the local population.[45] In turn, they suffered only two casualties, both army sergeants, one of whom was wounded and the second killed.[46] With a political accommodation that permitted the orderly transfer of power from President Chamoun to his successor worked out by Deputy Under-Secretary of State Robert Murphy, relative calm returned to the country permitting the withdrawal of all US troops during the month of October.[47] The Lebanese crisis of 1958 was over.

While some commentators have criticized the action of the United States on political grounds,[48] few observers have registered legal objections to the landing of US troops.[49] The strongest basis for their introduction into Lebanon, of course, was the existence of a formal invitation from Lebanon's recognized government.[50] The right of a State to furnish military assistance to another State pursuant to a request from the latter is universally recognized under international law. Provided that the right is not abused, as in the case of Lebanon,[51] it affords ample legal justification for the landing of troops. Collective self-defense under the United Nations Charter also justified the action taken by the United States.[52] It must be noted, however, that the factual basis for invoking this right was questioned in some quarters.[53]

Finally, the "protection of nationals" rationale, relied upon initially by the United States[54] but subsequently ignored by it and most commentators as well,[55] arguably provided additional support for the decision to send in the Marines.

Contrasting legal views about the availability of the protection of nationals rationale in the context of Lebanon are set out in forthright fashion in articles by the late Professors Potter and Wright, apparently the only two authorities to have considered the legal issues involved in a systematic fashion. Professor Potter, in an article entitled *Legal Aspects of the Beirut Landing*, suggests that:

... [a] plausible basis for "intervention" in the instant situation, as in so many such cases, is to be found in the right to use force for the protection of nationals, and their property, of the intervening state, in absence of ability or willingness of the local state to perform this function. While well established in principle, however, such a right obviously depends upon proof of the need for such action under the conditions cited. In the present case there seems to have been actual and serious danger to United States citizens and their interests, and some inability, though not unwillingness, on the part of the Lebanese Government to protect them. President Eisenhower did not fail to invoke this basis for United States action at Beirut.[56]

On the other hand, Professor Wright in *The United States Intervention in Lebanon,* concentrates exclusively upon the UN Charter norms which he regards as dispositive of the case stating:

[I]t has been suggested that the "self" which must be immediately menaced to permit self-defensive action [under Article 51 of the Charter] includes not only territory but also agencies of the government and its citizens in foreign territory. There have been many cases in which states have landed forces in foreign territory to protect embassies or other government agencies, as in the Boxer affair in 1900, or to protect the lives of their citizens. It is difficult to bring these extensions within the meaning of Article 51 of the Charter. The United States has, however, referred to the protection of American citizens in the Lebanon as one reason for its intervention in that country. To support this contention, it would be necessary to show that immediate danger to government agencies or American citizens in the Lebanon constituted "an armed attack" upon the United States.[57]

Wright's remarks urge that even if US citizens had been in clear and present danger, their country had no right to intervene forcibly to protect them. If this is true, then is it necessary to revisit and redraft Art. 51 and Art. 2(4) to allow States to intervene with force to protect their nationals and consulates?

To place the threat to US citizens into perspective, it must be remembered that for two months prior to the landing of Marines, civil strife had been rampant in Lebanon.[58] With 2,500 American nationals scattered throughout the country,[59] the possibility always existed that US citizens would get caught up in the fray.[60]

The *coup d'etat* in Iraq and the death of several citizens there[61] gave the United States all the more reason for concern over the fate of its citizens in the Middle East.[62] Murphy, who arrived in Lebanon several days after the first contingents of Marines, records that "[s]ince Berlin in 1945, I had not been in a more trigger-happy place than Beirut was at that time. Wild fusillades, bombings and arson were the order of the day and more especially the night."[63] Given this state of affairs, it is a happy, and indeed a near miraculous fact that no instances of harm to US citizens were recorded.[64]

The attitude of the US Embassy in Beirut, while admittedly self-serving to some extent, also affords a significant insight into the situation in Lebanon prior to the landing of US troops. Like all embassies, it had an emergency plan for such situations, which consisted of a three-phrase evacuation program. If, after the initial alert,

> ... the situation further deteriorated, Phase A would be put into operation. This called for the voluntary evacuation at government expense of dependents of members of the staff. At the same time the embassy would discreetly recommend that dependents of the local American community also be sent out of the country. Phase B called for the mandatory evacuation of all nonessential government personnel and their dependents, with a similar recommendation for the private American community. Phase C contemplated the evacuation of all American citizens from the crisis area.[65]

The Embassy placed Phase A into effect on 15 June, when the civil strife worsened, and declared Phase B operative immediately after the Iraqi *coup d'etat*.[66] Had Phase C thereafter been invoked, obviously a stronger factual predicate would have been laid to justify the measures of forcible protection subsequently taken. Yet simply because Phase C was not invoked, or just because no US citizens actually were harmed, does not mean that on 14 and 15 July, the key dates in question, US decisionmakers were not presented with a threat to US citizens sufficiently grave to justify, at least to themselves, the action they took.[67]

## B. The Congo. 1964.

The summer of 1960 saw the Congo (now Zaire) achieve independence from Belgium. Unhappily, within a week the Congolese Army mutinied against its Belgian officers and, following a complete breakdown of law and order,[68] Belgium, on 10 July 1960, sent paratroopers into the country to protect the lives and property of its nationals and other Europeans.[69] Shortly thereafter, the UN Security Council, calling upon Belgium to withdraw its troops, created a temporary security force whose mission was to cooperate with the Congolese government in the restoration of order.[70] This temporary force gradually metamorphosed into the United Nations Operation in the Congo (ONUC), which between July 1960 and its withdrawal on 30 June 1964 attempted the unenviable tasks of controlling civil strife, ending the secession of Katanga, the country's largest province, and creating conditions conducive to the establishment of a strong and viable modern State.[71]

While ONUC achieved its second objective—ending the secession of Katanga—it was unable to fashion a strong central government capable of maintaining civil peace by the time of its withdrawal.

Indeed, in the spring of 1964 several separate revolts had broken out, the most serious in the Eastern Congo, where in late May, Albertville fell to rebels. Thereafter events moved rapidly. On 30 June 1964, the fourth anniversary of the Congo's independence, the UN force withdrew and the government of Prime Minister Cyrille Adoula resigned. Nine days later a new government, headed by Moise Tshombe, took office. As the tempo of rebellion increased, however, the rebels on 5 August seized Stanleyville and, two weeks later, Paulis. Proclaiming a revolutionary regime, they named Christophe Gbenye, a former Minister of Interior, as President. An unending round of executions thereupon began,[72] during which:

> [w]ave after wave of 'intellectuals' or 'counterrevolutionaries' or 'American agents' were assassinated in all the main towns held by the rebels. The lack of cohesion and control permitted diverse groups to seize the occasion to liquidate their rivals on various pretexts. Many of the executions were public, performed in front of Lumumba monuments, with grotesque cruelty, including disemboweling of still living victims, consumption of the heart, liver and other portions, and various tortures.... In Stanleyville, Paulis, and Kindu alone, the executions totalled close to 10,000; in all, there were probably at least 20,000.[73]

This reign of terror apparently was as purposeless as it was despicable. "The mediocre talents and often pathological character of [the] rebel leaders," Professor Young has noted, "rendered them incapable of directing or controlling social tensions which they unleashed, even in the interest of consolidating their own newly won power."[74]

After six weeks, the tide began to turn. The forces of the central government, the Armee Nationale Congolaise (ANC), "reinforced by Katanga gendarmes and spearheaded (in most but not all cases) by small contingents of mercenaries,"[75] put the rebel army to rout. Seeking to snatch victory—or at least a stalemate—from the jaws of defeat, Gbenye announced on 26 September that the approximately 1,600 foreigners remaining in the Stanleyville area, made up of "500 Belgians, 700 people of other European nationalities and 400 Indians and Pakistanis,"[76] would not be allowed to leave; his intention obviously was to use them as hostages for political bargaining purposes.[77] With the rebels thus holding "sixteen hundred trump cards,"[78] a feverish round of negotiations began involving not only the rebels and the central government, but also the United States, Belgium, Kenya, an Ad Hoc Commission on the Congo of the Organization of African Unity (OAU) and the International Committee of the Red Cross (ICRC).[79] Progress was not forthcoming and tensions heightened. By early November, the ANC, continuing its advance, neared Stanleyville.

When the ANC, preceded by white mercenary contingents, seized Kindu on 6 November, the plight of the hostages worsened still further, with Gbenye proclaiming that "all Belgian and American civilians would be treated as 'prisoners of war' in retaliation for the bombing of our liberated territory."[80] On 11 November, during a radio broadcast, Gbenye stated that "the British, Americans, Belgians and Italians must get ready to dig their own graves."[81] Three days later, utilizing the rebel newspaper *LeMartyr*, he threatened that "'we will make our fetishes with the hearts of the Americans and Belgians, and we will dress ourselves with the skins of the Americans and Belgians."[82] On the same day Radio Stanleyville announced that Dr. Paul Carlson, a U.S. medical missionary held by the rebels, had been sentenced to death for espionage.[83]

The above threats, moreover, were not just rhetoric. As Ambassador Stevenson subsequently recounted to the UN Security Council, by mid-November "the total of those thus already tortured and slaughtered amounted to 35 foreigners, including 19 Belgians, 2 Americans, 2 Indians, 2 Greeks, 1 Englishman, 1 Italian, 2 Portuguese, 2 Togolese and 4 Dutch, many of them missionaries who had spent their lives in helping the Congolese people."[84] The grim prospect that other hostages would meet a similar fate was strengthened by a captured telegram from a rebel general to an officer in charge of the hostages that had been held in Kindu. It ended: "'In case of bombing of region, exterminate all [Americans and Belgians] without requesting further orders. . . ."[85]

With the ANC now nearing Stanleyville, negotiations reached an impasse. Thomas Kanza, the representative of the rebels who had been in direct contact with the US Ambassador to Kenya, William Attwood, made it crystal clear that, in Professor Grundy's words, "the rebels were not about to surrender their only major bargaining lever."[86] According to Attwood, Kanza would not discuss evacuating the hostages, whom he termed "prisoners of war," until the ANC advance had been stopped and a cease-fire put into effect.[87] That this use of innocent civilians flatly violated the Geneva Conventions[88] did not bother the rebels, who considered themselves not bound by international agreements "written by whites."[89] Thus, political and legal arguments having failed, it became increasingly apparent that military measures would have to be used to extricate the hostages from their three month ordeal.[90]

These measures actually had been put in train in mid-November when US military planes transported the 545-man Belgian First Paratroop Battalion to Ile Ascension, where it was quartered by the British government.[91] After further unavailing efforts to secure the release of the hostages,[92] the paratroopers, with the express authorization of the central government,[93] landed at Stanleyville at dawn on 24 November and undertook an emergency rescue mission,[94] evacuating an estimated 2,000 people over a four-day period.[95] Included in this number were several hundred foreigners rescued during a follow-up landing at Paulis, 225 miles to the north.[96] The evacuees included "Americans, Britons and Belgians; Pakistanis, Indians, Congolese, Greeks, French, Dutch, Germans, Canadians, Spaniards, Portuguese, Swiss, and Italians; as well as citizens of Ghana, Uganda, Ethiopia, and the United Arab Republic."[97]

To justify US participation in the rescue operation,[98] the Department of State initially expressed the view that the action was taken "in exercise of our clear responsibility to protect United States citizens under the circumstances existing in the Stanleyville area."[99] At the United Nations, Ambassador Stevenson extended the rationale behind the action stating that, "[w]hile our primary obligation was to protect the lives of American citizens, we are proud that the mission rescued so many innocent people of eighteen other nationalities from their dreadful predicament."[100] Finally, President Johnson put the case in its broadest humanitarian terms when he assumed "full responsibility for those [decisions] made for our planes to carry the paratroopers in there in this humanitarian venture. We had to act and act promptly in order to keep hundreds and even thousands of people from being massacred."[101]

Of course, the Congo rescue operation, as the Department of State reiterated several times, was carried out "with the authorization of the Government of the Congo,"[102] and hence, technically, was not a case of unilateral forcible protection at all.[103] Nevertheless, viewing the operation in its total context, it is hard to avoid the conclusion that the United States treated the Congolese invitation more as an additional argument justifying its action than as the *sine qua non* of its legitimacy. The statement issued by the Department of State clearly was designed to show not only reliance upon an express invitation by the central government of the Congo, but also in compliance with all the requirements of the traditional doctrine of humanitarian intervention.[104]

> This operation is humanitarian—not military. It is designed to avoid bloodshed—not to engage the rebel forces in combat. Its purpose is to

accomplish its task quickly and withdraw—not to seize or hold territory. Personnel engaged are under orders to use force only in their own defense or in the defense of the foreign and Congolese civilians. They will depart from the scene as soon as their evacuation mission is accomplished.

We are informing the United Nations and the *Ad Hoc* Commission of the Organization of African Unity of the purely humanitarian purpose of this action and of the regrettable circumstances that made it necessary.[105]

Add to this statement the acknowledged fact that both the United Nations and the OAU were unable to cope with a situation which by mid-November required immediate action,[106] and one reaches the inescapable conclusion that if ever there was a case justifying the forcible protection of lives, the Congo rescue operation was it.

Reviewing the operation in retrospect, perhaps the United States should not have been as surprised as it was at the criticism heaped upon it for its role in this humanitarian venture.[107] In the debates that the operation engendered at the United Nations, the virulence of many African delegates can be attributed, in varying degrees, to four principal factors.[108] First, they argued that the rescue operation was rife with racism, in that not until the lives of the white hostages had been threatened did the United States become concerned,[109] and that while most of these hostages had been rescued hundreds of blacks had been slain.[110] When one considers what the world community's reaction would have been had the United States or other Western powers introduced troops immediately after the United Nations' withdrawal to protect those Congolese threatened by the rebels, however, such criticism must be regarded, to say the least, as unfair.

Since intervening earlier to protect Congolese surely would have been branded as a flagrant violation of the UN Charter, this supposed option was not really a viable one. Accordingly, the United States should not be criticized, either expressly or impliedly, for failing to intervene earlier on.[111] Moreover, the fact that the ANC slaughtered hundreds of blacks when it reached Stanleyville shortly after the airdrop is no argument that racist considerations motivated the rescue operation itself. The paratroopers, it should be noted, evacuated 400 Indians and Pakistanis as well as more than 200 Congolese,[112] and the vengeance meted out by the ANC while mopping up Stanleyville hardly would have been less had it reached the city hours or days later, especially if the hostages had been massacred in the meantime.

A second factor underlying the criticism put forth by many African delegates was the disrespect the rescue operation allegedly showed for the OAU and its mediation efforts.[113] Coming at a time when Pan-Africanism was riding high on the African continent, the failure to work through the regional organization to secure the release of the hostages engendered considerable ire. The airdrops, according to the delegate from the Congo Republic (Brazzaville), were clearly an attempt to humiliate the OAU.[114]

Such an attitude, while understandable, also is unjustified. Both the United States and Belgium had turned repeatedly to the OAU for assistance in obtaining the hostages release, but in every instance the OAU had proved to be either ineffective or uncooperative or both. This failure stemmed not only from the inherent weakness of the organization itself, but also, and perhaps primarily, from the resentment many African States had for the Tshombe government, a regime which they wished to see toppled. Given this anti-Tshombe attitude, the airdrops obviously would not have been approved had the United States and Belgium sought OAU authorization.[115] Moreover, seeking such authorization not only was unnecessary, given the central government's approval,[116] but would have removed the surprise element from the airdrops and thus, jeopardized the success of the entire rescue operation.

The third factor causing much African criticism was the memory of colonial injustices still fresh in the minds of many delegates. Such memories naturally were exacerbated by the dropping of paratroopers of the former colonial power, assisted by logistical support from one of the superpowers. As Attwood, in a passage worth quoting at length, put it:

> We saw the Stanleyville rescue operations as a dramatic effort to save hundreds of helpless, innocent people. It was humanitarian, and it was necessary, since all other attempts to release them had failed. And the operation had to take place before the ANC column entered the city, for the panicky Simbas would probably have mowed down the hostages before fleeing from the mercenaries.
>
> But if you could put yourself in the shoes of an average educated African, you got a quite different picture. When he looked at the Congo, he saw a black government in Stanleyville being attacked by a gang of hired South African thugs, and black people being killed by rockets fired from American planes. He did not know about the thousands of blacks who were tortured and murdered by the Simbas, but he did know that the mercenaries and their Katangan auxiliaries left a trail of African corpses in their wake.
>
> Even more galling to the educated African was the shattering of so many of his illusions—that Africans were now masters of their own continent, that the OAU was a force to be reckoned with, that a black man with a gun was the equal of a white man with a gun. For in a matter of weeks, two hundred swaggering white

mercenaries had driven through an area the size of France, scattered the Simbas and captured their capital; and in a matter of hours, 545 Belgians in American planes had defied the OAU, jumped into the heart of Africa and taken out nearly two thousand people—with the loss of one trooper.

> The weakness and impotence of newly independent Africa had been harshly and dramatically revealed to the whole world, and the educated African felt deeply humiliated: the white man with a gun, the old plunderer who had enslaved his ancestors, was back again, doing what he pleased, when he pleased, where he pleased. And there wasn't a damn thing Africa could do about it, except yell rape.[117]

Just what the United States could have done to avoid this verbal attack—short of foregoing participation in the rescue operation altogether—is difficult to imagine. Generalities to the effect that "it should have taken greater account of African sensitivities"[118] are fine, but they offer little guidance to decisionmakers, past or present. In sum, given the legacies of the colonial past, the United States could not have avoided African criticism for its part in the rescue operation, no matter how humanitarian its motives may have been.

Finally, the fourth factor disturbing many African delegates was the role the United States was playing in supporting the Tshombe government, a role which included the supplying of military equipment and advisers, the flying of intelligence and transport as well as occasional combat missions, and the general underwriting, through the US Embassy and the CIA, of the ANC's mercenary-led efforts to reestablish the central government's authority over the Congo.[119] African leaders, who originally had opposed the return of Tshombe and subsequently had condemned his central government, naturally resented any bolstering of his power, which was the inevitable by-product of the rescue operation.[120] As Grundy observes, "Africans hostile to Tshombe's cause would naturally seek to discredit the legitimacy of an operation that resulted in Tshombe's increased power."[121]

The four factors discussed above naturally exacerbated the criticism of the operation leveled at the United States and Belgium during the United Nations debates. Replying to accusations in the Security Council that often bordered on and sometimes reached the slanderous, Ambassador Stevenson flatly stated that:

> . . . [w]e have no apologies to make to any state appearing before this Council. We are proud of our part in saving human lives imperiled by the civil war in the Congo.

The United States took part in no operation with military purposes in the Congo. We violated no provision of the United Nations Charter. Our action was no threat to peace or to security; it was not an affront—deliberate or otherwise—to the OAU: and it constituted no intervention in Congolese or African affairs.[122]

His views, of course, received support from Belgium[123] and Great Britain,[124] with Bolivia,[125] Brazil,[126] and the Republic of China[127] also approving this instance of forcible protection. Admittedly, most States condemned the rescue operation, generally because they regarded it, in retrospect, either to have been counterproductive in lives saved[128] or to have served as a "pretext" for what they regarded as an illegal intervention in the Congo's affairs.[129] In general, they grounded their complaints more upon its political than its legal aspects.[130] The vague resolution finally adopted by the Security Council, "[d]eploring the recent events in [the Congo],"[131] not unsurprisingly contains no official condemnation of either Belgium or the United States.[132] Indeed, one writer actually has suggested that the resolution constitutes an implied if not an express approval of the rescue operation.[133]

Two issues relevant to any forcible protection action for human rights purposes, and especially to the Congo rescue operation, warrant further brief discussion. Namely, whether in the present case the operation was not counterproductive insofar as the saving of lives was concerned, and whether the operation was not used to impose or preserve a preferred government on the Congo.[134]

Insofar as the first issue is concerned, of the approximately 1,600 foreigners in the Stanleyville area only 27 were killed during the initial Stanleyville airdrops, and all 22 white hostages found dead at Paulis two days later had been killed by the rebels prior to that follow-up operation.[135] Having fled at the last minute, few if any of the rebels who carried out the massacre in Stanleyville apparently were killed by the paratroopers,[136] who themselves lost only one man.[137] The rebels and their supporters, it is true, suffered appalling casualties when the mercenary-led ANC troops who subsequently entered Stanleyville ran amok,[138] but such atrocities hardly can be attributed to the rescue operation itself and, in any event, would have been no less severe had the ANC fought its way into the city without the airdrop having taken place.

Similarly, although from the Stanleyville airdrop through the end of December "more than three hundred whites, eight of them Americans, were killed"[139] by the rebels, these deaths, which occurred throughout the entire Eastern Congo, cannot be attributed solely to the rescue operation having taken place.[140] On balance, then, while admittedly a matter of speculation not susceptible of absolute proof either way, the Congo rescue operation would appear to have saved far more lives than it lost.[141]

Insofar as the second issue is concerned, there is little doubt, as numerous commentators have pointed out in their respective fashions,[142] that the rescue operation's success contributed to the eventual downfall of the rebel regime. Since the rebels, contrary to international law, were using the hostages not only to prevent central government attacks but also to gain time to replenish their depleted arsenals, the rescue operation, by its very nature and success, obviously constituted a severe blow to their cause. However, the fact that the Stanleyville airdrop appears to have been coordinated with the ANC advance upon the city, frequently cited as authoritative evidence that the rescue operation was undertaken for political rather than humanitarian reasons,[143] certainly does not overcome the strong evidence that its primary objective actually was humanitarian in nature.[144] The reason for synchronizing the airdrop with the ANC advance was to reduce casualties and to avoid the rebels fleeing with the hostages. "The main purpose of the coordination," concludes Weissman, "was to assure the safety of the maximum number of hostages with the minimum cost."[145] The fact that a by-product of the rescue operation was the collapse of the rebel regime should not be read back to taint the entire mission, which as Ambassador Stevenson rightly stated was designed to save human lives.[146]

## C. The Dominican Republic. 1965

On 30 May 1961, an assassin's bullet struck and killed Rafael Trujillo, dictator of the Dominican Republic for over three decades. Trujillo's death presaged a period of unrest within the Dominican Republic that culminated four years later in violent revolution followed by forcible intervention by US (and subsequently Organization of American States [OAS]) forces. The purpose of this case study is to assess, in the context of the facts now available, the validity of the initial legal justification advanced by the United States in support of its intervention, that being the need to protect the lives of US nationals. To place the US argument in perspective, a short description of the events preceding and surrounding the crisis of 1965 is required.[147]

Following Trujillo's assassination, Dominicans, in the first free elections held in the country in nearly 40 years, elected as their President, Juan Bosch, founder of the left-of-center Dominican Revolutionary Party (PRD). The Kennedy Administration welcomed Bosch's election, dispatched Vice President Johnson to his inauguration in February 1963, and increased Alliance for Progress (AID) programs in an effort "to construct a 'showcase of democracy' in the

Caribbean as a contrast to neighboring Communist Cuba."[148] Bosch, unhappily, proved to be an ineffective leader once in office and soon came under heavy attack by opposition critics, especially for allowing Dominican communists to return from exile and reenter political life.[149] After just seven months in office he was ousted by an anti-communist *coup d'etat* on 25 September 1963.[150]

The Kennedy Administration reacted to the *coup d'etat* by suspending diplomatic relations with the Dominican Republic and halting all economic and military aid.[151] Such pressures had little effect upon the three-man junta that had replaced Bosch, however, and by mid-December the United States, with the Johnson Administration now in office, reversed its policy, recognized the new government, and resumed foreign assistance.[152]

Despite this development, the junta, which soon came to be dominated by Donald Reid Cabral, an anti-communist holding decidedly conservative views, lost popularity steadily during 1964. Reid, in an effort to stave off domestic criticism and improve the junta's reputation abroad, scheduled "free elections" for 15 September 1965, but his subsequent announcement that he intended to run for the presidency and would win constituted the "final straw."[153] By the late winter and early spring of 1965, only the timing and not the occurrence of another *coup d'etat*, this time to oust Reid, was in doubt.[154]

The uprising began in the early hours of Saturday, 24 April 1965, when "a small group of young colonels acting in concert with PRD leaders seized and imprisoned the Army Chief of Staff and declared themselves in revolt against the government."[155] The rebels, calling themselves the "constitutionalists," occupied the government radio station in Santo Domingo, the capital, and broadcast appeals calling for the ouster of Reid. When thousands of civilians took to the streets, the constitutionalist officers passed out arms to them in an apparent attempt "to broaden the base of the movement and counter any possible reaction from the bulk of the armed forces."[156] Actually, they had nothing to fear from the regular forces at this point, since the military's leaders, while responding to Reid's request for assistance with pledges of support, obviously were waiting for the dust to settle before committing either themselves or their troops.[157] Certainly they did nothing to crush the uprising against Reid, and the latter, after an unsuccessful attempt to obtain US military intervention on the morning of Sunday, 25 April,[158] resigned and went into hiding.[159]

Later that afternoon, reportedly after conferring by telephone with Bosch,[160] who at the time was living in Puerto Rico, the constitutionalists named Rafael Molina Urena, President of the Chamber of Deputies during Bosch's regime, as Provisional President.[161] Molina's subsequent announcement that he intended to hold office only until Bosch's return, which reflected a pro-Bosch rather than merely the anti-Reid view held by a majority of the constitutionalists, had the unfortunate effect of alienating many revolutionary leaders and driving not a few wavering military commanders into the anti-constitutionalist (or what came to be known as the "loyalist") camp. For, according to Slater:

> there no longer could be much doubt that a victory of the revolution would result in the direct return of Bosch to the Presidency, rather than in new elections as had originally been planned.[162] This was another matter, for the regular military detested and feared Bosch, judging, undoubtedly correctly, that a triumphant Bosch backed by the defecting constitutionalist military and what amounted to a well-armed civilian militia would probably seek to destroy their power and position in the Dominican Republic. As a result, by late Sunday afternoon the bulk of the military, particularly the key San Isidro Air Force Base dominated by [General] Wessin y Wessin, had decided to actively resist the revolution.[163]

The bombing of the National Palace and constitutionalist military encampments by planes from the San Isidro Air Base began about 4:30 P.M., plunging the Dominican Republic into civil war.[164]

By the following morning—Monday, 26 April—the military situation had reached a stalemate and civil authority had broken down completely. While sensational reports of atrocities allegedly committed by the constitutionalists subsequently proved to be wildly exaggerated,[165] the carnage in the streets of Santo Domingo nevertheless was great,[166] with an estimated 2,000 people losing their lives in the fighting during a four day period.[167] The military standoff prompted loyalist leaders to make their first request for US military intervention, a request that the United States denied.[168] The Department of State, however, instructed the US Embassy "to inform both sides in Santa Domingo that the US government had received requests from American citizens wishing to be evacuated, and that the U.S. requested an immediate ceasefire to permit a safe and orderly evacuation."[169] Preparations for this voluntary evacuation operation, which had been contemplated since the uprising began,[170] commenced Monday evening with the assembling and registering of US and other foreign nationals who wished to leave the country. Their actual evacuation—by land to the nearby port of Haina, from whence they were to be loaded aboard two ships of a US navy task force lying offshore, or by helicopter from the grounds of the Hotel Embajador to the decks of the *USS Boxer*—was scheduled for the following day.

On that day—Tuesday, 27 April—an unarmed detachment of about 50 Marines was sent ashore to secure the hotel grounds, establish a helicopter landing area therein, and to generally facilitate the evacuation process. All went reasonably smoothly and by 3:15 P.M. the operation, which involved ferrying out 1,172 of the 2,500 US nationals supposedly in the country, had been completed.[171] The only hitch occurred when a small band of constitutionalists arrived on the scene and engaged in a brief exchange of fire with unidentified persons on several upper story balconies of the hotel. Then, as Slater relates, they suddenly "burst into the hotel, lined the Americans [gathered in the lobby waiting to be evacuated] against the wall, and fired a number of machine-gun bursts over their heads." No one was hurt, and it later turned out that the rebels had not been seeking deliberately to terrorize the Americans but were looking for an extreme right-wing propagandist who had taken shelter in the hotel.[172] This incident, however, caused considerable concern at the US Embassy, whose "overwrought reporting" of it to Washington obviously influenced President Johnson's thinking and strengthened the hand of those officials who already were urging a much larger US military intervention.[173]

As the evacuation took place that Tuesday, the military tide slowly turned against the constitutionalists. Under continuous attack from General Wessin's planes since Sunday, they now had to contend with a force of tanks from San Isidro attempting to enter the city. Faced with impending defeat, the leading constitutionalists, including Provisional President Molina Urena, sought help from the US Embassy to mediate the conflict. Ambassador W. Tapley Bennett, no fan of ex-President Bosch and ever-fearful of a leftist takeover,[174] flatly refused, advising the constitutionalists to surrender.[175] Although they ignored his advice, a number of them, including Molina Urena, apparently conceded defeat, for they immediately sought political asylum at various Latin American embassies.[176] One did not. Surprisingly, Francisco Caamano, a career officer who had served as chief of the police riot squad under Trujillo and certainly was not known as a Bosch supporter, after a dramatic reply to Bennett, rushed from the embassy to rally the constitutionalist forces opposing Wessin's tanks at the Duarte Bridge.[177] Miraculously, the tide turned yet again: the tanks were driven back, the police stations fell, and by mid-afternoon of the next day—Wednesday, 28 April 1965—the city belonged to the constitutionalists.[178]

During this surprising turnaround, US helicopters continued to airlift evacuees from the Hotel Embajador to the *Boxer*.[179] As the constitutionalists solidified their control of the city, however, Colonel Benoit, the head of a new junta conducting the loyalist's operations, informed Ambassador Bennett that "the junta was in no position to guarantee the safety of Americans or other foreigners in Santo Domingo."[180] Accordingly, "the junta was requesting a United

States intervention."[181] While the junta's formal written request, submitted about 4 P.M. on the afternoon of the 28th, actually made no mention of the need to protect US nationals,[182] Bennett relied upon this argument in his now-famous "critic" telegram recommending the immediate landing of US Marines, which arrived in Washington about 5 P.M.[183] Shortly thereafter, President Johnson decided to land a contingent of armed Marines,[184] 536 of whom came ashore in the early evening.[185] In an address to the nation later that night, the President reported that military authorities in the Dominican Republic had informed the United States that the lives of its nationals were in danger, and that the assistance of US military personnel was necessary to guarantee their safety.[186] As a result, the President stated, he had ordered the Secretary of Defense "to put the necessary American troops ashore in order to give protection to hundreds of Americans who are still in the Dominican Republic and to escort them safely back to this country. This same assistance will be available to the nationals of other countries, some of whom have already asked for our help."[187]

The following day—Thursday, 29 April—additional Marines with heavy equipment landed, bringing total US forces in Santo Domingo to 1,700 men.[188] The next day military transports ferried two battalions of the 82nd Airborne Division to the San Isidro Air Base. They immediately took up positions along the east bank of the Ozama River, an area in which there were no US or other foreign nationals to be evacuated.[189] Yet, in his address to the nation that evening, 30 April, President Johnson again invoked the protection of nationals argument that he had made two nights earlier, noting that over 2,400 US and other foreign nationals already had been evacuated from the Dominican Republic.[190] More significantly, however, the President, for the first time, advanced a new argument for US intervention, namely, that "people trained outside the Dominican Republic are seeking to gain control" of the country. While not saying so explicitly, Johnson clearly intended to leave the impression that "outside" communists threatened to take over the Dominican Republic. In the face of this potential threat, he continued, the Organization of American States (OAS) had the "immediate responsibility" to take prompt action to achieve a ceasefire before such an "international conspiracy" could take control.[191]

On 1 May, after the apparent failure of a tenuous ceasefire between the two opposing factions, President Johnson ordered additional troops flown in, raising the number of US forces to 6,200. They proceeded to enter constitutionalist (but apparently not loyalist) territory in an attempt to enforce the ceasefire.[192] Nevertheless, in a written statement issued the same day the

President once again maintained that the mission of the troops was solely to protect and evacuate US and other foreign nationals.[193]

Warning of a "tragic turn" of events, President Johnson addressed the nation for a third time the following day. The President now publicly asserted that the Dominican revolution had been "seized and placed in the hands of a band of Communist conspirators . . . [m]any of them trained in Cuba. . . ."[194] To counter this alleged new development, the President reported that he had ordered an additional force of 6,500 men to proceed to the Dominican Republic. He did not attempt to justify their dispatch by continued reliance upon protection of nationals arguments. Instead, the President proclaimed what came to be known as the "Johnson Doctrine," namely, that "[t]he American nations cannot, must not, and will not permit the establishment of another Communist government in the Western Hemisphere."[195] To prevent such an occurrence, he announced, the United States was consulting with the OAS regarding proposals for a multilateral response to this new threat posed by the Dominican crisis.[196]

In the event, on 6 May 1965, the OAS, which much earlier had adopted a resolution calling for a ceasefire and the establishment of a neutral zone "within which the nationals of all countries will be given safe haven,"[197] approved a US-sponsored resolution creating an InterAmerican Force.[198] This force, largely made up of US troops that numbered over 23,000 by the middle of May, eventually ended hostilities, established a provisional government and supervised general elections before finally departing the Dominican Republic on 21 September 1966.[199] During this time, the OAS legal umbrella, not the protection of nationals rationale, gradually became the principal, if not exclusive, US justification for the continued presence of its troops in the Dominican Republic.[200]

Whether the OAS officially legitimized or merely acquiesced in the introduction of US troops has been the subject of much scholarly debate,[201] as has been the legitimacy of the OAS operation itself.[202] While both issues are beyond the scope of the present study—which focuses upon the current status of the right of forcible protection—it should be underscored that the OAS never criticized, much less condemned, the initial US action of sending troops to the Dominican Republic to protect the lives of its nationals and other foreigners. Nor, for that matter, did the United Nations.[203]

Criticism of the US action in general, however, was widespread. Senator Fulbright, Chairman of the Committee on Foreign Relations, who dramatically broke with President Johnson over the Dominican Republic even before he took issue with the latter's policy in Vietnam, argued in the Senate that the

Administration had "cooked up" an invitation to intervene on the questionable grounds that the lives of US nationals were endangered.[204] While admitting that "Santo Domingo was not a particularly safe place to be in the last days of April 1965," the Senator contended that the "danger to American lives was more a pretext than a reason for the massive US intervention. . . ."[205] Had the protection of US and other foreign nationals been the real reason for US action, he argued, the United States could have sent in troops "promptly and then withdrawn them and the incident would soon have been forgotten."[206]

Scholarly comment almost unanimously agreed with the Senator's appraisal.[207] Although regarding "[t]he initial landing of four hundred Marines [to be] a permissible self-defense measure to protect the United States nationals,"[208] Professor Nanda pointed out the obvious, that:

> the United States' action was not limited in its objective [to] protecting the lives of its nationals; furthermore, it was not limited in its scope or duration either. Hence, there are serious doubts that it met the required criterion of proportionality to justify the United States' claim that since it had dispatched armed forces primarily to protect its citizens, the United States' use of coercive measures in the Dominican Republic should be considered a permissible use of self-defense.[209]

Professor Friedmann took much the same view, although his conclusion had a much harder edge. While acknowledging, like Nanda, that "[t]here is respectable authority for the view that the original limited intervention to protect US citizens from imminent danger, in a situation of anarchy, did not violate international law,"[210] he believed the massive build-up and continued presence of US forces in the Dominican Republic to be "patently, by standards of international law, an illegal action. . . ."[211]

The present writer and almost all other participants at a 1972 conference that subsequently debated the Dominican crisis also expressed similar views,[212] essentially supporting the continued existence of a limited right of forcible protection,[213] while at the same time recognizing and warning against the possibilities of the doctrine's misuse.[214] Today, three decades after President Johnson ordered in US troops, one still may conclude, as a minimum common denominator, that "it is far easier to justify the initial American response than it is the prolonged American presence in the Dominican Republic."[215]

### D. Iran. 1980.

On 4 November 1979, several hundred armed Muslim fundamentalist students overran the US Embassy in Tehran and took more than five dozen diplomatic and consular staff, Marine guards and other US citizens hostage.[216] The Iranian government did nothing to prevent the takeover[217] or, subsequently, to secure the release of the hostages.[218] The militant students, among other demands, requested the United States to return the former Shah—who on 22 October had been allowed to enter the United States from his exile in Mexico to receive medical treatment—to Iran for trial, a demand that the United States rejected.[219]

The United States immediately protested the seizure of the Embassy and its staff, but when Prime Minister Bazargan, a secular moderate opposed by the religious extremists, resigned on 6 November, it found itself with no one in Iran to negotiate. Thereafter President Carter dispatched two emissaries from the private sector—former Attorney General Ramsey Clark and former Foreign Service officer William Miller—on a secret mission to Tehran in an attempt to open up channels of communication. Carrying a letter from the President on White House stationery addressed "Dear Ayatollah Khomeini," Clark and Miller got no further than Istanbul, Turkey, by which time the Ayatollah had learned of their trip and ordered that no one in Tehran should see them.[220] After a week in Istanbul, during which time they made dozens of fruitless calls to Tehran, they concluded that there would be no movement on Iran's part until a new constitution had been adopted and a new government put in place and thereafter returned to Washington.[221]

While this mission and other efforts to secure the return of the hostages were under way, the United States requested that the UN Security Council meet to discuss ways to obtain the hostages release. Eventually it did on 4 December unanimously approving a resolution that called for the hostages immediate release.[222] When this resolution went unheeded by Iran, the Council met again and on 31 December, adopted another resolution demanding that Iran should free the hostages.[223] It also decided to reconvene in January 1980, in the event of continued Iranian non-compliance, to discuss the imposition of sanctions under Articles 39 and 41 of the UN Charter. The Council met again on 13 January 1980, to consider a US draft resolution that would have mandated broad economic sanctions against Iran. A veto cast by the Soviet Union prevented its adoption and effectively removed the Security Council from the settlement process.[224]

In the meantime, the United States on 29 November 1979, instituted proceedings against Iran before the International Court of Justice, requesting the Court, pending its final Judgment in the case, to indicate certain provisional measures, first and foremost being that "the Government of Iran immediately release all hostages of United States nationality and facilitate the prompt and safe departure from Iran of these persons and all other United States officials in dignified and humane circumstances."[225] Acting with commendable alacrity, the Court took the case, heard oral argument by the United States (Iran did not appear at the hearing), and on 15 December unanimously ordered Iran to restore the Embassy to US control and to ensure the:

> immediate release, without any exception, of all persons of United States nationality who are or who have been held in the Embassy . . . or have been held as hostages elsewhere, and afford full protection to all such persons, in accordance with the treaties in force between the two States, and with general international law.[226]

The Court also enjoined both the United States and Iran not to take any action "which may aggravate the tension between the two countries or render the existing dispute more difficult of solution. . . ."[227] As it had in the case of the two Security Council resolutions,[228] Iran refused to obey the Court's Order.

Diplomatic efforts during the winter and early spring of 1980 were no more successful in achieving the hostages' release.[229] Most prominent among these efforts was the establishment of a five-member UN Commission of Inquiry that was to undertake a fact-finding mission to Iran to hear Iran's grievances and to allow for an early solution of the crisis. . . ."[230] The Commission traveled to Tehran in early March but returned without having made any progress. A seemingly promising initiative involving the transfer of the hostages from the militants holding the Embassy into Iranian governmental control also fell through in early April when religious elements within Iran's Revolutionary Council thwarted the efforts of President Bani-Sadr and Prime Minister Ghotbzadeh to end the crisis.[231] Thus, by mid-April 1980—over five months after the Embassy had been overrun and the hostages seized—"momentum for a negotiated solution seemed to have run out."[232]

On 24 April 1980, some days after the beginning of the sandstorm season, and the "mission cut off" date recommended by the Joint Chiefs of Staff due to the possibility of sandstorms, with knowledge that a main highway ran adjacent to Desert I, in the face of the failure to secure their release through diplomatic or judicial means, the United States launched a rescue mission designed to free the hostages and return them to the United States.[233] That evening (local time) eight Sea Stallion RH-53 helicopters lifted off from the *USS Nimitz* stationed in the Arabian Sea off the coast of Iran. They were to fly under cover of darkness over 500 miles inland to a previously-prepared airstrip codenamed "Desert I," there to rendezvous with six Hercules C-130 cargo aircraft carrying

90 commandos. After refueling and loading the commandos and their equipment, the helicopters were to proceed to a remote site in the mountains south of Tehran, where they would be camouflaged to avoid detection the following day. That evening, 25 April, "Delta Force" was to enter Tehran in local vans and trucks, free the hostages at the Embassy, and then be evacuated by helicopter to an abandoned airport outside of Tehran codenamed "Desert II." Leaving the helicopters, they would get aboard transport aircraft waiting for them and be flown out of Iran under heavy US air cover.

Unfortunately, while operating through a sandstorm, two of the eight helicopters encountered mechanical and navigational difficulties and never reached Desert 1.[234] A third helicopter experienced hydraulic problems, which upon inspection at the desert site proved incapable of on-site repair. With only five workable helicopters at hand and knowing that a minimum of six were needed to accomplish the actual rescue the following night, the mission commander decided to abort the operation. Tragically, during refueling operations prior to the withdrawal, one of the helicopters collided with a C-130 and the resulting explosion and fire killed eight crew members and wounded another five. The force thereupon withdrew in the remaining C-130s. Evidence suggests that Iran was not even aware that US forces had been in the territory until President Carter officially informed it of the failed rescue operation several hours later.[235]

In a nationally televised broadcast at 7 A.M. that morning, President Carter in describing the aborted rescue operation characterized it as a "humanitarian mission" and specifically disavowed any hostility towards the Iranian people.[236] According to the President, he "ordered this rescue mission prepared *in order to safeguard American lives*, to protect America's national interests, and to reduce the tensions in the world that have been caused among many nations as this crisis has continued."[237] The following day, in a report to the Congress, the President reiterated the humanitarian nature of the mission and briefly explained why he considered it justified under international law, stating that "[i]n carrying out this operation, the United States was acting wholly within its right, in accordance with Article 51 of the United Nations Charter, to protect and rescue its citizens where the government of the territory in which they are located is unable or unwilling to protect them."[238] The United States, in a contemporaneous report to the UN Security Council, also relied upon the protection of nationals rationale, claiming that the rescue operation was a permissible "exercise of its inherent right of self-defense, with the aim of extricating American nationals who have been and remain the victims of the Iranian armed attack on our embassy."[239]

The US legal argument, based upon the inherent right of self-defense that States still enjoy under Article 51, is a reprise of the argument the United States first advanced in the case of the seizure of the *Mayaguez* in 1975 and subsequently developed in the UN Security Council to justify Israel's raid on Entebbe in 1976.

Since Iran never took the failed US rescue operation to the Security Council, that body did not have the opportunity to debate or pass on either the legality of the operation or the validity of the US legal argument. Moreover, the reactions of States, while generally supportive of the United States,[240] shed little light on their views regarding the legal basis of the US action under international law.[241]

In the case of Iran, however, unlike the other incidents discussed in this Chapter, the International Court of Justice had the opportunity to consider, at least in passing, the question of what legal arguments, if any, were available to support such rescue operations. This opportunity arose from the fact, as will be recalled, that in its Order on provisional measures of 15 December 1979, the Court had instructed both Iran and the United States not to take any action that might exacerbate the dispute between the two countries.[242] The attempted rescue operation, of course, took place on 24 April 1980, over a month after the Court had held three days of hearings on the merits of the case and while it was in the course of preparing its Judgment issued exactly a month later. Thus, it could be argued that the operation constituted the international law equivalent of contempt of court, especially if the Court were to have found that it violated the UN Charter.

In the event, as the late Judge Dillard remarked, "[w]hat the Court did was very gentle. It chided the United States for its rescue operation but didn't pass judgment on it."[243] While stating that it could not "fail to express its concern in regard to the United States' incursion into Iran," the Court nevertheless pointedly passed up the opportunity to question its legality, noting merely that it considered itself "bound to observe that an operation undertaken in those circumstances, from whatever motive, is of a kind calculated to undermine respect for the judicial process in international relations . . . ."[244] This mild slap on the wrist, as the late Professor Stein notes in his perceptive critique of this aspect of the Court's Judgment, "was coupled with an express disavowal of any finding that the rescue attempt was unlawful."[245] To quote from its Judgment:

> [T]he Court must point out that neither the question of the legality of the operation of 24 April 1980, under the Charter of the United Nations and under

general international law, nor any possible question of responsibility flowing from it, is before the Court.[246]

Thus, as Stein aptly concludes, the Court:

[L]eft to another day, a day one suspects will never come, a definitive statement of its views regarding the law governing the use of force in defense of the lives of nationals abroad.[247]

Should the day ever arrive when the Court addresses this question, however, its decision may well turn on its acceptance or rejection of the US argument in the Hostages Case—that the forcible protection of nationals abroad is a proper exercise of the inherent right of self-defense against armed attack authorized by Article 51 of the UN Charter—rather than on whether such actions constitute an exception to the prohibition against the use of force found in Article 2(4) or are otherwise permissible under general international law.[248]

This characterization of the legal question, after all, seems to have been "accepted without question by the Court,"[249] which not only mentions its being asserted by the United States before the Security Council,[250] but also refers twice to the "armed attack on the United States Embassy"[251] and the "armed attack by the militants ... and their seizure of Embassy premises and staff...."[252] Professor Stein has called attention to what he labels the Court's:

tantalizing suggestions that the category of "armed attacks" under Article 51 of the UN Charter extends well beyond major armed assaults.... If, indeed, the Court's references to "armed attack" were studied rather than casual, operations such as the rescue mission are lawful not because the right of self-defense under the UN Charter is coextensive with the preexisting customary law right of self-defense, which extended beyond defense against 'armed attack' . . ., but because the right of self-defense against armed attack has arisen.[253]

The two dissenting judges in the Hostages Case appear to have accepted the majority's analytical framework as well. Thus, Judge Morozow, after criticizing "the so-called rescue operation," which he labeled "an invasion of the territory of the Islamic Republic of Iran,"[254] maintained that the Court should have drawn attention to the undeniable legal fact that Article 51 of the Charter establishing [sic] the right of self-defense, may be invoked only "if an armed attack occurs against a member of the United Nations." It should have added that . . . there is no evidence that any armed attack had occurred against the United States.[255]

Judge Tarazi, who prefaced his remarks on this score with the observation that "[i]t is not my intention to characterize [the rescue] operation or to make any legal value judgment in this respect,"[256] nevertheless reflected in his opinion some of Judge Morozow's concerns about attempts to treat the operation as a self-defense response to an armed attack.[257] The legal framework for debate on the question is in place should the issue arise in some future case.[258]

Surprisingly, scholarly comment on the legality of the rescue operation has been relatively sparse. One US writer declared categorically that it was "a flagrant violation of international law,"[259] while another of his colleagues found it to be "preemptively illegal."[260] A German scholar, rejecting the US self-defense argument, concluded that "it was from the very beginning nothing but a violation of the prohibition of the use of force and of Iran's territorial integrity."[261] Professor Ronzitti, who repeatedly refers to the rescue operation and the *Hostages Case* in his monograph,[262] presumably holds the same opinion, since he reaches the general conclusion that "the right to intervene to protect one's own citizens abroad does not exist."[263]

Two more detailed legal studies of the rescue operation reach the contrary conclusion, each perhaps by a different legal path. In the first, while finding the US self-defense argument "subject to considerable difficulties,"[264] a British author nevertheless regards the operation as legally justified pursuant to a "restrictive" interpretation of Article 2(4), *i.e.*, that it was not a use of force against the political independence or territorial integrity of Iran, or in any other manner inconsistent with the purposes of the United Nations.[265]

In the second, Professor Schachter, who also believes that "an armed rescue action to save lives of nationals . . . is not prohibited by article 2(4) when the territorial government is unable or unwilling to protect them and the need for instant action is manifest,"[266] applies this test to the rescue operation and concludes that "the action taken did not violate the U.N. Charter or international law."[267]

It is not entirely clear from his exposition, however, whether his finding that Article 2(4) was "no problem" is grounded upon the belief that the rescue operation represented "an exception to the prohibition of article 2(4)"[268] or, alternatively, that it constituted an exercise of legitimate self-defense.[269] On balance, both the approach and language of his seminal chapter on the subject are somewhat confirmed by his subsequent writings.[270] It is suggested that Professor Schachter justifies the Iranian rescue operation not by a restrictive reading of Article 2(4), but rather by an expanded concept of the right of self-defense under Article 51.

Finally, as in the case of the Lebanese crisis discussed earlier in this Chapter,[271] some mention of the factual predicate behind its invocation by the United States during the Iranian crisis seems warranted here. While this issue has not received much attention in Iranian crisis postmortems,[272] an adequate factual showing that the lives or safety of the hostages were in imminent danger—that, technically, the requirement of the "necessity" of the rescue operation had been met[273]—is the *sine qua non* of its being a valid exercise of the right of forcible protection. Put more pointedly by former Under Secretary of State Christopher, the question becomes: "was the United States legally justified in undertaking the rescue mission in April 1980 . . . even though the hostages, *at that moment,* may not actually have been in imminent danger?"[274]

The answer to this question is made more difficult in the case of Iran by the fact that the real or apparent threat to the lives and safety of the hostages was not short-lived, requiring a decision as to whether to undertake a rescue mission to be made once and for all within a relatively narrow time frame, but continued for a period of many months. Thus, this case differs markedly from the other instances surveyed in this Chapter, especially the Dominican Republic crisis, where US decisionmakers had relatively little time to assess the facts before deciding whether or not to mount a rescue mission. It also differs from these other instances in that here the foreign government involved was not just unable, but blatantly unwilling, to do anything to protect the lives and safety of US nationals, thus accentuating the actual and potential danger to them.

Since, as the Hostages Convention reaffirms in its Preamble, hostage-taking is *par excellence* an "act which endangers innocent human lives,"[275] it is difficult to deny the fact that the US hostages at the Embassy were in "imminent danger" immediately after their seizure on 4 November 1979, a seizure that, it will be recalled, was endorsed and confirmed by the Ayatollah Khomeini within a fortnight. They were bound, blindfolded, paraded before TV cameras and threatened with trial and possible execution. Clearly the "necessity" requirement permitting a rescue mission could have been satisfied easily at that time.

If once satisfied, however, must the necessity requirement be satisfied again on 24 April 1980, when the actual rescue operation took place? Secretary Christopher's rhetorical question, perhaps shaped by the fact that it was raised in the context of his summary and evaluation of Professor Schachter's contribution to a joint publication effort, implies an affirmative answer.[276] The latter's analysis takes the position that:

[t]he illegality of their [prolonged] detention and the failure of international organs to obtain their release should not be enough to legitimize the use of force to effect their release. To allow the use of force in the absence of imminent peril would imply a "necessity" to use force to redress a legal wrong [which the UN Charter does not permit]. It would be significantly different from the necessity of self-defense to repel an attack or to save lives.[277]

Professor Schachter's attempt to transmute a permissible exercise of the right of forcible protection into an illegal use of force to redress a legal wrong, using the passage of time and possible improvement in the treatment of the hostages as an alchemist's converter, is not persuasive on a number of grounds. The taking of hostages being a wrongful act under international law, to then deny the State of the hostages' nationality the right to forcibly protect the hostages simply because the State that has seized the hostages has lessened its threat to the hostages' lives or limbs—evidenced, perhaps, by having placed them in an ordinary prison or permitted Red Cross access—is to eliminate an important sanction against the hostage-taking State. It improves the hostage takers negotiating position, and thereby encourages similar acts in the future.

Second, if "any taking of hostages is so grave a criminal act that a rescue action is instantly justified in law," (a position Professor Schachter apparently rejects but admits has "appeal" since to him "[i]t appears realistic and practical"[278]), why should any remedial steps taken by the hostage-taking State—short of the unconditional release of all hostages—in effect, reduce the wrongfulness of the hostage-taking State's act.

Finally, although there appears to be little if any State practice on point, there is no data that suggests that any State has acknowledged a diminution of its right to protect its nationals who have been illegally detained by another State merely because they have been held for some time and the threat to their lives and safety may have diminished somewhat since their wrongful detention commenced. Certainly the United States never took this position during the Iran crisis. Indeed, as Professor Stein perceptively points out, "[i]n the *Hostages* case, the United States made no effort to demonstrate to the Court that the rescue mission was undertaken in response to a new or more imminent peril to the hostages' lives."[279]

Even assuming, *in arguendo*, that international law required the United States to demonstrate that the hostages actually were in imminent danger at the time of the rescue operation, that burden of proof certainly would appear to have been met. As President Carter noted when initially explaining his reasons for ordering the mission, "the steady unraveling of authority in Iran and the mounting dangers that were posed to the safety of the hostages themselves" made the attempt "a necessity . . . ."[280] Secretary of Defense Brown seconded the President's remarks, stressing the "danger posed to the hostages by the deteriorating security situation in Iran."[281] Furthermore, he added, "[w]e have considerable concern for the physical and psychological effects on the hostages of prolonged captivity."[282] Secretary Christopher, who subsequently reviewed what he had believed to be the risks to the hostages "not in retrospect, with the benefit of hindsight, but at the time of the crisis, when decisions actually had to be made," spelled out US concerns in far more detailed fashion before concluding that, "[b]y any objective measure, it was certainly reasonable for the United States to operate on the assumption that the hostages were in grave, even mortal, peril at the time of the rescue mission."[283]

Professor Schachter, who believes the question of whether the hostages were in imminent danger at the time of the rescue operation to be unanswerable, even with hindsight, takes a "margin of appreciation" approach to the matter. "The pertinent point," he observes, agreeing with Christopher:

> is whether, at the time, the US government had reason to fear that in the emotional atmosphere of Iranian revolutionary ferment the hostages would be executed, with or without a trial. As a general rule, it seems reasonable to recognize that the state whose nationals are imprisoned as hostages should have wide latitude to make the decision whether they are in extreme danger.[284]

Applying this approach to the publicly available facts, he concludes that:

> whether or not the hostages were actually in extreme danger, the conditions were such as to lead the US government to believe they were. Faced with this fact and the not unrealistic conclusion at the time that peaceful means offered no promise of release, the United States had reasonable grounds to consider military action necessary to effect a rescue. On these premises, the action taken did not violate the Charter or international law.[285]

With this conclusion, if not with all his reasoning in reaching it, few reasonable observers can disagree. Moreover, by spelling out and applying a "margin of appreciation" approach to the determination of whether the requirement of necessity was satisfied in the case of the rescue operation in Iran, Professor Schachter has made an important contribution towards refining one of the criteria that will be used in judging the validity of future claims by States to exercise the right of forcible protection of their nationals abroad.

Fundamentally, as in the Iran case, a state's embassy and/or consulate constitutes the sovereign property of the foreign state which occupies it. If an embassy or consulate is attacked by foreign nationals, it constitutes an attack on the occupying state (the United States in the Iran case).

An attack on a state justifies a "self-defense" response against the attackers/occupiers of the state's embassy or consulate to secure the building and the rescue of its nationals per Article 51 of the UN Charter.

## NOTES

1. Information about the forcible protection of nationals abroad by States other than the United States — principally France — is hard to obtain and often fragmentary or inaccurate. Moreover, with the one exception of Entebbe, such instances appear to have generated little legal debate either on the international level or within the States concerned. For a necessarily cursory and undoubtedly incomplete series of case studies of non-US forcible protection of nationals abroad, *see* Chapter V.

2. Background information about the crisis as well as detailed descriptive accounts of it may be found in M. Agwani, The Lebanese Crisis, 1958 (1965); L. Meo, Lebanon: Improbable Nation (1965); and F. Qubain, Crisis In Lebanon (1961) [hereinafter cited as Qubain]. For differing views on the legal issues involved, compare Potter, *Legal Aspects of the Beirut Landing,* 52 Am. J. Int'l L. 727 (1958) with Wright, United States Intervention in the Lebanon. 53 *id.* 112 (1959). For a useful monograph, prepared under the supervision of the present writer and drawn upon throughout this chapter, see R. Osborne, The Lebanese Intervention and International Law, 31 Mar. 1969 (unpublished thesis in US Naval War College Library). *See also* C. Thayer, Diplomat ch. III (1959) for a vivid account of the actual intervention.

3. According to the official census, Lebanon's population consists of 392,000 Christians and 383,000 Muslims. L. Meo, *supra* note 2, at 229 n.1. *But see* text at and accompanying note 4 *infra.*

4. The most recent estimates place the population at 2,800,000. The Middle East and North Africa 1989, at 617 (36th ed. 1990). With a higher birthrate and lower emigration, most informed observers believe that Muslims now account for about 60% of the total population.

5. Qubain, *supra* note 2, at 17.

6. M. Agwani, *supra* note 2, at 1-2.

7. Qubain, *supra* note 2, at 18.

8. "The people of Lebanon enjoy one of the highest standards of living in the Middle East." *Id.* at 3.

9. *Id.* at 35-37.

10. *Id.* at 38.

11. *Id.* at 38-44.

12. *Id.* at 42.

13. Joint Resolution of 9 March 1957, § (1957). 2, 71 Stat. 5, *reprinted in* 36 DEP'T ST. BULL. 481.

14. *See* L. Meo, *supra* note 2, at 117-20.

15. R. Garnet, Intervention and Revolution 140 (1968).

16. The violence began in Tripoli, where according to unsubstantiated reports of the opposition, 168 of their members were killed. Qubain, *supra* note 2, at 74. It soon spread. For a succinct account, *see* R. Osborne, *supra* note 2, at 22-23:

Violence in Tripoli led to armed rebellion. On 9 May demonstrations began followed by a burning of the US Information Library. On 12 May the violence reached Beirut. Barricades were set up with burning oil drums. The road to Damascus was barred and a curfew was introduced. Commerce and industry came to a standstill and the large volume of tourists disappeared from the country. When the news of the upheaval in Tripoli reached Beirut, the United National Front held a meeting and the decision was made for armed revolt. On 13 May the United National Front attacked the Presidential Palace at Bayt al-Din. The Cairo radio began urging Lebanese Moslems to seize areas where they were in control and accede to the United Arab Republic. The country was sliding toward anarchy.

17. Despite Chamoun's demands that the army promptly put down the rebellion and end the strike, General Fuad Chebab, the commander-in-chief, refused to commit the army against what he considered a mass protest rather than subversion. From May to July he used his 6,000-man army to patrol the streets and to prevent clashes between Christians and Muslims. He wanted at all costs to keep the army, which was about two-thirds Christian and one-third Muslim, above the political fray that threatened to split the county. R. Garnet, *supra* note 15, at 144.

18. While the civil strife which occurred in Lebanon from May through July of 1958 went well beyond Garnet's "mass protest," *see text* accompanying notes 16 and 17 *supra*, it never really degenerated into civil war. Moreover, throughout the crisis an element of unreality, if not farce, often prevailed. Thus, according to Qubain:

[h]ad the Lebanese crisis not had such tragic aspects, it could have been easily described as a comic opera. There was something unreal about the whole affair-a succession of scenes taken virtually *in toto* from Ruritania: an army that would not fight; opposition leaders officially declared 'rebels,' with warrants out for their arrest, blandly walking the streets of Beirut in broad daylight with no one laying so much as a finger on them; pitched battles between the army and 'rebel' forces stopped, so that army trucks could bring water to the rebels and move their wounded to hospitals; a president virtually a prisoner in his own palace for over two months; a parliament that could not meet; opposition leaders, each with a private army of his own, establishing virtually independent government in his locality—levying taxes and administering justice; and a crisis that was long on bitter words, but short on actual casualties.

19. For President Chamoun's statement to the press reiterating such charges, *see* M. Agwani, *supra* note 2, at 74-76.

20. For the Lebanese complaint to the Security Council, *see* 13 U.N. SCOR Supp. (Apr.-Jun. 1958) at 33, U.N. Doc. S/4007 (1958), *reprinted in* M. Agwani, *supra* note 2, at 120-21.

21. 13 U.N. SCOR (823d mtg.) at 4, U.N. Doc. StP.V. 823 (1958), *reprinted in* M. Agwani, *supra* note 2, at 124.

22. 13 U.N. SCOR (823d mtg.) at 22-23, U.N. Doc. S/P.V. 823 (1958), *reprinted in* M. Agwani, *supra* note 2, at 147-59.

23. 13 U.N. SCOR Supp. (Apr.-Jun. 1958) at 47, U.N. Doc. S/4023 (1958), *reprinted in* M. Agwani, *supra* note 2, at 198.

24. Curtis, *The United Nations Observation Group in Lebanon*, 18 Int'l Org. 738, 751-52 (1964). Other observers are much more critical of UNOGIL's operations. *See* Kerr, *The Lebanese Civil War*, in The International Regulation of Civil War 65, 85-89 (E. Luard ed. 1972); R. Murphy, Diplomat Among Warriors 402 (1964); and Qubain, *supra* note 2, at 143-52.

25. D. Eisenhower, The White House Years: Waging Peace 1956-1961, at 267 (1965).
26. 39 DEP'T ST. BULL. 31 (1958).
27. D. Eisenhower, *supra* note 25, at 270 (emphasis added). *See also* text *infra* accompanying note 32.
28. Qubain, *supra* note 2, at 115. *See* Baghdad Reports Americans Slain, N.Y. Times, July 16, 1958, at 15, col 1. *See also* C. Thayer, *supra* note 2, at 27.
29. Kerr, *supra* note 24, at 77.
30. For a graphic description, *see* C. Thayer, *supra* note 2, at 33-36.
31. Kerr, *supra* note 24, at 77.
32. *See supra* text at note 27. According to one key official who thereafter was instrumental in achieving a settlement of the crisis, President Eisenhower did not even mention the need to protect nationals when in a White House briefing he:

> elaborated a little on his purpose in ordering US Marines to land in Lebanon. He said that sentiment had developed in the Middle East, especially in Egypt, that Americans were capable only of words, that we were afraid of Soviet reaction if we attempted military action. Eisenhower believed that if the United States did nothing now, there would be heavy and irreparable losses in Lebanon and in the area generally. He wanted to demonstrate in a timely and practical way that the United States was capable of supporting its friends.

R. Murphy, *supra* note 24, at 398.

33. 39 DEP'T ST. BULL. 181 (1958) (emphasis added).
34. *Id.* at 182.
35. *Id.* at 184.
36. Explaining the landing of Marines he argued that:

> [t]heir presence is designed for the sole purpose of helping the Government of Lebanon at its request in its efforts to stabilize the situation brought on by the threats from outside, until such time as the United Nations can take the steps necessary to protect the independence and political integrity of Lebanon. *They will also afford security to the several thousand Americans who reside in that country.* 13 U.N. SCOR (827th mtg.) at 7, U.N. Doc. S/P.V. 827 (1958), *reprinted in* 39 DEP'T ST. BULL. 186 (1958) (emphasis added).

37. Ambassador Lodge's statement before the Security Council on 18 July 1958, to the effect that the "[f]orces of the United States now in Lebanon at the specific request of the lawfully constituted Government of Lebanon would not remain if their withdrawal were requested by that Government," 13 U.N. SCOR (833d mtg.) at 10, U.N. Doc. S/P.V. 833 (1958), *reprinted in* 39 DEP'T ST. BULL. 196 (1958), demonstrates beyond doubt that the protection of nationals rationale had been discarded after three days of use. One explanation for the shift in legal justifications, of course, might be that over the 15-18 July period the safety of US nationals had been secured, thus depriving the United States of the factual basis for continued reliance upon this rationale.

38. R. Murphy, *supra* note 24, at 399-400. *See supra* note 17. *Cf.* D. Eisenhower, *supra* note 25, at 265, who places the Lebanese army at 9,000 men.

39. D. Eisenhower, *supra* note 25, at 286. "In support of these troops, the entire Sixth Fleet, consisting of about 70 ships with 40,000 men, moved to the east Mediterranean." Qubain, *supra* note 2, at 115.

40. According to President Eisenhower, the decision to have the troops occupy only Beirut and its airfield was:

> ... a political one which I adhered to over the recommendations of some of the military. If the Lebanese army were unable to subdue the rebels when we had secured their capital and protected their government, I felt, we were backing up a government with so little popular support that we probably should not be there.

D. Eisenhower, *supra* note 25, at 275 n.8. Would that subsequent Presidents had taken a similar approach when committing United States forces to the assistance of various governments in later years!

41. Qubain, *supra* note 2, at 120.
42. For a description of their "low profile" activities, *see* Kerr, *supra* note 24, at 81-83.
43. In one semi-humorous incident, "two American soldiers in a jeep lost their way and strayed into the rebel-held quarter of Beirut called El-Basta. Local irregulars surrounded their car, disarmed them and took them to their chief, Satib Salam, who served them Coca-Cola and gave them a kindly lecture about interference in the domestic affairs of foreign countries. They were then sent off in their jeep, minus their weapons." *Id.* at 90 n.12.
44. Qubain, *supra* note 2, at 119-20. *See also id.* at 130.
45. "Two other points should perhaps be emphasized in this connection: (1) that on several occasions American troops, while on duty, were shot at by snipers, but in most cases, in accordance with their instructions, did not return the fire and (2) that not a single Lebanese suffered any injury of any kind—whether in his person or property—as a result of US military action." *Id.* at 121.
46. Schulimson, Marines in Lebanon: 1958, at 32 (Historic Branch, G-3 Division Headquarters, US Marine Corps, 1966). *Accord,* Kerr, *supra* note 24, at 90 n.13; R. Murphy, *supra* note 24, at 408; and Qubain, *supra* note 2, at 120.
47. The withdrawal began on 8 October 1958, and was completed in less than three weeks. 39 DEP'T. ST. BULL. 650-51 (1958).

> On October 25, 1958, the final withdrawal of United States troops took place, almost without public notice. This lack of attention contrasted vividly with attitudes in the early days of our intervention when some international critics were crying that America's purpose was to establish a permanent and imperialistic foothold in the Middle East.

D. Eisenhower, *supra* note 25, at 288.

48. *See, e.g.,* Curtis, *supra* note 24, at 754.
49. *But see* Wright, *supra* note 2.
50. "The most plausible ground for the recent landing of military forces of the United States near Beirut is to be found in the invitation of the duly elected Government of Lebanon . . . ." Potter, *supra* note 2. According to Wright, "[t]he American declaration that it would withdraw when requested by Lebanon and its actual withdrawal when so requested indicate that this was the justification mainly relied upon." Wright, *supra* note 2, at 124 n.38. *See supra* text at and accompanying note 37.
51. Responding to the argument that the right to intervene by invitation may be the subject of abuse, Qubain concludes that:

> [t]his was clearly not the case with respect to the landing of American troops in Lebanon. Free elections had already taken place without the slightest interference from the troops, and a new President, supported and accepted by all factions, was elected. Furthermore, . . . the presence of American troops did serve a constructive

purpose in Lebanon itself, and contributed to the calming of the tense atmosphere in the area. Qubain, *supra* note 2, at 101.

52. *See generally supra* text at notes 32-37. President Eisenhower, who recognized that any action by the United States must conform "with the Charter of the United Nations," obviously relied upon the concept of collective self-defense. D. Eisenhower, *supra* note 25, at 271. Describing his briefing of Congressional leaders, he notes that at one point Secretary of State Dulles "had to explain Article 51 of the United Nations Charter, which permitted a country to act on an emergency basis pending the first opportunity to turn the problem over as soon as the United Nations was able to act." *Id.* at 272.

53. *See supra* text at note 24. For a strong argument supporting the collective self-defense thesis, *see* Qubain, *supra* note 2, at 123-26.

54. *See supra* text at notes 32-37.

55. *See, e.g.*, Kerr, *supra* note 24, and Qubain, *supra* note 2.

56. Potter, *supra* note 2, at 728.

57. Wright, *supra* note 2, at 117.

58. *See supra* text at and accompanying notes 16-18. Of course, this fact cuts two ways. Questioning the motives for the action of the United States in a debate in the British Parliament, Mr. Hugh Gaitskell, leader of the opposition, tellingly remarked "that if it [the justification for US action] was simply the lives of Americans, then they have been in some danger throughout all these last weeks while the civil war has been taking place in Lebanon." 591 Parl. Deb., H.C. (5th ser.) 1249 (1958).

59. *See supra* text at note 33. "In addition to our embassy personnel and other government employees, a good many Americans lived in Lebanon, most of them as teachers, missionaries, and businessmen. Beirut also was a popular seaside resort which attracted Americans residing throughout the Middle East and many tourists." R. Murphy, *supra* note 24, at 398.

60. For instances of US citizens being trapped by crossfire, *see, e.g.*, C. Thayer, *supra* note 2, at 23. That they were not intentionally the targets of the anti-Chamoun forces seems apparent from the statement of Mr. Sa'ib Salam, the opposition leader, made immediately after the landing of US troops. "Our national Lebanese liberation movement is proud of the fact that it has not threatened foreigners or their property in the two months of an all-out bloody revolution, because its only aim is to get rid of [President Chamoun]...." *See* M. Agwani, *supra* note 2, at 295.

61. *See supra* text at note 28.

62. It is worth noting in this regard, however, that while the United States chartered "four commercial aircraft to provide transportation for Americans who wish[ed] to leave Iraq," it apparently never contemplated forcible action to protect them at that time. Indeed, five days after the *coup d'etat* the US Ambassador seemed quite content with assurances from the revolutionary regime "that they will honor their promise to protect American lives and property. Assurances have also been given that those Americans wishing to leave Iraq will be allowed to depart freely and that all necessary precautions shall be taken to assure safe departure." 39 DEP'T. ST. BULL. 199 (1958).

Also worthy of note is the fact that Great Britain, while accepting the protection of nationals rationale advanced by the United States in the case of Lebanon, 591 Parl. Deb., H.C. (5th ser.) 1243 (1958) (Mr. Lloyd), did not adopt it herself when justifying the subsequent dispatch of British troops to Jordan. *Id.* at 1438-39 (Prime Minister). But see the remarks of an opposition spokesman to the effect that "[t]here would, in my view, be only one justification for entering Jordan with troops. That is if British personnel were in danger and it was our duty to preserve the lives of British persons in Jordan. Then, I can visualize our putting troops in for that sole purpose." *Id.* at 1304 (Mr. Crossman).

63. R. Murphy, *supra* note 24, at 400.
64. R. Osborne, *supra* note 2, at 61-62.
65. C. Thayer, *supra* note 2, at 9-10.
66. *Id.* at 20, 28. *See supra* text at note 26.
67. R. Osborne, *supra* note 2, at 74-75 (emphasis deleted):

> Although a stronger case could be made if "Phase C" had been set, which required the evacuation of all Americans from the crisis area, it appears that a moment for deliberation did not exist and an immediate danger did exist after the Iraqi coup in which Americans were killed. The rebels in Lebanon had clearly announced their intent to violently overthrow the western aligned government and therefore it would be reasonable to assume that Americans would be harmed. The threat existed although no Americans were harmed, but a threat is sufficient to justify the exercise of a reasonable degree of self-defense.

68. For a description of this breakdown and a day-by-day account of its aftermath, *see* A. Merriam, Congo: Background of Conflict ch. VI (1961).

69. For Belgium's legal justification of this action, *see* McNemar, *The Postindependence War in the Congo*, in The International Law of Civil War 244, 273 (R. Falk ed. 1971), who quotes Prime Minister Gaston Eyskens as stating that:

> The Belgian troops intervened when there was imminent danger and the government found itself in a situation of absolute necessity. The Belgian government like any government has a duty to observe a rule of international ethics and international law which imposes upon a country the protection of its nationals. The Belgian government intervened solely to prevent bloodshed and to offer the protection which was necessary for the preservation of human lives.

The above author, who acknowledges the continued existence of the right of forcible protection in such cases, nevertheless concludes that:

> The Belgian case was weak on two grounds. The failure to seek Congolese consent was a violation of a specific treaty commitment and the aggravation of an extremely sensitive colonial issue. Second, the Belgian actions in Katanga were more extensive than necessary for the protection of nationals and significantly contributed to the province's ability to remain independent.

*Id.* For discussion of the question of consent and the principle of proportionality, *see infra* text at notes 102-104 & 142-146.

70. S.C. Res. 143, 15 U.N. SCOR Supp. (July-Sept. 1960) at 16, U.N. Doc. S/4387 (1960).

71. For a succinct account of ONUC's operations, *see* L. Miller, World Order and Local Disorder 66-116 (1967).

72. "One [witness] said the rebels carried out thousands of executions during their occupation of Stanleyville. He said that 'every day, any time of the day, some Congolese was being dragged to the Lumumba monument and executed.' Their hands were tied behind their backs and they were hacked to death with machetes. The more illustrious of those killed had their hearts cut out and eaten in public by the rebels." The Times (London), Nov. 25, 1964, at 12, col 2.

73. Young, *The Congo Rebellion*, Africa Report 6, 11 (April 1965). Another commentator concludes that "[a]t least 18,000 Congolese were executed by the rebels." Grundy, *The Stanleyville Rescue: American Policy in the Congo*, 56 Yale Rev. 242, 247 (1967).

74. Young, *supra* note 73, at 11.

75. *Id.* at 10. On the mercenaries and the key role they played in turning the tide of battle, *see* I. Colvin, The Rise and Fall of Moise Tshombe ch. XII (1968); D. Reed, 111 Days in Stanleyville ch. 10 (1965). There is little doubt that, like most mercenary contingents, they quickly filled their quotas in the looting and wanton murder departments. One mercenary is reported to have admitted that "in Kindu we must have shot at least three thousand people. I'll be honest with you: most of them unnecessarily." *Id.* at 180. *See also infra* text accompanying note 138.

76. D. Reed, *supra* note 75, at 8.

77. Case Studies In African Diplomacy, No. 1, The Organization of African Unity and the Congo Crisis 1964-65, at 32 (C. Hoskyns ed. 1969). *See infra* text at note 86.

78. *See* the title of Chapter 4 of D. Reed, *supra* note 75.

79. For an insider's view of these negotiations, *see* W. Attwood, The Reds and the Blacks 195-217 (1967).

80. I. Colvin, *supra* note 75, at 190.

81. *Id.*

82. 19 U.N. SCOR (1174th mtg.) at 15, U.N. Doc. S/P.V. 1174 (1964) (Ambassador Stevenson), *reprinted in* 52 DEP'T. ST. BULL. 18 (1965).

83. D. Reed, *supra* note 75, at 192.

84. 19 U.N. SCOR (1174th mtg.) at 15-16, U.N. Doc. S/P.V.1174 (1964), *reprinted in* American Foreign Policy—Current Documents 1964, at 777 (1967). *See infra* text accompanying note 90.

85. *Id.* at 16, reprinted in 52 DEP'T. ST. BULL. 18 (1965). Fortunately, "the mercenary-led column captured Kindu, 300 miles south [of Stanleyville], just in time to prevent the mass murder of twenty-four Europeans. (Hundreds of Congolese 'intellectuals' had already been burned alive there by the . . . [rebels].)" W. Attwood, *supra* note 79, at 207. *Compare supra* text accompanying note 75.

86. Grundy, *supra* note 73, at 247. *See supra* text at notes 77-78.

87. W. Attwood, *supra* note 79, at 213. Attwood states that he was not authorized to discuss military operations, but points out that in any event it would have been impossible to impose a cease-fire so late in the day. "I doubt if . . . [Kanza] realized that nothing now could have stopped the gung-ho mercenary-led column from taking Stanleyville—not even Tshombe himself standing in the road and waving his arms." *Id.*

*Compare* Attwood's recollection that Kanza "said the ANC advance had to be stopped and a cease-fire put into effect before we could talk about the hostages," *Id.* (emphasis added), *with* Garnet's inaccurate and misleading assertion that "[t]here is little doubt from Attwood's own account that had the United States ordered Tshombe to stop bombing Stanleyville, *the US and Belgian hostages would have been released.*" R. Garnet, *supra* note 15, at 251 (emphasis added). Attwood's "own account," of course, indicates nothing of the kind.

88. *See, e.g.*, Geneva Convention Relative to the Protection of Civilian Persons in Time of War, Aug. 12, 1949, art. 3, 6 UST. 3516, T.I.A.S. No. 3365. "The rebels' action in holding and threatening hostages is in direct violation of the Geneva Conventions and accepted humanitarian principles." 19 U.N. SCOR Supp. (Oct.-Dec. 1964) at 189, U.N. Doc. S/6062 (1964) (statement by US Government), *reprinted in* 12 M. Whiteman, Digest of International Law 212 (1971).

89. On 25 September, when an ICRC delegation flew to Stanleyville for two days of talks with the rebels about releasing the hostages, Gbenye and his associates professed not to know "what the International Committee of the Red Cross was. When told about the Geneva Conventions and particularly the ban on holding people as hostages, they said they had not

heard about that, either. In any case, they added, they did not consider themselves as bound by the Geneva rules. The conventions, they scoffed, were 'written by whites.' " D. Reed, *supra* note 75, at 115.

90. On their ordeal, *see generally id. passim*. Ambassador Stevenson subsequently refuted what he termed "the astonishing thesis" that the threats to their lives were not real.

> The threats were very real indeed; they had been carried out in the past and we had every reason to expect that they would continue to be carried out in the future. From mid-August onward after the rebel forces had taken Stanleyville, seizing and holding foreigners as hostages became a deliberate act of rebel policy, and in the following months this medieval practice was widely applied. Many of those hostages were deliberately killed. By the time the Belgian paratroopers arrived in Stanleyville, and before the outlaws even knew of their impending arrival, the total of those thus already tortured and slaughtered amounted to 35 foreigners. . . .

19 U.N. SCOR (1174th mtg.) at 15-16, U.N. Doc. S/P.V. 1174 (1964), *reprinted in* 52 DEP'T. ST. BULL. 18 (1965). *See supra* text at note 84.

91. The Belgian Foreign Ministry confirmed this development on 20 November, adding by way of explanation that "[t]he Belgian and American Governments have considered it their duty in view of the threat to their nationals and civilians in general in the region of Stanleyville to take preparatory measures in order to be able to effect, if necessary, a humanitarian rescue operation." 51 DEP'T. ST. BULL. 840 (1964), *reprinted in* American Foreign Policy—Current Documents 1964, at 767 (1967).

92. *See* W. Attwood, *supra* note 79, at 209-14.

93. Prime Minister Tshombe, in a note to the United States dated 21 November 1964, stated that the Congo Government had decided:

> to authorize the Belgian government to send an adequate rescue force to carry out the humanitarian task of evacuating the civilians held as hostages by the rebels, and to authorize the United States Government to furnish necessary transport for this humanitarian mission. I fully appreciate that you wish to withdraw your forces as soon as your mission is accomplished.

19 U.N. SCOR Supp. (Oct.-Dec. 1964) at 187-88, U.N. Doc. S/6062 (1964), *reprinted in* American Foreign Policy—Current Documents 1964, at 768 (1967).

According to his biographer, Tshombe recalled that three weeks earlier "'the United States and Belgium, fearing that the army advance would be too slow to rescue the hostages, [had] asked my authorisation to organise a parachute attack on Stanleyville.'" I. Colvin, *supra* note 75, at 189. Thus, as in the case of the Dominican Republic, *see infra* text at notes 181-183 and accompanying note 186, an invitation to undertake a rescue operation apparently was solicited.

94. For a vivid description of the actual operation, *see* D. Reed, *supra* note 75, ch. 19. Reed and Colvin state that 22 white hostages were killed and at least 40 wounded (*Id.* at 259; I. Colvin, *supra* note 75, at 194), while Attwood places the number of dead at 27. W. Attwood, *supra* note 79, at 217. Apparently the discrepancy stems from the fact that five of the wounded later died. D. Reed, *supra* at 259. Three of the dead, including ironically Dr. Paul Carlson, were United States nationals. American Foreign Policy—Current Documents 1964, at 772 (1967).

95. 52 DEP'T. ST. BULL. 16 (1965) (Ambassador Stevenson), *reprinted in* American Foreign policy—Current Documents 1964, at 776 (1967).

96. 19 U.N. SCOR Supp. (Oct.-Dec. 1964) at 195, U.N. Doc. S/6068 (1964) (Letter from Ambassador Stevenson to the President of the Security Council), *reprinted in* American Foreign Policy—Current Documents 1964, at 771 (1967). For a description of this operation, *see* D.

Reed, *supra* note 75, *at* 267-69. Prior to it, the rebels had killed 22 white hostages. *Compare infra* text at note 97.

Subsequent estimates of the total number of hostages rescued during the four day period ranged even higher than the figures given in the text. "The rescue operation was undertaken on November 24. As a result, more than 1,300 non-Congolese and over 1,000 black Africans were rescued from Stanleyville. In subsequent air and ground rescues, another 1,600 non-Congolese were saved." 52 DEP'T. ST. BULL. 222 (1965) (Assistant Secretary of State Williams).

97. *See supra* note 95. The Times (London), Nov. 28, 1964, at 8, col 1, reported that in the four day operation 80 white hostages had been killed in Stanleyville and Paulis. *Compare supra* text accompanying note 94 and at *infra* notes 135-136.

98. For a comprehensive treatment of Belgium's legal justification of its participation in the operation, see Gerard, *L'Operation Stanleyville-Paulis Devant le Parlement Belge et les Nations Unis*, 3 Revue Belge De Droit International 242 (1967). According to the author, the Belgian Government consistently maintained that the right of self-defense guaranteed States by Article 51 of the United Nations Charter included the right of forcible protection of a State's nationals abroad. *Id.* at 254-56. *See supra* text accompanying note 69. The British government's position was the same. 702 Parl. Deb., H.C. (5th ser.) 911 (1964) (Mr. Thomson): "We take the view that under international law a state has the right to land troops in foreign territory to protect its nationals in an emergency if necessary."

99. 19 U.N. SCOR Supp. (Oct.-Dec. 1964) at 188, U.N. Doc. S/6062 (1964), *reprinted in* 12 M. Whiteman, *supra* note 88, at 211.

100. 19 U.N. SCOR (1174th mtg.) at 13, U.N. Doc. S/P.V. 1174 (1964), *reprinted in* 52 DEP'T. ST. BULL. 17 (1965).

101. 51 DEP'T. ST. BULL. 846 (1964).

102. *See supra* note 99. *See also* Cleveland, *The Evolution of Rising Responsibility*, 52 DEP'T. ST. BULL. 7, 9 (1965). For the Congolese note authorizing the operation, see *supra* text accompanying note 93.

103. A point repeatedly made by Professor Brownlie and other critics of the doctrine of humanitarian intervention. *See, e.g.*, Brownlie, *Thoughts on Kind-Hearted Gunmen*, in Humanitarian Intervention and The United Nations 139, 143-44 (R. Lillich ed. 1973).

104. These requirements have been summarized conveniently by Farer, *The Regulation of Foreign Intervention in Civil Armed Conflict*, 142 Recueil Des Cours (Hague Academy of International Law) 297, 394 (1974-II), as follows:

>(1) that there be an immediate and extensive threat to fundamental human rights;
>
>(2) that all other remedies for the protection of those rights have been exhausted to the extent possible within the time constraints posed by the threat;
>
>(3) that an attempt has been made to secure the approval of appropriate authorities in the target State;
>
>(4) that there is a minimal effect on the extant structure of authority (e.g., that the intervention not be used to impose or preserve a preferred regime);
>
>(5) that the minimal requisite force be employed and/or that the intervention is not likely to cause greater injury to innocent persons and their property than would result if the threatened violation actually occurred;
>
>(6) that the intervention be of limited duration; and
>
>(7) that a report of the intervention be filed immediately with the Security Council and where relevant, regional organisations.

105. 19 U.N. SCOR Supp. (Oct.-Dec. 1964) at 189, U.N. Doc. S/6062 (1964), *reprinted in* 12 M. Whiteman, *supra* note 88, at 212-13.

106. *See supra* text at notes 80-90. "It is clear from the statements of the rescued persons themselves that further delay would have meant an even greater number of wanton and tragic killings. Time, for the lives of those people, was calculable only in minutes." 19 U.N. SCOR Supp. (Oct.-Dec. 1964) at 195, U.N. Doc. S/6068 (1964) (Letter from Ambassador Stevenson to the President of the Security Council), *reprinted in* American Foreign Policy—Current Documents 1964, at 771 (1967). *Accord,* 19 U.N. SCOR Supp. (Oct.-Dec. 1964) at 194, U.N. Doc. S/6067 (1964) (Letter from the Belgian Ambassador to the President of the Security Council): "All [rescued hostages] stress their conviction that they owe their lives only to the intervention *in extremis* of the Belgian paratroops."

*See also* the statement by Under Secretary of State Ball that prior to the airdrop "the situation was deteriorating to the point where we felt that it couldn't hold very much longer, and, in fact, Mr. Hoyt, who is our consul in Stanleyville and who has been one of the hostages for 3 months, has told us, first of all, that it was the opinion of everyone there that if this had gone 24 hours longer they would all have been executed—they were going to be lined up against the wall—and, secondly, that only the airdrop saved their lives." 51 DEP'T. ST. BULL. 843 (1964).

107. A quarter century ago the present writer, perhaps unduly reflecting official US reaction, remarked that "the criticism heaped upon the United States for its role in this humanitarian venture comes as something of a surprise." R. Lillich, *Intervention to Protect Human Rights,* 15 McGill L.J. 205, 214 (1969) *But see* R. Falk, Legal Order in a Violent World 326 (1968).

108. These factors are taken from an excellent review of the UN debates found in a Note, *The Congo Crisis 1964: A Case Study in Humanitarian Intervention,* 12 Va. J. Int'l L. 261, 266-74 (1972), written by Howard L. Weisberg, Esq., Class of 1973, University of Virginia School of Law and Member of the Maryland and District of Columbia Bars, under the supervision of the present writer.

109. The following quote from a speech by the delegate from the Congo Republic (Brazzaville) is illustrative: "Why, in a conflict in which the Congolese are fighting between themselves, should there be no concern for the safety of the civilian population in general and why should the fate of the whites be the sole consideration?" 19 U.N. SCOR (1170th mtg.) at 14, U.N. Doc. S/P.V. 1170 (1964). One writer, reviewing the operation, has suggested, somewhat cynically, that "[t]he State Department's humanitarian concerns were aroused only when it appeared that Americans and Europeans might be the next victims." R. Garnet, *supra* note 15, at 249. *See infra* text at note 111.

110. They were slain, of course, not by the Belgian paratroopers, but by the white mercenary-led ANC that reached Stanleyville several hours after the airdrop began. The time of the ANC's arrival has been put at "soon after nine o'clock" by I. Colvin, *supra* note 75, at 194, and as "[a]t 10:30 a.m." by D. Reed, *supra* note 75, at 261. *See infra* text at and accompanying note 138.

111. Garnet's criticism of the United States' slowness in acting (*see supra* text accompanying note 109) seems particularly unfair in view of his caustic comments on the rescue operation itself. *See* R. Garnet, *supra* note 15, at 250-51. One can imagine what his reaction to an earlier humanitarian intervention would have been!

112. 19 U.N. SCOR (1173d mtg.) at 12, U.N. Doc. S/P.V. 1173 (1964). *See generally supra* text at notes 95-97.

113. *See supra* text at note 79. *See also supra* text at notes 86-90.

114. 19 U.N. SCOR (1175th mtg.) at 23, U.N. Doc. S/P.V. 1175 (1964).

115. When Attwood informed President Kenyatta of Kenya, who was chairman of the OAU Ad Hoc Commission on the Congo, "that the paratroopers might have to mount a humanitarian rescue operation as a last resort," the latter "look pained" and replied that "'that would be very bad....'" W. Attwood, *supra* note 79, at 214. Later, in response to Attwood's plea to remain friends, he stated frankly that "'[w]e can be friends... only if you stop being friends with Tshombe." *Id.* at 215.

116. *See supra* text at and accompanying note 102.

117. W. Attwood, *supra* note 79, at 218-19. Omitted at the end of the second paragraph of the above quote are parentheses containing the following sentence: "The orgy of looting and killing that followed the capture of Stanleyville by the ANC was so bad that the Belgian paratroop commander was glad to pull his men out of the city for fear they'd start fighting the mercenaries." *Id.* at 218. *See infra* text at and accompanying note 138.

118. R. Falk, *supra* note 107, at 326. In a clause preceding the extract quoted in the text, Falk notes that the adverse African reaction "does not mean that the United States should have refused to join in the rescue. . . ." *Id.* Elsewhere he observes that "[t]he case for intervention is not altogether capricious since the alternative may be to allow one's countrymen to be slaughtered without cause." *Id.* at 329. Although his view is less than crystal clear on this point, it appears that Falk is troubled less by the legality than by "the appearances of the Stanleyville Operation. . . ." *Id.* at 331. *Cf.* Grundy, *supra* note 73, at 251, who affirms the operation's legality more explicitly, but who nevertheless criticizes it from from a political perspective, concluding that the United States "was fortunate in getting off as easily as it did in the Congo." *Id.* at 255.

119. *See generally* S. Weissman, American Foreign Policy in the Congo 1960-1964, at 226-46 *passim* (1974).

120. Whether it actually was a by-product of the rescue operation or one of its principal objectives is discussed at *infra* notes 142-146.

121. Grundy, *supra* note 73, at 251.

122. 19 U.N. SCOR (1174th mtg.) at 13, U.N. Doc. S/P.V. 1174 (1964), *reprinted in* American Foreign Policy—Current Documents 1964, at 777 (1967).

123. 19 U.N. SCOR (1173d mtg.) at 3-10, U.N. Doc. S/P.V. 1173 (1964). *See supra* text accompanying note 98.

124. 19 U.N. SCOR (1175th mtg.) at 3-4, U.N. Doc. S/P.V. 1175 (1964). *See supra* text accompanying note 98.

125. 19 U.N. SCOR (1183d mtg.) at 14, U.N. Doc. S/P.V. (1964). "Bolivia thinks that this was clearly a rescue operation, regrettable from the political point of view of sovereignty, but essential morally and duly authorized by the legally responsible Government of the Congo."

126. 19 U.N. SCOR (117th mtg.) at 19-20 U.N. Doc. S/P.V. 1177 (1964):

> Such an operation finds its justification in the very objective which inspired it, which was to frustrate the perpetration of a crime, recognized as such by international law and by all the norms of conduct governing relations among States, which consists in the use of innocent civilians as hostages, as a bargaining point in wartime. . . . Therefore the humanitarian action taken to save the lives of the hostages seems legitimate to the delegation of Brazil, both in regard to its means and to its motivations.

127. 19 U.N. SCOR (1177th mtg.) at 26, U.N. Doc. S/P.V. 1177 (1964): "In the circumstances, my delegation is fully satisfied with the statements made in this Council by the repesentatives of Belgium and the United States that the operation was necessary to save the lives of the hostages, and that it was a humanitarian mission, and nothing more."

128. *See infra* text at notes 135-141.

129. "[I]t is repugnant to use as a pretext the uncertainty of the fate of some 1,500 foreigners in order to attack a country and to interfere in its domestic affairs. . . ." 19 U.N. SCOR (1178th mtg.) at 10, U.N. Doc. S/P.V. 1178 (1964) (Morocco). Several other States used the same or similar language. "The use of the term 'pretext,' " as has been pointed out, actually "suggests a recognition of the concept of humanitarian intervention [or forcible protection], for such a charge tacitly admits the legitimacy of the subject matter to which that pretense is applied." Note, *supra* note 108, at 269. *See infra* text at notes 142-146.

130. Attempting to rebut an earlier assertion of this thesis, *see* R. Lillich, *Humanitarian Intervention: A Reply to Dr. Brownlie and a Plea for Constructive Alternatives*, in Law and Civil War in The Modern World 229, 243 (J.N. Moore ed. 1974), Professor Farer states that "to have legal significance for [Lillich, the African complaints] would apparently have to have assumed the form of flat claims of illegality." Farer, *supra* note 104, at 396. This characterization of the present writer's views obviously goes too far and reveals Farer, as is his wont upon occasion, once again setting up a straw man for easy demolition. Surely the fact that only a handful of States condemned the rescue operation on legal grounds is not *entirely* irrelevant to an assessment of its legality under international law, which after all is the issue at hand.

131. S.C. Res. 199, 19 U.N. SCOR Supp. (Oct.-Dec. 1964) at 328, U.N. Doc. S/6129 (1964) (100-1), *reprinted in* American Foreign Policy—Current Documents 1964, at 786 (1967).

132. Replying to a suggestion by the Ghanaian delegate that the resolution impliedly condemned the rescue operation, Ambassador Stevenson stated: "I think it is quite clear from the statements made during this debate that the overwhelming majority of the members of this Council do not so interpret that paragraph of the resolution. The fact that my delegation has voted for the resolution as amended makes it perfectly clear that we do not so interpret it." 19 U.N. SCOR (1189th mtg.) at 12, U.N. Doc. S/P.V. 1189 (1964), *reprinted in* American Foreign Foreign-Current Documents 1964, at 789 (1967).

Farer faults the present writer for "[finding] comfort in the failure of the Security Council to condemn Humanitarian Intervention as such or the United States and Belgium, as if Security Council condemnation of those States were a conceivable option in the world of 1964." Farer, *supra* note 104, at 396-97. His point may be well-taken, but it does not take one very far. The fact that the Security Council condemned neither the operation nor the States undertaking it certainly has *some* relevance. Even in "the world of 1964" the censure of a permanent member of the Security Council for an illegal use of force was not out of the question, as witness the formal condemnation of Great Britain the same year for a reprisal it had undertaken against Yemen. S.C. Res. 188, 19 U.N. SCOR Supp. (Apr.-Sept. 1964) at 9, U.N. Doc. S/5650 (1964) (9-0-2). *See* Lillich, *supra* note 130, at 244.

133. "After the Congo debates, the legal principle of Article 2(4) remains, but what that Article means has been altered by political evaluation. There is now an unwillingness on the part of the world community to read Article 2(4) as an absolute prohibition on the use of force in humanitarian intervention." Note, *supra* note 108, at 274.

134. *Compare* the fifth and fourth requirements, respectively, of the traditional doctrine of humanitarian intervention, as summarized by Farer in the *supra* text accompanying note 104.

135. D. Reed, *supra* note 75, at 268.

136. According to Ambassador Stevenson, "only a very small number of rebels were killed as a consequence of that operation and these only in self-defense or because they were at the moment resisting attempts to rescue the hostages." 19 U.N. SCOR (1174th mtg.) at 12, U.N. Doc. S/P.V. 1174 (1964), *reprinted in* American Foreign Policy—Current Documents 1964, at 776 (1967). *Cf.* D. Reed, *supra* note 75, at 259: "As far as anyone could tell, none of the Simbas who carried out the massacre was killed by the paratroopers. They all ran at the last minute." *Compare infra* text at and accompanying note 138.

137. *Id.* at 264. "Two men were wounded by gunfire and three were injured in the drop. None of the American airmen was hurt." *Id.*

138. *See supra* text accompanying note 117. *See also* D. Reed, *supra* note 75, at 264:

> The mercenaries and the ANC were running wild in Stanleyville. They shot every Congolese they saw. They looted homes and stores.... A mercenary patrol paid a visit to the city zoo. They found that the lions were ravenously hungry. Gleefully, they released the lions, who ran off into the city.

Colonel Laurent, the mild-mannered commanding officer of the paratrooper regiment, was horrified. "I never saw such a bloodbath in my life," he said. "No prisoners were taken. They were shot up, cut up or beaten to death. It was brutal."

Laurent did not want the young paratroopers to see what was going on. He ordered his men to return to the airfield as soon as they had rescued everyone.

139. *Id.* at 273.

140. Although one "revisionist" historian, misciting Reed for support, has contended that the airdrops themselves "resulted in the execution of perhaps 300 whites. . . ." S. Weissman *supra* note 119, at 248.

141. In response to a complaint about "the terrible massacre" that occurred at Stanleyville, the British minister responsible replied that "[i]n my view, if the troops which were advancing overland to Stanleyville had advanced without the intervention of this aerial operation, I am convinced that the loss of life would have been much greater than it has been." 702 Parl. Deb., H.C. (5th ser.) 1278-79 (1964) (Mr. Thomson). For further speculations pro and con, see S. Weissman, *supra* note 119, at 253.

Colvin concludes that "[a] parachute drop was probably necessary," but that instead of the tactics that were adopted "[t]he parachute drops should have been planned in triple strength within hours of each other at Stanleyville, Paulis and Bunia." I. Colvin, *supra* note 75, at 196. As events transpired, the delay in mounting the Paulis airdrop caused many additional casualties there; moreover, a contemplated airdrop on Bunia never took place. D. Reed, *supra* note 75 at 271-72.

142. *See, e.g.,* R. Garnet, *supra* note 15, at 250; R. Falk, *supra* note 107, at 333; Farer, *supra* note 104, at 394-96; Grundy, *supra* note 73, at 250-52; and S. Weissman, *supra* note 119, at 249-51.

143. *See, e.g.,* Professor Frey-Wouters, *Remarks,* in Humanitarian Intervention and the United Nations, *supra* note 103, at 58 n.5.

144. Even Weissman acknowledges that "[t]he rescue motivation seems to have been predominant. . . ." S. Weissman, *supra* note 119, at 252 n.106. *See also id.* at 251, where he contends that a "secondary objective" of the rescue operation was to help the ANC recapture Stanleyville.

145. *Id.* at 250. *See supra* text accompanying note 106.

146. *See supra* text at note 122.

147. For background information about the crisis as well as detailed descriptive accounts of it, *see* T. Draper, The Dominican Revolt (1968); D. Kurzman, Revolt of the Damned (1965); A. Lowenthal, The Dominican Intervention (1972); J. Slater, Intervention and Negotiation (1970); and T. Szulc, Dominican Diary (1965). *See also* J. Moreno, Barrios In Arms (1970). For differing views on the legal issues involved, *compare* Fenwick, *The Dominican Republic: Intervention or Collective Self-Defense,* 60 Am. J. Int'l L. 64 (1966), *with* Bohan, *The Dominican* Case: Unilateral Intervention, 60 *id.* 809 (1966). For a useful monograph, prepared under the supervision of the present writer and drawn upon throughout this Section, *see* J. Tuttle, The Case Study of the Dominican Crisis—1965: The Legality of the United States Action (1969) (unpublished thesis, U.S. Naval War College Library).

148. T. Szulc, *supra* note 147, at 13. How much assistance actually was given, as opposed to being authorized, is not entirely clear. *See* J. Slater, *supra* note 147, at 13-14 and accompanying note.

149. For a sampling of opposition criticism—reasoned, biased and vitriolic—*see* J. Moreno, *supra* note 147, at 18-19.

150. Slater absolves Bosch of serious charges of maladministration, observing that "it is far from clear that anyone could have survived [as President], at least without making such far-reaching concessions to the forces of reaction as to make survival almost pointless. As Jose Figueres has put it, 'God Himself would have done a bad job in the Dominican Republic.'" J. Slater, *supra* note 147, at 15.

151. American Foreign Policy: Current Documents 1963, at 322 (1967).

152. *Id.* at 359. The reversal of policy was in train long before President Kennedy's assassination. "Thus, the usual interpretation of this period, seeing great significance in the fact that Johnson recognized the Dominican junta only three weeks after the assassination of Kennedy and stressing the sharp contrast between the Kennedy and Johnson policies toward the coup, is quite wrong." J. Slater, *supra* note 147, at 16-17.

153. *Id.*, at 19.

154. Indeed, US Ambassador W. Tapley Bennett, who had become increasingly concerned over the deteriorating situation in the Dominican Republic, wrote prophetically to the Department of State in early April that "[l]ittle foxes, some of them red, are chewing at the grapes.... A diminution of our effort or failure to act will result in a bitter wine." *Quoted in* R. Stebbins, The United States In World Affairs 1965, at 74-76 (1966). Both Bennett and Reid were in receipt of intelligence reports about planned coups, but they did not anticipate one before June, when campaigning for the presidential election was scheduled to start. Center for Strategic Studies (Georgetown University), Dominican Action—1965: Intervention or Cooperation?, at 9 (1966).

155. J. Slater, *supra* note 147, at 19.

156. *Id* at 22.

> Until that point, the civilians working with the constitutionalists were mostly middle-class, college-educated students, lawyers, engineers, technicians, and young businessmen, frustrated by a system in which they had no purpose and no meaningful future. With the passing out of the arms large sectors of the urban lower class joined the ranks, giving the movement something of a mass base as well as providing most of the *actual combatientes*.

157. The case of General Wessin, who commanded most of the Dominican Republic's tanks and 1,500 of its Army's crack troops, best illustrates the response of the military leaders to Reid's appeal. Neither the tanks nor the troops moved from the San Isidro Air Base while Reid remained in office. Center for Strategic Studies (Georgetown University), *supra* note 154, at 11.

158. Draper, *supra* note 147, at 55-56.

159. *Id.* at 57; J. Slater, *supra* note 147, at 22.

160. J. Slater, *supra* note 147, at 23 note.

161. T. Draper, *supra* note 147, at 57.

162. In 1968, Antonio Martinez Francisco, the Secretary General of the PRD during the revolution, said that the original agreement between Bosch and sympathetic military men called for a military junta to rule the country temporarily after the overthrow of the Reid government, pending the holding of new elections within ninety days. Once Reid had fallen, Martinez charges, Bosch ignored the agreement and called for a return to 'constitutionality,' that is, the immediate restoration of his Presidency.

J. Slater, *supra* note 147, at 23 note.

163. *Id.* at 23-24.

164. *Id.* at 25.

165. *See infra* text at notes 172-173. President Johnson, relying upon such reports, subsequently claimed that "some 1,500 innocent people were murdered and shot, and their heads cut off..." Johnson, *An Assessment of the Situation in the Dominican Republic*, 53 DEP'T. ST. BULL. 19, 20 (1965). As Slater observes:

> not only was not a single American attacked but there were remarkably few constitutionalist atrocities of any sort. What few attacks did occur were highly selective, aimed almost exclusively at a few extreme rightists, and then mainly at their

property. Indeed, many more innocent citizens died as a result of the Air Force bombing and strafing than at the hands of the constitutionalists.

J. Slater, *supra* note 147, at 33.

166. For a graphic description of the scene in Santo Domingo at about this time, *see* Szulc, *supra* note 147, at 18:

> [I]n the ancient Dominican capital blood was flowing freely. Rebel army units and civilian bands were firing across the city at the positions of the Wessin forces. Planes streaked overhead, machine gunning the streets and dropping bombs on the rebels and the civilian population. Casualties were mounting and hospitals were filling up with the wounded.

167. *Id.* at 18 (four day period of April 25-28); J. Moreno, *supra* note 147, at 29 (four day period of April 27-30).

168. T. Szulc, *supra* note 147, at 20-21.

169. A. Lowenthal, *supra* note 147, at 85.

170. Johnson, *supra* note 165, at 21. "The Commander of Task Group 44.9, Captain Dare, had been ordered as early as 25 April to proceed to the vicinity of the Dominican Republic and prepare to evacuate approximately 1,200 United States nationals if this action should become necessary." Tuttle, *supra* note 147, at 28, citing Dare, *Dominican Diary*, 91 US Naval Institute Proc. 37, 38 (Dec. 1965). Moreover, on the following day—26 April—the Department of Defense had put on alert a Marine brigade at Camp Lejeune and the 82nd Airborne Division at Fort Bragg. T. Szulc, *supra* note 147, at 29.

171. *See generally* T. Szulc, *supra* note 147, at 31-34, and Dare, *supra* note 170, at 38-41.

172. J. Slater, *supra* note 147, at 33.

173. Szulc concludes that:

> [T]he embassy's reports on this incident must have been greatly exaggerated because President Johnson later spoke of armed rebels running up and down the hotel's corridors firing into rooms and closets. Actually, nothing of the sort had occurred, but this overwrought reporting by the embassy evidently helped increase the President's concern and pushed the United States closer to the ultimate decision to intervene militarily in the Dominican Republic.

T. Szulc, *supra* note 147, at 33-34. Other accounts reinforce Szulc's views. *See* T. Draper, *supra* note 147, at 105-06, and A. Lowenthal, *supra* note 147, at 90 & 204 n.27.

174. US policy even before the revolution had frowned on the return of Bosch to the Presidency, and after the revolution began nowhere was that policy more faithfully implemented than at the US Embassy:

> [T]he State Department had assigned the two top embassy positions to conservatives who instinctively distrusted not only Bosch but the PRD in general, and who had almost no ties with even the moderate left. 'Tap didn't seem to know anyone to the left of the Rotary Club,' one embassy official is quoted as remarking, while William Connett, the Deputy Chief of Mission, 'seemed to be ill at ease with people who were not correctly dressed.'

J. Slater, *supra* note 147, at 25.

175. Although there is absolutely no doubt that Bennett refused US mediation and made the accusations mentioned in the text [accusations that PRD officials had allowed "communists" to take advantage of the movement and had tolerated looting and atrocities], the former Ambassador has denied he told the constitutionalists to surrender. However, not only the constitutionalists but Martin [J. Martin, *Overtaken By Events* 653 (1966)] maintain that he did so.

J. Slater, *supra* note 147, at 227 n.24.

176. *Id.* at 29.

177. A participant at the now famous embassy confrontation vividly recalls that at the moment when Bennett labeled the revolution 'Communist' and told the leaders to surrender, a big, barrelchested man whom he had never seen before jumped to his feet and said, 'Son of a bitch! I know what *I'm* going to do.' It was Francisco Caamano, and he was not going to strangle Bennett on the spot as the startled assemblage for a moment feared, but was on his way to the bridge to rally his forces for a last-ditch stand. *Id.* at 29-30.

178. For a succinct account of this turn of events, see *id.* at 30.

179. T. Szulc, *supra* note 147, at 42.

180. *Id.* at 44.

181. *Id.* Needless to say, in making their second request for US intervention the junta was motivated by factors beyond just the protection of US nationals. One such factor was their own personal safety. "That night, when the first contingents of the 82nd Airborne Division arrived at San Isidro, they found the 'strong man' of the Dominican armed forced, the dreaded Wessin y Wessin, in tears: 'If you had not come,' he cried, 'they would have killed us.'" J. Slater, *supra* note 147, at 30-31.

182. A. Lowenthal, *supra* note 147, at 101-02. See *infra* text accompanying note 186.

183. *Id.* at 102-03; T. Draper, *supra* note 147, at 118-21; and J. Slater, *supra* note 147, at 30.

184. Speaking of this decision at a news conference on 17 June 1965, the President noted that "[i]t was a decision we considered from Saturday until Wednesday evening. But once we made it, in the neighborhood of 6:00 or 6:30 that evening, they landed within one hour." Johnson, *supra* note 165, at 21.

185. Dare, *supra* note 170, at 42. The President, according to one commentator, authorized the landing of only 500 Marines. A. Lowenthal, *supra* note 147, at 103. Other commentators give the number of Marines landed that evening as about 400. T. Szulc, *supra* note 147, at 73.

186. 52 DEP'T. ST. BULL. 738 (1965), American Foreign Policy: Current Documents 1965, at 956 (1968) [hereinafter cited as American Foreign Policy - 1965]. Actually, although Colonel Benoit had made such representations to Ambassador Bennett, they were not contained in the junta's written request. See *supra* text at notes 180-182. Their omission so concerned Under Secretary of State Thomas Mann that, following President Johnson's decision to land US troops, he purportedly called Bennett and asked him to obtain from Benoit "a written statement for the record asking for US military assistance to restore order and specifically mentioning the need to protect American lives." A. Lowenthal, *supra* note 147, at 104. Accordingly, by early Thursday morning, 29 April 1965, Benoit dispatched a follow-up communication to the US Embassy:

> Regarding my earlier request, I wish to add that American lives are in danger and conditions of public disorder make it impossible to provide adequate protection. I therefore ask you for temporary intervention and assistance in restoring order in this country.

Senate Comm. on the Judiciary, 89th Cong., 1st Sess., Organization of American States Combined Reports on Communist Subversion 114 (Comm. Print 1965).

As Szulc notes—and as Mann, of course, well knew—Benoit's request, "if nothing provided the legal justification for a United States landing if Washington chose to play it that way. It was somewhat reminiscent of the 1958 situation in Lebanon, where United States Marines landed at the request of President Camille Chamoun to help him restore order." T. Szulc, *supra* note 147, at 44. *Compare supra* text at and accompanying notes 37, 50 & 93, and *infra* text at and accompanying note 204.

187. 52 DEP'T. ST. BULL. 738 (1965), American Foreign Policy-1965, *supra* note 186, at 956.

188. T. Szulc, *supra* note 147, at 73.

189. Id. at 78.
190. 52 DEP'T. ST. BULL. 742 (1965), American Foreign Policy - 1965, *supra* note 186, at 956. According to the President, US troops eventually evacuated 5,600 people from 46 countries from the Dominican Republic. Johnson, *supra* note 165, at 20.
191. 52 DEP'T. ST. BULL. 742, American Foreign Policy - 1965, *supra* note 186, at 956-57. The US Representative to the OAS, Ellsworth Bunker, had made a similar argument before the OAS Council of Ministers earlier the same day. *Id.* at 957-58.
192. T. Szulc, *supra* note 147, at 90.
193. 52 DEP'T. ST. BULL. 743 (1965), American Foreign Policy - 1965, *supra* note 186, at 959.
194. *Id.* at 745, American Foreign Policy - 1965, *supra* note 186, at 962-63.
195. *Id.* at 746, American Foreign Policy - 1965, *supra* note 186, at 963.
196. *Id.*, American Foreign Policy - 1965, *supra* note 186, at 963-64.
197. For the text of this resolution, *see* Senate Comm. on For. Rels., 89th Cong., 1st Sess., Background Information Relating to the Dominican Republic 52 (Comm. Print 1965).
198. For the text of this resolution, *see* 52 DEP'T. ST. BULL. 862 (1965). The vote on the resolution, which required a two-thirds majority, was 15 for, 5 against (Chile, Ecuador, Mexico, Peru and Uruguay), and one abstention (Venezuela). *Id.*
199. N.Y. Times, Sept. 23, 1966, at 3, col 1.
200. *See, e.g.,* the remarks of the Legal Adviser along these lines in Meeker, *The Dominican Situation in the Perspective of International Law.* 53 DEP'T ST. BULL. 60, 62 (1965):

> We landed troops in the Dominican Republic in order to preserve the lives of foreign nationals — nationals of the United States and many other countries. We continued our military presence in the Dominican Republic for the additional purpose of preserving the capacity of the OAS to function in the manner intended by the OAS Charter.

201. *See generally* Humanitarian Intervention and the United Nations, *supra* note 103, at 76-82 *passim*. There is no doubt that "the US attempted to legitimize its military action by securing approval of the OAS." Frey-Wouters, *The Prospects for Regionalism in World Affairs*, in 1 The Future of the International Legal Order 463, 536 (R. Falk & C. Black eds. 1969). Whether the various OAS resolutions constituted legitimation or merely acquiescence, however, is another matter. Prof. Frey-Wouters believes the Dominican intervention an example of how the United States often has sought OAS approval to provide "a multilateral legitimacy for essentially unilateral US action." *Id.* at 539.
202. *See e.g.*, A. Thomas & A. Thomas, *Working Paper*, in The Dominican Crisis 1965 - Legal Aspects 1 (Hammarskjold Forum, J. Carey ed. 1967); McLaren, *The Dominican Crisis: An InterAmerican Dilemma*, 4 Canadian Y.B. Int'l L. 178 (1966); and Nanda, *The United States Action in the 1965 Dominican Crisis: Impact on World Order - Part II*, 44 Denv. L.J. 225 (1967).
203. On 21 May 1965, the United States, Great Britain, Bolivia, China, Netherlands, and Northern Ireland all voted against a Soviet Union-sponsored resolution initially submitted to the Security Council on 4 May that would have condemned what it labeled US armed intervention in the internal affairs of the Dominican Republic. 20 U.N. SCOR (1214th mtg.) at 22, U.N. Doc. S/6328 (1965). Great Britain stated it "fully understood the reasons for the United States emergency action" and thanked the United States for evacuating British subjects from the country, 2 UN Monthly Chron., No. 6 at 6 (1965), while France, acknowledging US interest in protecting its nationals there, cautioned that "such operations must be limited in objective, duration, and scale, or run the risk of becoming armed intervention, for which there appeared to be no need in this case." *Id.* at 7. France's position seemed to recognize the necessity of the US action, while gently questioning its proportionality. On these two limitations on the right of forcible protection, *see* "Nanda, *The United*

*States Action in the Dominican Crisis: Impact on World Order - Part I*, 43 Denv. L.J. 439, 462-71 (1966), who concludes that "while the necessity of the [US] action can be defended on humanitarian grounds, the proportionality cannot be justified." *Id.* at 479. *Compare infra* text at note 209.

204. 111 Cong. Rec. 23855, 23857 (1965):

> In midafternoon of April 28 Col. Pedro Bartolome Benoit, head of a junta which had been hastily assembled, asked again, this time in writing, for US troops on the ground that this was the only way to prevent a Communist takeover; no mention was made of the junta's inability to protect American lives. This request was denied in Washington, and Benoit was thereupon told that the United States would not intervene unless he said he could not protect American citizens present in the Dominican Republic. Benoit was thus told in effect that if he said American lives were in danger the United States would intervene. And that is precisely what happened.

*Compare supra* text accompanying note 186.

205. 111 Cong. Rec. 23857 (1965).
206. *Id.* at 23858.
207. *But see, e.g.*, Fenwick, *supra* note 147.
208. Nanda, *supra* note 203, at 471.
209. *Id.* at 472. Compare *supra* text accompanying note 203.
210. Friedmann, *United States Policy and the Crisis of International Law*, 59 Am. J. Int'l L. 857, 867 (1965), citing Waldock, *The Regulation of the Use of Force by Individual States in International Law*, 81 Recueil des Cours (Hague Academy of International Law) 451, 467 (1952).
211. Friedmann, *supra* note 210, at 869. He subsequently reiterated and elaborated his views as follows:

> There was a general consensus on the original US position of intervening to protect American lives and property and the sending in of a battalion; that is, it can be justifed . . . in the limited sense that it is strictly limited to nationals, and therefore it is an extension of national interests intervention. That had been previously stated by international lawyers as a justifiable cause of intervention. . . .
>
> Then came the radical shift which Johnson made by his famous statement that totally altered the situation and made it clear, I think, beyond a shadow of a doubt, that the subsequent massive and prolonged intervention was contrary not only to the U.N. Charter but to the OAS Charter; namely, intervention in the internal affairs of another small power by a big power, in order to effect a change of political regime.

Remarks, in Humanitarian Intervention and the United Nations, *supra* note 103, at 81-82.

212. Lillich, Remarks, in *id.* at 10:

> When you are talking about evacuating citizens, this is a limited objective, and, of course, you must evacuate them as rapidly as possible. Applying this to the Dominican context, . . . it would, I would assume, justify perhaps the first day or so, but it wouldn't justify the 22,000 Marines for six months.

For the views of other participants, *see id.* at 76-82.

213. *See* text accompanying note 211.

214. For a particularly outspoken warning, *see* Rogers, *Remarks*, in Humanitarian Intervention and the United Nations *supra* note 103, at 72:

> We see the constant misuse of the excuse of protection of one's own nationals for great power purposes, most recently, of course, in the movement of the Sixth Fleet into the Bay of Bengal—which was justified for a short moment by Kissinger's preposterous idea that it

was going to be used for the protection of US nationals—a shocking rationalization for a great power ploy.

215. R. Lillich, *Forcible Self-Help by States to Protect Human Rights*, 53 Iowa L. Rev. 325, 344 (1967).

216. For background information about the hostage crisis as well as detailed descriptive accounts of it, *see, e.g.*, J. Bill, The Eagle and the Lion: The Tragedy of American-Iranian Relations (1988); W. Christopher et al., American Hostages in Iran: The Conduct of a Crisis (1985) [hereinafter cited as Christopher]; G. Sick, All Fall Down: America's Tragic Encounter with Iran (1985). *See also* The Iranian Hostage Crisis: A Chronology of Daily Developments, Report Prepared for the Committee on Foreign Affairs, US House of Representatives, by the Congressional Research Service, Library of Congress, 97th Cong., 1st Sess. (1981).

217. Case Concerning United States Diplomatic and Consular Staff in Tehran (US v. Iran) (Merits), 1980 I.C.J. 3, 30-33 (Judgment of May 24) [hereinafter cited as Hostages Case-Merits].

218. *Id.* at 33-35. On 18-20 November 1979, however, Iran did release 13 women and black hostages "not considered spies." Their release was a unilateral Iranian gesture, not the result of negotiations. "[It] was probably seen in Tehran as a step to portray the regime as humanitarian and intent only on exposing the US government and its 'nest of spies.'" Saunders, *Diplomacy and Pressure. November 1979-May 1980*, in Christopher, *supra* note 216, at 79. Although another hostage who became ill was released in July 1980, Saunders, *The Crisis Begins*, in Christopher, *supra*, at 68, Iran continued to hold the remaining 52 hostages until their release on 20 January 1981 following the so-called Algiers Accords, 20 I.L.M. 223 (1981).

219. The Ayatollah Khomeini, the de facto head of Iran's revolutionary government, endorsed the students' demands in a decree issued on 17 November expressly declaring that "the premises of the Embassy and the hostages would remain as they were until the United States had handed over the former Shah for trial and returned his property to Iran." Hostages Case-Merits, *supra* note 217, at 34.

220. He learned of their trip from a report on the NBC evening news that Press Secretary Jody Powell had attempted to dissuade the network from carrying. Saunders, *Diplomacy and Pressure*, in Christopher, *supra* note 216, at 76. Saunders is justifiably critical of NBC's action, taken despite the knowledge that it might jeopardize a sensitive mission.

221. *Id.* at 76-77.

222. S.C. Res. 457, 34 U.N. SCOR, Res. & Dec. at 24, U.N. Doc S/RES/457 (1979).

223. S.C. Res. 461, 34 U.N. SCOR, Res. & Dec. at 24-25, U.N. Doc. S/RES/461 (1979). Eleven States voted for the resolution, with the Soviet Union, Czechoslovakia, Kuwait and Bangladesh abstaining. 80 DEP'T. ST. BULL. 68 (Feb. 1980).

224. The text of the draft resolution may be found in 80 DEP'T. ST. BULL. 70-71. Ten States voted for the resolution, the Soviet Union and the German Democratic Republic voted against it, Bangladesh and Mexico abstained, and China did not participate. *Id.*

225. Case Concerning United States Diplomatic and Consular Staff in Tehran (US v. Iran) (Provisional Measures), 1979 I.C.J. 7, 12 (Order of Dec. 15) [hereinafter Hostages Case-Provisional Measures]. *See generally* Mendelson, *Interim Measures of Protection and the Use of Force by States*, in The Current Legal Regulation of the Use of Force 337 (A. Cassese ed. 1986).

226. Hostages Case-Provisional Measures, *supra* note 225, at 21.

227. *Id.*

228. *See supra* text at notes 222-223.

229. They are described in considerable detail in Saunders, *Diplomacy and Pressure*, in Christopher, *supra* note 216, at 102-45.

230. Hostages Case-Merits, *supra* note 217, at 21.

231. *See* Saunders, *Diplomacy and Pressure*, in Christopher, *supra* note 216, at 135:

> After an 8-3 vote in the Revolutionary Council, the issue was taken to Khomeini on April 6. Confirmed reports told us that Khomeini had asked whether the recommendation of the Revolutionary Council [to transfer the hostages] was unanimous. When he was told that there were three negative votes—Ayatollah Beheshti and two other clerics—Khomeini refused to approve the Council's recommendation.

232. *Id.*

233. For inside descriptions of the rescue operation and why it failed, *see* C. Beckworth & D. Knox, Delta Force (1983); P. Ryan, The Iranian Rescue Mission: Why It Failed (1985); Sick, *Military Operations and Constraints*, in Christopher, *supra* note 216, at 154-64. *See also* the 78 page study by the Special Operations Review Group, headed by Admiral J. L. Holloway, III, entitled "Rescue Mission Report," distributed in Washington, D.C., during the summer of 1980.

234. The first landed in the desert, with its crew being taken aboard another helicopter that proceeded to the landing site. The second returned to the *USS Nimitz*. Sick, *Military Operations and Constraints*, in Christopher, *supra* note 216, at 158.

235. *Id.* at 159. At 1 A.M. [EST] on 25 April the White House issued an announcement of the operation's failure, whose purpose and timing was "intended to insure that Iran would not mistake the events at Desert I for an invasion attempt and retaliate against the hostages." *Id.*

236. 80 DEP'T. ST. BULL. 38 (June 1980).

237. *Id.* (emphasis added).

238. Letter from the President to the Speaker of the House and the President Pro Tempore of the Senate, 80 DEP'T. ST. BULL. 42, 43 (Jun 1980).

239. 35 U.N. SCOR Supp. (Apr.-Jun.) at 28, U.N. Doc. S/13908 (1980) (Letter from Ambassador McHenry to the President of the Security Council).

240. Great Britain, Italy and the other European Community Member States supported the US action, as did Australia, Canada, Egypt, Israel and Japan. *See* N. Ronzitti, Rescuing Nationals Abroad Through Military Coercion and Intervention on Grounds of Humanity 45-47 (1985). In addition to Iran, the Soviet Union, China and Cuba, as well as India, Pakistan and Saudi Arabia, condemned it. *Id.* at 47-48.

241. *But see* the Italian statement justifying the action under international law which, while "hardly a model of legal logicality," appears to reject the US self-defense argument and rest instead upon a State's purported inherent right to resort to self-help in such cases. *Id.* at 46. As explained by Professor Ronzitti, the Italian view seems to be that:

> The Charter does not abrogate a State's right to resort to self-help, including the use of armed force, which belongs to it under customary international law. The Charter simply suspends the right to resort to self-help, since it entrusts the Security Council with the task of safeguarding the rights of member States. Whenever this mechanism does not function, for example when the action of the Security Council is paralysed by veto, the States are free to resort to self-help, under the terms permitted by customary international law.

*Id.* at 46-47. For evaluation of the viewpoint reflected in the Italian statement, one that has received support in the past from legal commentators, including the present writer, but has not attracted widespread, if any, support from States, *see* text at *supra* notes 54-57.

242. *See supra* text at note 227.

243. Dillard, Remarks, in The Iran Crisis and International Law: Proceedings of the John Bassett Moore Society of International Law Symposium on Iran 33 (R. Steele ed. 1981) [hereinafter cited as The Iran Crisis and International Law].

244. Hostages Case-Merits, *supra* note 217, at 43.

245. Stein, *Contempt, Crisis, and the Court: The World Court and the Hostage Rescue Attempt*, 76 Am. J. Int'l L. 499, 500 (1982). While the Court did not expressly find the rescue operation to be lawful, a slight tilt towards the recognition of a right of forcible protection of nationals abroad may be discernible, at least to some observers, from its failure to condemn the US action per se. *See* Lillich, *Remarks*, in The Iran Crisis and International Law, *supra* note 243, at 29 & 32. This point is noted and discussed in N. Ronzitti, *supra* note 240, at 61. In view of the Dissenting Opinions of Judges Morozov and Tarazi that condemned and challenged its legality respectively, *see infra* text at notes 254-257, one might have expected the Court to have denounced the rescue operation had a substantial number of the 13 judge majority believed that it violated the UN Charter. Thus, as in the case of the dog that did not bark in the Sherlock Holmes story, the Court's silence on the question of whether a right of forcible protection exists may not be entirely without signifcance. *Cf.* N. Ronzitti, *supra*, at 67-68:

> The silence of the Court certainly does not imply that it acquiesces in the theory of the legality of a rescue mission through the use of force. However, the Court did not block the process leading to the creation of a new rule legitimizing recourse to force to protect nationals abroad, which would have been the case if it has censured the use of force in those circumstances.

246. Hostages Case-Merits, *supra* note 217, at 43.
247. Stein, *supra* note 245, at 500 n.7.
248. The two main and several other arguments are canvassed in this chapter.
249. Jeffery, *The American Hostages in Tehran: The I.C.J. and the Legality of Rescue Missions*, 30 Int'l & Comp. L. Q. 717, 723 (1981).
250. Hostages Case-Merits, *supra* note 217, at 18. *See supra* note 239.
251. *Id.* at 29.
252. *Id.* at 42.
253. Stein, *supra* note 245, at 500-501 n.8. This reading, of course, may require reassessment in light of the Court's later pronouncements on armed attack in the Case Concerning Military and Paramilitary Activities In and Against Nicaragua (Nicar. v. US) (Merits), 1986 I.C.J. 14 (Judgment of June 27).
254. Hostages Case-Merits, *supra* note 217, at 55.
255. *Id.* at 56-57.
256. *Id.* at 64.
257. "One can only wonder, therefore, whether an armed attack attributable to the Iranian Government has been committed against the territory of the United States, apart from its Embassy and Consulates in Iran." *Id.* at 64-65.
258. *But see supra* text accompanying note 253.
259. Schweppe, *Iran: World Court Ruling of December 15, 1979 and May 24, 1980*, 14 Int'l Law. 529, 529 (1980).
260. Boyle, *International Law as a Basis for Conducting American Foreign Policy: 1979-1982*, 8 Yale J. World Pub. Order 103, 130 (1982). *See also* F. Boyle, World Politics and International Law 200 (1985).
261. Schweistfurth, *Operations to Rescue Nationals in Third States Involving the Use of Force in Relation to the Protection of Human Rights*, 23 German Y.B. Int'l L. 159, 179 (1980).
262. N. Ronzitti, *supra* note 240, at 12, 41-49, 57 & 61-62.
263. *Id.* at 65.
264. Jeffery, *supra* note 249, at 725.
265. *Id.* at 725-26, *citing* L. Henkin, How Nations Behave 142 (2d ed. 1979).

266. Schachter, *International Law in the Hostage Crisis*, in Christopher, *supra* note 216, at 332. Much of the material in Professor Schachter's chapter is taken, often *in haec verba*, from one of his earlier articles. *See* Schachter, *Self-Help in International Law: US Action in the Iranian Hostages Crisis*, 37 J. Int'l Affairs 231 (1984). *See also* Schachter, *The Right of States to Use Armed Force*, 82 Mich. L. Rev. 1620, 1628-33 (1984).

267. Schachter, *International Law in the Hostage Crisis*, in Christopher, *supra* note 216, at 334.

268. *Id.* at 331.

269. Professor Schachter introduces his discussion of the topic with the proposition that "article 51 seems on first blush to provide an adequate legal basis for the employment of military force after the seizure," *id.* at 328, and later devotes considerable space to considering whether the requirement of "necessity" for self-defense had been met, i.e. whether the hostages were actually in imminent danger at the time of the operation. *See infra* text at notes 284-285.

270. *See e.g.*, O. Schachter, International Law in Theory and Practice 126, 128, 144 (1991).

271. *See supra* text at notes 56-66.

272. *But see* Lillich, *Remarks*, in The Iran Crisis and International Law, *supra* note 243, at 28 & 39; Stein, *supra* note 245, at 522-23 & n.99. *See also* Professor Schachter's consideration of the issue discussed *infra* at notes 277-285.

273. "The requirement of 'necessity' for self-defense is not controversial as a general proposition," Schachter, *International Law in the Hostage Crisis*, in Christopher, *supra* note 216, at 329, and it long has been thought applicable in the context of the forcible protection of nationals abroad. *See, e.g.*, Waldock, *supra* note 210, at 467, who formulated three requirements governing the right of forcible protection as follows: "There must be (1) an imminent threat of injury to nationals, (2) a failure or inability on the part of the territorial sovereign to protect them and (3) measures of protection strictly confined to the object of protecting them against injury." He adds that "[e]ven under customary [international] law only an absolute necessity could justify an intervention to protect nationals." *Id.*

For an unusual but interesting examination of the necessity requirement arguing that necessity and not self-defense is the proper legal justification of the right of forcible protection, *see* Raby, *The State of Necessity and the Use of Force to Protect Nationals*, 26 Can. Y.B. Int'l L. 253 (1988).

274. Christopher, *Introduction*, in Christopher, *supra* note 216, at 12.

275. Paragraph 3 of the Preamble to the International Convention Against the Taking of Hostages, Dec. 17, 1979, G.A. Res. 34/146, 34 U.N. GAOR Supp. (No. 46) at 245, U.N. Doc. A/34/46 (1980), incorporates G.A. Res. 31/103, 31 U.N. GAOR Supp. (No. 39) at 186, U.N. Doc. A/31/39 (1977), which in Paragraph 4 of its Preamble contains the language quoted in the text.

276. *See infra* text at note 274.

277. Schachter, International Law in the Hostages Crisis, in Christopher, *supra* note 216, at 332.

278. *Id.*

279. Stein, *supra* note 245, at 522-23. In a footnote to the statement in the text, he goes one step further:

> None of the documentation submitted to the Court suggested the existence of a new threat to the hostages; indeed, the US assertion that the mission had been carried out "in exercise of its inherent right of self-defense with the aim of extricating American nationals who have been and remain the victims of the Iranian armed attack on our Embassy," [1980] ICJ Rep. 3, para. 32, tends to negate the existence of a new threat to the hostages.

*Id.* at 523 n.99.

280. *See supra* note 236.

281. 80 DEP'T. ST. BULL. 40 (June 1980).
282. *Id.*
283. *See supra* note 274.
284. Schachter, *International Law in the Hostage Crisis,* in Christopher, *supra* note 216, at 334.
285. *Id.* He pointedly adds: "Whether or not the rescue action was wise in a political and military sense is, of course, a different matter."

# Chapter V

## Case Studies of Non-United States Forcible Protection of Nationals Abroad

There have been at least 15 instances since the adoption of the United Nations Charter in 1945 where legal commentators have claimed that the doctrine of "protection of nationals abroad" has, or could have, been invoked by States other than the United States to justify forcible measures undertaken in other States.[1] In most of these cases, the State involved relied primarily upon a government request or an international agreement and only secondarily, if at all, upon the protection of nationals doctrine to justify its actions. Moreover, even when a State invoked the doctrine it rarely advanced specific international law arguments justifying it. The principal exception occurred during the Suez Crisis in 1956, when Great Britain claimed, inter alia, that its actions against Egypt were taken to protect the lives and property of British nationals and as such was an exercise of its inherent right of self-defense under Article 51 of the UN Charter.[2]

Since the Suez crisis there has been very little discussion in international or national forums about the legality of a State's use of forceful means to protect its nationals in another State, aside from various U.S. forays into other countries. The extended debate over Israel's Entebbe operation being a rare exception.

While the international law discourse emanating from these instances is scant, and the data about them often fragmentary, they serve to round out the international perspective showing that the United States is not alone in supporting and, more importantly perhaps, actually invoking the "forcible protection of nationals" doctrine.[3]

## A. Suez Crisis. 1956.

Great Britain has justified its 1956 action in the Suez Crisis as necessary for the protection of its nationals. Selwyn Lloyd, Secretary of State for Foreign Affairs, argued that "self-defense undoubtedly includes a situation where the lives of the State's nationals abroad are in imminent danger."[4] Asked what armed attack had occurred against Great Britain to justify the invocation of Article 51 of the UN Charter, Mr. Lloyd maintained that the British government was not foreclosed from taking action to "protect the lives of British subjects abroad unless and until they are expressly authorized by the United Nations to do so."[5] He countered that "it would be a travesty of the Charter to say that no intervention can take place until our nationals are actually being attacked and perhaps killed."[6] His comments included three criteria for when a protection of nationals operation would meet the requirements of customary international law. "The first is where there is an imminent threat of injury to our nationals.... The second is where there is a failure or inability on the part of the territorial sovereign to protect the nationals in question. The third is where the measures of protection are strictly confined to the object of protecting the nationals against injury."[7] These situations are reflected in the self-defense portions of articles 39, 40 and 41 of the UN Charter.

During UN debates, however, other goals also were emphasized, although Great Britain consistently invoked the protection-of-nationals rationale. In the words of Sir Pierce Dixon, the British representative to the United Nations, "British and French lives must be safeguarded. I again emphasize. . . that we should certainly not want to keep any forces in the area for one moment longer than is necessary to protect our nationals, to help bring the fighting to an end and to deal with the very real danger of fighting across the Canal."[8] This justification for the British operation at Suez has been dismissed by almost all commentators as utterly without merit and illustrative of how the right of forcible protection may be open to abuse.[9]

## B. Belgium in the Congo. 1960.

The Congo gained its independence from Belgium on 30 June 1960. On 5 July, Congolese troops mutinied and attacked Belgian subjects and other Europeans. Belgian paratroops entered the Congo on 10 July to evacuate Belgian nationals and other foreigners.[10] The next day, the provincial government of Katanga proclaimed its independence. The central government, in a letter to the UN Secretary-General reacting to the Belgian action and the Katangese secession, requested military assistance from the United Nations and claimed that the dispatch of Belgian troops to the Congo violated the treaty of friendship that the two countries had signed on 29 June 1960. Under the terms of that treaty, Belgian troops could intervene only at the express request of the Congolese government.[11]

In the Security Council, M. Pierre Wigny, the Belgian Foreign Minister, cited numerous reports of rape and other atrocities by Congolese troops against Belgian nationals. He stated that "we had a right to intervene when it was a question of protecting our compatriots, our women, against such excesses. We had the most imperative duty to do so."[12] He explained that the operation in the Congo was purely humanitarian and strictly proportionate to the objective of protecting Belgian lives,[13] and that Belgium would withdraw its troops as soon as, and to the extent that, the United Nations effectively ensured the maintenance of order and the safety of all foreigners.[14]

On 14 July 1960, the Security Council adopted a resolution calling upon Belgium to withdraw its troops from Congolese territory.[15] Subsequent resolutions urged the Belgian government to withdraw with haste and requested that all States refrain from actions that might undermine Congo's territorial integrity or political independence.[16]

Prime Minister Lumumba of the Congo, in a letter dated 31 July 1960, informed the Security Council that UN troops, with the help of the Congolese army, could protect all foreign nationals removing the need for the Belgian presence.[17] The Security Council thereupon once again demanded that Belgium withdraw its troops from Katanga "under speedy modalities determined by the Secretary-General."[18]

The Belgian actions in the Congo seem to be a legitimate use of force for the protection of nationals. The French, British, and Italian governments all approved and expressed their appreciation.[19] The French representative, M. Berard, stated that "[t]heir mission of protecting lives and property is the direct result of the failure of the Congolese authorities and is in accord with a recognized principle of international law, namely, intervention on humanitarian grounds."[20] Several nations were critical. Predictively, the Soviet Union and several other States, including Tunisia, Poland and Argentina, denounced the protection-of-nationals rationale as a device to mask an illegal armed intervention.[21]

### C. France in Mauritania. 1977.

On 1 May 1977, Polisario guerrillas took six French nationals hostage during an attack on the city of Zouérate, an important mining town in northeastern

Mauritania. Over the course of 1977, the rebels made advances and destroyed vital economic centers in Mauritania and on 25 October they took two more French nationals as hostages. Consequently, in November 1977 France sent ten Jaguar bombers to Mauritania in support of the approximately 12,000 French troops who were assisting the Mauritanian army in its fight against the Polisario Front.[22] This extensive French military operation in support of the Mauritanian government, known as Operation Lamentin, continued until May 1978.

The first air strikes by the French planes occurred on 12-13 December 1977, after Polisario forces attacked a train carrying iron ore from Zouérate to the port of Nouadhibou. France responded with a second air strike on 18 December after a Polisario assault on a Mauritanian garrison near the border with Western Sahara.[23] On 23 December, negotiations between French officials and Polisario representatives led to the Polisario release of the eight French hostages to UN Secretary-General Kurt Waldheim in Algiers.[24]

France invoked humanitarian justifications for the air strikes that it had undertaken at the request of the Mauritanian government.[25] A letter by M. Jacques Leprette, the French representative to the UN, to the president of the Security Council, stated that "[i]n the face of the persistent threats directed against our compatriots in undisputed Mauritanian territory... it is the duty of the French government, as it would be the duty of any Government with respect to its nationals abroad, to provide protection for them."[26] The strikes were dual-purposed. They were a response to the abduction of French nationals, and were also a part of Operation Lamentin to combat the Polisario Front in Mauritania.[27] Because no rescue mission occurred, however, the invocation of the forcible-protection doctrine seems primarily a pretext for the French use of force to support the Mauritanian government.

### D. France and Belgium in Zaire. 1978.

As in 1964,[28] the lives of numerous European citizens, primarily Belgian and French, were put at risk in Katanga during disturbances caused by activities of the "gendarmes kantangais" who fought for the independence of the province.[29] On 11-12 May 1978, Katangese rebels had entered the province, arriving from Angola through Zambia, and occupied the city of Kolwezi. During this operation and its aftermath, they killed about 900 people, including an estimated 120 Europeans.[30] The lives of French and Belgian citizens, therefore, were obviously endangered.[31]

On 19 May French troops were air-dropped just to the north of Kolwezi, with Belgian troops landing in a separate operation the following day.[32] Both

France and Belgium justified their actions as responses to the request for military assistance by the Zairian government.[33] Indeed, Belgian Prime Minister Tindemans actually stated before the Belgian Parliament that Zaire "was a sovereign State where Belgium could not simply interfere at will and that, consequently, an authorization from the Zairian authorities was required before Belgium could proceed with its rescue operation."[34] This statement represents a far more restrictive approach to the forcible-protection-of-nationals doctrine than the Belgian Foreign Minister had taken during the 1960 Congo operation.[35] On the other hand, French president Giscard d'Estaing justified the operation as a normal exercise of the legitimate and inalienable right of France to protect its citizens abroad.[36]

Most Belgian troops withdrew on 22 May, by which time they had evacuated 2,269 people to Europe.[37] The French operation, however, continued until 15 June.[38] Neither action was debated in the Security Council, although several European countries expressed their appreciation to France and Belgium, implicitly endorsing their actions.[39] There seems little doubt that the operations undertaken were justifiable under the protection-of-nationals rationale.

### E. France in Mauritania. 1978.

In May 1978, French Jaguar bombers struck Polisario rebels near the city of Zouérate during the final stages of Operation Lamentin. In June 1978, Foreign Minister Louis de Guiringaud of France stressed that the location of the air strikes against the Polisario forces had occurred on Mauritanian territory where French nationals were endangered.[40] Although the 1978 operation did not involve an evacuation of French nationals, presumably the nationals were indirectly protected by the assistance to the Mauritanian government in opposing the Polisario Front.

As in case of the 1977 French air strikes in Mauritania, discussed in Section C, France did not mount a rescue operation, but rather sought to assist the recognized Mauritanian government against Polisario insurgents through military measures. The 1978 French air strikes, again then appear pretextual if the claim is humanitarian intervention.

### F. France in Chad. 1978.

Visible Chadian unrest began in July 1977, mainly in the area of Bardaï in northern Chad, caused by the rebel group Frolinat (Front de libération rationale du Tchad).[41] By February 1978, the rebels controlled the strategic cities of

Faya-Largeau and Fada. According to M. Olivier, the French Secretary of State to the Foreign Minister, the 4,000 French nationals in Chad, the majority of whom lived in the capital city N'Djamena, and in southern Chad, were not in immediate danger.[42] He informed the French Parliament that the Chadian government had extended measures to ensure their safety, with the help of the French "coopérants" who were present in Chad under the terms of a cooperation accord that the two States had signed on 6 March 1976.[43]

French Cooperation Minister Robert Galley, however, did not rule out the possibility that the Frolinat propaganda campaign being diffused over seized Chadian radio stations might necessitate a rescue operation to evacuate French nationals.[44] When the rebels approached to within 250 km of N'Djamena in April 1978, he invoked the 1976 cooperation accord to justify any French action taken against the rebellion, which was lead and armed largely from outside the country.[45] At the request of the Chadian government, France also increased the number of coopérants to help train the Chadian army and sent supplementary units to protect the army training centers.[46] Altogether, France deployed 2,500 troops to Chad as part of this action, called Operation Tacaud, including a regiment of parachutists, two infantry companies, one Marine infantry company, and several supporting tactical airplanes and Jaguar bombers.[47] Foreign Minister Guiringaud described their objective as helping the legitimate government find a political compromise to the rebellion.[48]

After three French coopérants were killed, the French government reacted vigorously.[49] As Foreign Minister Guiringaud indicated, the French presence in Chad was both at the request of the government and because French civilians and coopérants were in danger.[50] Although French troops closely guarded the army training centers and communities with large concentrations of French nationals,[51] they made no attempt to stage an evacuation. On 27 April, French Jaguars provided air cover to Chadian troops defending the city of Salal,[52] and on 19 May over 100 French troops gave decisive help to Chadian forces opposing Frolinat advances at Ati.[53] French forces lent support to Chadian forces in other battles, although the number of French actively engaged never exceeded 200 to 300 troops.[54] Because French troops deployed in Operation Tacaud made no effort to evacuate French nationals but, rather simply helped the Chadian army turn back Frolinat rebels in several important battles, to classify the French operation as a case of forcible protection is tenuous.

## G. France in Chad. 1979.

The relations between the Chadian government and rebel factions worsened over the winter of 1978-79, so again the Chadian government requested the assistance of France in its defense against armed rebellion.[55] According to the Minister of Foreign Affairs Louis de Guiringaud, on 15 February France began preparations to evacuate its nationals.[56] This time, after four French nationals in Chad were killed in the fighting, the French forces in N'Djamena helped repatriate about 2,500 French nationals, virtually the entire French population of Chad. Nationals from many other countries were also repatriated.[57] Because this operation was carried out exclusively by French "coopérants" already in Chad at the request of its government, this evacuation does not warrant categorization as an instance of forcible protection.

## H. France in Mauritania. 1979.

In 1979 France again conducted an air operation over the Mauritanian-ruled area of the Western Sahara. The French Minister of Foreign Affairs Guiringaud advised Parliament that involvement occurred to counter the armed-rebel operations that violated the Mauritanian border and not to target the Saharan people.[58] "One cannot claim that our military action in Mauritania, which was in conformity with article 51 of the UN Charter in particular, has been contrary to the international obligations of France, nor to the requirements of international law," he stressed.[59]

The government of Mauritania in this instance had requested support from France against outside aggression. Although the French Foreign Minister emphasized that France needed to protect its citizens,[60] the safety of foreign nationals in Mauritania was, at best, a secondary factor in France's actions. Almost consistently, France's actions are difficult to justify by exclusive reference to the protection-of-nationals-abroad doctrine.

## I. France in Gabon. 1990.

Riots erupted in Libreville, the Gabonese capital, when opposition supporters accused the government of having killed Joseph Rendjambe, the leader of the P.G.P. (Parti gabonais du progrès) opposition party, who was found dead on 22 May 1990.[61] Order also collapsed in Port-Gentil, where 10 foreigners, including seven French nationals who were working at the Elf-Aquitaine oil refinery, were taken hostage for 12 hours on 23 May.[62] On 24 May, France deployed approximately 600 Marines from their permanent station near Libreville who were there under the terms of a defense and military assistance treaty signed by the two countries on 17 August 1960.[63] France dispatched an additional 200 troops to Gabon, including parachutists based at Calvi, in Corsica, and infantrymen based at Nîmes. All these acts were in conformity with the treaty:[64] which required that the Gabonese government issue a specific request before France could deploy its forward-deployed forces, or introduce new troops into the country.[65] By 25 May the fighting had largely ceased, and on 29 May oil production resumed at the Elf refinery. The threat to French nationals in Gabon having passed, and on 1 June France withdrew most of its forces.[66]

French Minister of Foreign Affairs Roland Dumas stated that the French mission in Gabon was solely to protect the nearly 2,500 French nationals living in Port-Gentil and to repatriate those who wished to leave.[67] By the end of the rescue mission, named Operation Requin,[68] approximately 1,800 French nationals had been evacuated to Paris.[69] Despite the fact that there may have been other reasons for the French action, the evacuation of over two-thirds of the French nationals living in Port-Gentil identifies this as being a legitimate case of forcible intervention.[70]

## J. France and Belgium in Rwanda. 1990.

On 1 October 1990, several thousand armed soldiers of the Rwandan Patriotic Front invaded Rwanda from Uganda. As the rebels approached Kigali, the capital, where they sought to overthrow President Habyarimana, the Rwandan government requested military assistance from France and Belgium.[71] Both countries responded immediately to the request. On 4 October, Belgium dispatched 540 Belgian paratroops and France dispatched 300 French Foreign Legion paratroops to Rwanda,[72] where approximately 650 French and 1,600 Belgian citizens were living.[73] The Rwandan government then specifically asked Belgium to help protect the airport in Kigali. After securing it, the 150 French Foreign Legion troops and 150 Belgian paratroopers[74] evacuated nearly 1,000 European and US nationals.[75] Belgium withdrew its troops on 2 November 1990,[76] with France withdrawing its forces a few weeks thereafter.[77]

Belgian Prime Minister Martens subsequently explained before the Commissions on Foreign Affairs and National Defense of the Belgian Parliament that the government's concern had been the security of the Belgian citizens in Rwanda, which had led to the humanitarian action for their protection and, if they chose to leave, evacuation.[78] Although the widespread anarchy in

Rwanda led to an extended Belgian and French military presence, their initial actions, taken at the request of the Rwandan government, certainly qualify as a legitimate case of forcible protection.

### K. France in Chad. 1990.

On 10 November 1990, the Chadian opposition leader Idriss Déby, formerly the Commander-In-Chief to the dictatorial president Hissène Habré, rebelled against the Habré regime.[79] France, which considered the affair an internal Chadian matter,[80] nevertheless proceeded without a request from the Chadian government to transfer a company of 150 parachutists on 16 November from N'Djamena, the capital, to Abéché, in eastern Chad. These men reinforced the 350 French troops stationed there and combined they were expected to ensure the security of French citizens should Déby's forces approach.[81] They achieved this objective. When Abéché fell to the rebels on 29 November, France flew in a company of parachutists from Corsica, as well as Foreign Legion troops from the Central African Republic, to protect both French nationals and other foreigners in N'Djamena[82] and prepare for their evacuation.[83] By early December,[84] they had evacuated approximately 1,600 foreigners, including between 960 and 1,120 French nationals.[85] France made no effort to oppose Déby, who, having entered N'Djamena on 1 December, had installed himself as president, Habré having fled the country.[86]

Unlike the 1978 and 1979 French actions in Chad (discussed in Sections F and G respectively), in this instance neither followed a request by the Chadian government nor was it pursuant to the cooperation accord. It surely can be justified under the protection-of-nationals abroad doctrine, however.

### L. France and Belgium in Zaire. 1991.

Zairian soldiers mutinied in September 1991 when hyperinflation rendered their paychecks worthless.[87] Although Europeans were not targets, some of them fell victim to random pillaging. France thereupon dispatched 1,200 Foreign Legion troops aboard military transport planes on loan from the United States; Belgium sent 500 paratroopers.[88] These forces arrived in Brazzaville, in the Republic of the Congo, on 23 and 24 September and, after crossing the Zaire River, proceeded to Kinshasa, Zaire.[89]

After securing the airport, the forces shuttled French and Belgian nationals from Kinshasa to safety in Brazzaville. They then proceeded to Kolwezi, a large mining center in the Katanga region 1,500 km southeast of Kinshasa.[90] Their mission was to begin the evacuation of the 3,500 French nationals and 3,000 Belgians in Zaire,[91] of whom 650 and 2,000 respectively lived in Katanga.[92] The evacuation of over 9,000 foreign nationals from over 30 European, African and Middle Eastern countries was completed on 2 October.[93] This was not a complete evacuation. Some foreigners chose to remain.

Violence in Zaire resumed on 22 October when President Mobutu arbitrarily dismissed Prime Minister Tshisekedi, at which point the Belgian, French and U.S. authorities strongly recommended a complete evacuation. This was done and France withdrew its last soldiers on 31 October, with the last Belgian troops leaving on 4 November 1991.[94]

According to U.S. Secretary of State James Baker, the foreigners' safety had depended on the temporary presence of French and Belgian troops.[95] While President Mobutu accused France of seeking to destabilize Zaire,[96] Karl I Bond, then the leader of the United Opposition Parties, acknowledged the humanitarian nature of the rescue operations.[97] Like the 1978 operation in Zaire (discussed in Section D) the 1991 actions of both France and Belgium in Zaire appear to be a legitimate case of forcible protection.

## M. France and Belgium in Zaire. 1993.

In late January 1993, the Zairian army began an armed mutiny, with several foreigners being killed during ensuing riots.[98] In mysterious circumstances related to the mutiny, the French Ambassador to Zaire, Philippe Barnard, was killed. At the time, 3,000 Belgian and 1,000 French nationals still remained in Zaire. Belgian Minister of Foreign Affairs Willy Claes recommended that Belgians leave the country for Brazzaville, in the Republic of the Congo. The Belgian government also stated that any decision regarding the evacuation of foreign nationals from Zaire would be made in coordination with the other member States of the European Community, and that Belgium and France would furnish the majority of any troops that might be dispatched.[99] Subsequently, Belgium decided to send 550 troops to Kinshasa. According to Prime Minister Jean-Luc Dehaene, the operation was coordinated with France.[100] Foreign Minister Claes emphasized that the joint action was limited to the evacuation of civilians, primarily the 1,500 Belgians living in Kinshasa.[101]

While Zairian Prime Minister Tshisekedi, recently reinstated to office, requested Belgian military assistance, President Mobutu strongly opposed any Belgian presence by deploying air-defense forces to the N'Djili airport in Kinshasa to prevent Belgian military planes from landing. Mobutu even put his presidential yacht at the disposal of those foreigners seeking evacuation to

## Case Studies of Non-United States Forcible Protection of Nationals Abroad

Brazzaville, in an effort to make any Belgian action unnecessary.[102] In any event, the Belgian evacuation forces remained in Brazzaville and never crossed into Zaire.

On 29 January, however, France deployed 150 Marine infantry troops from their station in Bangui, in the Central African Republic, to Kinshasa via Brazzaville. The same day, 12 of these Marines secured the French Embassy and evacuated 400 French nationals from Kinshasa.[103] French troops began to withdraw on 4 February after Zairian troops loyal to Mobutu had quelled the mutiny. Belgian forces left Brazzaville the next day. While the latter never actively engaged in any rescue operation, the French did, making their actions seem a proper case of forcible protection. Interestingly, the French justified their involvment on such grounds.

### N. Multinational Evacuation Operation in Rwanda. 1994.

Security Council Resolution 872 of 5 October 1993 authorized a 1,000-man multinational force to monitor peace between the Rwandan government and rebel forces.[104] By early April 1994 the UN contingent included 2,500 troops from over 20 countries.[105] When armed bandits threatened to kill any foreigner unable to prove that he was not Belgian[106] and the UN peacekeepers suffered casualties, including 10 Belgian peacekeepers who were hacked to death by Rwandan soldiers,[107] seven Western States organized an operation that began on 8 April, with the purpose of evacuating Rwanda's foreign community.

The number of States involved and the scale of the evacuation effort made the multilateral action in Rwanda unique. France sent 460 troops and five transport planes,[108] while Belgium sent 750 troops (in addition to the 430 Belgian troops already participating in the UN operation)[109] and nine airplanes, including seven C-130 transport planes and two Boeing 747s.[110] Italy sent 80 troops and three C-130 transport planes. Germany and Canada each sent one transport plane and the Netherlands sent four planes.[111] Additionally, the United States kept one ship with 330 Marines on alert off the Kenyan coast and also provided two transport planes to assist in the evacuation.[112] By April 15, 1994 Belgian, French and Italian troops had withdrawn after evacuating over 3,900 foreigners from Kigali.[113] Although the number of participating States distinguishes this rescue operation from other ones considered in this chapter, in essence it constituted a legitimate case of collective, albeit not UN, forcible protection.

## O. France in the Central African Republic. 1996.

On 19 May 1996, fighting broke out in Bangui, the capital of the Central African Republic, between government forces and mutineers who were protesting a governmental decision to place the armory under the command of the presidential guard.[114] At the behest of President Félix Patassé, France initially deployed 800 troops of its 1,400 troops currently stationed in the country to Bangui.[115] On 20 May, these forces were supplemented with 550 members of the French Foreign Legion and additional French paratroopers stationed in Gabon.[116]

The stated mission of the French forces was to protect the 2,500 French nationals in the country, 1,500 of whom were in Bangui. By 23 May, however, the situation had so deteriorated that M. Jacques Godfrain, French Minister of Cooperation, announced that the objectives of Operation Almandin II had been expanded to include protecting the democratically-elected government of President Patassé.[117] French Defense Minister Charles Millon justified this decision under the defense agreement with Central African Republic.[118]

France received political support of its expanded mission from Cameroon, Gabon, and Senegal, all of which are former French colonies with democratically-elected presidents.[119] In the streets of Bangui, however, French forces faced violent protests against their efforts to support President Patassé. Nevertheless, France eventually employed 2,300 troops to evacuate 3,000 foreigners, primarily French but also including US, Japanese, and Lebanese nationals.[120] Because the French actions were in response to an invitation by the President of the Central African Republic and consistent with the defense agreement between the two countries, they shed little light on the forcible-protection-of-nationals-abroad doctrine per se.

## NOTES*

*The author wishes to acknowledge the research assistance provided by Ms. Eva Rieter, LL.M., Class of 1996, and Mr. Michael Coco, Class of 1998, University of Virginia School of Law, in the preparation of this Chapter.

1. The situation in the Congo (Belgian and US rescue operations) and the Israeli raid on Entebbe in 1976 are not considered in this Chapter, but are discussed in the Conclusion. Other instances that have been mentioned in the literature provide little guidance because protection of nationals abroad arguments either were not raised or were not relevant. *See, e.g., Loyola,* 1976, where French citizens, taken hostage in Somalia, were freed when French soldiers responded to Somali fire but remained within the territory of Djibouti, then a French colony; *Mogadishu,* 1977, where the Somali government consented to the use of German commando units to rescue German citizens taken hostage on a Lufthansa airplane; *Larnaca,* 1978, where Egypt did not

# Case Studies of Non-United States Forcible Protection of Nationals Abroad

invoke the protection of nationals rationale to justify its operation in Cyprus to rescue Egyptians taken hostage aboard a Cypriot airplane, but simply explained its action as necessary to fight terrorism; and *Bangkok*, 1981, where Thai authorities permitted Indonesian forces to storm an Indonesian airplane to rescue civilians taken hostage by terrorists.

  2. *See infra* text accompanying notes 4-8.

  3. For an instructive account of the political context of the French, Belgian and British military presence in Africa, *see* generally A. Rouvez, Disconsolate Empires (1994).

  4. 558 Parl. Deb., H.C. (5th ser.) 1565 (1956).

  5. *Id.* at 1566.

  6. *Id.*

  7. *Id.*

  8. 11 U.N. SCOR (749th mtg.) at 24, U.N. Doc. S/P.V. 749 (1956).

  9. Higgins, *International Law and Civil Conflict*, in The International Regulation of Civil Wars 169, 175-76 (E. Luard ed. 1972).

  10. 15 U.N. SCOR (873d mtg.) at 34-35, U.N. Doc. S/P.V. 873 (1960).

  11. 15 U.N. SCOR Supp. (Jan.-Dec.) at 11, U.N. Doc. S/4382 (1960).

  12. 15 U.N. SCOR (877th mtg.) at 18, U.N. Doc. S/P.V. 877 (1960).

  13. *Id.* at 30. The Belgian representative to the Security Council cited the fact that Belgium had only 1,400 troops present in Leopoldville as evidence that Belgian objectives did not extend beyond the protection of its nationals, since the number of troops would have been insufficient to subdue and control that city's population of 350,000. *Id.* at 29.

  14. *Id.* at 30.

  15. S.C. Res. S/4387, 15 U.N. SCOR Supp. (Jan.-Dec.) at 16, U.N. Doc. S/P.V. 873 (1960).

  16. S.C. Res. S/4405, 15 U.N. SCOR Supp. (Jan.-Dec.) at 34-35, U.N. Doc. S/P.V. 879 (1960). The Secretary-General, reporting on the implementation of these resolutions, referred to a letter of the Belgian Foreign Minister that summarized the position of his government regarding the legal justification for the intervention:

> Belgian troops were obliged to intervene solely in order to save the lives of fellow-countrymen who were in great danger, lacking any of the protection which a State must afford to private individuals.
>
> This intervention implies no interference in the internal affairs of the Congo. It is temporary in nature.
>
> These rescue duties come to an end as soon as United Nations troops arrive in a given region to take over and, at the same time, to assume responsibility for the safety of individuals.

Second Report of the Secretary-General on the Implementation of Security Council Resolutions S/4387 of 14 July 1960 and S/4405 of 22 July 1960, 15 U.N. SCOR Supp. (Jan.-Dec.) at 48, U.N. Doc. S/4417 (incorporating Doc. S/4417 Corr.1) (1960).

  17. 15 U.N. SCOR Supp. (Jan.-Dec.) at 38-39, U.N. Doc. S/4414 (1960).

  18. S.C. Res. S/4426, 15 U.N. SCOR Supp. (Jan.-Dec.) at 92, U.N. Doc. S/P.V. 886 /d (1960).

  19. For praise of Belgian efforts in the Congo by the French representative to the UN, *see* 15 U.N. SCOR (873d mtg.) at 27-28, U.N. Doc. S/P.V. 873 (1960); for approval by the British representative, *see id.* at 25-27; and, for approval by the Italian representative, *see id.* at 22-25.

  20. *Id.* at 28.

  21. *Id.* at 37 (Soviet representative); *id.* at 12 (Tunisian representative); *id.* at 30 (Polish representative); and *id.* at 32 (Argentine representative).

22. Rouvez, *supra* note 3, at 167.

23. *Id.*

24. *Les otages du Polisario sont libérés: M. Waldheim les reconduit d'Alger à Paris*, Le Monde, Dec. 24, 1977, at 1, col. 6.

25. 32 U.N. SCOR Supp. (Oct.-Dec.) at 103, U.N. Doc. S/12503 (1977).

26. *Id.*

27. Rouvez, *supra* note 3, at 167-68.

28. For a description of the 1964 US-Belgian intervention in the Congo, see Chapter IV, Section B.

29. C. Alibert, Du Droit de se faire justice dans la société internationale depuis 1945, at 253 (1983).

30. Rouvez, *supra* note 3, at 336.

31. French President Giscard d'Estaing estimated the composition of the European population in Kolwezi to be about 1,700 Belgians, 400 French, 150 Italians, 150 British, 150 Greeks and a few other foreign nationals. Manin, *L'Intervention française au Shaba*, 1978 Annuaire Français de Droit International 159, 165. The Belgian Prime Minister Léo Tindemans stated that 1,800 Belgians lived in Kolwezi and more than 6,000 in the province of Katanga. Salmon & Vincineau, *La pratique du pouvoir exécutif et le contrôle des chambres législatives en matière de droit international (1977~1978)*, 15 Revue Belge de droit international 433, 633 (1980), *citing* A.P., Sénat, séance du 22 mai 1978, at 1424,-25 and A.P., Chambre, 22 mai 1978, at 2113. Underscoring the purely humanitarian nature of the rescue operation that eventually took place, the Belgian Prime Minister also asserted that Belgium would not leave behind nationals of other countries who wished to leave Kolwezi. *Id.*

32. As in the Congo in 1964, both the French and the Belgians were supported by the United States, which furnished logistical assistance and C-141 planes. These US airplanes were used for the long-range transport of heavy equipment, such as helicopters and mobile refueling units, thereby greatly facilitating French and Belgian evacuation efforts. *See* Rouvez, *supra* note 3, at 338.

33. Manin, *supra* note 31, at 171.

34. Salmon & Vincineau, *supra* note 31, at 632, *quoting* A.P. Sénat, séance du 22 mai 1978, at 1424-25 (author's translation).

35. *See supra* text accompanying note 12.

36. Manin, *supra* note 31, at 169.

37. Rouvez, *supra* note 3, at 336. No figures are available as to the nationalities of the people evacuated by the Belgians.

38. No figures are available as to the number or nationalities of the people evacuated by the French.

39. *See, e.g.,* Secretary of State Genscher: "[T]he [German] federal government has . . . expressly, and as one of the first, expressed its thankfulness towards the French and Belgian governments for their commitment to the saving of lives." 93. Sitzung, den 1. Juni 1978, Verhandlungen des Deutschen Bundestages, 8. Wahlperiode, Stenografische Berichte, Band 106, Plenarprotokolle 8/87-8/101, 26 Apr.-23 Jun. 1978, at 7320.

40. Guiringaud, Minister of Foreign Affairs, J.O. Sénat, séance du 16 juin 1978, at 1448. Article 3 of the Convention of Military Training Between France and Mauritania, signed on 10 and 27 December 1977, provided that French troops in Mauritania remained under French jurisdiction but "could not in any case be associated with the preparation or execution of war operations, or with the maintenance of order." J.O. du 6 novembre 1985, at

12,480. This treaty makes no mention of the use of French troops in Mauritania to protect French nationals.

41. For a description of France's strategic interests in Chad and the Cold War context, *see* Rouvez, *supra* note 3, at 151-64.

42. J.O. Sénat, séance du 19 mai 1978, at 892.

43. *Id.* "Coopérant" refers to French military personnel who are stationed in, and provide technical assistance to, States with which France has cooperation agreements. Although coopérants come from all branches of the French military, the majority are from the Army.

44. *Id.*

45. J.O. Sénat, séance du 12 mai 1978, at 817.

46. *Id.*

47. Rouvez, *supra* note 3, at 154.

48. J.O. Sénat, séance du 16 juin 1978, at 1448.

49. *Id.* at 1446.

50. *Id.* at 1448.

51. *Id.*

52. *Id.*

53. J.O. Assemblée Nationale, 3e séance du 9 novembre 1978, at 7417.

54. J.O. Sénat, séance du 16 juin 1978, at 1448.

55. J.O. Assemblée Nationale, 3e séance du 9 novembre 1978, at 7417.

56. Charpentier, *Pratique française du droit international*, 1979 Annuaire Français de Droit International 905, 908, *citing* 'Réponse du Ministre des Affaires Etrangères à Q.E Vivien, no. 14007,' J.O. Assemblée Nationale, 10 mai 1979, at 3612.

57. *Id.* No figures are available as to the number or nationalities of the other foreigners evacuated by the French.

58. Response to question of Mr. Odru, no. 3859, J.O. Assemblée Nationale, séance du 6 avril 1979, at 2438.

59. *Id.* (author's translation). For a discussion of the defense cooperation agreement between France and Mauritania, *see supra* text accompanying note 40.

60. Response of the Minister of Foreign Affairs to Mr. Vivien, no. 9548, and to Mr. Odru, no. 5239, J.O. Assemblée Nationale, séance du 3 mars 1979, at 1380.

61. Rouvez, *supra* note 3, at 180.

62. Gabon: émeutes et pillages à Libreville et à Port-Gentil, Le Monde, May 26, 1990, at 3, cols. 1-5.

63. *Renforts français au Gabon*, Le Monde, May 25, 1990, at 1, col. 6. The Franco-Gabonese defense accord had been revised in 1974. Rousseau, *Chronique des faits internationaux*, 94 R.G.D.I.P. 1035, 1071 (1990).

64. Rousseau, *supra* note 63.

65. Deux accords de sécurité avec Paris, Le Monde, May 26, 1990, at 3, cols. 3-4.

66. Rouvez, *supra* note 3, at 181.

67. *Plus des deux tiers des Français ont quitté Port-Gentil*, Le Monde, May 29, 1990, at 7, cols. 1-4.

68. Guérivière, *Mission presque accomplie*, Le Monde, June 1, 1990, at 6, cols. 3-6.

69. Le Monde, *supra* note 67.

70. No figures are available as to the nationalities of other foreigners evacuated by the French.

71. *Des accrochages entre forces régulières et rebelles on eu lieu dans la capitale, Kigali*, Le Monde, Oct. 6, 1990, at 4, cols. 3-6. Rwanda did not have a defense accord with either France or

Belgium, although approximately 20 Belgian troops were stationed in the country to provide logistical assistance. Guérivière, *Le geste "humanitaire" de la Belgique*, Le Monde, Oct. 6, 1990, at 4, col. 3.

72. Rouvez, *supra* note 3, at 343. The French Foreign Legion troops were flown to Rwanda from their station in Bangui, in the Central African Republic. *Des accrochages entre forces régulières et rebelles on eu lieu dans la capitale, Kigali*, Le Monde, *supra* note 71.

73. *Des accrochages entre forces régulières et rebelles on eu lieu dans la capitale, Kigali*, Le Monde, *supra* note 71.

74. Rousseau, *Chronique des faits internationaux*, 95 R.G.D. I. P. 439, 479 (1990).

75. *Foreign Missions In African Lands*, N.Y. Times, Apr. 11, 1994, at A13, col. 1. No breakdown of this figure by nationalities is available.

76. Vincineau & Ergec, *La pratique du pouvoir exécutif et le contrôle des chambres législatives en matière de droit international (1988-1990)*, 24 Revue Belge de droit international 132, 208 (1991).

77. Rousseau, *Chronique des faits internationaux*, 95 R.G.D.I.P. 721, 746 (1991). When rebels seized part of the city of Ruhengeri near the Ugandan border on 22 June 1991, 100 French paratroopers returned to Rwanda to evacuate French nationals and other foreigners. Rouvez, *supra* note 3, at 345.

78. Vincineau & Ergec, supra note 76, at 207-08, citing A.P., Chambre, 6 octobre 1990, at 3-4.

79. *L'entre-deux-guerres*, Le Monde, Dec. 4, 1990, at 3, cols. 5-6.

80. Rouvez, *supra* note 3, at 163.

81. *La France renforce son dispositif "Epervier" au Tchad*, Le Monde, Nov. 17, 1990, at 36, col. 4.

82. Rouvez, *supra* note 3, at 163.

83. *'On a laissé faire Idriss Déby' reconnaît le ministre français de la coopération*, Le Monde, Dec. 5, 1990, at 4, cols. 4-6.

84. Rouvez, *supra* note 3, at 163.

85. Le Monde, *supra* note 83. No figures are available as to the number or nationalities of the people evacuated by the French.

86. *Decembre 1990 dans le monde*, Le Monde, Jan. 9, 1991, at 14, cols. 1-4.

87. Hearing Before the Subcomm. on African Affairs of the Senate Comm. on Foreign Relations, 102d Cong., 1st Sess. 2 (1991) (Statement of Herman J. Cohen, Assistant Secretary of State for African Affairs) [hereinafter Hearing].

88. N.Y. Times, *supra* note 75.

89. *Le président Mobutu demande aux militaires de rentrer dans les casernes*, Agence France Presse, Sept. 25, 1991, *available in* LEXIS, Europe Library, Presse File.

90. *Id.*

91. Rousseau, *Chronique des faits internationaux* 96 R.G.D.I.P. 369, 403 (1992).

92. *Supra* note 89.

93. Stegic, *Un deuxième français tué à Kinshasa*, Agence France Presse, Jan. 29, 1993, *available in* LEXIS, Europe Library, Presse File. Specific figures as to the number or nationalities of the people evacuated are unavailable for either the French or Belgian rescue operations.

94. *Supra* note 89.

95. Hearing, *supra* note 87, at 3.

96. *Supra* note 93.

97. *Supra* note 89.

98. *Supra* note 93.

99. Navarro, *La garde presidentielle prend le contrôle d'une partie de Kinshasa, selon Bruxelles*, Agence France Presse, Jan. 29, 1993, *available in* LEXIS, Europe Library, Presse File.

100. *Id.*
101. *Id.*
102. Rouvez, *supra* note 3, at 352.
103. *Id.*
104. 48 U.N. SCOR (3288th mtg.) at 102, U.N. Doc. S/INF/49 (1993).

105. The number of UN peacekeepers had been increased pursuant to Security Council Resolution 893, which was adopted on 6 January 1994. S.C. Res. 893, 49 U.N. SCOR (3326th mtg.), U.N. Doc. S/Res/893 (1994).

106. Most Foreigners out of Rwanda, AP Online, Apr. 15, 1994, *available in* LEXIS, News Library, Arcnws File.

107. Belgium admits it had more troops in Rwanda, Reuters World Service, Apr. 16, 1994, *available in* LEXIS, News Library, Arcnws File.

108. Rouvez, *supra* note 3, at 355. However, the *N.Y Times*, *supra* note 75, reported that France sent 700 troops to Rwanda to protect foreigners.

109. Reuters World Service, Apr. 16, 1994, *supra* note 107. Rwanda, however, only had given permission for Belgium to send 400 paratroopers, according to Belgian Colonel Gilbert Hertoghe. *Id.*

110. Rouvez, *supra* note 3, at 355.
111. *Id.*
112. *Id.*

113. Rwanda Slaughter Continues, AP Online, Apr. 15, 1994, *available in* LEXIS, News Library, Arcnws File. According to a Belgian government source, it was unclear how many foreigners chose to remain in Rwanda. Shaw, Most Foreigners out of Rwanda, Rebels threaten Foreign Troops, AP WorldStream, Apr. 15, 1996, *available in* LEXIS, News Library, Arcnws File. Figures are unavailable as to the nationality of the evacuees.

114. Paris says 'necessary measures' taken in Bangui, Reuters World Service, May 19, 1996, available in LEXIS, News Library, Crnws File.

115. These 1,400 French troops were present in the Central African Republic according to the terms of a 1960 defense treaty between the two countries. Representing the second largest permanent French military presence in Africa, after that in Djibouti, they were not authorized to participate in the maintenance of law and order, but were permitted to protect foreign nationals. *1,400 soldats français*, Le Monde, May 21, 1996, at 4, cols. 2-3.

116. France sends more troops to Central African Republic, Deutsche Presse-Agentur, May 20, 1996, *available in* LEXIS, News Library, Crnws File.

117. *US, French Troops Protect Westerners Caught in Mutiny*, Wash. Post, May 23, 1996, at A38, cols. 3-4. President Patassé was elected in 1993 in the Central African Republic's first free elections. Mutiny Rocks Africa Republic: US, French Evacuate Capital, Newsday, May 22, 1996, *available in* LEXIS, News Library, Crnws File. The Minister of Cooperation stated that France had a duty to honor the request for assistance from President Patassé based on the defense agreement between the two countries. *See* Le Monde, *supra* note 115. This agreement, however, like many such agreements between France and its former African colonies, provides that the purpose of the French presence in the country is to protect foreign nationals by taking positions around sensitive points such as airports, and to assist the Central African Republic against external aggression. *Id.* Nevertheless, Minister of Cooperation Jacques Godfrain declared in 1995 that France now "[w]ill intervene [in Africa] each time an elected democratic power is overthrown by a *coup d'état* if a military cooperation agreement exists."

French, *France's Army Keeps Grip in African Ex-Colonies*, N.Y. Times, May 22, 1996, at A3, cols. 1-4.

118. M. Millon: 'assurer la libre circulation et la sécurité,' Agence France Presse, May 20, 1996, *available in* LEXIS, Europe Library, Presse File.

119. Intervention militaire française a Bangui: Les expatriés quittent le Centrafrique, *Le Monde*, May 24, 1996, at 1, cols. 5-6.

120. Specific figures as to the number or nationalities of the people evacuated are unavailable for the French rescue operation.

# Appendix I

## A Chronological List of Cases Involving the Landing of United States Forces to Protect the Lives and Property of Nationals Abroad Prior to World War II*

This Appendix contains a chronological list of pre-World War II cases in which the United States landed troops in foreign countries to protect the lives and property of its nationals.[1] Inclusion of a case does not necessarily imply that the exercise of forcible self-help was motivated solely, or even primarily, out of concern for US nationals.[2] In many instances there is room for disagreement as to what motive predominated, but in all cases included herein the US forces involved afforded some measure of protection to US nationals or their property.

The cases are listed according to the date of the first use of US forces. A case is included only where there was an actual physical landing to protect nationals who were the subject of, or were threatened by, immediate or potential danger. Thus, for example, cases involving the landing of troops to punish past transgressions, or for the ostensible purpose of protecting nationals at some remote time in the future, have been omitted. While an effort to isolate individual fact situations has been made, there are a good number of situations involving multiple landings closely related in time or context which, for the sake of convenience, have been treated herein as single episodes.

The list of cases is based primarily upon the sources cited following this paragraph. Additional sources are noted occasionally under individual cases. In those relatively few instances where the authorities are in conflict

---

* The author wishes to acknowledge the research assistance provided by George T. Yates, III, Esq., Member of the California and New York Bars, in the preparation of this Appendix.

about the character or details of a particular landing, the majority view generally has been followed. In each case, moreover, an attempt has been made to provide information as precise as possible about the nature of the threat to US nationals, the size of the force landed, the duration of its stay, the number of troops, nationals and other persons killed or wounded, and the extent of property loss or damage.

## Sources

1. *Annual Reports of the Secretary of the Navy* [hereinafter cited as *Annual Report*].
2. T. Bailey, *A Diplomatic History of the American People* (7th ed. 1965) [hereinafter cited as *Bailey*].
3. S. Bemis, *A Diplomatic History of the United States* (1936) [hereinafter cited as *Bemis*].
4. J. Clark (U. S. Solicitor of the Department of State), *Right to Protect Citizens in Foreign Countries by Landing Forces* (3d rev. ed. 1934) [hereinafter cited as *Clark*].
5. 117 *Cong. Rec.* S5637-47 (daily ed. April 26, 1971) (remarks of Senator Goldwater).
6. Department of State Historical Studies Division, Research Project No. 806A: *Armed Actions Taken by the United States without a Declaration of War 1789–1967* (1967) [hereinafter cited as *Dep't of State*].
7. *Dictionary of American History* (J. Adams ed. 1940) [hereinafter cited as *Dictionary*].
8. H. Ellsworth, *One Hundred Eighty Landings of United States Marines 1800–1934* (US Marine Corps Historical Section 1934) [hereinafter cited as *Ellsworth*].
9. G. Hackworth, *Digest of International Law* (1943) [hereinafter cited as *Hackworth*].
10. D. Knox, *A History of the United States Navy* (1936) [hereinafter cited as *Knox*].
11. *Message of the President and Accompanying Documents*, Part I, Papers Relating to Foreign Affairs, H.R. Exec. Doc. No. 1, 40th Cong., 3d Sess. (1868-69) [hereinafter cited as *Message and Documents*].
12. W. Miller & J. Johnstone, *A Chronology of the United States Marine Corps 1775–1934* (US Marine Corps Historical Branch 1965).
13. J. B. Moore, *International Law Digest* (1906) [hereinafter cited as *Moore*].
14. M. Offutt, *The Protection of Citizens Abroad by the Armed Forces of the United States* (1928) [hereinafter cited as *Offutt*].
15. C. Paullin, *Diplomatic Negotiations of American Naval Officers, 1778–1883* (1912) [hereinafter cited as *Paullin*].
16. J. Rogers, *World Policing and the Constitution* (1945) [hereinafter cited as *Rogers*].
17. R. Rotberg, *Haiti: The Politics of Squalor* (1971) [hereinafter cited as *Rotberg*].
18. O. Spaulding, *The United States Army in War and Peace* (1937) [hereinafter cited as *Spaulding*].
19. Staff of House Comm. on Foreign Affairs, 91st Cong. 2d Sess., *Background Information on the Use of United States Armed Forces in Foreign Countries* (Comm. Print 1970) [hereinafter cited as *Background*].
20. U.N. SCOR Supp. (Apr.–Jun. 1965) at 89, U.N. Doc. S/6331 (1965) (letter from Ambassador Stevenson to the President of the Security Council).

# Appendix I

*Case No. 1*, 1831–1832 — Falkland Islands

In July and August 1831, Louis Vernet seized three American ships at port in the Falkland Islands, while acting as the civilian and military governor of the islands under the authority of the Government of Buenos Aires. Late in November, Captain Duncan, sailing on the U. S. sloop *Lexington*, arrived at Buenos Aires and notified its American consul of his intention to proceed to the Falkland Islands to protect American citizens and commerce. Argentina protested claiming that the United States had no right to use the Falklands or its surrounding territorial waters.

Despite the protest, Duncan set sail for the Falklands, upon learning that Vernet had plundered the schooner *Harriet*, arriving off Berkley Sound on 28 December 1831. The American force remained inactive until 1 January 1832. On that day the *Lexington* proceeded to the port of St. Louis, where a small landing force of 17 men went ashore to release the American vessels and their crews, and arrest their captors. A reinforcement party landed from two small boats a short time later. The two parties took seven prisoners and dispersed the other inhabitants.

Since nearly all the American citizens in the islands wished to leave, Captain Duncan agreed to give them passage to Montevideo. He sent a guard of 12 Marines ashore to protect the Americans and their property while they were making preparations to depart. This force returned aboard ship on 2 January 1832. A smaller force landed daily until 5 January. On 21 January, a party of Americans consisting of 20 men, 8 women, and 10 children boarded the *Lexington*, which sailed the same day.

Upon reaching Montevideo on 7 February 1832, Duncan surrendered the prisoners on the condition that the Buenos Aires Government assume responsibility for their acts.

Sources: *Ellsworth* 76; *Offutt* 20-22; 1 *Moore* 298-99.

*Case No. 2*, 1833 — Argentina

In October 1833, insurrection broke out in Argentina. Violence was especially severe in the area around Buenos Aires. Although the United States had no diplomatic officers or consular agents in Buenos Aires, there were some American citizens residing in the city. Daniel Gowland, an American businessman, informed the commander of an American naval vessel stationed in the harbor of the situation's gravity and requested that the Navy provide protection for both US citizens and any foreign nationals not then represented by naval forces.

Five days later, on 21 October, an American flagship commanded by Commodore M. T. Woolsey arrived at Buenos Aires. Since the United States had no political agent on shore, Woolsey immediately sent Commander Isaac McKeever to reside in the city so as to keep him informed of developments. Until 31 October there were only occasional outbursts, but on that date a widespread disturbance began. Woolsey landed a force of 43 officers, Marines, and seamen, putting them under McKeever's command. They remained ashore until 15 November 1833, when peace was restored to the city.
Source: *Ellsworth* 9-10.

*Case No. 3, 1835–1836 — Peru*
The revolution which began in Peru in February 1835 led to American intervention by the end of the year. General Salaverry, anxious to gain control of the government, induced disturbances to distract attention from his secret organization of a revolutionary army. He deposed President Obregoso and proclaimed himself Head of State on 25 February 1835. Obregoso proved to be more entrenched than Salaverry expected. He was able to reorganize those forces which remained loyal to him and then opposed Salaverry. The ensuing conflict created deplorable conditions throughout Peru, especially in the capital city, Lima, and the chief port, Callao.

On 6 December 1835, several American citizens in Lima petitioned the US chargé d'affaires for a landing party to protect them and their property. The chargé d'affaires did not take any action until 10 December, when he requested that a force from the frigate *Brandywine* be landed at Callao and sent to guard the US consulate at Lima; four men landed on the same date. Shortly after their arrival, both factions temporarily withdrew from the city, leaving it without military or civil government for several days. Under these circumstances, the chargé d'affaires requested that more Marines be sent to protect foreign residents. On 17 December, the rest of the Marine guard from the *Brandywine* came ashore. Several days later the British and French also made landings. These forces prevented a general plunder of the city, especially in the foreign quarter — where no houses were disturbed. The American force returned aboard ship on 24 January 1836.

On 31 August 1836, the *Brandywine* returned to Callao to land one man who then proceeded to Lima to guard the American consulate. He remained ashore until 2 December 1836.
Source: *Ellsworth* 137-38.

## Appendix I

*Case No. 4, 1841 — Peru*
In 1841, Lieutenant A. Bigelow, commander of the US schooner *Shark*, intervened between two warring factions in upper Peru to save the lives and property of Americans and other foreigners.

Source: *Knox* 159.

*Case No. 5, 1852 — Argentina*
Early in 1852, revolution again swept the Republic of Argentina. The US chargé d'affaires at Buenos Aires, John S. Pendleton, believed that an American naval presence was needed urgently. In response to Pendleton's communications, Commodore Isaac McKeever marshaled a force of Marines and proceeded from Montevideo to Buenos Aires. On 2 February, McKeever, the British admiral, the senior naval officers of France, Sardinia, and Sweden, and all the accredited diplomats in Buenos Aires met. At the meeting, they decided to apply to the local authorities for permission to land such forces as the circumstances might require. Permission was not granted.

On the next day, when it became known that the rebels had won a victory over the forces of General Rosas and were marching toward Buenos Aires, panic spread throughout the city. Permission to land forces was urged again and this time granted. British, French and American forces were stationed as guards for various foreign residents and diplomats. Pillagers plundered the city. Disorder was widespread. During the transitional period American Marines and sailors patrolled the streets, killing four pillagers. This ended the looting. By 12 February, with the new provisional government in control and order restored, the Americans withdrew to their ships.

Source: *Ellsworth* 10-13.

*Case No. 6, 1852–1853 — Argentina*
A small disorder arose in Buenos Aires on 11 September 1852. This insurrection was not nearly as violent as the one earlier in the year.[3] Nevertheless, American interests were endangered so on 17 September a Marine guard landed to protect the US consulate. This force remained until about April 1853.

Source: *Ellsworth* 13.

## Forcible Protection of Nationals Abroad

*Case No. 7, 1853* — Nicaragua
In 1852, a dispute arose between the local government of San Juan del Norte (Greytown) and the Accessory Transit Company, an American-owned company chartered in Nicaragua, over the title to a piece of property at Puntas Arenas. On 8 February 1853, the city council ordered the company off the land. Before either side had taken any further action, the America sloop *Cyane* arrived in San Juan on 10 March. An armed force of 24 Marines was sent ashore to protect American citizens and their interests. After several days the controversy apparently was settled and the landing party was recalled on 13 March. Shortly thereafter the *Cyane* sailed north.
Sources: Clark 58-59; Ellsworth 120; Offutt 32.

*Case No. 8, 1854* — China (Shanghai)
Commodore Perry visited Shanghai, after his first visit to Japan in 1853. By 7 September 1853, the Taiping rebellion had become full blown; the city was captured by the insurgents and skirmishing near Shanghai was constant. In response to these events, Perry left behind the US sloop-of-war *Plymouth* before sailing to Japan in 1854.

The Imperial Chinese forces were encamped around the city, and their fleet was anchored in the river. They committed petty hostilities toward foreigners, with the army tearing down structures at construction sites and stealing building materials, and the navy firing without warning and searching all boats on the river. The general in command of the Imperial troops advised foreigners that he was no longer able to protect foreign interests and that they must protect themselves.

On 8 March 1854, a privately owned American pilot boat was fired upon. The Imperial forces seized the vessel, hauled down the American flag and maltreated the crew. In response, Commodore Kelly of the *Plymouth* threatened to kill the commanding officer of the Imperial vessel. This threat resulted in the release of six prisoners and the return of the American boat.

The attacks on foreigners continued, however, and by 3 April more affirmative action was necessary. A small body of British Marines moved on the Imperialists but was driven back. The British immediately landed another 150 seamen and Marines, and the Americans landed about 60 the following day. These men were joined by about 30 volunteers from American merchant vessels, as well as volunteers from the foreign quarter of the city. On the same evening, the United States sent ashore an additional force of 11 men to guard the American mission grounds. This combined force succeeded in driving the Imperial troops into their encampments.

## Appendix I

On 4 April, the British and Americans sent a note to the Imperialists advising them that if by 4 P.M. they did not evacuate their encampments in the vicinity of the Race Course, the scene of the most recent hostilities, the joint forces would be obliged to destroy them. The Chinese ignored the warning and the attack began at the appointed hour. The combined forces were victorious over the Imperialists, who left a number of men dead and wounded in their retreat. The American casualties included two killed and four wounded. The British lost one man with three others wounded. The bulk of the American force withdrew; however, two guard forces, 35 men at the American consulate and 11 at the American mission, remained ashore until 15 June. The last of the joint forces patrolling the Race Course area reembarked two days later.

Sources: *Clark* 57-58; *Ellsworth* 21-22; *Knox* 185; *Offutt* 28-31.

*Case No. 9, 1854* — Nicaragua

Shortly after the departure of the USS *Cyane* from Nicaragua in March 1853,[4] the dispute between the city of San Juan del Norte and the American residents flared once again. The local authorities set afire some of the Accessory Transit Company buildings on the Puntas Arenas property and stole some of the firm's goods. In May 1854, in trying to seize the US minister to Central America, Solon Borland, a mob cut his face. The American consul demanded reparation for these wrongs, but to no avail.

The *Cyane* returned to San Juan on 9 July to force reparations. Still unable to obtain any satisfactory response, Commander Hollins, of the *Cyane*, sent a landing party of 18 seamen and Marines ashore on 12 July to seize the arms and ammunition of the town and to post a proclamation declaring that the town would be bombarded the following day if the demands were not met. The *Cyane* opened fire at 9 A.M. on 13 July. There were three different bombardments during the day. At 4 P.M., the landing party from 12 July went ashore to complete the destruction by fire. The force then withdrew. Although most of the town was destroyed, no lives were lost because the inhabitants had fled.

Subsequently Nicaragua asserted claims for the damage incurred during the bombardment of Greytown. The following is a portion of Secretary of State Marcy's response to the Nicaraguan minister, dated 2 August 1854:

> If Nicaragua chooses to maintain the position you assume in your note to me, that her citizens who incorporated themselves with the community at San Juan are still in friendly relations with her and entitled to her protection, then

she approves by an implication which she is not at liberty to deny [the acts] of that political establishment planted on her own soil and becomes responsible for the mischiefs it has done to American citizens. It would be a strange inconsistency for Nicaragua to regard the organization at San Juan as a hostile establishment on her territory and at the same time claim the right to clothe with her nationality its members.

The United States also refused to pay the claims of French citizens growing out of the bombardment.[5]

On 4 December 1854, President Pierce communicated the facts of the incident to the Congress in his annual message. The President, the Congress, and the Secretary of the Navy approved Commander Hollins' conduct. In fact, he was commended for the prompt and efficient execution of his duties.

Sources: *Clark* 59; *Ellsworth* 121-22; *Knox* 183-84; 2 *Moore* 414-18.

*Case No. 10, 1854* — China (Ning-Po)
The United States made another landing in China at Ning-Po in 1854. On 20 July, two armed boats landed to deliver letters to the American consul and a missionary. Believing some disturbance was about to occur at Ning-Po, the Americans landed an additional 12 Marines the following day. These forces remained ashore for two days, acting as a guard. When it became apparent that no disorder was going to take place, they returned to the ship on 23 July.

Source: *Offutt* 31.

*Case No. 11, 1855* — China
The United States, dissatisfied with the failure of the Chinese authorities to provide adequate protection for American citizens in that country, maintained naval vessels in the area so that assistance might be rendered when necessary. On 8 March 1855, one such vessel put in to Shanghai, where local conditions were reported to be chaotic. No landing was made until 19 May, when 41 men went ashore to protect the lives and property of American citizens. They reembarked two days later.

Source: *Ellsworth* 23.

*Case No. 12, 1855* — Uruguay
An uprising in 1855 brought severe fighting to Montevideo, Uruguay, and on 25 November 1855, Commander W. F. Lynch of the sloop-of-war *Germantown* landed a force of seamen and Marines to protect the lives and property of

# Appendix I

American residents. Britain, France, and Spain, who had warships present in the harbor, also sent detachments to protect their nationals. Notable was the fact that Captain Lynch, an American and the senior naval officer of all the foreign forces, assumed the command of a joint column which occupied the customshouse without resistance. As the fighting intensified, more Americans were called ashore on 27 November, bringing the total to about 100. The reinforcements withdrew the same day.

By 29 November, the Uruguayan Government had succeeded in putting down the revolution and the original American landing force reembarked the following day. During reembarkation the American commander noticed that the Uruguayan Government forces were preparing to kill the insurgents, even though the latter had capitulated and had been disarmed. The Marines commanded by Lieutenant Nicholson interposed themselves between the Government troops and the insurgents, thereby preventing the slaughter.

Subsequently, Lynch received a note from the Uruguayan Government thanking him for his action in protecting the customhouse and the lives and property of the foreign residents.

Sources: *Ellsworth* 160-61; *Offutt* 36-37.

*Case No. 13, 1856 — Colombia (Panama)*
On 19 September 1856, a disturbance occurred in the Panamanian legislative assembly which seemed certain to lead to armed conflict between the two political factions. Commodore Mervine, commander of the Pacific Squadron, requested that the American consul inform Governor Fabriga that he wished to land some men to protect American citizens during the impending conflict. The Governor granted the request and Mervine sent ashore 160 men and a field gun to occupy the railroad station.[6] The American presence had such a dampening effect that the battle never occurred. The American forces reembarked on 22 September.

Source: *Offutt* 37-38.

*Case No. 14, 1856 — China*
In the autumn of 1856, fighting between the British and the authorities of Canton seemed inevitable. Fearing injury to Americans and their property, the American consul requested that Commander A. H. Foote of the sloop Portsmouth send a force to look after these interests. Foote sent 83 men from the Portsmouth who landed at Canton about 23 October. When this first force proved inadequate, an additional force of about 67 men was landed

from the sloop-of-war Levant around 27 October. On 28 November, a supplementary force of 29 Marines was landed from the steam sloop USS *San Jacinto*. This detachment remained ashore only two days. About this time the decision was made to withdraw the forces because several Americans had participated in a British assault on the Chinese without orders, and the United States wished to maintain its neutrality.

While Foote was arranging the American withdrawal, his boat was fired on five times as he passed Chinese installations on the river. On the following day, 16 November, the sloop Portsmouth was brought up from Whampoa to the nearest fort and the Americans immediately opened fire in retaliation. The fighting escalated, and on 20 November, Foote landed 287 men who took one fort by assault. When about 3,000 Chinese soldiers attempted to retake the fort, the American forces repulsed them. On the following day, two more forts were captured, and on 22 November, the last fort surrendered. The landing party returned to their ships that afternoon, but landed again the following day to occupy the forts and complete their destruction. This work continued until 6 December 1856, when the entire force withdrew. Chinese casualties amounted to about 250, while the Americans had 29 men killed or wounded.

Sources: *Clark* 60-61; *Ellsworth* 24-27; *Knox* 186-87; *Offutt* 38-39.

*Case No. 15, 1858 — Uruguay*
When a revolution broke out in Uruguay in January 1858, the Government of Uruguay requested that foreign troops be landed to protect the lives and property of foreign residents. Detachments from the frigate USS *St. Lawrence* and sloop-of-war *Falmouth* landed on 2 January 1858, and joined British naval forces in holding the two consulates and the customhouse in Montevideo. The American forces showed strict neutrality toward both political factions and confined themselves to protecting foreigners. On 27 January, about ten days after the revolutionary movement fell apart, the Marines withdrew without incident. On the day of the American withdrawal, an increased British force landed.

Sources: *Ellsworth* 161; *Offutt* 39-40; *Rogers* 103.

*Case No. 16, 1859 — China*
In the summer of 1859, it was reported among the Chinese at Shanghai that some coolies had been kidnapped and taken aboard a French merchant vessel. These reports led to a general disturbance directed against foreigners. At that time the side-wheel steamer USS *Mississippi* had arrived off Woosung and the

## Appendix I

American consul and several American merchants requested assistance in protecting their lives and property. On 31 July, the captain of the *Mississippi* sent ashore an armed party of 60 Marines to offer protection and restore order. Having accomplished their objective, the Americans reembarked on 2 August 1859.
Sources: *Clark* 62; *Ellsworth* 27-28; *Knox* 189; *Offutt* 41.

*Case No. 17, 1860 — Angola (Portuguese West Africa)*
When it appeared that the natives would attack the Portuguese settlement at Kisembo, Angola (Portuguese West Africa), the American residents requested assistance from the sloop-of-war USS *Marion* which was lying in the harbor. On 1 March 1860, several officers and about 40 seamen and Marines went ashore to guard the American factories during the night. The force was withdrawn the following day.

On 3 March, another force of 50 men was landed to protect American interests during a battle between the natives and the Portuguese. The natives made several attempts to burn the American factories, but the force from the *Marion* prevented them from achieving their objective. The next day, the natives having been defeated, the Americans withdrew. It should be noted that the Americans remained neutral throughout the conflict, their only function being that of a guard force.
Sources: *Clark* 62; *Ellsworth* 7; *Offutt* 41-42.

*Case No. 18, 1860 — Colombia (Panama)*
On 27 September 1860, an insurrection began in the outskirts of Panama City. After consulting with the American consul, and at the request of the military *intendente* and the agent of the Panama Railroad, Commander William D. Porter of the sloop-of-war USS *St. Mary's* landed a Marine guard to protect railroad traffic and American interests. The necessity of the force was demonstrated by the fact that six white inhabitants already had been killed and three wounded by stray bullets. The force landed and occupied the railroad station without opposition. The Governor of Panama turned over the city to the joint occupation of American and British forces the following day. On 29 September 1860, an additional force of 50 seamen landed to reinforce the Marine guard. These forces were not withdrawn until 7 October, when the insurrection had come to an end.
Sources: *Clark* 62-63; *Ellsworth* 46; *Knox* 189; *Offutt* 42.

## Forcible Protection of Nationals Abroad

*Case No. 19, 1864 — Japan*
In the summer of 1864, Robert H. Pruyn, United States minister to Japan, went to Yedo (Tokyo) to negotiate a settlement of American claims for several acts of hostility committed by Japan against the United States. A force of 65 seamen and Marines from the sloop USS *Jamestown* was landed on 14 July 1864, to act as a guard for Pruyn during the three weeks of negotiations, the Japanese being unable to guarantee his safety. According to Pruyn, however, he requested the guard not only to insure his safety but also to facilitate his work.
Source: *Offutt* 44-45.

*Case No. 20, 1865 — Colombia (Panama)*
Although the revolution which erupted in Panama on 9 March 1865, was unanticipated by American officials, it so happened that the USS St. Mary's was anchored in the harbor ready to render assistance to protect American lives and property. The American consuls who requested that a force be sent ashore first sought permission from Vice President Calancha, the acting Head of State. Since it was his government that was about to be overthrown, he readily granted permission. A detachment of Marines was sent to occupy the American consulate overnight. When foreign residents were not the object of any violence, the Marines returned to their ship the following morning.
Source: *Offutt* 48.

*Case No. 21, 1868 — Japan (Hiogo)*
Subsequent to the opening of the ports of Osaka and Hiogo on 1 January 1868, Japanese hostility toward foreigners became so noticeable that certain vessels of the Asiatic Squadron under the command of Rear Admiral Bell were stationed in the area so that they could offer assistance if American interests were threatened.

On 27 January, war broke out between two Japanese factions, one favoring greater commercial relations and the other wishing to restrict commerce with other nations. The leader of the former faction, the Tycoon, was defeated, and on 31 January he sought shelter for the night on board the steam sloop-of-war USS *Iroquois*.[7] On the following day, the foreign ministers were compelled to leave Osaka and they went aboard the *Iroquois* to Hiogo.

Hiogo also was experiencing trouble at this time. On 4 February, Japanese soldiers attacked a group of foreign residents and wounded a crew member of the screw sloop-of-war USS *Oneida*. In order to protect the foreign settlement,

*Appendix I*

the treaty powers present at the time made a joint landing. The American force withdrew on 8 February 1868.
Sources: *Clark* 64-65; *Ellsworth* 103-04; *Offutt* 50-51.

*Case No. 22, 1868 — Uruguay*
Two landings were made at Montevideo, Uruguay, in February 1868. At that time two-thirds of the city's 70,000 inhabitants were foreigners. In conjunction with the actions of commanders of other foreign squadrons,[8] and at the request of Governor Flores, Rear Admiral Davis landed a force of 50 Marines and seamen on 7 February, to protect foreign residents as well as the customhouse during a political disturbance. The force withdrew the following day, but another force of 50 officers and men had to be landed on 19 February to protect foreign residents from the rioting which occurred after the assassination of Flores. This force did not reembark until 26 February 1868, when the President of the Republic requested their withdrawal.
Sources: *Ellsworth* 161-63; *Offutt* 52.

*Case No. 23, 1868 — Japan (Nagasaki)*
At the request of the American consul in Nagasaki, a small force from the sloop-of-war USS *Shenandoah* landed on 8 February 1868 to protect the consulate during demonstrations against foreigners in that city.
Sources: *Ellsworth* 104; *Offutt* 51.

*Case No. 24, 1868 — Japan (Yokohama) (April)*
Antiforeign feeling was so strong in Yokohama that the foreign diplomatic officers in the city, representing France, Great Britain, Italy, Prussia, and the United States sought protection for the foreign settlement from their respective naval vessels then present in the harbor. The commanders of these vessels held a conference and decided upon a joint landing, which took place on 4 April 1868. The American contribution was a party of 25 Marines from the side-wheel gunboat USS *Monocacy* and the USS *Iroquois*. Two weeks later another detail of Marines reinforced them. The entire Marine guard withdrew on 12 May 1868.
Sources: *Ellsworth* 104; *Offutt* 51.

*Case No. 25, 1868 — Colombia (Panama)*
On 7 April 1868, while local police and Colombian troops were absent from Aspinwall (Colon), a crowd gathered in the streets of that city making rioting seem probable. An agent of a steamship company requested that the commanding officer of the screw gunboat USS Penobscot land a force to protect passengers and goods in transit. In compliance with this request, a force of two officers and 12 seamen went ashore. They were withdrawn as soon as the need for protection had passed.
Source: *Offutt* 52.

*Case No. 26, 1868 — Japan (Yokohama) (July)*
Attacks on foreigners in Yokohama continued. At a meeting on 8 July 1868, the foreign ministers of France, Great Britain, Italy, The Netherlands, Prussia, and the United States decided that in view of the city's disturbed state of affairs it would be necessary to establish four posts of foreign guards. These guards were to assist foreigners who might be attacked or who might request assistance, and observe the state of affairs in the foreign settlement. Under no circumstances, however, were the guards to interfere with the activities of the Japanese, except to defend foreigners. France, Great Britain, The Netherlands, and the United States each had the responsibility to maintain one post. The number of men furnished by each country was: France 11; Great Britain 16; The Netherlands 16; and the United States 21. All these measures were taken with the approval of Higashi Kuze Chiujio, the Japanese Minister of Foreign Affairs. The American force arrived in Yokohama about 13 July 1868 and remained until the danger ceased.
Sources: Letter from R.B. Van Valkenburgh to Hon. William H. Seward (July 22, 1868), reprinted in *Message and Documents* 780-1; *Offutt* 52.

*Case No. 27, 1868 — Japan (Niigata)*
The Marine guard of the screw steamer USS Piscataqua went ashore at Niigata on about 25 September 1868 to protect the lives of some American citizens during local riots. They remained for several days.
Sources: Letter from R. B. Van. Valkenburgh to Hon. William H. Seward (September 25, 1868), reprinted in *Message and Documents* 823-5; *Offutt* 52.

## Appendix I

*Case No. 28, 1873 — Colombia (Panama) (May)*
In 1873, at the request of the American consul and several American and other foreign residents, American forces landed in Panama to protect American citizens and their property during revolutionary disturbances. On 7 May 1873, as opposing political factions fought over control of the government, a force of 100 men with two field guns went ashore to occupy the Panama Railroad station. This force's orders restricted its activity to the protection of the railroad and its property. When the consul requested that an additional force of 150 Marines be sent into the city to protect foreign residents, Admiral Steedman refused because he lacked consent from the local authorities. The next day, having obtained the consent of both contending factions, Steedman sent a force of 100 men into the city to protect the foreigners. This force withdrew on 11 May when open hostilities ceased. The detachment at the railroad station remained until 22 May 1873.

Sources: *Ellsworth* 46-47; *Offutt* 60-61.

*Case No. 29, 1873 — Colombia (Panama) (September)*
By 24 September 1873, it seemed certain that the same factions which had clashed in May would renew hostilities.[9] The Panamanian Governor notified the US consul that his government was no longer able to protect the Panama Railroad as guaranteed by the 1846 Treaty.[10] Under these circumstances, Admiral Almy landed 130 men to occupy the railroad station, reinforcing this party with another 60 men during the night. These troops reassured the foreign residents and secured safe transit of the isthmus for the passengers, freight, and specie carried by four steamship lines, two of which were not American-owned. American forces boarded trains as necessary to ensure this vital connection between the Atlantic and Pacific Oceans. Hostilities ended on 6 October, and two days later all American forces withdrew, save for a detail of 30 men which remained to guard the railroad station for several more days.

Sources: *Ellsworth* 47-48; *Offutt* 61-62.

*Case No. 30, 1874 — Hawaii*
A dispute over accession to the throne of the Sandwich Islands led to rioting on 12 February 1874. In compliance with the request of the Hawaiian Minister of Foreign Affairs, Commander Belknap of the screw sloop USS Tuscarora landed a force of 150 officers and men. The force's mission was to protect not only the interests of American citizens, but also to help restore order. The American presence did dispel the disorderly crowds, and the inauguration of King David

proceeded without further incident. A portion of the U. S. forces withdrew on 16 February, and the remaining 33 men left on 20 February 1874. Subsequently, the Hawaiian Government extended a resolution of thanks for the American effort. This act was unsurprising as many consider King David to have owed his throne to the American intervention—Dowager Queen Emma having had such strong support that she may well have ascended otherwise.
Sources: *Ellsworth* 92; *Offutt* 62-64.

Case No. 31, 1876 — Mexico
General Gonzalez, leader of revolutionary forces, informed the U. S. consul at Matamoros, Mexico, that he intended to abandon that city because federal forces were approaching. There being no other civil authority, the consul requested that a small force from the screw sloop-of-war *USS Lackawanna* be landed to police Matamoros and protect foreign interests until Mexican authority could be restored. The force landed on 18 May 1876, and remained until after the arrival of the federal forces.
Sources: *Clark* 67-68; *Offutt* 64.

Case No. 32, Egypt — 1882
During the summer of 1882, trouble developed between the British and the Egyptians, and on 11 July 1882, the British bombarded Alexandria. As great fires raged in the city, mobs began looting and destroying what remained of it, while the Arabs sought to kill every Christian they could find. Scores of people were slaughtered. In an attempt to restore order, the British landed 1,100 men on 13 July.

Either that day or the following day the United States landed 70 Marines, 50 seamen and 6 officers to protect American interests. A portion of this force guarded the US consulate while the remainder, as well as a small detachment of Germans which had been landed to protect the German hospital, aided the British forces. One of the major tasks was to extinguish the many fires and capture the numerous incendiaries who roamed the streets.

Most of the Americans were recalled on 15 July, the remainder being withdrawn on 18 July, save for one detail of Marines that remained ashore until 24 July. Two of the three American vessels departed from Alexandria on 20 July, when the British reported that they had the city completely under control. The third vessel did not depart until 29 August.
Sources: *Ellsworth* 75; *Offutt* 65-66.

# Appendix I

*Case No. 33, 1885 — Colombia (Panama) (January)*
Early in 1885 a revolution in Panama threatened transit on the Panama Railroad. In January 1885, the President of Colombia announced that his provincial government was no longer capable of protecting the railroad property. At the request of the general superintendent and the US consul at Colon, Commander Clark of the screw gunboat USS *Alliance* landed 13 Marines to guard the railroad station on 18 January. They withdrew the following morning.
Sources: *Ellsworth* 48; *Offutt* 66-67.

*Case No. 34, 1885 — Colombia (Panama) (March)*
A more serious revolution than the one of January 1885 took place in Panama in March of that year. On 16 March 1885, insurgents led by Aizpuru captured Panama City, whereupon Colombian troops stationed at Colon marched to drive out the revolutionaries. In their absence from Colon, however, another revolutionary force under the leadership of Prestan took over that city. It was not until 1 April that the Colombian forces returned to Colon and defeated Prestan. By this time Aizpuru had reoccupied Panama City and succeeded in cutting off rail traffic; he controlled most of the city and the isthmus along the railroad line.

A force of seamen and Marines arrived in Colon, acting under the orders of Admiral Jouett, the commander of the US Atlantic Squadron. The first American landing force of 17 Marines went ashore 16 March 1885 to protect American interests after the Colombian forces had departed for Panama City, leaving the foreign residents of Colon without adequate protection. Later the same day an additional 13 men landed. Then again on 17 and 19 March 1885, more men went ashore.

On 30 March, a group of insurgents at Colon seized the American steamer Colon of the Pacific Mail Line. A small force from the wooden steamer USS *Galena* recaptured the ship and returned her to her owners on the same day. The following day, 31 March, a force of 140 seamen and Marines from the *Galena* landed to guard American property and fight the fires that were spreading over much of Colon. Unfortunately, most of the town could not be saved. At about the same time, a landing party went ashore at Panama City.

On 10 April 1885, Admiral Jouett sent a force to open the railroad line and occupy the cities of Colon and Matachin. The expeditionary force, included 750 seamen and Marines who had been sent from New York, landed at Colon in two sections on 11 and 15 April. As soon as the first section of the expeditionary force arrived it went to Panama City, and by the following day had restored the trains to service. The second section relieved the forces at Colon, while two more companies of Marines under Commander McCalla moved from Colon to Panama City.

When McCalla arrived in Panama City it was occupied by Aizpuru. Fearing that a battle between his forces and the national troops would destroy Panama City, McCalla, on 24 April, ordered up the garrison from Colon and the reserve battalion of Marines from the squadron to occupy most of the city. After arresting Aizpuru, he compelled him to sign an agreement that fighting should not take place in Panama City. No fighting ensued, but this is likely the result of a conference between the nationalist leaders, Aizpuru and Admiral Jouett, on 29 April, where Aizpuru and his forces capitulated. As the national authority of Colombia was reestablished, the American forces began to withdraw, the last Marines leaving the Isthmus on 25 May.

Sources: *Ellsworth* 48-51; *Offutt* 67-70.

*Case No. 35, 1888* — Korea
Unsettled political conditions in Korea kept American naval vessels in Korean territorial waters throughout 1888. One landing was made in June at the request of the US Minister to Korea who feared a disturbance in Seoul. A detachment of 25 seamen and Marines from the third USS *Essex*, a wooden screw steamer, landed at Chemulpo on 19 June and marched to the capital to protect American residents. On 30 June, when the city was again quiet, the American force withdrew.

Sources: *Clark* 68; *Ellsworth* 59; *Offutt* 71.

*Case No. 36, 1888–1889* — Samoa
In September 1888, there was a revolt in Samoa against the Government of Tamasese. Mataafa, leader of the opposition, proclaimed himself King and civil war ensued. The subsequent fighting endangered the lives and property of all foreign residents, the former especially in jeopardy considering the cannibalistic customs of some of the natives.

By November the situation had become so serious that the US consul requested that the commander of the gunboat USS *Nipsic*, which was then in the harbor at Apia, land a suitable force of Marines for the protection of American citizens and the US consulate. A landing party of 11 Marines went ashore on 14 November 1888, remaining until 20 March 1889. The Germans also made landings during the disturbance.

Sources: *Clark* 68-69; *Ellsworth* 146.

# Appendix I

*Case No. 37, 1889* — Hawaii
There was a revolution in progress in the Hawaiian Islands in 1889. By summer the situation had so declined that the American Minister feared for the safety of foreign residents and legations. Therefore, the second USS *Adams*, a wooden screw gunboat, landed a guard of Marines on 30 July 1889, to protect American interests. They were stationed at the American legation and returned aboard ship the following day.
Source: *Ellsworth* 92-93.

*Case No. 38, 1890* — Argentina
There was a revolution in the area around Buenos Aires in July 1890. A small detachment of Marines landed to protect the American consulate and the U. S. Minister's residence. They remained ashore until 30 July 1890.
Source: *Ellsworth* 13.

*Case No. 39, 1891* — Haiti (Navassa Island)
For several years the Navassa Phosphate Company, an American firm engaged in gathering guano from Navassa Island, suffered from labor troubles with its native workers. In the spring of 1891, those troubles expanded to threaten American lives. When the commander of the first USS *Kearsarge*, a screw sloop-of-war, reached the island, he determined that the situation demanded prompt action. He landed a detachment of Marines on 2 June to protect American lives and property. On 20 June, after most of the laborers had returned to work, the Marines returned to their ship.
Sources: *Clark* 69-70; *Ellsworth* 119; *Offutt* 71.

*Case No. 40, 1891* — Chile
In 1891, civil war broke out in Chile between the supporters of President Balmaceda and the Congressional party. After the Congressionalists captured the city of Valparaiso, they endangered the lives and property of foreign residents: even foreign legations and consulates were being treated with contempt. The American Minister, Patrick Egan, applied to Admiral George Brown for a suitable guard for the American consulate. On 28 August, Brown sent ashore 30 seamen and 18 Marines from the cruiser USS *San Francisco* and 36 seamen and 18 Marines from the fourth USS *Baltimore* (C-3) to protect the consulate and its refugees. These forces withdrew two days later.

Eventually the Congressionalists were victorious. They were also very resentful of the American intervention because US neutrality during the conflict had worked to the advantage of Balmaceda. They were especially irritated that the American Minister had given asylum to Balmaceda's supporters. Many incidents followed, including one in which two Americans were killed and 18 wounded. Finally, after lengthy negotiations, the governments of Chile and the US reached a peaceful settlement of their differences.

Sources: *Annual Report 1891*, at 158-59; Bemis 757-58; Ellsworth 16-20; Knox 326-27; Offutt 72.

*Case No. 41, 1893* — Hawaii
When Queen Liliuokalani informed her cabinet that she planned to promulgate a new autocratic constitution by royal edict, some of her ministers informed the prominent American residents of the islands. These Americans requested the support of the US Minister, John H. Stevens, and the protection of the US Navy. Stevens arranged to have a detachment from the fifth *USS Boston*, a protected cruiser, land at Honolulu on 16 January 1893, for the ostensible purpose of protecting American lives and property. Curious to their stated purpose, the Americans were not stationed near American property, but rather were located where they might most easily intimidate the Queen.

The American presence served its function and on 17 January, Liliuokalani's opponents deposed her and established a provisional government under the presidency of Sanford B. Dole. The provisional government requested that the United States assume the role of a protectorate over the islands. Mr. Stevens complied with the request and raised the American flag on 1 February. The *Boston* landed another detachment of Marines that same day, increasing the number of American forces in Honolulu to about 150 men. Subsequently, there was a change of administrations in Washington, with President Cleveland disavowing the actions of Mr. Stevens. On 1 April 1893, the American flag was hauled down and the landing force withdrew.

Sources: Baily 429-33; Ellsworth 93; Offutt 72-73.

*Case No. 42, 1894* — Brazil
On 6 September 1893, a large section of the Brazilian navy revolted against the Brazilian Government. Initially, the insurgents were quite successful and maintained close control over the harbor at Rio de Janeiro. During this period Admiral da Gama succeeded Admiral Mello as commander of the insurgent naval forces at Rio de Janeiro. Once in power, on 1 December 1893, da Gama vainly attempted to blockade the port. Since he was unsuccessful in

# Appendix I

maintaining a blockade, da Gama then sought to prevent vessels from going to the docks.

The United States had assembled a powerful squadron at Rio de Janeiro under the command of Rear Admiral Benham, and on 29 January 1894, one of these cruisers, the third USS *Detroit* (C-10), stood in toward the docks alongside several American steamers. The insurgents had forbade American vessels from going to the city piers. Benham advised the commanders of the American steamers that, since the insurgents lacked the status of belligerents, they were *ultra vires* in interfering with commerce. He announced that he would protect those American vessels which wished to go alongside the wharves. With this promise, a vessel moved toward the pier. When one of the insurgent gunboats suddenly fired at this American merchant vessel, Benham fired a shot which struck under the insurgent's bow. This shot was followed by another exchange, after which Benham advised the insurgents that he would sink their vessel if they fired again. There was no more firing and the American merchantmen unloaded without loss of life or property. Subsequently, the revolt failed.

Sources: *Knox* 327; 6 *Moore* 438-39; *Offutt* 74-75.

*Case No. 43, 1894 — Nicaragua*
The unsettled political conditions surrounding José Santos Zelaya's overthrow of President Roberto Sacasa in 1893 presented a further occasion for American intervention in Nicaragua. Once the lives and property of all foreigners residing in the country were in jeopardy, two American cruisers, the fourth USS Columbia (C-12) and the *USS Marblehead* (C-11), were stationed in Nicaraguan waters to lend aid in case of an emergency.

Early on the morning of 6 July 1894, the US consul at Bluefields requested that a force be landed for the protection of American interests. A detachment of Marines from the *Marblehead* landed the same day, and on 31 July, an additional landing party from the *Marblehead*, the Marine guard and a company of seamen from the *Columbia*, reinforced the original landing party. Both parties withdrew on 7 August.

Source: *Ellsworth* 122.

*Case No. 44, 1894–1896 — Korea*
Much of the fighting during the Sino-Japanese War took place on the Korean peninsula. The USS *Baltimore* (C-3) was instructed to proceed to Chemulpo, the port of Seoul, in order to watch developments and give assurance to American missionaries living in the area. On 23 July 1894, the US Minister at

Seoul sent telegrams requesting an armed guard to protect the legation. A force of 55 men landed and arrived in Seoul in two sections on 25 and 26 July. They reported that the situation in the capital was critical. The Marine force of 22 men remained until 26 September, when it was relieved by another detachment of 18 Marines. The latter force withdrew on 29 October, and four days later on 2 November 1894, the Marine guard of the second USS *Charleston* (C-2) landed.

Although the war between China and Japan ended in 1895, the legation guard remained. The force from the *Charleston* served until 25 March 1895, when a force from the USS *Detroit* (C-10) relieved them. After the force from the *Detroit* departed on 19 June, there was no guard until 11 October 1895, when the Marine guard from the gunboat USS *Yorktown* (PG-1) landed. On 29 November, a force of Marines from the first USS *Machias* (PG-5), a schooner-rigged gunboat, landed and the next day the *Yorktown* force withdrew. The *Machias* force remained ashore until 3 April 1896, when the United States ceased to maintain a legation guard at Seoul.

Sources: *Background* 53; *Ellsworth* 59-60; *Offutt* 75-76.

Case No. 45, 1894–1895 — China (Newchwang)
In October 1894, the third USS *Petrel* (PG-2), a fourth-rate gunboat, was dispatched to Newchwang (also known as Yingtze and Yenkow), China, in order to protect the city's foreign residents. Special problems arose because the city is located on the Liao River, which is closed to navigation from November until April by ice floes. Since it was necessary to remain there all winter, they beached the vessel and constructed a fortress around it large enough to include all the foreign residents.

It was reported that, although the American force never confronted hostile Chinese or the Japanese forces, its presence prevented the outbreak of rioting on several occasions, and strengthened the local governor's authority. The governor, the foreign consuls, and residents agreed that "Fort Petrel" had given them a significant advantage in their efforts to protect life and property.

The *Petrel* arrived at Newchwang on 12 November 1894, just as the winter freeze was setting in, and it departed with the spring thaw on 24 April 1895.

Source: *Offutt* 77-79.

Case No. 46, 1894–1895 — China (Tientsin)
A force of 51 Marines left the USS *Baltimore* (C-3) at Chefoo on 4 December 1894, and proceeded in the direction of Tientsin. They were to guard the US

## Appendix I

legation if rioting should erupt in Tientsin during the Sino-Japanese War. This precaution was taken in view of the rioting which had occurred in Peking on the approach of the Japanese army. The force reached the US gunboat *Monocacy* on 6 December, and remained alongside a Tientsin dock until the war ended. Germany, Great Britain, Russia, France, Italy and Spain also sent similar forces. The American force withdrew on 16 May 1895, six days after peace was declared.

Sources: *Ellsworth* 30-32; *Offutt* 76-77.

*Case No. 47, 1895 — Colombia (Panama)*
In March 1895, the US consul at Panama reported that a Mexican known as Garcia had landed in Colombia, at the border of Costa Rica, with the intention of capturing the town of Bocas del Toro. The second USS *Atlanta*, a protected cruiser, was dispatched from Colon, arriving on 7 March. Having conferred with Colombian authorities, Captain Cromwell of the *Atlanta* determined that the national forces had the situation under control and he stood offshore the following day.

Upon his return to the town late on the afternoon of 8 March 1895, Cromwell learned that Garcia's attack of the town during the day had met with defeat at the hands of the nationalists. Beaten but not dissuaded, Garcia threaten to return and ignite the town that night, leading the American consular agent at Bocas del Toro to request that a force be sent ashore for the protection of the consular agency and American property. Cromwell sought permission from the local governor who failed to respond. Still, Cromwell sent 70 men ashore that night to occupy the consulate and an American warehouse. (The governor, who was at the consulate when the landing force arrived, expressed his approval the following day.) The night passed without incident, and on 9 March, with assurance from local authorities that they could handle the problem, the force withdrew at noon that day.

Sources: *Ellsworth* 51-52; *Offutt* 79-81.

*Case No. 48, 1896 — Nicaragua*
When Zelaya's first term as President of Nicaragua expired in 1896, he forced his reelection, causing a new wave of political unrest. At Corinto, the locus of the disorder, the Nicaraguan commandant, after informing the American consul that his forces were inadequate to protect foreigners and their property, requested that the British and Americans land forces for the protection of their

nationals. Both countries followed this advice. The American landing party of 34 Marines and sailors went ashore on 2 May, and there remained until 4 May.
Source: *Ellsworth* 122-23.

*Case No. 49, 1898* — Nicaragua
The fighting between Zelaya and his political opponents continued, and in February 1898 there was another landing of American forces for the protection of the lives and property of American citizens. A party of 33 seamen and Marines went ashore at San Juan del Sur on 7 February. They remained until the following day when the commander of the Nicaraguan Government forces gave assurances that his forces were capable of protecting the foreign community.
Source: *Ellsworth* 123.

*Case No. 50, 1898* — Spain (Spanish-American War)
The Spanish-American War (21 April–10 December 1898) has been cited as a prime example of American intervention for humanitarian reasons. Clearly, the American people were aroused by reports of Spanish acts of inhumanity in Cuba. Most poignant were tales of the concentration camps. The camps were a response to the Spanish military authorities' conclusion in 1896 that it would be impossible to suppress the on-going revolution as long as the rebels received the aid of civilians throughout the country. Therefore, they ordered the populace placed in camps surrounded with barbed wire fences. Unfortunately, proper hygienic precautions were not observed and many thousands died. The American press reported numerous incidents of cruel and inhumane treatment. The "yellow" press in particular maintained that Spain was waging "uncivilized" war.

In his war message to the Congress on 11 April 1898, President McKinley summarized the reasons for US intervention as follows:

> First. In the cause of humanity and to put an end to the barbarities, bloodshed, starvation, and horrible miseries now existing there, and which the parties to the conflict are either unable or unwilling to stop or mitigate. It is no answer to say this is all in another country, belonging to another nation, and is therefore none of our business. It is specially our duty, for it is right at our door.

# Appendix I

Second. We owe it to our citizens in Cuba to afford them that protection and indemnity for life and property which no government there can or will afford, and to that end to terminate the conditions that deprive them of legal protection.

Third. The right to intervene may be justified by the very serious injury to the commerce, trade, and business of our people, and by the wanton destruction of property and devastation of the island.

Fourth, and which is of the utmost importance. The present condition of affairs in Cuba is a constant menace to our peace, and entails upon this Government an enormous expense. With such a conflict waged for years in an island so near us and with which our people have such trade and business relations; when the lives and liberty of our citizens are in constant danger and their property destroyed and themselves ruined; where our trading vessels are liable to seizure and are seized at our very door by war ships of a foreign nation, the expeditions of filibustering that we are powerless to prevent altogether, and the irritating questions and entanglements thus arising — all these and others that I need not mention, with the resulting strained relations, are a constant menace to our peace, and compel us to keep on a semiwar footing with a nation with which we are at peace.

Despite Spain's frantic, last-minute efforts to avoid it, the US Congress voted to declare war on 19 April. On 25 April, McKinley signed the resolution declaring war to have existed since 21 April 1898.

Sources: *Bailey* ch. 31; Message from the President to the Congress, [1898] *Foreign Rel. U. S.* 750, 757-58 (1901); 6 *Moore* 211-36.

### Case No. 51, 1898–1899 — China

At the end of the Sino-Japanese War, a movement against the "aggressive spirit of Western civilization" swept through China. Antiforeign feeling swelled so strongly that the diplomatic community in Peking became concerned for the safety of foreigners in the country. The US Minister to China requested that a force be landed to guard the legation in Peking and the consulate in Tientsin. On 4 November 1898, a force of 18 Marines landed and proceeded to Peking. Another landing party of 30 Marines went to Tientsin on 12 November. By the middle of the following March, conditions had improved significantly, and all Marines withdrew on 15 March 1899.

Source: *Ellsworth* 32-33.

## Forcible Protection of Nationals Abroad

*Case No. 52, 1899* — Nicaragua

On 4 February 1899, a new revolution led by General Juan P. Reyes flared in Nicaragua. President Zelaya requested that an American naval ship be sent to San Juan del Norte on 9 February. By this time the British consul had cabled his government requesting that a vessel be sent to San Juan and Bluefields.

When the second USS *Marietta* (PG-15), a schooner-rigged gunboat, arrived at San Juan del Norte on 12 February 1899, the revolutionaries were already in possession of the town. The situation grew tense when Reyes attempted to compel foreign merchants to pay custom charges and port dues to his agent. Consular agents of the United States, Great Britain, Norway and Sweden refused to sanction such payments. At the request of the foreign merchants, a force of about 17 Marines and sailors from the *Marietta* and a small force from a British vessel landed at San Juan del Norte. The revolution collapsed within a few days and the force from the *Marietta* reembarked on 5 March 1899.

By the end of March, however, there was again trouble over the payment of duties at San Juan and Bluefields. The Zelaya government was attempting to collect duties under threat of "action," this time from foreign merchants who had already paid duties to the insurgents under protest. Martial law was imposed. The cruiser USS *Detroit* was sent to Bluefields and soon thereafter a peaceful settlement was reached.

Sources: Clark 72; Ellsworth 123-24; [1899] *Foreign Rel. U. S.* 554, 560 (1901); Offutt 82-83.

*Case No. 53, 1899* — Samoa

A disturbance in the Samoan Islands over succession to the throne was the basis for American intervention for the protection of the US consulate and other American interests in the islands. The struggle was between the son of the former king, Malietoa Tanu, favored by the British and Americans, and Mataafa, the candidate preferred by the Germans.

When the fourth USS *Philadelphia* (C-4) reached Apia, Samoa, on 6 March 1899, the situation ashore was menacing. Indeed the British already had landed a force to protect their consulate. Rear Admiral Albert Kautz, commander of the Pacific Squadron, landed a force of 25 men from the cruiser *Philadelphia* on 13 March to protect the US consulate in view of the Mataafaistas' warlike preparations. A force of Marines landed to relieve the seamen the following day. The group of seamen, increased to 65 men, took over defensive positions outside Apia, with smaller parties being stationed inside the town. The Mataafa forces attacked on 15 March, and both the *Philadelphia* and the British cruiser *HMS Royalist* bombarded the hills behind the town. During the conflict, the American vessel boarded numerous refugees. Amidst scattered firing on 23 March, Malietoa was installed as King. British and American reinforcements landed on 24 March, bringing the total of the combined forces to 250 men.

On 1 April, a joint party of 60 Americans and 62 Britons, accompanied by four interpreters, two Mormon missionaries, and about 150 friendly natives, reconnoitered the island to plan a breaking up of one of Mataafa's camps near Vailele. In the engagement that followed, four seamen were killed, two of them American and two British. The wounded included two British and five American seamen. Subsequently, the British and American forces carried out reprisals against the hostile natives. Hostilities ceased on 13 May 1899, and two days later the Americans reembarked.

Sources: *Clark* 72; *Ellsworth* 146-49; *Knox* 369-71; *Offutt* 83-85.

*Case No. 54, 1900* — China (Boxer Rebellion)

The Boxer uprising of 1900 was by no means a sudden, unanticipated attack. Chinese resentment against foreign encroachment was longstanding, and there had been an increasing number of attacks on foreigners nearing the century's end. During the winter of 1898–1899, the legations of the European nations and the United States were compelled to call upon their respective governments for guards. These forces were largely withdrawn by the spring of 1899.

The Boxers were, in fact, only one of several patriotic groups especially resentful of foreign exploitation. The common goal of such groups was to wipe out "the barbarians" and their Christian converts. Eventually, they attracted the support of the Dowager Empress and the Imperial Army. Initially they confined their acts of pillage and murder to missionaries and other foreign residents located in outlying provinces, but by 1 June 1900, they were bold enough to attack the foreign legations in Peking.

The situation in Peking was critical. The United States force of 56 Marines sent ashore in May,[11] was inadequate. Much larger forces were needed. Between 24 June and 24 July 1900, 231 foreigners were killed. For a month all communication between Peking and the outside world was severed. The Western Powers and Japan agreed that the situation demanded a large interventionary force. While more than 15,000 American troops were ordered to China, only some 5,000 or 6,000 had arrived prior to Peking's capture in August 1900. Other nations also had increased their ranks gradually, so that by 8

August, a column of more than 19,000[12] soldiers began the advance from Tientsin[13] to Peking.

The relief expedition engaged the Chinese in a fierce battle near Peking on 13 August. On the following day the Allies entered the city and ended the siege. Negotiations between the Chinese and foreign representatives lasted for more than a year, and on 7 September 1901, the final protocol was signed. The withdrawal of foreign troops began ten days later.

Sources: *Bailey* 481-82; *Bemis* 486-87; *Ellsworth* 33-39; *Offutt* 85-89; *Spaulding* 390-92.

*Case No. 55, 1900–1941* — China (Peking)
In response to the US Legation's request for assistance at Peking after the outbreak of the Boxer Rebellion,[14] a force of 56 Marines from the *USS Oregon*, Battleship No. 3, and *USS Newark* (C-1), a protected cruiser, landed, arriving at Peking on 29 May 1900. After the rebellion ended, the United States decided to maintain a permanent guard of soldiers at the American legation. American officials justified this action under Articles VII and IX of the Boxer Protocol of 1901,[15] which had been negotiated after the Boxer Rebellion. The size of the guard was increased during times of trouble, as during the Chinese revolution which lasted from 11 October 1911 until 5 July 1912.

On 25 November 1941, President Roosevelt announced that the United States would withdraw all American troops from China, including the legation guard. However, the outbreak of war with Japan on 7 December 1941, somewhat delayed the implementation of this order.

Sources: *Ellsworth* 38-39; [1941] 5 *Foreign Rel. U. S.* 583, 589 (1956); *Offutt* 86, 89.

*Case No. 56, 1901* — Colombia (Panama)
Revolution swept Panama once again in 1901. By November the state of affairs was so precarious that the Governor advised Lieutenant Commander McCrea of the gunboat *USS Machias* (PG-5) that his forces could no longer assure the safety of Americans and their property or the free transit of the Isthmus. Thereupon, McCrea landed a force at Colon to occupy the property of the Panama Railroad on 20 November. Two days later another force of 248 men landed from the second *USS Iowa* (BB-4) at Panama City. These forces worked with British and French forces which also were present. Troops escorted all trains, and contending factions entered into agreements to assure the safety of passengers and property on the trains. On 29 November, about 300 American seamen and Marines and a detachment from the French cruiser *Le Suchet*

# Appendix I

occupied Colon. American forces began to reembark on 2 December, and by 4 December all of them had withdrawn.
Sources: *Ellsworth* 52-53; *Offutt* 89-92.

*Case No. 57, 1902 — Colombia (Panama) (April)*
During the Panamanian revolution of April 1902, the United States served as a neutral intermediary. The United States's services were varied. On 16 April, one section of a company of seamen from the *USS Machias* (PG-5) landed at Bocas del Toro to protect American residents and their property. On the night of 17 April, the insurgent Liberals and the Colombian Nationalists met on board the *Machias*, at which time all agreed that the Nationalist forces would surrender the city to Commander McCrea, who in turn would surrender it to the Liberals. Once this agreement was carried out on the 18th, the Americans withdrew to their ship, leaving a small guard of Marines to protect American property until the Liberals could guarantee its safety. With the arrival of more Nationalist troops on 20 April, the situation reversed itself and McCrea transferred the city back to the Colombian Nationalist authorities, maintaining the peace until they were established. All US forces withdrew on 22 April 1902.
Sources: *Ellsworth* 54-55; *Offutt* 92-93.

*Case No. 58, 1902 — Colombia (Panama) (September)*
Due to the continued activity of the revolutionary forces in Panama during late 1902 disturbances continued. By September the United States was compelled to intervene once again to restore and maintain free transit of the Isthmus. On 17 September, a detachment of seamen from the second *USS Cincinnati* (C-7) went ashore at Colon, while another force landed at Panama City. Together they were able to guard all the trains crossing the Isthmus. Reinforcements from the first *USS Panther* (AD-6), an auxiliary cruiser, and the *USS Wisconsin* (BB-9) landed on 23 and 30 September, respectively. All troops were present to protect the lives and property of Americans, and assist in maintaining rail traffic. By 12 November, the Nationalist forces having begun to make heavy gains over the rebels, the Colombian Government was able to assure the safety of American interests. On that date the Americans began to withdraw, and on 18 November 1902, the last Marine battalion embarked. A peace treaty between the opposing political parties was signed on board the battleship *Wisconsin* three days later.
Sources: *Ellsworth* 55-56; *Offutt* 94-96.

## Forcible Protection of Nationals Abroad

*Case No. 59, 1903 — Honduras*

The political unrest which beset Honduras in 1903 was the result of an effort by President Bonilla's political opponents, both within his own country and in Nicaragua, to oust his government, or at least discredit it, prior to the presidential election.

During this period of unrest, the United States stationed a squadron of five naval vessels in Honduran waters to protect American interests. At the request of the American consul at Puerto Cortés, a guard of 13 Marines landed on 23 March 1903 to guard the U. S. consulate in that city. The guard withdrew on 30 or 31 March. Another detachment of 30 Marines landed at Puerto Cortés to guard the steamship wharf on 24 March. They embarked on 26 March.

Source: *Ellsworth* 94-95.

*Case No. 60, 1903 — Dominican Republic*

A revolutionary outbreak occurred in the Dominican Republic during March and April 1903. The cruiser *USS Atlanta* was dispatched to Santo Domingo City to protect US interests during the insurrection. The vessel arrived on 30 March, and two days later a party of 29 Marines went ashore. The detachment was quartered in the house of the American consul general. Its presence was intended to prevent unnecessary bloodshed. The revolution soon ended and the Marines returned to the ship on 21 April 1903.

Sources: *Clark* 73; *Ellsworth* 66; *Offutt* 96.

*Case No. 61, 1903 — Syria*

Both the Moslem and Christian communities experienced difficulties in Syria in September 1903. Two American vessels, the second *USS Brooklyn* (CA-3), a heavy cruiser, and the cruiser *USS San Francisco*, were in the harbor of Beirut at the time. Admiral Cotton of the *Brooklyn*, believing an uprising likely, prepared to land a force to protect the US consulate. The need for the force that Cotton contemplated did not arise, but at the request of the American consul a guard of Marines and a few sailors did land on 7 September 1903, remaining ashore five days.

Source: *Ellsworth* 155.

*Case No. 62, 1903-1914 — Panama*

It is unclear whether the United States landed troops in Panama during the revolution of 1903 more to protect the lives and property of its citizens, or to

# Appendix I

encourage the on-going revolution. However, there is no doubt that the United States welcomed the change of governments, having had its treaty proposal for the construction of a Panamanian canal rejected by the Colombian Senate in August 1903.

By the autumn of 1903, the United States anticipated a revolution. The Navy Department instructed its ships to keep in readiness. The revolution which began on 3 November was successful. On that day, the rebels captured the 500 Colombian troops who landed at Colon and sent them by special train to Panama. The Colombians, so outraged at this use of the American-controlled railway to aid the revolutionaries, notified the US consul on 4 November that, if the two generals who were in charge of those troops were not released by 2 P.M., the Colombians would bombard Colon and kill every American citizen in the town. Just prior to the appointed hour, 42 men were landed with instructions to occupy a stone building owned by the railroad. Many Americans sought refuge there, while others boarded two steamers made available for their protection. Although it seemed certain that the Colombian troops would attack, their commander, Colonel Torres, changed his mind and offered to withdraw his troops if the American landing party were reembarked. The Americans consented and returned to their ship.

On the following morning, 5 November, when it was discovered that the Colombians had not withdrawn as far as had been promised, the US force again went ashore. The American commander protested the breach of the agreement, asserting the United States's neutrality and stressing that its only interests were protecting American citizens and maintaining rail traffic across the Isthmus. With effort, officials of the new Panamanian Government convinced Torres to withdraw his troops. During his preparations, a second force of Marines landed. The first landing party returned to their ship and the newly-arrived force reembarked the next day, 6 November.

Marines were stationed on the Isthmus almost continuously from 4 November 1903 to 21 January 1914 in order to protect American interests, especially the construction of the Panama Canal.

Sources: *Background* 54; *Ellsworth* 134-36; *Knox* 374-76; *Offutt* 96-99.

*Case No. 63, 1904 — Dominican Republic*
When revolution erupted in the Dominican Republic in 1904, Commander Dillingham of the USS *Detroit* (C-10) arrived with orders to negotiate a peaceful settlement, and to protect Americans and their property. Although

there is scant proof, it seems that Dillingham also was told to support the incumbent regime as much as possible.

Upon his arrival at Puerto Plata on 2 January, Dillingham discovered that a British vessel was already present. Small detachments from both ships went ashore to prevent any fighting in the city. After an engagement just outside the city ended in defeat for the rebels, they quickly retreated from Puerto Plata.

On 11 February, the American Clyde Line steamer *New York*, was unloading cargo at Santo Domingo when the insurgents fired upon her. Two American naval vessels were present. While one of them opened fire on the rebels, detachments from both ships gave chase. They secured a written pledge from the rebels that they would not further molest the *New York*, after which the Americans returned to their ships.

It was largely through the presence of the American naval vessels and the offers of diplomatic offices by the naval commanders that the contending factions reached settlement. The peace conference terminating the revolt was held on board the *Detroit* in June.

Sources: *Clark* 73-74; *Ellsworth* 66-69; *Knox* 376; *Offutt* 99-100; *Annual Report 1904*, at 540.

## Case No. 64, 1904–1905 — Korea

On 5 January 1904, a force of 102 Marines landed in Korea and proceeded to Seoul, where they established a guard for the American legation during the Russo-Japanese War. The force returned aboard ship 11 November 1905, some two months after the peace treaty had been signed.

Source: *Ellsworth* 60.

## Case No. 65, 1904 — Morocco

In 1904 the United States intervened upon learning that a bandit, Raisuli, had kidnapped Ion Perdicaris, an alleged American citizen and his stepson, a British subject, from their villa three miles from Tangier on the evening of 18 May. Christians residing in the area feared that this event presaged a wave of hostilities against them.

When the American naval squadron, under Rear Admiral French E. Chadwick, arrived in Tangier, the Admiral and the American consul general met with the Minister of Foreign Affairs for Morocco. Since the situation remained tense, three or four Marines landed on 30 May to protect the consulate. On 22 June, Secretary of State Hay, at the direction of President Roosevelt, sent a telegram to the consul advising that the US Government "wants

Perdicaris alive or Raisuli dead." Subsequently it was discovered that Roosevelt knew that Perdicaris was not an American citizen.

Raisuli released the hostages upon payment of a ransom. The Marines withdrew to their ship on 26 June 1904.

Sources: *Bemis* 576; *Ellsworth* 8; [1904] *Foreign Rel. U. S.* 503 (1905).

*Case No. 66, 1904 — Panama*

In 1904 an insurrectionary movement in Panama posed a threat to Americans and their property. On 17 November, the force of Marines that was sent to Ancon, Panama, occupied several houses, thereby inserting themselves in a strategic position should there be serious rioting. Their protection did not become necessary because the revolt collapsed, and the Marines withdrew without incident on 24 November.

Source: *Offutt* 101-02.

*Case No. 67, 1905 — Dominican Republic*

In 1905, while the patrol yacht *USS Scorpion* (PY-3) was anchored in the river off Santo Domingo, her commander, Lieutenant Commander Hilary P. Jones, went ashore alone and unarmed, to quiet the unruly crowd which had threatened the life of the Dominican President and the American Minister. The crowd acted in response to a false rumor that an armed force of American seamen was about to seize the city.

Source: *Knox* 376-77.

*Case No. 68, 1906–1909 — Cuba*

Immediately following Thomas Estrade Palma's election as President of the Republic of Cuba in August 1906, his political opponents revolted against his government. In this moment of turmoil Palma requested that the United States send warships to Havana and Cienfuegos in order to protect the lives and property of foreign residents.[16] President Roosevelt sent Secretary of War Taft to Cuba. By 29 September, he had established a provisional government under the authority of the American President.

On 13 September, the American chargé d'affaires at Havana ordered American forces to land at Havana and Cienfuegos as rioting seemed imminent and he feared that American interests and property might be endangered. The 120 seamen and Marines who landed at Havana withdrew the next day at the order of President Roosevelt. The situation at Cienfuegos being more serious, the force landed and there remained, being reinforced on 24 September. Their mission was to guard American sugar plantations. These men returned to their ships when a larger force arrived on 30 September.

The Marines remained active throughout the early stage of the crisis. The Marine forces serving in Cuba in 1906 numbered 2,892 men. On 1 November 1906, all the Marines, save for one regiment, withdrew and army troops assumed their functions.

The US Army then played the main role in this intervention in Cuba. A force of 5,394 men, designated as the Army of Cuba Pacification, was sent to Cuba in October 1906. These men patrolled the island and worked with the local authorities. The presence of this force effectively restored the peace. The force remained until 23 January 1909.

Sources: *Background* 54; Ellsworth 62; 2 Hackworth 327; Knox 377; Offutt 102-03; Spaulding 401-02.

*Case No. 69, 1907 — Honduras*

American naval vessels were sent to the eastern coast of Central America for the protection of American interests when Honduras and Nicaragua went to war in 1907. The *USS Marietta* (PG-15) arrived at Trujillo, Honduras, on 18 March, and discovered that the town, occupied by Nicaraguan troops, was likely to be attacked by the Hondurans at any moment. A force of 10 men from the gunboat *Marietta* went ashore to protect American interests, including the consulate. The commanding officer of the *Marietta* instructed the ensign in command of the guard "to extend protection to the citizens of other neutral powers if asked to do so by their consular representatives." The Nicaraguan general, Estrada, was advised of the detail's assignment and assured of its neutrality.

Another force from the *Marietta* landed at Ceiba on the same day. On 26 March, a somewhat larger detachment landed at Puerto Cortés and proceeded to San Pedro on 5 April, where the men served as a guard for American interests. On 10 April, reinforcements from the *USS Paducah* (No. 18), were sent to Trujillo and Ceiba and a small party landed at Puerto Cortés. Finally, on 18 April, a body of Marines went to Laguna.

All of these forces withdrew by 21 May, except for the Marines at Laguna, who remained until 23 May. On that date they removed to Cholma, where they were stationed for the protection of foreign property until 8 June 1907.

Sources: Ellsworth 95-96; 2 Hackworth 328; Offutt 103-04.

# Appendix I

*Case No. 70*, 1910 — Nicaragua

The armed revolt led by General Juan J. Estrada against José Madriz, President of Nicaragua, which began about the time of Madriz's inauguration on 21 December 1909, alarmed the American residents of Bluefields, and provided the basis for American intervention in Nicaragua.

The Estrada forces controlled Bluefields, where numerous foreigners resided. The gunboats USS *Paducah* (No. 18) and USS *Dubuque* (No. 17) were at anchor off Bluefields during this period of unrest. When the Nicaraguan gunboat *Maximo Jeraz* arrived at the city on 16 May 1910, the commander of the *Paducah*, W. W. Gilmer, issued a proclamation advising both factions that no fighting would be tolerated within Bluefield's city limits. (His objective was to safeguard the lives and property of foreign residents and other noncombatants.) In pursuit of calm, he further advised both factions that no more than 100 armed men would be allowed in Bluefields; the number sufficient to police and preserve order. Finally, he warned that the United States would not allow bombardment of the city, since such destruction would not serve any military end.

On 18 May, Gilmer landed a force of 100 men to enforce his decree. He instructed them to use "every effort to maintain peace and order, resorting to force only in the case of absolute necessity." This landing party being considered inadequate, Gilmer sent the *Dubuque* to Colon, Panama, on 27 May, to embark another 206 Marines. The vessel returned to Bluefields on 30 May, and Gilmer landed the newly arrived Marines the following day. All of the forces reembarked on 5 June 1910.

There was one more landing during the 1910 crisis. On 9 August 1910, a force of 29 men landed at Bluefields and remained on shore until 4 September 1910.

Although Gilmer was instructed to maintain US neutrality and is considered to have followed orders, the Madriz faction protested bitterly to the United States about the American involvement. In Madriz's opinion Gilmer's actions at Bluefields clearly helped the Estrada forces to maintain control over the city.

Sources: *Clark* 75-77; *Ellsworth* 124-25; 2 *Hackworth* 328; *Offutt* 104-07.

*Case No. 71*, 1911 — Honduras

The United States, Great Britain and Germany made landings in Honduras following its revolutionary disturbances that began on 22 July 1910. The uprising was so severe that on 3 November, the President of Honduras, Miguel Dávila, requested American assistance for the protection of foreigners at Amapala. In accord with this request, the unarmored protected cruiser USS

*Tacoma* (CL-20) and the gunboat USS *Marietta* (PG15) were dispatched to Honduras.

On 26 January 1911, the *Tacoma* arrived at Puerto Cortés and landed a force of 60 men. By this time, the threat to foreigners had been manifested by the death of one American noncombatant during the capture of Ceiba the night before. The commander of the *Tacoma*, learning that the insurgents were marching toward Puerto Cortés, and anxious to prevent any fighting within the city, issued an order prohibiting hostilities within the city limits. He warned both factions that he would forcibly enforce the prohibition. To the commander of the Government troops which occupied Puerto Cortés, he advised that if a superior revolutionary force should appear, the commander was expected to surrender the town or wage battle outside. On 28 January, the *Marietta* and the British second-class protected cruiser, HMS *Brilliant*, arrived to enforce these policies.

The United States was successful in preventing much loss of life and property through the establishment of neutral zones, and the peaceful transfer of towns between factions. On 31 January, the Government forces evacuated Puerto Cortés, leaving it under the control of the combined (British and American) forces, who then allowed General Christmas, leader of the revolutionary forces, to occupy the town on 1 February. A joint force of 72 American and British seamen went by train to San Pedro, where they executed a similar transfer of San Pedro to the insurgents. Once guards were aboard on all trains in the disturbed area, peace was soon restored. It is not clear exactly how long American forces remained ashore, but it appears that most of them withdrew 1 February 1911, the day that the *Marietta* sailed from Puerto Cortés.

On 28 January 1911, President Dávila requested American intervention in order to terminate the war. The United States, offering mediation, sent a special commissioner, Thomas C. Dawson, to arrange the terms of a peaceful settlement. Conferences were held on board the *Tacoma*, the final agreement being reached on 4 March.

Sources: *Annual Report 1911*, at 99; *Clark* 77-78; *Offutt* 107-09.

# Appendix I

*Author's Note*
*Incidents Related to the Chinese Revolution of 1911*
*and the Establishment of the Chinese Republic:*
Case Nos. 72-84; 87-88; 90-91; 96-97; 100; 106;
108-111; 113-116; 118-120; 122; 124-126;
128-130; 132; 134-136; 138-145

The Chinese revolution of 1911 against the Manchu Dynasty resulted from widespread mistrust among the Chinese people of the Central Government and a fear that China was about to be divided among foreign powers. More specifically, the people were concerned about the Government's strong stand with regard to the construction and control of the main railroad lines in the provinces, the conclusion of foreign loans, and the refusal of Government officials to convene an extra session of the National Assembly to discuss the budget and loans. In short, the Government appeared insensitive to popular demands.

Open revolt broke out in September 1911, and by year's end the revolutionary military leaders had established a new government in southern China and the Yangzte provinces. The revolutionary government convened a new national assembly whose members unanimously elected Dr. Sun Yat-sen Provisional President of the Republic of China on 29 December 1911. At the end of the year Yüan Shinkai, commander of the Manchu forces, agreed to an armistice and entered into negotiations with the republican leaders. The emperor abdicated on 12 February 1912. Subsequently, Sun Yat-sen resigned the presidency and Yüan was elected in his place. The Nanking Parliament promulgated a provisional constitution in March 1912, and in April the government was transferred to Peking.

Revolutionary disturbances threatening foreign nationals and their property began in 1911 and continued throughout most of the decade. Outbreaks of violence intensified in 1920, and reached a climax in 1927.

Sources: *Dep't of State* 7-8; [1912] *Foreign Rel. U. S.* 46-48 (1919).

*Case No. 72*, 1911 — China (Wuchang)
On 11 October 1911, the day before the revolutionaries seized Wuchang, a landing party of 11 armed men, accompanied by the American consul general, attempted to go ashore to evacuate some American missionaries. Opposing soldiers on the shore, however, initially prevented them from landing. When they did land on 11 October, a Chinese rebel officer informed them that

neither ingress nor egress would be permitted, but that all foreigners would be protected. The force then returned aboard ship.

Source: *Clark* 83.

*Case No. 73*, 1911–1912 — China (Peking)

The disorder of the Chinese revolution of 1911 caused the US to reinforce the guard at its legation in Peking with several companies of Marines from 11 October 1911 until 5 July 1912. On 15 October 1911, the force numbered 127 men, 10 days later the total was 220. The American Minister at Peking requested a further increase, and on 2 December 1911 another 100 men were landed, bringing the total to 320.

Early in 1912 the US became concerned that Peking's railway link with the sea might be severed. Therefore, the commanding general of the Philippine Division was ordered to dispatch more than 500 men from the Philippines and make them available according to the wishes of the American Minister at Peking. Many of these troops had arrived at Wuhu and Nanking by 21 January. On 3 March, the American Minister requested that they be sent to Peking, shortly thereafter they arrived. By 6 March, the American Minister had telegraphed for additional troops.

On 8 March, a company of Marines was dispatched from Taku to Peking to relieve the army troops in that city.17 About 11 March, after the disturbances in Taku had quieted, the remaining company of Marines stationed in that city were ordered to Peking to relieve another detachment of troops.18 This action brought the total number of Marines in Peking to about 500.

Around 27 April, the American force in Peking was reduced by about two companies, but this condition did not last long. By 22 May 1912, the American Minister at Peking had requested that the former force of 500 men be reestablished, since general uneasiness prevailed in the city. The next day two companies of expeditionary troops were dispatched from Manila to Peking.

Sources: *Clark* 84-86; *Offutt* 89.

*Case No. 74*, 1911 — China (Hankow)

On 13 October 1911, the US chargé d'affaires at Peking reported that the native population of Hankow had been engulfed by the revolution, the most serious outbreak until that time. On the same day a force of 10 men went ashore at Hankow to guard the works of the Standard Oil Company. One among this number stood guard at the US consulate.

Sources: *Clark* 83; [1912] *Foreign Rel. U. S.* 49 (1919).

# Appendix I

*Case No. 75, 1911 — China (Foochow)*
A landing party went ashore at Foochow on 7 November 1911, to protect the US consulate and the property of American citizens.

Source: *Clark* 83.

*Case No. 76, 1911 — China (Nanking)*
On 7 November 1911, a force of 11 unarmed men went ashore at Nanking and proceeded to the US consulate; another 30 men remained at the waterfront. The entire force withdrew shortly after landing.

On 16 November 1911, an unarmed guard was stationed at the American consulate in Nanking. The guard, whose presence was necessitated by unsettled conditions, remained until the American citizens had been evacuated from the city.

Source: *Clark* 83.

*Case No. 77, 1911 — China (Woosung)*
Guards were sent to Woosung to protect the American Cable Company's cable hut around 7 November 1911.

Source: *Clark* 83.

*Case No. 78, 1911 — China (Chinkiang)*
Two American landings occurred at Chinkiang on 9 November 1911. First, the USS *Decatur* (DD-5) landed one section of infantry, and, second, the USS *New Orleans*, a protected cruiser, landed a force for the protection of the US consulate and American citizens and their property.

Source: *Clark* 83.

*Case No. 79, 1911 — China (Wuhu)*
Both the gunboat USS Helena and the supply ship USS *Supply* were at Wuhu about 17 November 1911. The Supply landed a force as a precautionary measure because, even though there was no disorder, it was reported that there were many robbers in the area. Protection was extended to all foreigners. The force withdrew on 22 November 1911.

Source: *Clark* 84.

*Forcible Protection of Nationals Abroad*

*Case No. 80, 1911–1912 — China (Taku)*
At the request of the American Minister, at Peking, the fourth USS *Saratoga* (CA-2) left Shanghai on 29 November 1911 for Taku, where one company of Marines landed for the protection of the Methodist Mission.

On 4 March 1912, the American Minister telegraphed the Commander of the Asiatic Fleet:

> The situation in north China is very grave, practically no government. Mutinous troops have been rioting in Peking, Tientsin and elsewhere. Local authorities [in] Tientsin19 have requested foreign powers to police [the] city. Can you send a vessel to Taku?

Two days later the Asiatic Commander reported to the Secretary of the Navy that two companies of Marines on board the second USS *Cincinnati* (C-7) and *U.S.S. Abarenda* (AC-13) had been dispatched to Taku. The company on board the collier *Abarenda* remained in Taku until 8 March, when they were sent to Peking. By 11 March, the Taku disturbances had quieted freeing the remaining company of Marines for dispatch to Peking.[20]
Source: *Clark* 84-85.

*Case No. 81, 1911 — China (Yochow)*
One officer and 12 armed men landed in the vicinity of Yochow on 4 December 1911, to escort a group of missionaries to that city.
Source: *Clark* 84.

*Case No. 82, 1912 — China (Kiukiang)*
A landing force from the USS *Elcano* (PG-38) went ashore at Kiukiang on 7 March 1912, to protect concessions.
Source: *Clark* 85.

*Case No. 83, 1912 — China (Swatow)*
The second USS *Monterey* (BM-6), a monitor, landed a force at Swatow on 16 March 1912, to save a woman and some children who were endangered by fighting between government and revolutionary forces. The government forces allowed the Americans to extract them safely.

On 3 April 1912, another force of nine men landed at Swatow to guard the "Butterfield & Swire's residence," and the German consulate.
Source: *Clark* 86.

## Appendix I

*Case No. 84, 1912 — China (Nanking)*
The USS *Pompey* (AF-5), a torpedo boat tender, landed a force of men at Nanking on 12 April 1912, to protect American interests. They were withdrawn after a short time, even in advance of the order from the Commander-in-Chief of the Asiatic Fleet to do so. Their speedy withdrawal suggests that the perceived threat to American interests probably never materialized.
Source: *Clark* 86.

*Case No. 85, 1912 — Cuba*
In May 1912 there was a revolt of blacks in Cuba, organized by the "Independientes de Color." The uprising quickly became more serious than the Cuban Government wished to admit. When Cuban officials seemed unable to control the situation, the United States asserted its right to intervene for the maintenance of order, pursuant to Article III of the 1903 Treaty.[21] The American Government expressed concern for the safety of the lives and property of the large number of US citizens residing in Cuba.

The disturbances centered in the far eastern part of the island near the US Naval Station at Guantánamo Bay, to which the United States had sent about 2,000 additional men by the end of May. While many of them remained on the base, there were several landings during the crisis. Cuban President José Miguel Gómez requested that there be no landings, even for the protection of American citizens, because he felt that such action by the United States would tend to discredit his government at home and abroad. Nevertheless, four companies of Marines were sent into the province of Oriente on 5 June, despite the fact that there had not yet been any injury to Americans or their property. Faced with the *fait accompli,* Gómez left the American forces to protect foreign property interests and then withdrew his own troops so that they could be used against the rebels. At the request of the British chargé d'affaires in Washington, the US Department of State requested that "such American protection as might be available to American lives and property should likewise be extended to British subjects."

There also were two landings at Nipe Bay, Cuba. On 10 June 1912, a force of 28 Marines landed there and then traveled by rail to the site of the Spanish-American Iron Works at Woodfred, Cuba, to protect American property. Two days later, a similar detachment landed to relieve the first force, which then reembarked. This second detachment remained until 14 July. One other detachment went ashore on 19 June 1912, at El Cuero, Cuba, where it remained until 1 July. Apparently all the American forces on Cuban territory withdrew near the middle of July 1912.

The Cuban Government began to assert its reign in the area by the end of June. The gradual withdrawal of the American reinforcements from the United States base at Guantánamo Bay was under way by the middle of July, the last of them reembarking 5 August 1912.

Sources: *Bailey* 499-500; *Clark* 98-101; *Ellsworth* 62-63; 2 *Hackworth* 328-29; *Offutt* 109-11.

*Case No. 86, 1912–1925 — Nicaragua*
The revolt of 1912, one of the most serious in the history of Nicaragua, was led by the Minister of War, General Luis Mena, who had obtained control over most of the country's military supplies before the uprising. Therefore, the rebellion, which actually began 29 July 1912, when Mena attempted to seize the capital city, Managua, was especially hard fought.

As the revolt progressed, widespread fear among foreigners for the safety of their lives and property grew. The British consul general asked the US Minister to Nicaragua for US assistance in protecting his nationals. Requests for protection also came from two American corporations, one of which already had suffered property losses at the hands of the insurgents. When these facts were presented to the Nicaraguan Government, the Minister of Foreign Affairs replied to the US Minister that his government was fully occupied with the revolution and would be unable to afford protection to foreigners. He requested that the United States land forces to protect the lives and property of its citizens, and, indeed, to extend protection to all the inhabitants of the country.

On 3 August 1912, the first American force of 102 men landed at Corinto and traveled to Managua to guard the American legation and protect American interests. As the situation worsened, there were many more landings.[22] By the time the last ship arrived on 14 September, 2,350 seamen and Marines were ashore in Nicaragua. In the words of the acting Secretary of State, Huntington Wilson, the United States intended "to take the necessary measures for an adequate legation guard at Managua, to keep open communications, and to protect American life and property," as well as "to contribute its influence in all appropriate ways to the restoration of lawful and orderly government in order that Nicaragua may resume its program of reforms unhampered by the vicious elements who would restore the methods of Zelaya." Admiral Sutherland reported that his forces had extended their protection not only to Americans and other foreigners, but also to "all reputable Nicaraguans."

## Appendix I

Apparently, the American presence did help curtail what might have been a more lengthy struggle. Most of the fighting ended early in November, and the American force had been largely withdrawn by the time that the new president was elected on 14 November. Two battalions were withdrawn on 21 November and the last battalion on 13 January 1913. However, on 9 January 1913, a legation guard of 105 men was detailed for duty at Managua. This guard was maintained at the legation until 3 August 1925.[23]

Sources: *Clark* 119-22; *Ellsworth* 125-27; 2 *Hackworth* 331; *Offutt* 111-17.

*Case No. 87, 1912* — China (Kentucky Island)
During the four years that he ruled, Yüan was able to delay the further disintegration of China. He faced formidable opposition, however. On several occasions the United States found it necessary to land forces to protect American lives and property.[24] When Yüan died on 6 June 1916, he was succeeded by Li Yüan-hung, who was deposed during World War I.

On 24 August 1912, Admiral Nicholson ordered one company of Marines from the submarine tender USS *Rainbow* (AS-7) to go ashore on Kentucky Island to protect American lives and property. They withdrew two days later.

Source: *Ellsworth* 40-41.

*Case No. 88, 1912* — China (Camp Nicholson)
On 26 August 1912, Admiral Nicholson deemed it necessary to land a force of Marines at Camp Nicholson for the protection of American lives and property during a disturbance. The landing party remained ashore until 30 August.

Source: *Ellsworth* 41.

*Case No. 89, 1912* — Turkey
Rioting broke out in the Turkish capital in the autumn of 1912 as the victorious Balkan troops began to push the Turks back to Constantinople. These events endangered the lives and property of all Christians. The Diplomatic Corps decided to land about 2,500 men and 26 guns to protect foreign residents and their interests. Among troops who landed on 18 November 1912, were detachments from British, French, German, Russian and Italian warships. There was also a small detail from the USS *Scorpion* (PY-3), which landed to guard the US legation. According to a communication of the Navy Department to the Secretary of State, the men from the *Scorpion* reembarked on 3 December 1912.

Sources: [1912] *Foreign Rel. U. S.* 1352, 1353 (1919); *Offutt* 109 n. 112.

*Case No. 90, 1913* — China (Shanghai)
Civil war in China continued. When the southern forces attacked the arsenal at Shanghai on 28 July 1913, the naval forces of several countries, including the United States, landed troops for the protection of foreign citizens and their property. Vice Admiral Nawa of the Imperial Japanese Navy was the senior officer present. By 12 August, most of the members of the landing parties had returned to their ships without ever having engaged either southern or northern forces.
Source: *Clark* 87.

*Case No. 91, 1913* — China (Chapei)
Fighting between the Chinese and the Indians at Chapei endangered the lives and property of foreign residents. After the Chinese drove out the Indian police, who were protecting the Indian settlement, the foreign consuls on 29 July 1913, warned both sides that they would have to cease firing into and over the settlements. On the next day, the consuls called forth a force of Marines to preserve order in the city. On the same day, the Chinese Minister of Foreign Affairs expressed his appreciation to the Minister in Pehng, advising him that the American presence in Chapei had rendered protection to all the people in that locality. The American force withdrew 17 August 1913.
Source: *Clark* 86.

*Case No. 92, 1913* — Mexico
In 1913 Mexico underwent another period of political unrest, accompanied by considerable fighting among various factions. The United States had warned American citizens to leave the country, but unfortunately not all of them followed this advice. The situation became so severe by September that a rescue operation was deemed necessary to assist the stragglers who now wished to depart.

On 5 September 1913, the USS *Buffalo*, an auxiliary cruiser, landed four Marines and an American consular agent at Ciaris Estero. These men proceeded to the Richardson Construction Company's headquarters in the Yaqui Valley to escort to the coast those Americans and foreigners who wished to leave. Twelve Americans and 83 others availed themselves of the opportunity. The landing party and the refugees returned to the ship two days later.
Source: *Ellsworth* 115-16.

## Appendix I

*Case No. 93, 1914* — Haiti (January)
The United States landed forces in Haiti to protect Americans and their property during a period of political unrest that led to the abdication of President Oreste on 27 January 1914, as General Zamor came to power. In three separate landings on 27-29 January, a total of 120 seamen and Marines went ashore at Port-au-Prince to guard the U.S. consulate and protect foreign interests. At the same time the French and Germans landed 15 and 35 men, respectively. The French force was reinforced on 6 February. All of these international forces reembarked on 9 February, the day after General Zamor, the successful revolutionary leader, was elected President of Haiti.

A landing party of Marines from the composite gunboat USS *Wheeling* (PG-14) subsequently went ashore at Port-de-Paix, Haiti, on 16 February, to protect American and foreign interests. They remained ashore for six days.

Théodore, one of the minor rebel leaders who had been defeated, evacuated Cap-Haïtien on 20 February, leaving no force to maintain order in the town. At the request of the foreign consuls, who feared looting and widespread disorder, the commander of the *Wheeling* landed an armed force of 65 men for the protection of all foreigners and their property on the same day. On 21 February, the landing party returned aboard ship, save for a small guard of Marines who remained several days longer at the American consulate. Théodore and Zamor continued to fight, the former succeeding to the presidency in October 1914.
Sources: Clark 111-12; Ellsworth 88; Offutt 117-18; Rotberg ch. IV.

*Case No. 94, 1914* — Haiti (October)
The Zamor government, which came to power in Haiti in February 1914, found itself faced with revolution in October. The revolution began in the northern part of the country and quickly spread to the other regions. On 19 October 1914, the US Minister at Port-au-Prince reported that the commander of the cruiser USS *Tacoma* (CL-20) had landed an armed force of 117 men at Cap-Haïtien for the protection of foreigners and their property. Moreover, Zamor and his followers had been given refuge at the US consulate in that city. Reinforcements were sent to the city on 24 October, but they were withdrawn the same day. A portion of the original force at Cap-Haïtien, 24 men, returned aboard ship on 28 October, the others remaining ashore until 7 November.

By 29 October, the US Minister reported heavy fighting and looting and requested that naval vessels be sent for the protection of foreign interests. Accordingly, the third USS *Hancock* (AP-3), with an armed force of 800 Marines, was dispatched to the city, arriving there 30 October. The Department of State instructed the American Minister to land such Marines from this vessel as were necessary to protect life and property. He was informed that the USS *Kansas* (BB-21) had been dispatched to Port-au-Prince, and instructed that upon the arrival of that vessel he should make similar dispositions for the protection of life and property in Gonaïves and Saint-Marc. Apparently, no landings were necessary.

The French Minister at Port-au-Prince gave refuge to some of the cabinet members of the fallen government. Fearing a mob attack, he requested that the American Minister make arrangements to assist in the defense of the French legation should it become necessary. Thus, the American Minister called up a detail of signalmen from the transport *Hancock* and stationed them at the French legation on 2 November. Order finally was restored by 6 November.

Sources: *Clark* 112; *Ellsworth* 88-89; [1914] *Foreign Rel. U.S.* 354-57, 386 (1922); *Offutt* 118.

*Case No. 95, 1915–1934 — Haiti*

President Théodore was ousted by Vilburn Guillâume Sam in March 1915, the latter holding office only four months before a new revolution occurred. The forces of the revolution proved too strong for Sam and he sought refuge in the French legation. This action did not deter his opponents, who forcibly entered the legation on 28 July, seized Sam and dragged him into the street where they decapitated him.

On 9 July 1915, prior to Sam's death, the United States had sent ashore a landing party from the cruiser USS *Washington* (CA-11) at Cap-Haïtien to quell a disturbance in that city. While the *Washington* was en route to Port-au-Prince on 27 July, the commander of the vessel received word from the American Minister of the serious state of affairs in the capital. The *Washington* arrived at Port-au-Prince on 28 July, after Sam's execution. Two battalions of Marines, about 140 men, landed immediately to protect foreigners and their property. Admiral Caperton of the *Washington* found his force insufficient and called for reinforcements. Another 100 Marines landed at Port-au-Prince on 29 July to preserve order and protect legations. On the next day a party of Haitians attacked the American forces and killed two men. Thereupon, a force of 500 Marines was dispatched to Haiti, landing at Port-au-Prince in early August. With the addition of two more forces landed on 15 and 31 August, the total number ashore amounted to nearly 2,000 Marines. The American forces took no offensive action against the Haitians unless provoked. However, there were numerous confrontations with the Cacos, or hill bandits, who tried to cut off supplies and communications.

# Appendix I

On 12 August 1914, Haiti elected Dartiguenave its new president. United States forces remained in the country to assist in its stabilization. The program proved effective and a large portion of the American occupation forces were withdrawn in May 1916. American casualties in Haiti, from the time of the first landing in 1915 until October 1920, were 13 killed and 28 wounded. A force of about 500 Marines remained in Haiti until 15 August 1934, when President Franklin Roosevelt ordered their withdrawal.

Sources: Clark 112-13; Ellsworth 89-91; 2 Hackworth 329-30; Knox 380; Offutt 124-27; Rotberg ch. IV

*Case No. 96, 1916 — China (Nanking)*
A landing party of seamen from the USS *Quiros* (PG-40), a schooner-rigged composite gunboat, went ashore at Nanking on 29 March 1916 to quell a riot on the premises of the International Export Company. The seamen returned to their ship when the riot was under control.
Source: Clark 88.

*Case No. 97, 1916 — China (Swatow)*
A few Marines were stationed at the US consulate at Swatow during the night of 30 March 1916, to safeguard the chief of police, the Taoyin's family, and the assistant salt commissioner of Chacchowfu, all of whom had sought refuge there. A few Marines also were sent to the German consulate, the agreed meeting place of foreign residents in case of trouble. Although several Chinese were killed, the disorders were not as great as had been feared, there being only minor looting. The American force withdrew the following day.
Source: Clark 87-88.

*Case No. 98, 1916 — Dominican Republic*
In 1916 General Desiderio Arias, Dominican Secretary of War, launched a rebellion against the government of President Juan Isidro Jiménez, which thrust the Dominican Republic into a state of anarchy. Since an important objective of both factions was to gain control over Santo Domingo, much of the fighting took place in the capital city. The U.S. legation, being in the direct line of fire, was struck by shells several times. Thereupon, the American Minister requested that a naval force be sent for the protection of American citizens.

A force consisting of two companies of Marines (about 280 men) landed at Santo Domingo on 5 May 1916. By this time, the rebels had succeeded in impeaching Jiménez and were in control of the capital. There was widespread fighting, however, as the President's forces tried to regain the city. Some members of the first landing parties guarded the US legation, while others guarded the Haitian legation — where many foreigners had taken refuge. On 6 May, the American minister reported that the President's forces had been unable to take the city, and that the situation had become so chaotic that the American forces were preparing to occupy the capital and disarm the rebels. The United States soon landed another seven companies of Marines and the city was occupied without serious difficulty on 15 May 1916, the rebels having withdrawn to the interior to establish a new headquarters at Santiago.

Having quieted the capital, the Americans made plans for the pacification of the interior. Several landing parties of Marines were transferred from Puerto Plata and Santo Domingo to Monte Cristi. Another regiment of Marines from the United States landed at Monte Cristi on 21 June. Five days later, an expedition started toward Santiago. Fortunately, a peaceful settlement was negotiated before the Marines reached the city, enabling the American force to enter Santiago without opposition on 6 July. The peak strength of American occupation forces was three regiments, or approximately 3,000 men.

American occupation forces remained in the Dominican Republic until 17 September 1924. During this time 140 Marines were killed or died from disease, accident and other causes. Another 55 men were wounded in action.

Sources: *Clark* 109-10; *Ellsworth* 69-71; 2 *Hackworth* 331; *Knox* 380.

*Case No. 99, 1917–1922* — Cuba

In February 1917, there were disorders in Cuba arising from a dispute over the results of the presidential election of 1 November 1916. The Liberals maintained that their candidate had won, but the Conservatives, who were in power, contested the election and refused to surrender the offices. Rioting began on 11 February 1917, resulting in widespread looting and destruction of property, most American-owned. There was evidence of organized revolution in Camagüey and Santa Clara provinces.

From 12 February onward there were numerous landings in Cuba by American forces.[25] Most of the fighting had subsided by 20 May, the date of the inauguration. While the majority of the American forces had withdrawn by 24 May, on 4 June there were about 600 Marines and sailors in Cuba. The number was high because three additional regiments had landed after 24 May. On 28

*Appendix I*

August, the remaining forces withdrew with the exception of 220 men at Camagüey and 120 men at the US Naval Station at Guantánamo Bay. The force at Camagüey withdrew on 15 February 1922.

Sources: *Clark* 101-07; *Ellsworth* 63-64; 2 *Hackworth* 330; *Offutt* 133-37.

*Case No. 100, 1917 — China (Chungking)*
A landing party from an American gunboat went ashore at Chungking on 3 December 1917, to guard the US consulate during a period of political unrest. The guard remained for two days and two nights. British and Japanese guards also landed at the same time to guard their respective consulates during the crisis.

Source: 2 *Hackworth* 332.

*Case No. 101, 1918 — Soviet Union*
The Russian revolution of 1917 eventually brought turmoil to all parts of the Russian Empire. The effects of the overthrow of the Czarist Government by the Bolsheviks spread to the far eastern part of the country including Vladivostok, where the almost constant fighting between the Czech and Bolshevik forces exposed the foreign residents of Vladivostok to considerable danger.[26]

On 29 June 1918, the Czechs occupied the city and assumed complete control, arresting members of the Red Guard, Austrians and Germans. On the same day, the United States established a guard of 32 Marines at the American consulate. Britain and China also landed forces. Conditions in the city remained unstable, and on 6 July representatives of Japan, Great Britain, China, France and the Czechoslovak Army issued a proclamation stating that, while the authority of the Czechs still would be recognized, the Allied Forces assembled intended to take measures to defend the city against all dangers, both internal and external. The American consulate guard remained until 10 August 1918.

Sources: *Ellsworth* 141-42; 2 G. Kennan, *Soviet-American Relations, 1917–1920,* at ch. VI (1958).

*Case No. 102, 1918–1920 — Soviet Union*
In August 1918, the United States landed about 7,000 men at Vladivostok to assist in the city's occupation. Their mission was to enforce the proclamation of 6 July 1918,[27] and maintain order in Vladivostok. This force remained until January 1920.

Source: *Background* 55.

*Case No. 103, 1919* — Soviet Union

A landing party of 32 Marines from the USS *New Orleans*, a protected cruiser, went ashore at Tyntuke Bay, near Vladivostok, on 30 July 1919, to protect American interests during new disturbances. This force returned aboard ship 1 August 1919.

Source: *Ellsworth* 142.

*Case No. 104, 1919* — Honduras

During August and September 1919, there was much political unrest in Honduras and revolution loomed. On 8 September, a landing force from the USS *Cleveland* (C-19) went ashore at Puerto Cortés to protect the lives and property of Americans and other foreign residents. They cooperated with the forces of Honduras in maintaining order in a neutral zone, designated by the Military Commander of Puerto Cortés, which the armed forces of both factions were forbidden to enter. The revolutionary forces captured the towns of Puerto Cortés, La Curva and La Laguna on 11 September. There was no further fighting or disorder and the Americans began to return to their ship. The remainder of the force withdrew on 12 September 1919. Both factions agreed to a truce, and free elections were held in October. General Lopez Gutierrez, the revolutionary leader, was elected President with more than 75 percent of the votes.

Sources: *Clark* 114; [1919] 2 *Foreign Rel. U. S.* 377-95 (1934).

*Case No. 105, 1920–1922* — Soviet Union

The United States landed a force of 18 Marines on 16 February 1920, to guard the American radio station on Russian Island in the Bay of Vladivostok. A guard similar to this one was maintained until 19 November 1922.

Source: *Ellsworth* 143.

*Case No. 106, 1920* — China (Kiukiang)

On 14 March 1920, the commanding officers of the gunboats USS *Elcano* (PG-38) and *Samar* (PG-41), having consulted with the British consul, landed a force to quell a local riot at Kiukiang and protect lives. The force remained ashore about two hours.

Sources: *Clark* 88; 2 *Hackworth* 332.

# Appendix I

*Case No. 107, 1920 — Guatemala*

Civil war between the Government and Unionist forces caused the United States to intervene in Guatemala in 1920. Fearing a bombardment of Guatemala City and concerned about the threat both to the foreign legations and US property, the US Minister, on 9 April 1920, requested that the commander of the gunboat USS *Tacoma* (PG-32) (ex-CL-20) send a guard for the legation. On the same day the *Tacoma* landed a force of 40 men supplemented by an additional force of 50 men from the sixth USS *Niagara* (SP-136), an armed patrol yacht. The forces arrived at Guatemala City on 10 April. Both warring factions approved of the American presence. On 13 April, the *Tacoma* landed another force of 13 men at the request of the American consular agent to guard the cable station. This guard reembarked the next day. On 20 and 21 April, the United States withdrew 29 sailors, the others remaining ashore until 27 April 1920. Two naval vessels were stationed in Guatemalan waters for several days thereafter.

Sources: *Clark* 111; 2 *Hackworth* 331.

*Case No. 108, 1920 — China (Lakeside)*

The USS *Quiros* (PG-40) landed a force to guard the property of the American Mission at Lakeside, apparently church-owned property, on 25 June 1920. One American missionary was killed and property valued at about $1,500 was looted and destroyed. The force returned aboard ship two days later.

Source: *Clark* 89.

*Case No. 109, 1920 — China (Wuchow)*

The Kwantung forces attack of Wuchow in June 1920 endangered the lives of foreign residents. To protect them a force of six men landed on 26 June 1920. The men escorted the wife and child of Dr. Levell and three nurses, all of whom were associated with the Wuchow People's Mission Hospital, to a place of safety. Most of, if not all, of these five people were American citizens.

Source: *Clark* 89.

*Case No. 110, 1920 — China (Yochow)*

On 30 June 1920, the patrol commander of the first line destroyer USS *Upshur* (DD-144) reported his landing of a force to guard the American Mission Compound at Yochow. The mission was church-owned property.

Source: *Clark* 89.

*Case No. 111, 1920* — China (Tungchow)
At the request of the American Mission at Tungchow, a force of 12 Marines landed on 20 August 1920 to guard the mission for a few days.
Sources: *Clark* 89; 2 *Hackworth* 332.

*Case No. 112, 1922* — Nicaragua
In early 1922 political conditions in Nicaragua became unsettled, and the US legation at Managua required an increase in the Marine guard to counter anticipated disturbances. On 25 January 1922, a landing party of 31 Marines went ashore. A second party of 53 men reinforced the first group on 29 January. An additional force of 47 Marines landed on 8 February and proceeded to Managua. Apparently the situation improved because all but 40 of the 131 men returned aboard ship on 11 February.

A revolt actually broke out in May 1922. The legation guard played an important role in preventing loss of life as the rebels had contemplated destruction of Managua. The United States offered its good offices, enabling the rival parties to reach a peaceful settlement without bloodshed.
Source: *Ellsworth* 128.

*Case No. 113, 1922* — China (Peking)
A new phase of the civil war in northern China began on 28 April 1922, when fighting commenced near Machang between the Chang Tso-lin and Chihli forces. The fighting ended in June with the restoration of Li Yüan-hung to the presidency.[28]

At the commencement of the fighting, there were about 800 Americans living in and around Peking outside the legation quarter. Anticipating danger to American citizens and their property, a force of 156 seamen and Marines from the second USS *Albany* (CL-23) landed at Chinwangtao on 27 April 1922. When they arrived in Peking the following day, they were added to the legation guard, bringing its strength to more than 500 men. The force remained until 25 May 1922.
Sources: *Clark* 89; *Ellsworth* 41; [1922] 1 *Foreign Rel. U. S.* 681, 694-96 (1938).

*Case No. 114, 1922* — China (Shanghai)
On 5 May 1922, a battalion of Marines commanded by Captain Roy C. Swink landed from the USS *Huron* (CA-9) at Taku and proceeded to Shanghai to protect American interests. They remained there until 11 May 1922.
Source: *Ellsworth* 41.

## Appendix I

*Case No. 115, 1922 — China (Tientsin)*
The American Minister at Peking received reports on 4 May 1922, that the Chihli forces had won victories at Kuan and Machang and were within 20 miles of Tientsin. Fearing possible violence in the city, Admiral Strauss of the USS *Huron* landed about 150 Marines armed with machine guns at Tientsin the following day. The force withdrew on 15 May 1922.
Source: [1922] 1 *Foreign Rel. U. S.* 698-99, 705 (1938).

*Case No. 116, 1922 — China (Tungchow)*
Fearing possible violence from retreating Fengtien forces, the American Minister at Peking sent a detachment of Marines to Tungchow on 5 May 1922. Their mission was to protect American citizens and their property.
Sources: *Clark* 89; 2 *Hackworth* 332.

*Case No. 117, 1922 — Smyrna (Izmir, Turkey)*
During the war between Turkey and Greece in 1922, the United States found it necessary to intervene for the protection of American lives and property, including the consulate, at Smyrna. As the Turkish forces advanced and the Greeks withdrew, much of the city was burned and the US consulate was destroyed. A total of four naval vessels were dispatched to Smyrna and made landings. In three landings from three different vessels on 7, 8 and 9 September 1922, about 55 men went ashore. Both the Greek and Turkish authorities consented to the landings. The men withdrew in three groups on 13, 14 and 16 September. A fourth vessel landed a guard for the American consulate on 16 September. These men reembarked on 2 October, their ship departing Smyrna on 21 October 1922.
Sources: *Background* 56; *Clark* 129-30; 2 *Hackworth* 333.

*Case No. 118, 1922 — China (Foochow)*
The American consul at Foochow requested a landing force on 4 October 1922, when a threat of military invasion by the southern forces arose. A landing party of 48 men from the light minelayer USS *Rizal* (DM-14) went ashore the next morning. Later the same day, they were joined by about an equal number of British and Japanese troops. The force withdrew within a few days.

On 11 October 1922, a force of 30 men and 2 officers from the *Rizal* again landed at Foochow after the city was captured by the southern forces. Admiral Anderson held a conference with fleet officers and local American representatives and together they formulated a joint plan for the protection of American nationals in Foochow and Nantai. According to a report of the American consul, "[t]his plan provided for the stationing of a force of 30 Marines at the consulate, with the forces of the naval vessel in port at Pagoda as a reserve; and for the concentration of all Americans, in case of danger, at three concentration centers on Nantai Island, where they would receive military protection."

Source: *Clark* 89-90.

*Case No. 119, 1923* — China (Masü Island)
A party of four Marines from the first USS *Asheville* (PG-21) landed at Masü Island on 14 February 1923, to protect Americans who were threatened by bandits. The force withdrew 19 February 1923.

Source: *Clark* 90.

*Case No. 120, 1923* — China (Tungshan)
On 15 November 1923, a detachment of eight Marines went to Tungshan, a suburb of Canton, to protect American missionaries during fighting between Chinese forces. The guard withdrew after several days.

Source: *2 Hackworth* 332.

*Case No. 121, 1924* — Honduras
A contest for the presidency of Honduras in 1924 brought much political unrest to that country. Fearing an outbreak of violence, the United States dispatched several vessels, one of which landed a small force at Amapala. The force traveled to Tegucigalpa, the capital, to protect the American legation.

There were numerous landings in February and March. Fearing that the insurgents would attack the town of La Ceiba, the United States landed a force of 59 men on 28 February, to protect the American consulate. This force declared the compound of the Standard Fruit and Steamship Company neutral ground and gave refuge there to Americans and other foreigners. Both of the contending factions were notified of this action and advised that the United States intended to remain neutral in the conflict.

On 29 February, a force of 35 men from the USS *Denver* (C-14) landed at La Ceiba, remaining ashore until 3 March. A combined force of 41 men from two vessels was landed at Tela and established a neutral zone on 3 March. These men returned to their ships on 7 March.

## Appendix I

At the request of the American consul at Puerto Cortés, who reported that the situation was critical, the *Denver* landed a force of 167 men at Puerto Cortés on 4 March to establish a neutral zone. These men returned aboard ship 6 March. On the day after this force departed, a force of 70 men landed and remained two days.

Several more landing parties went ashore at La Ceiba. A party of 41 men landed on 8 March. Another force of 86 Marines and seamen went ashore at La Ceiba and proceeded to Mazapon to establish a neutral zone. A force of 24 men from the *Denver* landed on 9 March. All three of these forces returned aboard their ships on 13 March.

Fighting temporarily ended early in March, but events necessitated one more landing. On 18 March, the American Minister at Tegucigalpa reported widespread looting, the loss estimated at $400,000. Among foreign residents, the British and Chinese suffered the greatest property losses, but at least two American-owned stores were looted. The American legation and consulate were fired at and the American Minister believed that the lives of all Americans in the city were in imminent danger. Having obtained the permission of the Commandante, an American force of 176 men landed at San Lorenzo on 18 March. Part of the force proceeded to Toncontín and established a radio station, while the remainder traveled to Tegucigalpa. That city fell to the rebels on 28 April, and shortly thereafter order was reestablished. The force returned aboard ship 30 April 1924.

Sources: *Clark* 115-17; *Ellsworth* 96-98; 2 *Hackworth* 331.

### Case No. 122, 1924 — China (Shanghai)

Beginning 3 September 1924, there was intermittent fighting between the Chekiang and Kiangsu forces in the vicinity of Shanghai, the nearest battle taking place about nine miles from the city. This fighting was the beginning of a new civil war in northern China, one that resulted in the overthrow of President Tsao Kun and the establishment of a provisional government.

As a precautionary measure, several foreign nations with naval vessels in the harbor landed forces on 9 September. These forces included approximately 260 Americans, 360 Britons, 500 Frenchmen, 400 Japanese and 100 Italians. Also present was a force of about 1,000 men from the Shanghai Volunteer Corps. These troops took-up stations in the city so that they could protect foreigners in the event that fighting occurred. Many refugees also sought protection in the city, there being from six to seven thousand new arrivals daily beginning 29 August 1924. By 23 October 1924, the danger having passed, the refugees began returning to the rural districts. The American force withdrew the same day.[29]

Sources: *Clark* 90; [1924] 1 *Foreign Rel. U. S.* 361, 371, 383 (1939); 2 *Hackworth* 332-33.

*Case No. 123*, 1924 — Honduras
Disorder returned to Honduras in September 1924. Threats of murder, looting and burning endangered American lives and property. On 10 September, the second line cruiser *USS Rochester* (CA-2) landed a force of 111 men at La Ceiba and then proceeded to Tela. The Governor, believing that the presence of American forces would ensure the preservation of order, requested that the Marines be left ashore, but they withdrew 15 September 1924.

Source: *Clark* 117.

*Case No. 124*, 1924 — China (Tungchow)
By 24 October 1924, the Kiangsu forces having captured Peking, staged a successful *coup d'état* against the government of President Tsao Kun. The unsettled political condition and a report that the Shensi troops at Tungchow were acting lawlessly caused the US legation at Peking to send a force of 10 Marines that day to protect about 100 American citizens in Tungchow.

Sources: *Clark* 90; [1924] 1 *Foreign Rel. U. S.* 385 (1939).

*Case No. 125*, 1924 — China (Peking)
The unsettled state of affairs following the overthrow of President Tsao Kun[30] caused the American legation in Peking to request that the Commander in Charge of the Asiatic Fleet provide reinforcements for the legation guard. A landing party of 125 Marines arrived in Peking on 28 October 1924. A second detachment of 100 men arrived on 4 November 1924.

Source: Clark 90.

*Case No. 126*, 1924–1926 — China (Shanghai)
By 1925 it became apparent that the provisional government of China, established in 1924, had not successfully unified the country, including the northern region. The Chihli forces retained much power in the Yangtze Valley and Chang Tso-lin was the virtual ruler of Manchuria, having established his headquarters at Tientsin in the autumn of 1924. On 2 January 1925, the American Minister at Peking reported that the provisional government of

## Appendix I

Marshal Tuan, Provisional Chief Executive and Prime Minister of China, could not endure much longer without Chang's support. Another consideration was Inspector General of the Chinese Army, Feng Yu-hsiang's, seizure of Peking in October 1924. In short, the political situation in northern China remained quite unstable.

The various factions clashed regularly around Shanghai as early as January 1925, and the lives and property of foreigners in the city were in great danger. The American consul general at Shanghai reported that the United States and others landed sailors in the city on 15 January 1925. The American force took a position with the French as guards of interned Chinese soldiers at the Haig Reserve School. (The force withdrew 24 January). On 19 January, the Heads of Legation to China met at a meeting in Peking:

> Resolved, that with a view to maintaining the neutrality of Shanghai and for the protection of foreign life and property therein the consular body are authorized, as an emergency measure and during the continuance of fighting and the presence of bodies of troops near Shanghai (but no longer) and without referring the matter to the diplomatic body, in their discretion to expel from the International Settlement (or to refuse admissions thereto to) Chinese military leaders (being any officer with the rank of general now or recently having active command of troops) and political chiefs who serve the internal affairs of such militarists who may, in the opinion of the consular body, use the Settlement for fitting out military expeditions or otherwise as a base of military operations or for political agitation.

The United States landed several forces at Shanghai to protect Americans and other foreigners residing in the city's International Settlement. The first party to land was a Marine detachment of 28 men from the gunboat USS *Sacramento* (PG-19) which went ashore 15 January, and remained there until 22 January. The Second Expeditionary Force, which was organized in the Philippines, landed at Shanghai on the day that the first force departed, remaining until 9 February. A period of relative calm ensued until 2 June, when a landing party of 127 men went ashore at Shanghai to protect foreign residents. They returned aboard ship 29 August. A Marine detachment of reinforcements from the second line cruiser USS *Huron* (CA-9) landed on 1 July, and remained ashore until 29 July. For the next five months there were no incidents. Then, on 30 December 1925, new outbreaks necessitated the landing of still another detachment of 69 men at Shanghai. They withdrew 12 March 1926.

Sources: *Background* 56; *Ellsworth* 42-43; [1925] 1 *Foreign Rel. U. S.* 588-89, 595-96 (1940); 2 *Hackworth* 332-33.

*Case No. 127, 1925 — Honduras*
An uprising in Honduras in April 1925 again resulted in American intervention. American lives and property at La Ceiba were endangered by the threat of Red Ochoa, some insurgent forces, to attack the city. The USS Denver (C-14), with the permission of the Governor and the Commandante, landed 165 men on 20 April. The American forces quickly declared the city a neutral zone: as hoped, all subsequent fighting took place outside the city. After having been ashore about 30 hours, the force reembarked the following day.
Source: Clark 117.

*Case No. 128, 1925 — China (Nanking)*
The revolutionary unrest in China was accompanied by labor disputes and strikes. On the morning of 7 June 1925, a large crowd, apparently comprised of the International Export Company's striking workmen, gathered outside the company's facility at Nanking and attempted to "rush" for the waterfront, on which the company's river water intake was located. At the request of the company's manager and the British and American consuls, the USS John D. Ford (DD-228) landed a small party at the plant. The strikers quickly abandoned the rush.
Source: Clark 91.

*Case No. 129, 1925–1926 — China (Hankow)*
In 1926, Cantonese forces invaded the Yangtze Valley and disrupted the region's organized government. Demonstrations and rioting, often directed against foreigners, were widespread. The situation of all foreigners residing in the area became perilous, especially since local authorities often were impotent to provide adequate protection. Therefore, the United States again landed forces on several occasions to preserve American lives and property. (Even before the above invasion the United States landed a force of 24 men at Hankow on 16 June 1925 as a part of the International Defense Force. These men were stationed in the former Russian Concession of the city.)

The city of Hankow fell into a state of disorder when the Cantonese were poised to move upon it in early September 1926. At the request of Chinese authorities, several landing parties from American naval vessels landed to restore order on 3 September. British, French, and Japanese forces also landed. Most of the American forces withdrew on 16 September; a small guard remained for

some time thereafter. As a precautionary measure, British, Japanese and American naval units landed at Hankow on 5 November 1926, and remained three days.
Sources: *Background* 56; *Clark* 91; *Offutt* 141-42.

*Case No. 130*, 1925 — China (Kiukiang)
The second USS *Stewart* (DD-224) landed a force of 20 armed men at Kiukiang on 17 June 1925, to protect American citizens during a period of revolutionary fighting in that city.
Source: *Clark* 90.

*Case No. 131*, 1925 — Panama
Rent increases in Panama City led to rent strikes and harassment of landlords. Tenants combined in order to hinder the collection of these increased rents. The disorder spread as various groups of workers went on secondary strike. When rioting broke out the Panamanian Government found it impossible to control the situation, much less afford protection to foreign residents. Many Americans appealed to the American chargé d'affaires in Panama and the Governor of the Canal Zone for protection against the threats of mob violence.

On 12 October 1925, at the request of the Panamanian Minister of Foreign Affairs, 600 American troops entered the city of Panama. Within three days relative peace was restored and the force was reduced to one battalion, which was quartered in the jail and police station in order to keep them from public view. The situation continued to improve and the remainder of the troops withdrew 23 October 1925.
Source: *Clark* 128-29.

*Case No. 132*, 1925–1926 — China (Tientsin)
During the period of revolutionary unrest in 1925 and 1926, American forces landed at Tientsin to protect Americans and their interests. At the request of the American legation, a force of 100 men was sent to Tientsin on 28 October 1925. An additional force of 127 men landed in the city on 9 November, and remained until 9 June 1926.
Sources: *Clark* 91; *Ellsworth* 42-43.

*Case No. 133, 1926* — Nicaragua

Shortly after the American legation guard withdrew from Managua on 3 August 1925, a new period of political unrest began in Nicaragua.[31] A band of government troops favoring the Conservative Party arrested various Liberal leaders, including the Minister of Finance. Their avowed purpose was to liberate the President from the alleged domination of the Liberal element. The leader of the revolutionary forces, General Chamorro, steadily increased the pressure on the Nicaraguan Government. The disturbances increased in number and intensity, except for an 11-day period in September when American naval vessels were present in Nicaraguan waters. Through highly questionable political maneuvering, General Chamorro succeeded in gaining executive power on 14 January 1926. The United States refused to recognize his government.

In May 1926, fighting erupted on the east coast of Nicaragua as the Liberals' violence increased in their opposition to Chamorro. The American Consul at Bluefields reported that the lives and property of all foreigners were endangered and requested the dispatch of an American naval vessel. On 7 May, a force of 213 men went ashore at Bluefields. Beginning on 28 May, this force gradually was withdrawn, the final group reembarking on 6 June. Intermittent landings of US forces for the protection of foreign lives and property took place throughout the remainder of 1926.

Sources: *Clark* 122-24; *Ellsworth* 128-31.

*Case No. 134, 1926* — China (Kiukiang)

When Kiukiang fell to the Cantonese forces on 4 November 1926, the inhabitants of the city resisted little. However, as a precautionary measure, British, Japanese and American naval units landed forces for the protection of foreigners. Subsequently, British sources reported further fighting during the Northern forces' counterattack at Kiukiang. By 6 November 1926, the Cantonese completely occupied the city and all was quiet. Consequently, the American forces returned aboard their ships.

Sources: *Clark* 91; [1926] 1 *Foreign Rel. U. S.* 650 (1941); 2 *Hackworth* 333; *Offutt* 142.

*Case No. 135, 1926* — China (Chingwangtao)

In the latter part of 1926 the fighting among the various Chinese revolutionary factions intensified to such an extent that the Commander of the Asiatic Fleet found it necessary to land a force at Chingwangtao, the center of trouble. The

## Appendix I

force of 127 Marines from the USS *Gold Star* (AG-12) landed on 7 November 1926, and remained five days.

Source: *Ellsworth* 43.

*Case No. 136, 1926* — China (Ichang)
On 17 December 1926, a small force from the American gunboat USS *Elcano* (PG38) landed at Ichang to protect US citizens and their property during a battle between the Cantonese and Northern forces. The men returned aboard ship when the conflict ended.

Source: *Offutt* 142.

*Case No. 137, 1926-1933* — Nicaragua
The Nicaraguan Congress named Adolfo Díaz President of Nicaragua on 11 November 1926. Six days later, the United States recognized his government. There were signs of rebellion from the beginning of his administration. Díaz called on the United States to provide protection for Americans and other foreigners in Nicaragua from the activities of the revolutionists. American officials believed that Díaz's real motive was to employ US assistance in support of his government. The American chargé d'affaires informed Díaz that the United States was not obligated to protect his government by physical means.

But, in view of the many requests from American citizens for protection, the United States did land a force of Marines and sailors on 23 December 1926 at Bluefields and Rio Grande Bar. The next day, additional forces went ashore at Puerto Cabezas, a stronghold of the Liberal revolutionaries. The United States established neutral zones in all these cities and required all Nicaraguans therein to disarm. The American force even censored radio transmissions in these zones until the Liberals registered a complaint with the U. S. Department of State. By 10 January 1927, the American force had established three more neutral zones at Pearl Lagoon, Prinzapulka and Rama. By month's end the American forces ashore and in the territorial waters of Nicaragua numbered about 5,000 men.

Having been obstructed from fighting in the eastern region of the country by the establishment of neutral zones, the Liberals turned their attention toward Managua. When it began to appear that the Liberals would succeed in cutting the capital city off from the sea, a force of 600 seamen landed at Corinto on 20 February to guard the railroad link to Managua. The United States also then established more neutral zones at Corinto, Managua and Grenada.

President Coolidge sent Secretary of State Stimson to Nicaragua as his personal representative. Stimson arrived 17 April 1927, and promptly met with American officials, Nicaraguan Government officials, and various leaders of the Liberal party in search of a peaceful settlement. In May, when it appeared that a settlement loomed, the US troops stationed themselves between the opposing factions so that their arms might be received in case of an agreement. An additional force of 800 Marines was landed to arrest the terrorism and marauding which was contributing to the general state of anarchy.

Consensus emerged, and on 15 May 1927, Stimson reported that the civil war in Nicaragua was over. Yet, the entire American force did not withdraw immediately. American troops remained to supervise elections and aid in the establishment and maintenance of the Guardia Nacional de Nicaragua. Indeed, the last of the American forces in Nicaragua did not depart until 2 January 1933.

Sources: *Clark* 124-27; *Ellsworth* 129-33; *Offutt* 137-40.

*Case No. 138, 1927* — China (Hankow)
Although the entire city of Hankow had fallen to the Cantonese forces on 3 September 1926, there were subsequent disturbances that the Cantonese could not control. On 3 January 1927, for instance, serious rioting occurred along the edge of the British concession at Hankow. The British authorities called on the local police, including several hundred Cantonese soldiers, for protection, but the police were unable to assert firm control over the situation even with the assistance of British ships on the river. That evening an American landing force of 50 Marines went ashore to protect American citizens and their property until evacuation could be arranged.

The American consul general reported on 5 January that the situation in Hankow was critical, with 20 or 30 American and British citizens having been evacuated already and three more fully-loaded ships scheduled to sail that evening. The next day about 60 more American and British women and children went aboard the *Kutwo*, an American naval vessel. American naval vessels also assisted in evacuating refugees from Kiukiang and Ichang via Hankow to Shanghai. By 19 January 1927, approximately 583 people had been evacuated from Hankow, including 83 Americans.

Sources: *Clark* 91; [1927] 2 *Foreign Rel. U. S.* 237, 239, 240, 248 (1942); *Offutt* 142.

# Appendix I

*Case No. 139, 1927* — China (Shanghai)

Violence broke anew in the International Settlement of Shanghai in 1927. The Expeditionary Battalion, consisting of three companies of Marines, landed at Shanghai on 9 February 1927, to reinforce the forces guarding the Settlement. A dramatic increase came when 1,250 Marines arrived 24 February. Although a few small parties went ashore for brief periods prior to 16 March, the entire force did not land until that date. With this addition, the total number of men in the foreign forces available for service at Shanghai numbered approximately 13,000, of whom approximately 7,000 were British.

On 21 March, the US consul general at Shanghai reported that outside the International Settlement in Chapei, turmoil existed. Laborers had attacked Chinese police stations. He also reported demonstrations in the streets of the Settlement. The Municipal Council declared a state of emergency and requested that foreign naval forces join local volunteers and police in defending the Settlement. American, Japanese and Dutch naval forces landed the same day. Approximately 1,500 Marines landed for the protection of American lives and property.

The disorder continued on 22 March. There were armed uprisings and numerous incidents of looting and burning in the Chinese territory adjoining the Settlement. The forces of General Pi Shu-cheng, commander of the Northern Troops in the Shanghai area, shot and killed a number of the agitators. Many foreigners, including Americans, were evacuated under police escort. The consul general at Shanghai reported that he was attempting to evacuate Americans in isolated areas without the use of military force. Nearly all foreigners in the northern area were evacuated by 23 March.

On 25 March a landing party of 62 Marines went ashore at Shanghai to patrol the Settlement. They returned aboard ship the following day. They landed once again on 31 March, and remained ashore until 3 April 1927.

Sources: Clark 91-92; Ellsworth 43; [1927] 2 *Foreign Rel. U. S.* 89, 90 (1942); 2 Hackworth 333.

*Case No. 140, 1927* — China (Nanking)

On 22 March 1927, when the entry of the Cantonese forces into the city of Nanking appeared imminent, the United States landed a force of 11 men from the USS Noa (DD-343) to protect the American consulate during any ensuing disturbances. It seemed quite likely that the Northern forces would riot should they be defeated or forced to withdraw. A signalman also was sent to Standard Oil Hill, the residence of Earle Hobard of Standard Oil Company. This measure insured communication between the consulate and the *Noa* at all times.

Trouble had been anticipated at Nanking many weeks before the actual outbreak of violence on 23 March. The foreign consuls at Nanking had been evacuating their nationals out of the danger zone to other cities, primarily Shanghai. By 23 March, around 100 American women and children had left, but 68 men, 153 women and 88 children still remained. As Nationalist soldiers began to enter the city, 104 women and 69 children were sent aboard the American destroyers, *Noa* and *USS Preston* (DD-327). In addition to these vessels, the British light cruiser *HMS Emerald* and three Japanese destroyers were present.

Six seamen from the *Preston* also were stationed at the Hill residence on 23 March. Looting and rioting broke out about 6 P.M. that night when about 10,000 defeated Northern soldiers, passing through the city to the Yangtze River, returned again to the city, having discovered it would be impossible to cross the river. The following day, Dr. J. E. Williams, an American citizen and Vice President of Nanking University, was killed. On the same day, Cantonese troops attacked the American, British and Japanese consuls, wounding the latter two. The American consular staff and 24 refugee foreigners who were under their protection escaped to the Hill residence before the consulate was looted.

During this entire time, Mr. Davis from the American consulate had tried in vain to contact a responsible Cantonese official to ensure the safety of all foreigners. The US forces were hesitant to move because they had been instructed to act only to protect life and not merely property. Therefore, when the Cantonese approached the Hill residence, the Americans did not request assistance from the *Noa* and the *Emerald* until attack was imminent. Shortly thereafter, the Cantonese attacked and the occupants requested landing forces from the ships.

When it appeared that the landing force would be unable to reach the Hill residence in time to save the occupants from the Cantonese, the *Emerald*, *Noa* and *Preston* shelled the area. The *Noa* and *Preston* then sent a landing force to rescue the 52 Americans and foreign refugees in the house.[32] However, the Hill group missed the landing force and was picked up by the British destroyer *HMS Wolsey* (D-98). There were no fatalities.

Immediately afterward, a conference of British and American naval officers was held on board the *Emerald*. They drew up a set of demands to the Cantonese requiring: (1) the protection of all foreigners still ashore and their evacuation by 10 A.M. the next day; (2) orders to protect foreign property; and (3) the

## Appendix I

presence of the Cantonese general commander on board the *Emerald* before 11 P.M. that night to arrange for the protection of foreigners.

Negotiations took place that night and the next afternoon. The Chinese replies were insolent and evasive. Indirectly, word came that General Chiang Kai-shek was coming to Nanking to take charge of the situation. Over 100 Americans (45 women, 90 men and 20 children), 17 British and several foreign nationals were still left in the city. Most of the Americans assembled at Nanking University. It finally was decided that if all foreign nationals were not released by late in the afternoon of 25 March, the USS *Isabel* (PY-10), the *Noa*, the *Emerald* and the *Wolsey* would begin firing on salient military points in Nanking. The Chinese general became alarmed, and by 4:30 P.M. British Marines and all but two British civilians were returned. The Americans also were released from the University and by 8 P.M. all were aboard the vessels.

During the incident, American ships had fired 34 rounds and the *Emerald* had fired 76. Six Chinese civilians and some soldiers had been killed. Only five business men and two missionaries remained in the city. A great part of the foreign population of Nanking, including people of many nationalities, had been saved by the American action.

Sources: Clark 92-93; [1927] 2 Foreign Rel. U. S. 146-70 (1942); 2 Hackworth 333; Offutt 142-49.

*Case No. 141, 1927* — China (Hankow)
At the request of the manager of the Standard Oil Company, a landing party of 24 seamen went ashore at Hankow on 27 April 1927, to quell a "fracas."
Source: Clark 93.

*Case No. 142, 1927* — China (Chinkiang)
On 22 May 1927, landing parties from the destroyers USS *John D. Ford* (DD-228) and the HMS *Wolverine* (D-78) went ashore at Chinkiang to fight a fire which began when a shell hit a Socony fuel oil tank. Apparently the shell had been fired by the Northern forces from the northern bank of the river during revolutionary disturbances in that city.
Source: Clark 94.

*Case No. 143, 1927* — China (Tientsin)
By June 1927, the Southern forces had pushed the civil war to the northern part of China. It seemed certain that the area around Tientsin would be the

next target of their attack. The American Minister to China reported that the lives and property of all US citizens were in danger. He suggested that additional forces be sent to Tientsin to afford Americans complete protection and ensure that there would be no repetition of the serious incidents which had occurred recently in South China.[33]

On 2 June 1927, a force of Marines about the size of one regiment sailed from Shanghai, arriving at Taku Bar two days later. On 6 June 1927, the force reached Tientsin, where they remained until the danger had passed.

Sources: Ellsworth 44; [1927] 2 Foreign Rel. U. S. 124-27 (1942).

## Case No. 144, 1927 — China (Canton)

A two-day revolt supported by the Communists began in Canton on 11 December 1927. The same day, a force of nine Marines landed and proceeded to the Hackett Medical College to evacuate U. S. citizens whose lives were endangered by the rebellion. Evacuated persons were taken to another part of the city where the rebels had not been active.

Source: Clark 94-95.

## Case No. 145, 1932 — China (Shanghai)

Following the outbreak of war between Japan and China, the American consul at Shanghai, fearing for the lives and property of Americans in the city, requested that additional forces be landed to assure their protection. On 5 February 1932, the U. S. transport *USS Chaumont* (AP-5) arrived at Shanghai and landed a force of 1,178 men. They remained ashore until 1 July 1932.

Source: Clark 97.

## Notes

1. Omitted are the instances considered at length in Chapter IV, where the United States has taken similar action in the post-World War II period.

2. Some readers may regard this Appendix as too inclusive. Prior lists, for instance, have contained as few as 69 cases compared to the 145 listed herein. See Wormuth, "The Nixon Theory of the War Power: A Critique," 60 Calif. L. Rev. 623, 654 (1972). *But see generally* Appendix A to Emerson, War Powers Legislation, 74 W. Va. L. Rev. 53, 88 111 (1971). If the present compilation errs in this respect, the reader can separate the wheat from the chaff quite easily.

3. *See* Case No. 5.

4. *See* Case No. 7.

5. *See* Perrin v. United States, 4 Ct. Cl. 543 (1868).

6. The United States took the position that American forces could be sent to occupy the railroad stations of the Panama Railroad Co. in the event of revolution under the following

# Appendix I

clause of Article 35 of the 1846 Treaty of Peace, Amity, Navigation, and Commerce with New Granada (United States of Colombia):

> And, in order to secure to themselves the tranquil and constant enjoyment of these advantages, and as an especial compensation for the said advantages and for the favours they have acquired by the 4th, 5th and 6th articles of this Treaty, the United States guarantee positively and efficaciously to New Granada, by the present stipulation, the perfect neutrality of the before mentioned Isthmus, with the view that the free transit from the one to the other sea, may not be interrupted or embarrassed in any future time while this Treaty exists.

6 C. Bevans, Treaties and Other International Agreements of the United States of America 1776–1949, at 879-80 (1971).

7. The executive officer of the *Iroquois* was none other than Alfred T. Mahan. *See* T. Mahan, from Sail to Steam 242-47 (1907).

8. Brazil, France, Great Britain, Italy and Spain.

9. *See* Case No. 28.

10. *See* Case No. 13.

11. *See* Case No. 55.

12. Of these forces, 8,000 were Japanese; 4,800 Russian; 3,000 British; 2,500 American; 800 French; 40 Italian and 25 Austrian.

13. Tientsin fell to the Allies on 14 July 1900.

14. *See* Case No. 54.

15.
Article VII

> The Chinese Government has agreed that the quarter occupied by the legations shall be considered as one specially reserved for their use and placed under their exclusive control, in which Chinese shall not have the right to reside and which may be made defensible.

Article IX

> The Chinese Government has conceded to the Powers, in the protocol annexed to the letter of the 16th of January 1901, the right to occupy certain points, to be determined by an agreement between them, for the maintenance of open communication between the capital and the sea. The points occupied by the powers are:
>
> Huang-tsun, Lang-fang, Yang-tsun, Tientsin, Chum-liang Ch'eng, Tang-ku, Lu-tai, Tangshan, Lan-chou, Chang-li, Ch'in-wang tao, Shan-hai Kuan.

1 C. Bevans, Treaties and Other International Agreements of the United States of America 1776–1917, at 306-07 (1968).

16. The United States had the right to intervene under Article III of the 1903 Treaty with Cuba, which stated:

> The Government of Cuba consents that the United States may exercise the right to intervene for the preservation of Cuban independence, the maintenance of a government adequate for the protection of life, property, and individual liberty, and for discharging the obligations with respect to Cuba imposed by the Treaty of Paris on the United States, now to be assumed and undertaken by the Government of Cuba.

6 C. Bevans, Treaties and Other International Agreements of the United States of America 1776-1949, at 1118 (1971).

17. *See* Case No. 80.

18. *See id.*

19. By 8 March 1912, the distribution of foreign troops in the vicinity of Tientsin was as follows: about 575 American, 1,200 British, 1,500 Japanese and 100 German troops, respectively, and about 200-225 Russian, Austrian, French and Italian troops combined.

20. *See* Case No. 73.

21. *See* Case No. 68 for the text of Article III.

22. American landings in Nicaragua, 1912:

(1) 3 August — A force of 102 men landed at Corinto and traveled by rail to Managua to guard the American legation and protect American interests.

(2) 14 August — Reinforcements numbering 354 men disembarked at Corinto and proceeded to Managua, arriving there 15 August. This force also was used to guard the legation.

(3) 28 August — A force of 351 seamen and Marines landed at Corinto for field service.

(4) 29 August — A force of 120 men landed at Corinto for duty ashore. They returned aboard ship 24 and 25 October 1912.

(5) 30 August — A force of 25 men went ashore at San Juan del Sur to protect the cable station and American interests from 30 August to 6 September 1912, and from 11 September to 27 September 1912.

(6) 4 September — A provisional regiment of 781 Marines disembarked at Corinto.

(7) 5 September — An additional force of 323 sailors and Marines landed at Corinto for duty in the field.

(8) 19 September — Another 50 men landed at Corinto.

(9) 3 November — A force of 21 men landed at San Juan del Sur. Twelve of these men were withdrawn on 5 November and the balance on 8 November.

23. *See* Case No. 112 for more information about the activity of the legation guard at Managua.

24. *See also* Case Nos. 82, 83, 84, 90 and 91.

25. Landings by American forces in Cuba, 1917:

(1) 12 February — A force of 32 men landed at Jobabo Anchorage to protect a sugar plantation near Trinidad. They reembarked 13 February.

(2) 13 February — A landing party of 17 men from the USS *Tucker* (DD-57) went ashore at Manzanillo to protect the American consulate. They were relieved on the same day by a similar force from the USS *Dubuque* (PG-17). The guard was withdrawn 15 February.

(3) 17 February — A force of 29 men from the USS *Paducah* (PG-18) disembarked and was quartered on the Cuban gunboat *24 de Febrero* until 20 February.

(4) 20 February — The 29 men quartered on board the Cuban gunboat *24 de Febrero* landed and occupied a house at Casilda until 22 March.

(5) 25 February — A force of 218 men landed at Guantánamo Bay. They were transported by water to Caimanera, where they embarked by train for Guantánamo City. With the exception of one detachment of Marines, they reembarked 6 March.

(6) 25 February — A force of more than 200 Marines from three different vessels went ashore at Guacanayabo Gulf at the dock of the Francisco Sugar Company of New York to protect the lives and property of American citizens. Each of the three detachments returned to their ship on a different date: 3, 4 and 7 March.

(7) 27 February — A force of 32 men landed at Nuevitas Bay and remained until 28 February.

(8) 5 March — A force landed at Santiago.

(9) 7 March — A force landed at Rio Canto to protect the Rio Canto Sugar Plantation. They returned aboard ship on 11 March.

## Appendix I

(10) 8 March — A force of 358 men landed at Santiago to protect the lives and property endangered by the revolutionaries' bombardment of the city. About 120 of these men returned to their ship on 17 March.

(11) 8 March — A force of 153 Marines and seamen went ashore at Santiago, returning to their ship 18 March.

(12) 8 March — A detail of 12 men landed at Santiago to guard the El Cobre mines.

(13) 9 March — A company of Marines went ashore at Santiago and remained ashore until 21 March.

(14) 9 March — A party of 122 men landed at Guantánamo Bay and traveled to Guantánamo City where they remained until 24 March.

(15) 9 March — Two companies of Marines landed at Santiago.

(16) 9 March — Additional men landed at Santiago to reinforce the party which had landed there on 5 March. This force was relieved on 10 March.

(17) 10 March — Eight men from the USS *Montana* (ACR-13), a first-class armored cruiser, landed and returned to ship daily at Caimanera until 23 March.

(18) 10 March — Another company of Marines landed at Santiago, remaining ashore until 18 March.

(19) 10 March — Small detachments landed at Preston and Lacajo where they remained until 12 March, when they were relieved by another landing party.

(20) 11 March — A force of 13 men landed at Guara and remained there until 23 March.

(21) 12 March — A force of 25 sailors and Marines was stationed at Banes and San Jeronimo to protect American interests. Part of the force reembarked on 15 March, the remainder on 20 March.

(22) 12 March — A landing party from the USS *Machias* (PG-5) relieved the detachments which had landed at Preston and Lacajo on 10 March.

(23) 13 March — A detachment of 20 Marines from the U. S. Naval Station at Guantánamo Bay was sent to Boquerón to protect American property. They remained until 24 March.

(24) 15 March — A small detachment landed at Nipe Bay to protect lives and property at San Jeronimo. They returned to ship on 18 March.

(25) 17 March — A force landed at Batey to guard the mill of the Manti Sugar Company. They reembarked 21 April, when they were relieved by a detachment of Marines.

(26) 19 March — A detachment of 20 men landed at Santiago to protect the El Cobre mines. They returned aboard ship 22 March.

(27) 19 March — A force of 100 men landed at Guantánamo Bay and proceeded to Guantánamo City, where they remained until 22 March.

(28) 20 March — A company of Marines went ashore at Daiquiri, where they remained until 23 May.

(29) 20 March — A force of 41 men landed from the USS *Machias* for duty ashore. Part of the force re-embarked the same day, with the remainder reembarking on 23 March.

(30) 21 March — A landing party of 18 Marines and sailors went ashore and remained until 23 March.

(31) 21 March — For several days small detachments were landed daily at Santiago to protect the Aguadores railroad bridge and the El Cobre mines.

(32) 22 March — A force of two infantry companies and special details landed at Santiago to relieve a detachment of Marines, re-embarking 23 March.

(33) 22 March — A company of Marines was sent to Guantánamo City. They returned aboard ship 23 May.

(34) 22 March — A company of Marines disembarked at Guantánamo Bay, remaining ashore until 30 March.
(35) 22 March — A force of 46 men landed to relieve forces at Preston, Guara and Nipe Bay. They returned aboard ship 25 March.
(36) 24 March — Fifty seamen landed at Cienfuegos, reembarking the same day.
(37) 24 March — A detachment of 18 Marines landed at Santiago to guard the El Cobre mines. They reembarked 28 March.
(38) 24 March — A small detachment landed at Santiago each night through 27 March to protect the Aguadores Bridge.
(39) 25 March — A detachment of 13 men landed at Guara, returning aboard ship 7 April.
(40) 27 March — A detachment of 10 men landed at Pelton, remaining until 2 April.
(41) 28 March — A small detachment landed daily at Cienfuegos for the protection of the Aguadores Bridge. Another force of 21 men landed there to protect the El Cobre mines. These men were relieved 15 April by a company of Marines.
(42) 31 March — A company of Marines landed at Nipe Bay to relieve various detachments. It reembarked 24 May.
(43) 15 April — A company of Marines landed to relieve a detachment at Cienfuegos.
(44) 25 April — A small force landed at Preston, returning aboard ship 26 April.
(45) 27 August — The Marine 7th Regiment disembarked at Guantánamo Bay and remained there until 28 August 1919.

26. From the beginning of World War I, the Czechs had fought in a special unit of the Russian army called the *Druzhina*. The Czech Corps was in the Ukraine when the Germans resumed their offensive against Russia in February 1918. The Czechs made arrangements with Bolshevik leaders to evacuate the Corps via the Trans-Siberian Railway and Vladivostok. Subsequently, the Bolsheviks changed their minds and decided to draft the Czechs into the Soviet army. The Czechs resisted and hostilities broke out on 26 May 1918.

27. *See* Case No. 101.
28. *See* Case No. 87.
29. *See also* Case Nos. 124 and 125.
30. *See* Case No. 124.
31. The U. S. Government announced its intention to withdraw the legation guard about 14 months prior to the actual date of withdrawal. At the request of President Martinez, who apparently believed that the guard was necessary to preserve order, the United States had delayed the withdrawal. Martinez sought to reverse the American decision but met with no success.
32. The occupants of the house included Mr. and Mrs. Hobart, several American civilians, two officers from the *Emerald*, five British civilians, two Scandinavians, two Russians, two Signalmen from the destroyers and the guard of six seamen from the *Preston*.
33. For example, the Nanking incident of March 1927. *See* Case No. 140.

# Appendix II

## A History of United States Navy Regulations Governing the Use of Force to Protect the Lives and Property of Nationals Abroad*

### CONTENTS

Introduction. . . . . . . . . . . . . . . . . . . . . . . . . . . . . . . . . . . . . . . . . . . . 187

I. Regulations and Instructions Relating to His Majesty's Service at Sea (llth Ed. 1772) . . . . . . . . . . . . . . . 188

II. Rules for the Regulation of The Navy of The United Colonies of North America (1775) . . . . . . . . . . . . 190

III. An Act for The Government of the Navy of the United States (1799) . . . . . . . . . . . . . . . . . . . . . . . . . 190

IV. United States Navy Regulations (1802). . . . . . . . . . . . . . . . . . . . 191

V. United States Navy Regulations (1814) . . . . . . . . . . . . . . . . . . . . 192

VI. United States Navy Regulations (1818) . . . . . . . . . . . . . . . . . . . . 192

VII. United States Navy Regulations (1821). . . . . . . . . . . . . . . . . . . . 193

VIII. United States Navy Regulations (1841) . . . . . . . . . . . . . . . . . . . 194

IX. United States Navy Regulations (1853). . . . . . . . . . . . . . . . . . . . 194

*The author wishes to acknowledge the research assistance provided by Stephen T. Bolton, Esq., Class of 1972, University of Virginia School of Law and Member of the Ohio Bar, and Captain J. Ashley Roach, USN, Office of the Legal Adviser, US Department of State, in the preparation of this Appendix. Punctuation and capitalization has been standardized to modern usage.

| | | |
|---|---|---|
| X. | United States Navy Regulations (1858) | 195 |
| XI. | United States Navy Regulations (1863) | 195 |
| XII. | United States Navy Regulations (1865) | 196 |
| XIII. | United States Navy Regulations (1869) | 197 |
| XIV. | United States Navy Regulations (1870) | 200 |
| XV. | United States Navy Regulations (1876) | 202 |
| XVI. | United States Navy Regulations (1893) | 203 |
| XVII. | United States Navy Regulations (1896) | 206 |
| XVIII. | United States Navy Regulations (1900 and 1905) | 208 |
| XIX. | United States Navy Regulations (1909) | 210 |
| XX. | United States Navy Regulations (1913) | 212 |
| XXI. | United States Navy Regulations (1920) | 215 |
| XXII. | United States Navy Regulations (1948) | 217 |
| XXIII. | United States Navy Regulations (1973) | 220 |
| XXIV. | United States Navy Regulations (1990) | 223 |
| Summary | | 226 |

*Appendix II*

# Introduction

The United States has long viewed military intervention in foreign countries to protect the lives and property of US nationals as a proper use of naval power.[1] US Navy Regulations dating back to 1775 have provided naval commanders with the authority to undertake such action. Additionally, throughout much of this period the accepted norms of international law countenanced such activity under such headings as self-preservation or nonpolitical intervention.[2]

In recent years, however, the international political and legal context has changed drastically. With the emergence of the United Nations and the post-colonial proliferation of independent States, new norms and new needs have been generated. For instance, under Article 2(4) of the UN Charter the use of force is proscribed, except when used in self-defense or when sanctioned by the United Nations. Article 51, however, preserves the possibility of the valid use of force in situations involving self-defense. At the same time, emergent nations have demonstrated an anti-colonial attitude bent on the elimination of many formerly accepted practices, such as intervention for the protection of foreign nationals and their property, which are now viewed as tools of imperialistic control.[3]

Despite this substantial shift in international norms, the regulations governing the conduct of the US Navy in this area remained essentially unchanged until 1973. With the promulgation of the 1973 and 1990 Regulations however, it appears that the Navy Regulations have become more congruent with the realities of present-day international life, thus attenuating much of the former criticism regarding their compatibility with contemporary international law.[4]

This Appendix constitutes a textual analysis of the regulations which have guided and continue to guide the US Navy in its use of force to protect the lives and property of US nationals abroad. The analysis proceeds with a listing of those regulations in each edition of US Navy Regulations that relate to the protection of nationals and then following each by a brief commentary addressed to the question of how each edition fits in with the overall development of the current Navy regulations.

The regulations analyzed in this study begin with the British Navy Regulations of 1749 and 1772 and continue with their offspring,[5] the US Navy Regulations of 1775, 1799, 1802, 1814, 1818, 1821, 1841, 1853, 1858, 1863, 1865, 1869, 1870,

1876, 1893, 1896, 1900, 1905, 1909, 1913, 1920, 1948, 1973 and 1990. Histories of the various editions of British or US Navy Regulations until 1973 are not available, for reasons partially explained in the paragraph that follows.

Although the Constitution grants Congress sole authority to issue regulations for the armed forces,[6] Congress, except for the first three Regulations of 1775, 1799 and 1800, merely ratified the rules compiled by the President and the Secretary of the Navy.[7] Even this limited supervisory rule was abdicated in 1862, when Congress gave the Secretary of the Navy the authority to issue regulations subject to the approval of the President.[8] As a practical matter, this delegation probably ensured that regulations were written and revised at the behest of senior naval officers.[9] In any event, records of the administrative process in the formulation of US Navy Regulations prior to 1973 are unavailable. Therefore, authorship and the intended results remain unclear for earlier regulations. This leaves the actual language of the regulations and the interpretations subsequently given to them by naval commanders as the only sources of interpretative standards.

As noted above, the regulations in force until 1973 did not differ greatly from those regulations in force during the nineteenth century. The 1973 and 1990 Regulations vary considerably from their predecessors by omitting out-of-date passages from earlier regulations. It is the purpose of the following analysis to examine the extent to which these new revisions have brought the US Navy Regulations into line with contemporary international law.

## I. Regulations And Instructions Relating To His Majesty's Service At Sea (llth ed. 1772)

### The Flag-Officer or Commander-in-Chief

Article VI. To direct the Naval Officers abroad, according to the Rules of the Navy. When he is in Foreign Parts, where Naval or other Officers are established, he is to conform himself, as much as possible, to the standing Rules of the Navy, in such Directions as he shall have Occasion to give them; and never to put them upon any extraordinary Expenses, unless the Service shall absolutely require the same.

### The Captain or Commander

Article XLII. Not to go into Port unnecessarily. He is not to go into any other Port than such as his Orders direct him, unless by inevitable Necessity,

# Appendix II

and then to make no unnecessary Stay there. If he is employed in a cruising Station, he is to keep the Sea the Time required by his Orders; but if he is compelled by any Accident to return sooner into Port, he is to send in Writing the Reasons thereof to the Secretary of the Admiralty, and also to the Commander-in-Chief, if any such be there, and to put to Sea again so soon as the Ship's Wants are supplied.

Article XLV. To demand English Seamen out of foreign Ships. When he meets with any Foreign Ship or Vessel, he is to send a Commission Officer to inquire if any Seamen, who are His Majesty's Subjects, be on Board her, and to demand all such, obliging their Masters to pay them their Wages to that Day. But this is to be done with civil and friendly Behavior on the Part of His Majesty's Officers, who are to be very careful not to offer any Violence or ill Treatment to the Subjects of His Majesty's Friends or Allies.[10]

## Commentary

The Eleventh Edition of *Regulations and Instructions Relating to His Majesty's Service at Sea*, established by His Majesty in Council in 1772, is the direct ancestor of all subsequent editions of US Navy Regulations. This text is a restatement of the Sixth Edition, published in 1749 to update British Navy Regulations from a code which originated during the reign of Henry VIII. The three articles cited above are identical in both the Sixth and Eleventh Editions.

Article VI is concerned with the relationship between a Flag-Officer or Commander-in-Chief and the agents of the British government already established in foreign ports. The "unless" clause at the end of the article qualifies the instructions to conform to the "Rules of the Navy" and the rule against extraordinary expenditures placing the needs of the service paramount. The Flag-Officer, as the senior officer present in foreign waters, is the person best-qualified to determine the needs of the service.

On the other hand, according to Article XLII, a Captain or Commander acting independently may not even enter a foreign port without orders unless "inevitable necessity" forces him to do so. Again the Captain is the person who determines whether inevitable necessity exists. The second sentence, dealing with a return from cruising station, refers to the home port of the ship.

Article XLV was the cause of much hostility in the United States, since it was the legal justification used for impressment of American sailors during the Revolutionary and Napoleonic wars. While this rule provided a vehicle whereby British sailors could be liberated from foreign employment, it often was used to conduct a forced draft.

## II. Rules For The Regulation Of The Navy Of The United Colonies Of North America (1775)

Article 21. If any ships of the Thirteen United Colonies shall happen to come into port in want of provisions, the warrant of a Commander-in-Chief shall be sufficient to the agent or other instrument of the victualling to supply the quantity wanted; and in urgent cases where delay may be hurtful, the warrant of the Captain of the ship shall be of equal effect.[11]

### Commentary

As stated in the Introduction to this Appendix,[12] for the most part these rules were copied from the British Regulations of 1749 and 1772. They are concerned with the prerogatives and responsibilities of command and matters affecting supply, discipline and conduct in action. Articles VI and XLV of the British Regulations were not included. The only provision which might be said to govern conduct in foreign ports short of an actual engagement is Article 21, which corresponds roughly to Article XLII of the British Regulations. Reference to purchases in foreign ports, however, is omitted. This omission was consistent with the coastal character of the continental Navy.

## III. An Act for the Government of the Navy of the United States (1799)

Article 18. Warrant for supply of provisions. If any ships of the United States shall happen to come into port in want of provisions, the warrant of the commander of the squadron, or of a captain where there is no commander of a squadron present, shall be sufficient to procure the supply of the quantity wanted, from the agent, or navy agent at such port.[13]

### Commentary

Article 18 is based on Article 21 of the 1775 Rules for the Regulation of the Navy of the United Colonies of North America, amended to reflect the independence won two decades earlier. Perhaps in recognition of the infant Navy's engagement in an undeclared war with France in the West Indies, any squadron commander's warrant was now sufficient even in non-urgent cases.

This provision was not included in the 1800 revision, which repealed the 1799 statute entirely.[14] No reason for this omission is apparent.

## IV. United States Navy Regulations (1802)

### Of the Duties of a Commander-in-Chief, or Commander of a Squadron

Article 16. When he is in foreign parts where naval or other officers are established, he is to conform himself as much as possible to the standing rules of the navy, in such directions as he shall have occasion to give them, and never to put them under any extraordinary expenses, unless the service should absolutely require the same.

### Of the Duties of a Captain or Commander

Article 40. He is not to go into any port, but such as are directed by his orders, unless necessitously obliged, and then not to make any unnecessary stay; if employed in cruising, he is to keep the sea the time required by his orders, or give reasons for acting to the contrary.[15]

### Commentary

Of the Duties of a Commander-in-Chief, Article 16, is almost an exact reproduction of Article VI of the 1772 British Regulations for the Flag-Officer or Commander-in-Chief. It allows an American Commander-in-Chief identical discretion as to expenditures as his British counterpart, and similarly ignores the situation of where provisions are located in a port where naval authorities are not established. It is reasonable to assume that both the British and American regulations were concerned more with the possibility of commanders putting into port too often or making extravagant purchases than with any danger of intervention by force in foreign countries.

Of the Duties of a Captain or Commander, Article 40, succeeded Article 18 of the 1799 Rules. It is a close paraphrase of Article XLII of the 1772 British Regulations for the Captain or Commander.

The reinsertion of both these articles may be explained by the fact that the US Navy by this time had become transoceanic and had begun a series of engagements in the Mediterranean using ships of substantial size and firepower. Visitation of foreign ports by necessity was thus a distinct possibility. There is no indication, however, that the necessity standard refers to anything other than matters concerning the administration and operation of the vessel itself.

## V. United States Navy Regulations (1814)

### Of the Duties of Commander of a Squadron

Article 16. When he is in foreign parts, where naval or other agents are established, he is to conform himself, as much as possible, to the standing rules of the navy, in such directions as he shall have occasion to give them; and he is never to put them under any extraordinary expenses, unless the service should absolutely require the same.

### Of the Duties of a Captain or Commander

Article 41. He is not to go into any port, but such as are directed by his orders, unless necessitously obliged, and then not to make any unnecessary stay; if employed in cruising, he is to keep the sea the time required by his orders, or give reasons for acting to the contrary.[16]

### Commentary

Article 16 is repeated from Article 16 of the 1802 Regulations governing the duties of a Commander-in-Chief or Commander of a Squadron with certain clarifying changes. "Agents" is substituted for "officers" who may be in foreign parts. The words "he is" are added at the beginning of the last clause, as are several commas.

Article 41 repeats Article 40 of the 1802 Regulations governing the Duties of a Captain or Commander.

## VI. United States Navy Regulations (1818)

### Commanders of Fleets or Squadrons

Article 15. Conform to established rules. He shall conform to the standing rules of the navy, in such directions as he shall give to established agents, and incur no expense that the public service does not render absolutely necessary.

### Regulations for the Promotion of Discipline, Cleanliness, etc.

Article 28. To visit no port without orders. He [the Captain] is not to go into any port, but such as may be directed by his orders, unless by absolute necessity, and then not to make any unnecessary stay. If employed in cruising, he is to keep the sea, the time required by his orders, or give reasons for acting to the contrary, to the Secretary of the Navy.[17]

### Commentary

Article 15 repeats the substance of Article 16 of the 1814 Regulations governing Squadron Commanders but with significant differences.

The section of the regulations was entitled "Commanders of Fleets or Squadrons" to reflect the increased size of the Navy in the preceding four years. The language referring to "foreign parts" was omitted, applying the regulation everywhere there were "established agents." This latter term replaced the phrase "where naval or other agents are established." "Extraordinary" was deleted from the last clause, which was reworded for clarity.

Article 28 is derived from Article 41 of the 1814 Regulations governing the duties of a Captain. The subject matter is now under the heading "Regulations for the Promotion of Discipline, Cleanliness, etc.," perhaps also reflecting the expanding navy. The remaining changes are for purposes of clarification. The report of reasons for not keeping to sea as required is now specified to be made to the Secretary of the Navy.

## VII. United States Navy Regulations (1821)

### Commanders of Fleets or Squadrons

Article 15. He shall conform to the standing rules of the navy, in such directions as he shall give to established agents, and incur no expense that the public service does not render absolutely necessary.

### Regulations for the Promotion of Discipline, Cleanliness, etc.

Article 28. He is not to go into any port but such as may be directed by his orders, unless by absolute necessity, and then not to make any unnecessary stay. If employed in cruising, he is to keep the sea the time required by his orders, or give reasons for acting to the contrary to the Secretary of the Navy.[18]

### Commentary

The 1821 Regulations are identical to the 1818 Regulations with respect to these articles.

## VIII. United States Navy Regulations (1841)

### Commanders of Vessels

Article 186. When directed to cruise, he is to keep the sea the time required by his orders, or produce satisfactory reasons for acting to the contrary.

Article 187. He is not to go into any port but such as may be designated or permitted by his instructions, unless from necessity, and then to make no unnecessary stay.[19]

### Commentary

The 1841 edition of the regulations was never approved by Congress, but evidently the Navy adhered to them as if they had been.

Article 28 of the 1821 Regulations concerning the Promotion of Discipline, Cleanliness, etc. was split into two articles, 186 and 187, in the 1841 Regulations. Reasons for failure to keep to the sea (Article 186) are no longer specifically to be submitted to the Secretary of the Navy. Entering an undesignated port is now permitted merely "from necessity." The other changes are for purposes of clarity.

The direction to conform to the standing rules of the Navy in Article 15 of the 1821 Regulations governing the duties of Commanders of Fleets or Squadrons is omitted from this and succeeding editions.

## IX. United States Navy Regulations (1853)

### Commanders of Vessels

Article 21. When directed to cruise, he is to keep the sea the time required by his orders, or produce satisfactory reasons for deviating from them.

Article 22. He is not to go into any port but such as may be designated or permitted by his instructions, unless from necessity, and then to make no unnecessary stay.[20]

### Commentary

Articles 21 and 22 are identical to Articles 186 and 187 of the 1841 Navy Regulations, except for a clarifying change to Article 21. If a Commander does not keep to the sea the time required by his orders, he must now produce satisfactory reasons for "deviating from them" rather than for "acting to the contrary."

## X. United States Navy Regulations (1858)

### Commanders of Vessels

Article 28. To keep the sea the time required by his orders. When directed to cruise, he is to keep the sea the time required by his orders, or produce satisfactory reasons for deviating from them.

Article 29. To visit no port not designated in his instructions. He is not to go into any port but such as may be designated or permitted by his instructions, unless from necessity, and then to make no unnecessary stay.[21]

### Commentary

Articles 28 and 29 are identical to Articles 21 and 22 of the 1853 Regulations.

## XI. United States Navy Regulations (1863)

### Article VI.

### General Duties of Line Officers

### The Commander-in-Chief of a Fleet or Squadron

To place himself in communication with the diplomatic agents of the United States.

On arriving within the limits of his station on foreign service, he is to place himself in communication with the diplomatic agents of the government of the United States thereabouts, and he is to afford them, on his own responsibility, such aid and cooperation in all matters for the benefit of the government as they may require, and as he may judge to be expedient and proper.

### Officers Commanding Vessels

To keep the sea the time required by his orders.

When directed to cruise, he is to keep the sea the time required by his orders, or produce satisfactory reasons for deviating from them.

To visit no port not designated in his instructions.

He is not to go into any port but such as may be designated or permitted in his instructions, unless from necessity, and then to make no unnecessary stay.[22]

## Commentary

That portion of the 1863 Regulations governing the duties of officers commanding vessels is identical to Articles 28 and 29 of the 1858 Regulations. However, that portion of the 1863 Regulations governing the duties of the Commander-in-Chief of a fleet or squadron reflects the different Navy of 1863. In contrast to Article 15 of the 1821 Regulations concerning commanders of fleets or squadrons, there is no mention of the "rules of the navy" or "expenses," but rather "co-operation in all matters for the benefit of the government." The emphasis shifted from the simple maintenance of ships in foreign waters to the implementation of foreign policy through the use of naval forces.

Moreover, the actions of the Commander-in-Chief are "on his own responsibility" and as he judges to be "expedient and proper." The regulations vest an individual commander with the discretion to aid and cooperate with diplomatic officials in foreign ports as he sees fit. Presumably, he may exceed their recommendations if he feels such action to be appropriate. This article, then, is the first instance where naval commanders were given the authority to take matters into their own hands and intervene in foreign lands to protect US nationals under the umbrella phrase "for the benefit of the government."

## XII. United States Navy Regulations (1865)
### General Duties of Line Officers
### The Commander-in-Chief of a Fleet or Squadron

Article 310. On arriving within the limits of his station on foreign service, he is to place himself in communication with the diplomatic agents of the government of the United States thereabouts, and he is to afford them, on his own responsibility, such aid and cooperation in all matters for the benefit of the government as they may require, and as he may judge to be expedient and proper.

### Officers Commanding Vessels

Article 346. Should he find it necessary to go into a port not designated or permitted by his instructions, he will make no unnecessary stay, and will report the cause of the necessity and of any delay that may occur.[23]

# Appendix II

## Commentary

These 1865 Regulations are the last of the original sailing instructions that were closely related to the 1775 and 1802 editions of the Regulations.

Article 310 repeats verbatim that portion of Article VI of the 1863 Regulations pertaining to the Commander-in-Chief of a fleet or squadron previously quoted.

Article 346 is based on that portion of Article VI of the 1863 Regulations pertaining to the duty of officers commanding vessels to keep to sea the time required by his orders. The revised version no longer prohibits entry into an undesignated port. The change in tenor reflects the Navy's increased role. For the first time, however, the commanding officer must report the cause of the necessity for entering the undesignated port and of any delay that may occur.

No longer is there a requirement to keep to the sea when directed to cruise.

## XIII. United States Navy Regulations (1869)

### Instructions for Officers, Afloat: Commander-in-Chief

Article 52. The Commander-in-Chief is not to attempt the arrest of a deserter, whatever may be his class, by sending an officer under his command after him, but he is to make the proper application to the civil authorities of the place where he may be.

Article 53. No Commander-in-Chief is ever to take upon himself the power of inflicting punishment upon the subjects of any civilized nation, with whom we have treaties, for any alleged violation of treaties or international law.

Article 54. In the absence of a United States Minister he is to enter into diplomatic discussions on all matters of this kind, with the nation which is supposed to be the aggressor, and will take the earliest opportunity to lay the correspondence before the United States Government.

Article 157. A Commander-in-Chief is on all occasions to do his utmost to protect American commerce in all quarters.

Article 165. If he finds an American seaman employed on board a foreign vessel who complains that he is there contrary to his will, he will institute all necessary inquiries, and if he finds that the said seaman is improperly detained, the Commander-in-Chief will apply to the proper authority to have him released and will give him a passage to the nearest American port.

Article 169. The Commander-in-Chief should observe himself that all under his command comply with the laws of blockade when a harbor or port is blockaded by a nation with whom we are at peace.

Article 170. He is to observe the strictest neutrality, and afford no assistance to either party not called for by the interests of humanity.

Article 171. He is at the same time to make every effort to protect the lives and property of American citizens that may be within the lines of the belligerents.

Article 172. In time of war, a Commander-in-Chief will cause all the laws of neutrality to be strictly observed by those under his command.

Article 173. A Commander-in-Chief will also take upon himself to exercise particular authority over all American letters-of-marque and privateers that come within the limits of his command, and will ascertain if they have made any fraudulent seizures or captured vessels belonging to neutral powers, which they had no right to capture.

Article 174. He will exercise his judgment as to what disposal to make of said privateers or letters-of-marque.

Article 175. In every case investigated by the Commander-in-Chief, he will send a report to the Secretary of the Navy as soon as possible.

Article 176. When on a foreign station, it is desirable that the best feeling should exist between the Commander-in-Chief of a United States fleet or squadron and the American Minister, Chargés and Consuls, but while every courtesy should be paid to these officials, it must be understood that the Commander-in-Chief is responsible to the Secretary of the Navy alone, for his acts.[24]

### Commentary

These regulations, which Secretary of the Navy George M. Robeson promulgated after the Civil War, are direct ancestors of the 1990 Regulations currently in effect. The most obvious explanation for the break between the 1865 and 1869 Regulations is the emergence of a powerful ironclad US Navy during the Civil War. Although the Royal Navy resumed its role as the most powerful afloat in the decade after the Civil War, the United States had become a significant force. Navy Regulations from 1869 to the present day have reflected this fact, dealing extensively with the duties of commanders in foreign waters and ports.

This edition of the regulations was in effect for only one year. Yet the direct ancestors of the articles quoted below from the 1990 Regulations all appear for the first time in 1869. Textually, these articles are the first "modern" Navy regulations. Geopolitically, they are an extension of the 1865 Regulations in that they reflect the Navy's increased awareness of its new foreign relations role.

Article 52 is a clear prohibition against sending forces ashore in a foreign land to pursue and arrest a deserter from a US ship, such matters are left to the local civil authorities.

Article 53 is repeated in conjunction with Article 54 in several other editions. The prohibition against retorsion or reprisal by a naval Commander-in-Chief acting on his own authority is restricted to "civilized nation[s], with whom we [the United States] have treaties." Presumably, "civilized" States meant European or Latin American ones. In any event, the regulation contains an open invitation to ignore treaties or international law with regard to "savage" nations such as Hawaii, most African tribal kingdoms, and most East Asian kingdoms. The article is thus narrow in its scope and permits a Commander-in-Chief to punish in most instances.

Article 54 requires diplomatic discussions with an alleged civilized aggressor with whom the United States has treaties. Those areas excluded from Article 53 are similarly excluded here. These articles establish the Commander-in-Chief as the arbiter of whether there has been a breach of treaty or violation of international law towards the United States. They further leave it to him to determine whether a nation is civilized. Freedom to use force is contingent on these determinations.

Article 157 appears in one form or another in all succeeding editions of the Regulations. It makes the US Navy the guardian of US commerce both on the high seas and in foreign waters. There is no element of discretion. A Commander-in-Chief must do everything he can to protect American commerce.

Article 165 corresponds roughly to Article XLV of the 1772 British Regulations. The US counterpart does not allow boarding, and it becomes operative only when a complaint is received. It may be implemented only by foreign authorities. The only affirmative actions a Commander-in-Chief may make in such a case are "necessary inquiries" and passage of the seaman to the nearest American port.

Article 169, in conjunction with the following seven articles, is repeated in some form in all succeeding editions of the regulations. In this edition Articles 169 through 176 should be read together.

Article 169 specifically requires compliance with the laws of blockade when the United States is at peace with the blockading nation. Article 170 commands that US naval forces shall remain neutral in the face of a blockade, except where assistance is called for in the interests of humanity. Article 171 gives the Commander-in-Chief the responsibility to protect the "lives and property of American citizens within the lines of the belligerents." Article 172 commands US forces shall remain neutral "in time of war" when the United States is not a party. Article 173 gives American Commanders-in-Chief jurisdiction over letters-of-marque and privateers operating in areas under their command and makes them a prize court of original jurisdiction. Article 174 authorizes judgment on letters-of-marque and privateers within the jurisdiction of a Commander-in-Chief. Article 175 requires that a report of such cases be sent to the Secretary of the Navy. Article 176 makes the Commander-in-Chief solely responsible to the Secretary of the Navy for his acts while on foreign station.

The thrust of these seven articles is that Commanders-in-Chief are urged to respect blockades by friendly nations and to comply with the laws of neutrality when the United States is not at war. At the same time, Commanders-in-Chief are authorized, on their own initiative, to intervene in wars to which the United States is not a party on humanitarian grounds. Commanders-in-Chief are also obliged to engage in forcible self-help for the protection of American lives and property, at least with respect to wars to which the United States is not a party. They must justify such actions only to the Secretary of the Navy.

## XIV. United States Navy Regulations (1870)

### Duties of Commander-in-Chief

Section 52. He will preserve, so far as in him lies, the best feeling and the most cordial relations with the ministers and consuls of the United States on foreign stations, and will extend to them every official courtesy. He will also duly consider such information as they may have to give him relating to the interests of the United States, but he will not receive orders from such sources, and he will be responsible to the Secretary of the Navy, in the first place, for his acts.

Section 53. He will not take upon himself the power of inflicting punishment upon the people of any civilized nation with whom we have treaties, for any violation, alleged or otherwise, of such treaties or of international law.

Section 54. In the absence of a diplomatic representative of the United States, he will enter into correspondence on matters of this kind with the authorities of the nation which may be supposed to have been the aggressor, and

# Appendix II

will take the earliest opportunity to communicate all the information in his possession to the government of the United States.

Section 55. He will do his utmost on all occasions to protect the commerce of the United States.

Section 94. During wars to which the United States is not a party, he shall himself observe the strictest neutrality between the belligerents, and shall require every one under his command to practice the like observance.

Section 95. He shall comply with the laws of blockade, when a harbor or port is blockaded by a nation with whom the United States is at peace, and will require the like compliance by all under his command.

Section 96. He shall at the same time make every effort to protect the lives and property of citizens of the United States within the lines of the belligerents, and will so instruct the Commanding Officers of his fleet or squadron.

### Officers Commanding Vessels

Section 247. When not acting under the orders of a superior officer, he will be governed by the regulations for the Commander-in-Chief, so far as they may be applicable to his case.[25]

### Commentary

Section 52 repeats the substance of Article 176 of the 1869 Regulations. Sections 53 through 55 repeat the substance of Articles 53, 54 and 157 of the 1869 Regulations. Section 94 generally repeats Articles 170 and 172 of the 1869 Regulations. The regulation clarifies the scope of responsibility by placing the context as "[d]uring wars to which the United States is not a party." Otherwise, it is a combination of the two earlier articles.

Section 95 repeats Article 169 of the 1869 Regulations, while Section 96 repeats Article 171 of the 1869 Regulations. In addition, the Commander-in-Chief is to extend his responsibility to the commanding officers of his squadron or fleet.

Section 247 incorporates the regulations for a Commander-in-Chief by reference, the first instance of such an incorporation, and there is no indication of a captain's responsibilities while on foreign station except as mentioned previously.

The most interesting aspect of the 1870 Regulations is what they do not include. Omitted from the 1869 Regulations are Article 52 on the arrest of deserters, Article 165 on American seamen held aboard foreign vessels, and

Articles 173, 174 and 175 on letters-of-marque and privateers. The "civilized nations" distinction is retained in Section 53, however, so that the right to conduct reprisals in many areas of the world remains along with the right of self-help to protect American lives and property.

## XV. United States Navy Regulations (1876)

### Instructions for Officers, Afloat: Commanders-in-Chief

Article 21. Punishment of people of any civilized nation. He will not inflict punishment upon the people of any civilized nation with whom the United States has treaties, for any violation, alleged or otherwise, of such treaties or of international law; but in the absence of a Diplomatic Representative, he will enter into correspondence with the authorities of the nation, and will take the earliest opportunity to communicate all the information in his possession to the Navy Department.

Article 22. Protection of commerce of the United States. He will do his utmost on all occasions to protect the commerce of the United States.

Article 49. Neutrality of the United States; Protection of lives and property. During wars in which the United States are neutral, he will observe the strictest neutrality and require the same of everyone under his command. He will comply strictly with the laws of blockade, when a harbor or port is blockaded by a nation with whom the United States is at peace, making every effort to protect the lives and property of citizens of the United States within the lines of the belligerents, and will so instruct the commanding officers of the vessels of his fleet or squadron.

### Officers Commanding Vessels.

Article 101. Acting singly. When acting singly, he will be governed by the regulations for the Commander-in-Chief, so far as they may be applicable to his case.[26]

### Commentary

Article 21 consolidates Sections 53 and 54 of the 1870 Regulations. Article 22 repeats Section 55 of the 1870 Regulations. Article 49 consolidates Sections 94, 95 and 96 of the 1870 Regulations. Article 101 repeats in substance Section 247 of the 1870 Regulations.

## Appendix II

### XVI. United States Navy Regulations (1893)

### A Commander-in-Chief

### Duties in Time of War

Article 276. To protect and convoy merchant vessels. He shall afford protection and convoy, so far as it is within his power, to merchant vessels of the United States and to those of allies.

Article 277. Duties during a war between civilized nations at peace with the United States. During a war between civilized nations with which the United States is at peace, he, and all under his command, shall observe the laws of neutrality and respect a lawful blockade, but at the same time make every possible effort that is consistent with the rules of international law to preserve and protect the lives and property of citizens of the United States wherever situated.

Article 278. To observe the principles of international law and treaty obligations. When the United States is at war, he shall require all under his command to observe the rules of humane warfare and the principles of international law. When dealing with neutrals, he shall cause all under his command to observe the rules of international law and the stipulation of treaties, and expect and exact a like observance from others.

Article 283. Intercourse with Foreigners.

1. Territorial authority. He shall exercise great care that all under his command scrupulously respect the territorial authority of foreign civilized nations in amity with the United States.

2. No armed force to be landed. No armed force for exercise, target practice, funeral escort, or other purpose shall be landed without permission from the local authorities; nor shall large bodies of men be granted leave to visit the shore without a similar permission; nor shall men be landed to capture deserters.

3. No target practice within. Great-gun target practice, even at floating targets, shall not take place within foreign territorial waters or at any point from which shots may fall therein, without permission.

Article 284. Violation of international law and treaty obligations. On occasions where injury to the United States or to citizens thereof is committed or threatened, in violation of the principles of international law or treaty rights, he shall consult with the diplomatic representative or consul of the United States, and take such steps as the gravity of the case demands, reporting immediately to the Secretary of the Navy all the facts. The responsibility for any action taken by a naval force, however, rests wholly upon the commanding officer thereof.

Article 285. Use of force. The use of force against a foreign and friendly State, or against anyone within the territories thereof, is illegal. The right of self-preservation, however, is a right which belongs to States as well as to individuals, and in the case of States it includes the protection of the State, its honor, and its possessions, and the lives and property of its citizens against arbitrary violence, actual or impending, whereby the State or its citizens may suffer irreparable injury. The conditions calling for the application of the right of self-preservation cannot be defined beforehand, but must be left to the sound judgment of responsible officers, who are to perform their duties in this respect with all possible care and forbearance. In no case shall force be exercised in time of peace otherwise than as an application of the right of self-preservation as above defined. It can never be exercised with a view to inflicting punishment for acts already committed. It must be used only as a last resort, and then only to the extent which is absolutely necessary to accomplish the end required.

Article 286. Landing an armed force in foreign territory. Whenever in the application of the above-mentioned principles it shall become necessary to land an armed force in foreign territory on occasions of political disturbance where the local authorities are unable to give adequate protection to life and property, the assent of such authorities, or of some one of them, shall first be obtained, if it can be done without prejudice to the interests involved.

Article 288. To protect the commerce of the United States. So far as lies within their power, Commanders-in-Chief and captains of ships shall protect all merchant vessels of the United States in lawful occupations, and advance the commercial interests of their country, always acting in accordance with international law and treaty obligations.

Article 289. Dealings with foreigners. He shall impress upon officers and men that when in foreign ports it is their duty to avoid all possible causes of offense to the authorities or inhabitants; that due deference must be shown by them to the local laws, customs, ceremonies, and regulations; that in all dealings with foreigners moderation and courtesy should be displayed; and that a feeling of good will and mutual respect should be cultivated.[27]

## Commentary

This edition of the regulations is the earliest to use the text still found in the 1948 Navy Regulations, which remained in force until 1973. The articles dealing with conduct and intervention in foreign lands reflect the policy of wide

## Appendix II

discretion intended to promote maximum flexibility expressed in the 1869, 1870 and 1876 editions.

This edition, however, is even more insistent on the duty to intervene in a foreign land when an American interest is threatened. Article 285 in particular sets forth the right of self-preservation as the justification for self-help by the United States. Although the doctrine of self-preservation must be read against the background of the times—1893 falls in the midst of the age of imperialism—it also must be remembered that similar language was retained through the 1948 edition of the regulations, which until 1973 were the law of the Navy.[28]

Article 277 corresponds in substance to Article 49 of the 1876 Regulations. For the first time the "civilized nations" qualification is applied to the neutrality and blockade rule, no longer confined to the punishment rule. See Article 21 of the 1876 Regulations. The responsibilities the article imposes upon a Commander-in-Chief remained unchanged.

Article 284 corresponds roughly to Article 21 of the 1876 Regulations. The thrust of the article is changed from punishment to prevention. The clear import here is that the Commander-in-Chief is to take only such action as is necessary to forestall injury to the United States or its citizens or to put a stop to harmful acts in progress. The necessity to report to the Secretary of the Navy is unchanged, but the responsibility for any action taken rests entirely with the Commander-in-Chief himself.

Article 285 is similar to Article 277 in that it is designed to give Commanders-in-Chief the authority to intervene in situations where US interests are threatened. Unlike Article 277 and its predecessors, Article 285 can be invoked in peacetime. All previous regulations permitting intervention in foreign countries to protect American lives and property either refer to a wartime situation or call for consultation with local authorities before action is taken, except in the most extreme circumstances. While the exercise of "sound judgment of responsible officers" may give rise to the use of force only as a last resort, and then only to the degree necessary to end the threat to American interests, the breadth of the right of self-preservation means that any prospect of violence that could threaten the United States or its citizens may be sufficient grounds for intervention by a naval force.

It is noteworthy that the "civilized nations" qualification is not included in this article. Instead, mention is made in the first sentence of "a foreign and friendly state." There is no indication, however, that application of Article 285 is in any way limited to friendly States. The essential prerequisite is the threat to US interests, wherever they are.

Article 286 requires the Commander-in-Chief to seek the assent of local authorities before he lands an armed force pursuant to Article 285. The wording of this article makes it clear that "local authorities" can mean any of the factions which might claim to rule a city or country. Also, assent is to be obtained only if it does not involve further danger to US interests. Thus, this article is not an important limitation on the discretion of the Commander-in-Chief. Article 286 is otherwise interesting because it is the first to mention consent rather than consultation when dealing with the prospect of armed intervention. If nothing else, it reflects a desire on the part of the United States to justify its actions through the consent of the authority structure in the locality in which it is intervening.

Article 288 repeats in substance Article 22 of the 1876 Regulations. The duty to protect the commerce of the United States is narrowed to include only merchant vessels in lawful occupations. Advancement of the commercial interests of the United States, which involves the policing of sea lanes and other tasks which ensure the free flow of commercial traffic, must be accomplished in accordance with international law and treaty obligations. The effect of this article is to make the protection of commerce a less-aggressive task. There is no attempt to hold all American ships inviolate, no matter what actions they take, as might be inferred from the earlier regulations.

Article 289 is a new rule requiring moderate conduct on the part of US Navy personnel while in foreign ports as invitees.

## XVII. United States Navy Regulations (1896).

### A Commander-in-Chief

### Duties in Time of War

Article 277. To protect and convoy merchant vessels. He shall afford protection and convoy, so far as it is within his power, to merchant vessels of the United States and to those of allies.

Article 278. Duties during a war between civilized nations at peace with the United States. During a war between civilized nations with which the United States is at peace, he, and all under his command, shall observe the laws of neutrality and respect a lawful blockade, but at the same time make every possible effort that is consistent with the rules of international law to preserve and protect the lives and property of citizens of the United States wherever situated.

# Appendix II

Article 279. To observe the principles of international law and treaty obligations. When the United States is at war, he shall require all under his command to observe the rules of humane warfare and the principles of international law. When dealing with neutrals, he shall cause all under his command to observe the rules of international law and the stipulation of treaties, and expect and exact a like observance from others.

Article 284. Intercourse with Foreigners.

1. Territorial authority. He shall exercise great care that all under his command scrupulously respect the territorial authority of foreign civilized nations in amity with the United States.

2. No armed forces to be landed. No armed force for exercise, target practice, funeral escort, or other purpose shall be landed without permission from the local authorities; nor shall large bodies of men be granted leave to visit the shore without a similar permission; nor shall men be landed to capture deserters.

3. No target practice without permission. Great-gun target practice, even at floating targets, shall not take place within foreign territorial waters or at any point from which shots may fall therein, without permission.

Article 285. Violation of international law and treaty obligations. On occasions where injury to the United States or to citizens thereof is committed or threatened, in violation of the principles of international law or treaty rights, he shall consult with the diplomatic representative or consul of the United States, and take such steps as the gravity of the case demands, reporting immediately to the Secretary of the Navy all the facts. The responsibility for any action taken by a naval force, however, rests wholly upon the commanding officer thereof.

Article 286. Use of force. The use of force against a foreign and friendly State, or against any one within the territories thereof, is illegal. The right of self-preservation, however, is a right which belongs to States as well as to individuals, and in the case of States it includes the protection of the State, its honor, and its possessions, and the lives and property of its citizens against arbitrary violence, actual or impending, whereby the State or its citizens may suffer irreparable injury. The conditions calling for the application of the right of self-preservation cannot be defined beforehand, but must be left to the sound judgment of responsible officers, who are to perform their duties in this respect with all possible care and forbearance. In no case shall force be exercised in time of peace otherwise than as an application of the right of self-preservation as above defined. It can never be exercised with a view of inflicting punishment for acts already committed. It must be used only as a last resort, and then only to the extent which is absolutely necessary to accomplish the end required.

Article 287. Landing an armed force in foreign territory. Whenever, in the application of the above-mentioned principles, it shall become necessary to land an armed force in foreign territory on occasions of political disturbance where the local authorities are unable to give adequate protection to life and property, the assent of such authorities, or of some one of them, shall first be obtained, if it can be done without prejudice to the interests involved.

Article 289. To protect the commerce of the United States. So far as lies within their power, Commanders-in-Chief and captains of ships shall protect all merchant vessels of the United States in lawful occupations, and advance the commercial interests of this country, always acting in accordance with international law and treaty obligations.

Article 290. Dealings with foreigners. He shall impress upon officers and men that when in foreign ports it is their duty to avoid all possible causes of offense to the authorities or inhabitants; that due deference must be shown by them to the local laws, customs, ceremonies, and regulations; that in all dealings with foreigners moderation and courtesy should be displayed; and that a feeling of good will and mutual respect should be cultivated.[29]

## Commentary

Articles 277, 278, 279, 284, 285, 286, 287, 289 and 290 of the 1896 Regulations are identical to Articles 276, 277, 278, 283, 284, 285, 286, 288 and 289, respectively, of the 1893 Regulations.

## XVIII. United States Navy Regulations (1900 and 1905)

### A Commander-in-Chief

### Duties in Time of War

Article 297. To protect and convoy merchant vessels. He shall afford protection and convoy, so far as it is within his power, to merchant vessels of the United States and to those of allies.

Article 298. Duties during a war between civilized nations at peace with the United States. During a war between civilized nations with which the United States is at peace, he, and all under his command shall observe the laws of neutrality and respect a lawful blockade, but at the same time make every possible

## Appendix II

effort that is consistent with the rules of international law to preserve and protect the lives and property of citizens of the United States wherever situated.

Article 299. To observe the principles of international law and treaty obligations. When the United States is at war, he shall require all under his command to observe the rules of humane warfare and the principles of international law. When dealing with neutrals, he shall cause all under his command to observe the rules of international law and the stipulation of treaties, and expect and exact a like observance from others.

Article 304. Intercourse with Foreigners.

1. Territorial authority. He shall exercise great care that all under his command scrupulously respect the territorial authority of foreign civilized nations in amity with the United States.

2. No armed force to be landed. No armed force for exercise, target practice, funeral escort, or other purpose shall be landed without permission from the local authorities; nor shall large bodies of men be granted leave to visit the shore without a similar permission; nor shall men be landed to capture deserters.

3. No target practice without permission. Great-gun target practice, even at floating targets, shall not take place within foreign territorial waters or at any point from which shots may fall therein, without permission.

Article 305. Violation of international law and treaty obligations. On occasions where injury to the United States or to citizens thereof is committed or threatened, in violation of the principles of international law or treaty rights, he shall consult with the diplomatic representative or consul of the United States, and take such steps as the gravity of the case demands, reporting immediately to the Secretary of the Navy all the facts. The responsibility for any action taken by a naval force, however, rests wholly upon the commanding officer thereof.

Article 306. Use of force. The use of force against a foreign and friendly State, or against any one within the territories thereof, is illegal. The right of self-preservation, however, is a right which belongs to States as well as to individuals, and in the case of States it includes the protection of the State, its honor, and its possessions, and the lives and property of its citizens against arbitrary violence, actual or impending, whereby the State or its citizens may suffer irreparable injury. The conditions calling for the application of the right of self-preservation cannot be defined beforehand, but must be left to the sound judgment of responsible officers, who are to perform their duties in this respect with all possible care and forbearance. In no case shall force be exercised in time of peace otherwise than as an application of the right of self-preservation as above defined. It must be used only as a last resort, and then only to the extent which is absolutely necessary to accomplish the end required. It can never be exercised with a view to inflicting punishment for acts already committed.

Article 307. Landing an armed force in foreign territory. Whenever, in the application of the above-mentioned principles, it shall become necessary to land an armed force in foreign territory on occasions of political disturbance where the local authorities are unable to give adequate protection to life and property, the assent of such authorities, or of some one of them, shall first be obtained, if it can be done without prejudice to the interests involved.

Article 309. To protect the commerce of the United States. So far as lies within their power, Commanders-in-Chief and captains of ships shall protect all merchant vessels of the United States in lawful occupations, and advance the commercial interests of this country, always acting in accordance with international law and treaty obligations.

Article 310. Dealings with foreigners. He shall impress upon officers and men that when in foreign ports it is their duty to avoid all possible causes of offense to the authorities or inhabitants; that due deference must be shown by them to the local laws, customs, ceremonies, and regulations; that in all dealings with foreigners moderation and courtesy should be displayed; and that a feeling of good will and mutual respect should be cultivated.[30]

### Commentary

These articles of the 1900 and 1905 Regulations are identical to their 1896 counterparts.

### XIX. United States Navy Regulations (1909)

### A Commander-in-Chief

### Duties in Time of War

Article 333. To protect and convoy merchant vessels. He shall afford protection and convoy, so far as it is within his power, to merchant vessels of the United States and to those of allies.

Article 334. Duties during a war between civilized nations at peace with the United States. During a war between civilized nations with which the United States is at peace, he and all under his command shall observe the laws of neutrality and respect a lawful blockade, but at the same time make every possible effort that is consistent with the rules of international law to preserve and protect the lives and property of citizens of the United States wherever situated.

Article 335. To observe the principles of international law and treaty obligations. When the United States is at war, he shall require all under his command to observe the rules of humane warfare and the principles of international law. When dealing with neutrals, he shall cause all under his command to observe the rules of international law and the stipulation of treaties, and expect and exact a like observance from others.

Article 340. Intercourse with Foreigners.

1. Territorial authority. He shall exercise great care that all under his command scrupulously respect the territorial authority of foreign civilized nations in amity with the United States.

2. No armed force to be landed. No armed force for exercise, target practice, funeral escort, or other purposes shall be landed without permission from the local authorities; nor shall large bodies of men be granted leave to visit the shore without a similar permission; nor shall men be landed to capture deserters.

3. No target practice without permission. Great-gun target practice, even at floating targets, shall not take place within foreign territorial waters or at any point from which shots may fall therein, without permission.

Article 341. Violation of international law and treaty obligations. On occasions where injury to the United States or to citizens thereof is committed or threatened, in violation of the principles of international law or treaty rights, he shall consult with the diplomatic representative or consul of the United States, and take such steps as the gravity of the case demands, reporting immediately to the Secretary of the Navy all the facts. The responsibility for any action taken by a naval force, however, rests wholly upon the commanding officer thereof.

Article 342. Use of force. Self-preservation. The use of force against a foreign and friendly State, or against anyone within the territories thereof, is illegal. The right of self-preservation, however, is a right which belongs to States as well as to individuals, and in the case of States it includes the protection of the State, its honor, and its possessions, and the lives and property of its citizens against arbitrary violence, actual or impending, whereby the State or its citizens may suffer irreparable injury. The conditions calling for the application of the right of self-preservation cannot be defined beforehand, but must be left to the sound judgment of responsible officers, who are to perform their duties in this respect with all possible care and forbearance. In no case shall force be exercised in time of peace otherwise than as an application of the right of self-preservation as above defined. It must be used only as a last resort, and then only to the extent which is absolutely necessary to accomplish the end required. It can never be exercised with a view to inflicting punishment for acts already committed.

Article 343. Landing an armed force in foreign territory. Whenever in the application of the above-mentioned principles it shall become necessary to land an armed force in foreign territory on occasions of political disturbance where the local authorities are unable to give adequate protection to life and property, the assent of such authorities, or of some one of them, shall first be obtained, if it can be done without prejudice to the interests involved.

Article 345. To protect the commerce of the United States. So far as lies within their power, Commanders-in-Chief and captains of ships shall protect all merchant vessels of the United States in lawful occupations, and advance the commercial interests of their country, always acting in accordance with international law and treaty obligations.

Article 346. Dealings with foreigners. He shall impress upon officers and men that when in foreign ports it is their duty to avoid all possible causes of offense to the authorities or inhabitants; that due deference must be shown by them to the local laws, customs, ceremonies, and regulations; that in all dealings with foreigners moderation and courtesy should be displayed; and that a feeling of good will and mutual respect should be cultivated.[31]

## Commentary

The substance of these articles is identical to that of the 1900 and 1905 Regulations.

## XX. United States Navy Regulations (1913)

### A Commander-in-Chief

### Duties in Time of War

Article 1632. To protect and convoy merchant vessels. The Commander-in-Chief shall afford protection and convoy, so far as it is within his power, to merchant vessels of the United States and to those of allies.

Article 1633. Duties during a war between civilized nations at peace with the United States. During a war between civilized nations with which the United States is at peace, the Commander-in-Chief and all under his command shall observe the laws of neutrality and respect a lawful blockade, but at the same time make every possible effort that is consistent with the rules of international law to preserve and protect the lives and property of citizens of the United States wherever situated.

Article 1634. To observe the principles of international law and treaty obligations. When the United States is at war, the Commander-in-Chief shall require all under his command to observe the rules of humane warfare and the principles of international law. When dealing with neutrals, he shall cause all under his command to observe the rules of international law and the stipulation of treaties, and expect and exact a like observance from others.

Article 1645. Intercourse with Foreigners.

1. Territorial authority. The Commander-in-Chief shall exercise great care that all under his command scrupulously respect the territorial authority of foreign civilized nations in amity with the United States.

2. No armed force to be landed. No armed force for exercise, target practice, funeral escort, or other purposes shall be landed without permission from the local authorities; nor shall large bodies of men be granted leave to visit the shore without a similar permission; nor shall men be landed to capture deserters.

3. No target practice without permission. Target practice with guns or torpedoes shall not take place without permission from the government of the country concerned within foreign territorial waters or at any point from which shots may fall or torpedoes enter therein.

Article 1646. Violation of international law and treaty obligations. On occasions where injury to the United States or to citizens thereof is committed or threatened, in violation of the principles of international law or treaty rights, the Commander-in-Chief shall consult with the diplomatic representative or consul of the United States, and take such steps as the gravity of the case demands, reporting immediately to the Secretary of the Navy all the facts. The responsibility for any action taken by a naval force, however, rests wholly upon the commanding officer thereof.

Article 1647. Use of force. Self-preservation. The use of force against a foreign and friendly State or against anyone within the territories thereof, is illegal. The right of self-preservation, however, is a right which belongs to States as well as to individuals, and in the case of States it includes the protection of the State, its honor, and its possessions, and the lives and property of its citizens against arbitrary violence, actual or impending, whereby the State or its citizens may suffer irreparable injury. The conditions calling for the application of the right of self-preservation cannot be defined beforehand, but must be left to the sound judgment of responsible officers, who are to perform their duties in this respect with all possible care and forbearance. In no case shall force be exercised in time of peace otherwise than as an application of the right of self-preservation as above defined. It must be used only as a last resort, and then only to the extent which is absolutely necessary to accomplish the end required. It can never be exercised with a view to inflicting punishment for acts already committed.

Article 1648. Landing an armed force in foreign territory. Whenever, in the application of the above-mentioned principles, it shall become necessary to land an armed force in foreign territory on occasions of political disturbance where the local authorities are unable to give adequate protection to life and property, the assent of such authorities, or of some one of them, shall first be obtained, if it can be done without prejudice to the interests involved.

2. Due to the ease with which the Navy Department can be communicated with from all parts of the world, no Commander-in-Chief, division commander, or commanding officer, shall issue an ultimatum to the representative of any foreign Government, or demand the performance of any service from any such representative that must be executed within a limited time, without first communicating with the Navy Department, except in extreme cases where such action is necessary to save life.

Article 1650. To protect the commerce of the United States. So far as lies within their power, Commanders-in-Chief, division commanders, and commanding officers of ships shall protect all merchant vessels of the United States in lawful occupations, and advance the commercial interests of this country, always acting in accordance with international law and treaty obligations.

Article 1651. Dealings with foreigners. The Commander-in-Chief shall impress upon officers and men that when in foreign ports it is their duty to avoid all possible causes of offense to the authorities or inhabitants; that due deference must be shown by them to the local laws, customs, ceremonies, and regulations; that in all dealings with foreigners moderation and courtesy should be displayed, and that a feeling of good will and mutual respect should be cultivated.[32]

### Commentary

Articles 1632, 1633, 1634, 1645, 1646 and 1647 repeat Articles 333, 334, 335, 340, 341 and 342 of the 1909 Regulations. Article 1648(1) repeats Article 343 of the 1909 Regulations. Article 1648(2) was added by Change No. 7 of September 15, 1916. It takes into account the Navy's use of radio communications. The sentence forbidding ultimatums to foreign governments without prior consultation with the Navy Department restricts the right of a Commander-in-Chief to apply the self-preservation doctrine. Henceforth, the right to self-preservation can be invoked by a Commander-in-Chief, acting on his own, only when it is a life-or-death situation calling for immediate action.

Article 1650 repeats Article 345 of the 1909 Regulations, except that the words "division commanders, and commanding officers" are substituted for the word "captains." This change reflects organizational growth in the Navy.

Article 1651 repeats Article 346 of the 1909 Regulations, except that the phrase "The Commander-in-Chief" is substituted for the pronoun "he," a change for clarity's sake only.

## XXI. United States Navy Regulations (1920)

### A Commander-in-Chief

### Duties in Time of War

Article 714. To protect and convoy merchant vessels. The Commander-in-Chief shall afford protection and convoy, so far as it is within his power, to merchant vessels of the United States and to those of allies.

Article 715. Duties during a war between civilized nations at peace with the United States. During a war between civilized nations with which the United States is at peace, the Commander-in-Chief, and all under his command, shall observe the laws of neutrality and respect a lawful blockade, but at the same time make very possible effort that is consistent with the rules of international law to preserve and protect the lives and property of citizens of the United States wherever situated.

Article 716. To observe the principles of international law and treaty obligations. When the United States is at war, the Commander-in-Chief shall require all under his command to observe the rules of humane warfare and the principles of international law. When dealing with neutrals he shall cause all under his command to observe the rules of international law and the stipulation of treaties, and expect and exact a like observance from others.

Article 721. Intercourse with foreigners.

1. Territorial authority. The Commander-in-Chief shall exercise great care that all under his command scrupulously respect the territorial authority of foreign civilized nations in amity with the United States.

2. No armed force to be landed. No armed force for exercise, target practice, funeral escort, or other purposes shall be landed without permission from the local authorities; nor shall large bodies of men be granted leave to visit the shore without a similar permission; nor shall men be landed to capture deserters.

3. No target practice without permission. Target practice with guns or torpedoes shall not take place without permission from the Government of the country concerned within foreign territorial waters or at any point from which shots may fall or torpedoes enter therein.

Article 722. Violation of international law and treaty obligations. On occasions where injury to the United States or to citizens thereof is committed or threatened, in violation of the principles of international law or treaty rights, the Commander-in-Chief shall consult with the diplomatic representative or consul of the United States, and take such steps as the gravity of the case demands, reporting immediately to the Secretary of the Navy all the facts. The responsibility for any action taken by a naval force, however, rests wholly upon the commanding officer thereof.

Article 723. Use of force. Self-preservation. The use of force against a foreign and friendly State, or against anyone within the territories thereof, is illegal.

The right of self-preservation, however, is a right which belongs to States as well as to individuals, and in the case of States it includes the protection of the State, its honor, and its possessions, and the lives and property of its citizens against arbitrary violence, actual or impending, whereby the State or its citizens may suffer irreparable injury. The conditions calling for the application of the right of self-preservation cannot be defined beforehand, but must be left to the sound judgment of responsible officers, who are to perform their duties in this respect with all possible care and forbearance. In no case shall force be exercised in time of peace otherwise than as an application of the right of self-preservation as above defined. It must be used only as a last resort, and then only to the extent which is absolutely necessary to accomplish the end required. It can never be exercised with a view to inflicting punishment for acts already committed.

Article 724. Landing an armed force in foreign territory.

1. Whenever, in the application of the above-mentioned principles, it shall become necessary to land an armed force in foreign territory on occasions of political disturbance where the local authorities are unable to give adequate protection to life and property, the assent of such authorities, or of some one of them, shall first be obtained, if it can be done without prejudice to the interests involved.

# Appendix II

2. Due to the ease with which the Navy Department can be communicated with from all parts of the world, no Commander-in-Chief, flag officer, or commanding officer shall issue an ultimatum to the representative of any foreign Government, or demand the performance of any service from any such representative that must be executed within a limited time, without first communicating with the Navy Department, except in extreme cases where such action is necessary to save life.

Article 726. To protect the commerce of the United States. So far as lies within their power, Commanders-in-Chief, division commanders, and commanding officers of ships shall protect all merchant vessels of the United States in lawful occupations, and advance the commercial interests of this country, always acting in accordance with international law and treaty obligations.

Article 727. Dealings with foreigners. The Commander-in-Chief shall impress upon officers and men that when in foreign ports it is their duty to avoid all possible causes of offense to the authorities or inhabitants; that due deference must be shown by them to the local laws, customs, ceremonies, and regulations; that in all dealings with foreigners moderation and courtesy should be displayed, and that a feeling of good will and mutual respect should be cultivated.[33]

### Commentary

Articles 714, 715, 716, 721, 722, 723, 724, 726 and 727 repeat Articles 1632, 1633, 1634, 1645, 1646, 1647, 1648, 1650 and 1651 of the 1913 Regulations.

### XXII. United States Navy Regulations (1948)

### Commanders-in-Chief and Other Commanders

Article 0505. Observance of International Law.

1. In the event of war between nations with which the United States is at peace, a commander shall observe, and require his command to observe, the principles of international law. He shall make every effort consistent with those principles to preserve and protect the lives and property of citizens of the United States wherever situated.

2. When the United States is at war, he shall observe, and require his command to observe, the principles of international law and the rules of humane warfare. He shall respect the rights of neutrals as prescribed by international law and by pertinent provisions of treaties, and shall exact a like observance from neutrals.

## The Senior Officer Present

Article 0613. Violations of International Law and Treaties. On occasions where injury to the United States or to citizens thereof is committed or threatened, in violation of the principles of international law or treaty rights, the senior officer present shall consult with the diplomatic or consular representatives of the United States, if possible, and shall take such action as the gravity of the situation demands. The responsibility for any action taken by a naval force, however, rests wholly upon the senior officer present. He shall immediately report all the facts to the Secretary of the Navy.

Article 0614. Use of Force Against a Friendly State.

1. The use of force by United States naval personnel against a friendly foreign State, or against anyone within the territories thereof, is illegal.

2. The right of self-preservation, however, is a right which belongs to States as well as to individuals, and in the case of States it includes the protection of the State, its honor, and its possessions, and the lives and property of its citizens against arbitrary violence, actual or impending, whereby the State or its citizens may suffer irreparable injury. The conditions calling for the application of the right of self-preservation cannot be defined beforehand, but must be left to the sound judgment of responsible officers, who are to perform their duties in this respect with all possible care and forbearance. In no case shall force be exercised in time of peace otherwise than as an application of the right of self-preservation as above defined. It must be used only as a last resort, and then only to the extent which is absolutely necessary to accomplish the end required. It can never be exercised with a view to inflicting punishment for acts already committed.

3. Whenever, in the application of the above-mentioned principles, it shall become necessary to land an armed force in a foreign territory on occasions of political disturbance where the local authorities are unable to give adequate protection to life and property, the assent of such authorities, or of some of them, shall first be obtained, if it can be done without prejudice to the interests involved.

Article 0620. Protection of Commerce of the United States. So far as lies within his power, acting in conformity with international law and treaty obligations, the senior officer present shall protect all commercial vessels and aircraft of the United States in their lawful occupations, and shall advance the commercial interests of this country.

Article 0622. Territorial Authority of Foreign Nations.

1. The senior officer present shall, in the exercise of his command, scrupulously respect the territorial authority of nations in amity with the United States.

2. Unless permission has been obtained from local authorities:

a. No armed force for exercise, target practice, funeral escort, or other purposes shall be landed.

b. No persons shall be allowed to visit the shore, except as necessary to conduct official business.

c. No men shall be landed to capture deserters.

3. Target practice with guns, torpedoes, rockets, guided missiles or other weapons shall not take place, without permission from the government of the country concerned, within foreign territorial waters and at any point from which projectiles, torpedoes, or missiles may enter therein.

Article 0623. Dealings with Foreigners. The senior officer present shall uphold the prestige of the United States. He shall impress upon officers and men that when in foreign ports it is their duty to avoid all possible causes of offense to the authorities or inhabitants; that due deference must be shown by them to the local laws, customs, ceremonies, and regulations; that in all dealings with foreigners, moderation and courtesy should be displayed; and that a feeling of good will and mutual respect should be cultivated.[34]

## Commentary

Article 0505 restates in substance Articles 715 and 716 of the 1920 Regulations. The old term "civilized nations" is finally dropped. The phrase was an anachronism and had become offensive to many countries by 1948. The phrase "principles of international law" takes the place of "the laws of neutrality and respect a lawful blockade." This change is not significant, since Article 715 had mentioned the "rules of international law." In short, Article 0505 reflects the same rules that had been used since 1893.

Article 0613 is a restatement of Article 722 of the 1920 Regulations, with minor alterations. "[T]he senior officer present" is substituted for the "Commander-in-Chief" in the first sentence. Consultation with diplomatic or consular representatives is to be had "if possible. . . ." The facts of the problem are to be reported to the Secretary of the Navy immediately, as in Article 722, but the change in priority is obvious. Again, this article is fundamentally the same as its 1893 counterpart.

Article 0614 repeats in substance Article 723 of the 1920 Regulations. The phrase "by United States naval personnel" is inserted in section 1 and the words "friendly" and "foreign" are reversed. Section 2 repeats the second paragraph of Article 723. Section 3 repeats verbatim Article 724 of the 1920 Regulations.

Article 0620 is a close paraphrase of Article 726 of the 1920 Regulations. Enforcement is now in the hands of the "senior officer present" and protection is extended to "all commercial vessels and aircraft. . . ." Otherwise the article is identical to its predecessor.

Articles 0622 and 0623 repeat the substance of Articles 721 and 727 of the 1920 Regulations.

## XXIII. United States Navy Regulations (1973)

### Commanders-in-Chief and Other Commanders

Article 0605. Observance of International Law. At all times a commander shall observe, and require his command to observe, the principles of international law. Where necessary to fulfillment of this responsibility, a departure from other provisions of Navy Regulations is authorized.

### The Senior Officer Present

Article 0914. Violations of International Law and Treaties. On occasions when injury to the United States or to citizens thereof is committed or threatened in violation of the principles of international law or in violation of rights existing under a treaty or other international agreement, the senior officer present shall consult with the diplomatic or consular representatives of the United States, if possible, and he shall take such action as is demanded by the gravity of the situation. In time of peace, action involving the use of force may be taken only in consonance with the provisions of the succeeding article of these regulations. The responsibility for any application of force rests wholly upon the senior officer present. He shall report immediately all the facts to the Secretary of the Navy.

Article 0915. Use of Force Against Another State.

1. The use of force in time of peace by United States naval personnel against another nation or against anyone within the territories thereof is illegal except as an act of self-defense. The right of self-defense may arise in order to counter either the use of force or an immediate threat of the use of force.

## Appendix II

2. The conditions calling for the application of the right of self-defense cannot be precisely defined beforehand, but must be left to the sound judgment of responsible naval personnel who are to perform their duties in this respect with all possible care and forbearance. The right of self-defense must be exercised only as a last resort, and then only to the extent which is absolutely necessary to accomplish the end required.

3. Force must never be used with a view to inflicting punishment for acts already committed.

Article 0916. Territorial Integrity of Foreign Nations. The senior officer present shall respect the territorial integrity of foreign nations. Unless permission has been obtained from foreign authorities:

a. No armed force for exercise, target practice, funeral escort, or other purposes shall be landed.

b. No persons shall be allowed to visit the shore, except as necessary to conduct official business.

c. No men shall be landed to capture deserters.

d. No target practice with guns, torpedoes, rockets, guided missiles or other weapons shall be conducted within foreign territorial waters or at any point from which projectiles, torpedoes or missiles may enter therein.

Article 0917. Dealings with Foreigners. The senior officer present shall uphold the prestige of the United States. He shall impress upon officers and men that, when in foreign ports, it is their duty to avoid all possible cause of offense to the authorities and inhabitants; that due deference must be shown by them to local laws, customs, ceremonies, and regulations; that moderation and courtesy should be displayed in all dealings with foreigners; that a feeling of good will and mutual respect should be cultivated.

Article 0920. Protection of Commerce of the United States. Acting in conformity with the international law and treaty obligations, the senior officer present shall protect, insofar as lies within his power, all commercial craft of the United States in their lawful occupations; and he shall advance the commercial interests of this country.[35]

### Commentary

Article 0605 is a rough paraphrase of Article 0505 of the 1948 Regulations. Its thrust, however, is somewhat different. By deleting the sentence exhorting the commander "to preserve and protect the lives and property of citizens of the United States wherever situated," the Article becomes less self-serving and appears to place primary emphasis upon observance of the principles of international law. Further evidence of this shift in emphasis is the statement that the commander is authorized to ignore other provisions of Navy Regulations where necessary for the fulfillment of his general responsibility to observe the principles of international law. Thus, the effect of the article is to make more explicit the subordination of Navy Regulations to the principles of international law.

The administrative history of this article clearly establishes that such subordination was the drafter's intent.

> The first sentence [of Article 0605] is a simple and straight forward statement reflecting the traditional Navy position with regard to international law. The second sentence provides necessary flexibility in those areas where a convention or treaty ratified by the United States might make other specific Navy Regulations inapplicable or inappropriate in a given circumstance. Because the present world situation is one in which rules in the international arena change so rapidly, and because the United States often takes a leading role in these changes, it is felt that flexibility is necessary in this general article.[36]

The second paragraph of Article 0505 was deleted from the 1973 Regulations "to make clear that Commanders shall observe international law" at all times. The 1973 revisers felt that "as currently phrased, [Article 0505] might support an interpretation which restricts the application of international law to situations of war or armed conflict." They correctly pointed out that "certainly this is true and has never been the Navy position."[37]

Article 0914 restates in substance Article 0613 of the 1948 Regulations. The only substantial change made is the insertion of a sentence emphasizing that in time of peace action involving the use of force is proscribed except in self-defense, as described in Article 0915.

Article 0915, defining the criteria by which a commander may be justified in the use of force in self-defense, roughly parallels Article 0614 of the 1948 Regulations. However, both the language and the thrust of the article have been altered somewhat. The more modern phrase "self-defense" is substituted for that of "self-preservation." The 1973 Regulation states that the right of self-defense "may arise in order to counter either the use of force or an immediate threat of the use of force." The 1948 Regulation states a much broader rationale, including "the protection of the State, its honor, and its possessions, and the lives and property of its citizens against arbitrary violence, actual or impending, whereby the State or its citizens may suffer irreparable injury." The deletion in the 1973 Regulation of language specifically authorizing the forcible protection of the lives and property of US nationals abroad indicates that the circumstances under which a commander may justifiably resort to force for such purposes are greatly restricted today.

The administrative history clearly indicates that the above changes were designed to bring the regulations into conformity with contemporary international law. Article 0614.1, Navy Regulations 1984, according to the drafters,

> discusses restraints on the use of force against a *friendly* State. It could be viewed by implication then that there are no prohibitions on the use of force against an *unfriendly* State. Such a distinction has no foundation in international law.[38]

Further, the drafting history refers to the applicable provisions of the UN Charter and to Security Council practice prescribing the permissible uses of force as the basis for these revised articles.

Article 0916 is a modernization of Article 0622 of the 1948 Regulations. The first sentence of Article 0916 is based on Article 0622, section 1. Respect for the territorial integrity of foreign nations is now properly extended to all nations, and is no longer limited by implications to those nations "in amity with the United States." Such was the drafters' intent:

> [Article 0622, section 1] contains a phrase limiting the article's general applicability to nations "in amity" with the United States. Such a grammatical construction could lead to the interpretation that the principles of this article do not apply to nations not in amity with the United States. This view is inconsonant with international law and the view of the United States.[39]

In the second sentence of Article 0916, "foreign" has been substituted for "local" to make clear just whose permission is required to do the subsequently listed acts. Subparagraphs a, b and c are duplicates of Article 0622, section 2, subparagraphs a, b and c of the 1948 Regulations. Subparagraph d is based on Article 0622, section 3, only grammatical changes have been made.

Article 0917, other than a minor repositioning of words in the penultimate clause, is almost a verbatim copy of Article 0623 of the 1948 Regulations.

Article 0920 restates in substance Article 0620 of the 1948 Regulations. The thrust of both articles is identical.

## XXIV. United States Navy Regulations (1990)

### Commanders-in-Chief and Other Commanders

Article 0705. Observance of International Law. At all times, commanders shall observe, and require their commands to observe, the principles of international law. Where necessary to fulfill this responsibility, a departure from other provisions of Navy Regulations is authorized.

## The Senior Officer Present

Article 0914. Violations of International Law and Treaties. On occasions when injury to the United States or citizens thereof is committed or threatened in violation of the principles of international law or in violation of rights existing under a treaty or other international agreement, the senior officer present shall consult with the diplomatic or consular representatives of the United States, if possible, and shall take such action as is demanded by the gravity of the situation. In time of peace, action involving the use of force may be taken only in consonance with the provisions of the succeeding article of these regulations. The responsibility for any application of force rests wholly upon the senior officer present. The senior officer present shall report immediately all the facts to the National Command Authority, keeping the operational chain of command and the Secretary of the Navy informed.

Article 0915. Use of Force Against Another State.

1. The use of force in time of peace by United States naval personnel against another nation or against anyone within the territories thereof is illegal except as an act of self-defense. Naval personnel have a right of self-defense against hostile acts or hostile intent (imminent threat to use force). This right includes defending themselves, their subunits and, when appropriate, defending US citizens, their property and US commercial assets in the vicinity.

2. The conditions calling for application of the right of self-defense cannot be precisely defined beforehand, but must be left to the sound judgment of responsible naval personnel who are to perform their duties in this respect with all possible care and forbearance. The use of force must be exercised only as a last resort, and then only to the extent which is absolutely necessary to accomplish the end required.

3. Force must never be used with a view to inflicting unlawful punishment for acts already committed.

Article 0916. Territorial Integrity of Foreign Nations. The senior officer present shall respect the territorial integrity of foreign nations. Unless permission has been obtained from foreign authorities:

a. No armed force for exercise, target practice, funeral escort or other purpose shall be landed.

b. No persons shall be allowed to visit the shore, except as necessary to conduct official business.

c. No persons shall be landed to capture deserters.

d. No target practice with guns, torpedoes, rockets, guided missiles or other weapons shall be conducted within foreign territorial waters or at any point from which projectiles, torpedoes or missiles may enter therein.

Article 0917. Dealings with Foreigners. The senior officer present shall uphold the prestige of the United States. He or she shall impress upon officers and enlisted personnel that, when in foreign ports, it is their duty to avoid all possible cause for offense to the authorities and inhabitants; that due deference must be shown by them to local laws, customs, ceremonies and regulations; that moderation and courtesy should be displayed in all dealings with foreigners; and that a feeling of good will and respect should be cultivated.

Article 0920. Protection of Commerce of the United States. Acting in conformity with international law and treaty obligations, the senior officer present shall protect, insofar as lies within his or her power, all commercial craft of the United States in their unlawful occupations.[40]

**Commentary**

Article 0705 is a nearly verbatim repetition of Article 0605 of the 1973 Regulations, the only difference being the substitution of the pronoun "their" for the pronoun "his." Similar changes in the interest of gender neutrality, made throughout the 1990 regulations, will not be mentioned below.

Article 0914 repeats in substance Article 0914 of the 1973 regulations. Under the 1990 Article, the senior officer present reports to the "National Command Authority, keeping the operational chain of command and the Secretary of the Navy informed." The 1973 Article requires a report only to the Secretary of the Navy.

Article 0915 includes a broader description of the right to use force as an act of self-defense than was found in Article 0915 of the 1973 Regulations. Under the 1990 Regulations, "[n]aval personnel have a right of self-defense against hostile acts or hostile intent (imminent threat to use force)," while under the 1973 Regulations the right "may arise in order to counter either the use of force or an immediate threat of the use of force." Further, under the 1990 Regulations, naval personnel may defend "themselves, their subunits and, when appropriate, . . . US citizens, their property and US commercial assets in the vicinity." In comparison, Article 0915 in the 1973 Regulations does not define the ambit of the right of self-defense.

Articles 0916 and 0917 are exact replicas of Articles 0916 and 0917, respectively, in the 1973 regulations.

Article 0920 omits the requirement that the senior officer present "shall advance the commercial interests of this country" but is otherwise a verbatim repetition of Article 0920 in the 1973 regulations.

## Summary

In summary, it can be seen that for nearly a century — between 1893 and 1973 — the Navy Regulations governing the use of force to protect US nationals and their property abroad remained virtually unchanged. With the promulgation of the 1973 Regulations, however, a shift in attitude toward the use of forcible self-help in such cases is evident. Omission of phrases relating directly to the protection of nationals, as well as the inclusion of positive statements relating to the supremacy of international law, indicate that the type of interventionary practice sanctioned by prior regulations no longer passes muster. The 1990 Regulations make no change in this regard. Just what measures of forcible self-help to protect nationals abroad remain permissible today is a controversial question, upon which it is hoped Chapters IV and V have shed some light.

### NOTES

1. *See* Woods, US Navy Regulations, International Law, and the Organization of American States, 22 Naval War College Rev. 66 (Feb. 1970).
2. *See* Chapter I. *See also* Woods, *supra* note 1, at 74-76.
3. *See generally* A. Bozeman, The Future of Law in a Multicultural World (1971).
4. For a pre-1973 discussion of ways to update US Navy Regulations in this area, see Woods, *supra* note 1, at 80-81.
5. Admiral Strauss notes that the 1775 Rules for the Regulation of the Navy of the United Colonies of North America, "were in the main based on the Regulations and Instructions Relating to His Majesty's Service at Sea (1772) and on An Act Relating to the Government of His Majesty's Ships . . . Vessels, and Forces by Sea (1749)." Admiral Strauss further states that "[e]ntire articles from these were taken verbatim; others were converted only to the extent that American political philosophy demanded; a few, but very few, were original." *See* Rules for the Regulation of the Navy of the United Colonies, Introductory Note, Naval Historical Foundation Reprint Series I, No. 1.
6. US Const. art. I, § 8.
7. Bolander, A History of Regulations in the United States Navy, 73 US Naval Institute Proceedings 1355, 1360 (1947).
8. Act of July 14, 1862, ch. 164, § 5, 12 Stat. 565 (1862) (codified as amended at 10 USC. § 6011 (1988)).
9. In 1981, Congress struck the words "with the approval of the President" from 10 USC. § 6011 (1988), leaving with the Secretary of the Navy sole authority to issue the regulations. *See id.*

# Appendix II

10. Regulations and Instructions Relating to His Majesty's Service at Sea, established by His Majesty in Council 2-3, 33, 34 (llth ed. London 1772).

11. Rules for the Regulation of the Navy of the United Colonies of North America 6 (1775); 3 Journals of the Continental Congress 1774-1789, at 380-81 (Ford ed. 1905).

12. *See* note 5 *supra*.

13. Act of March 2, 1799, ch. 24, § 1, 1 Stat. 711.

14. An Act for the better government of the Navy of the United States, Apr. 23, 1800, ch. 33, § 11, 2 Stat. 53 (1856).

15. Naval Regulations issued by Command of the President of the United States of America, January 25, 1802, at 3, 10 (date and place of publication unknown).

16. Naval Regulations, issued by command of the President of the United States of America 3, 9 (Washington, 1814).

17. Rules, Regulations and Instructions for the Naval Service of the United States 14, 29 (Washington, 1818).

18. "Rules, Regulations, and Instructions, for the Naval Service of the United States," in Letter from the Secretary of the Navy, at 20, 37 (Washington, 1821).

19. General Regulations for the Navy and Marine Corps of the United States, 1841, at 45 (Washington, 1841).

20. Orders and Instructions for the Direction and Government of the Naval Service of the United States, and for the Exposition of the Duties and Relations of Officers and Men in the several branches thereof 70-71 (Washington, 1853) (ruled "destitute of legal validity or effect" by the Attorney General on April 5, 1853, 6 Op. Atty Gen. 10, 19 [1856]).

21. "A Code of Regulations for the Government of the Navy," in Annual Report of the Secretary of the Navy, at 78 (Washington, 1858). This Code was prepared and laid before Congress for its approval pursuant to the Act of March 3, 1857, ch. 111, § 7, 11 Stat. 247 (1859). Such approval never was given. *See* Bolander, *supra* note 7, at 1360.

22. Regulations for the Navy of the United States, 1863, 55, 60-61 (Washington, 1863).

23. Regulations for the Government of the United States Navy, 1865, at 56, 62 (Washington, 1865).

24. Regulations for the Government of the United States Navy, 1868, at 7, 18-19 (Washington, 1869).

25. Regulations for the Government of the United States Navy, 1870, at 7, 11-12, 28 (Washington, 1870).

26. Regulations of the Government of the Navy of the United States, 1876, at 25, 27, 30, 35-36 (Washington, 1877).

27. Regulations for the Government of the Navy of the United States, 1893, at 65, 67-68 (Washington, 1893), *as amended,* US Navy Regulation Circular No. 13 (Aug. 15, 1894).

28. Other authorities have dealt at length with the changes in international law and practice between 1893 and recent times, especially as they affected the meaning of the regulations. *See* Woods, note 1 *supra*. *See also* Hallo, The Legal Use of Force . . . Short of War, 92 US Naval Institute Proceedings 88 (1966).

29. Regulations for the Government of the Navy of the United States, 1896, at 64, 65-66 (Washington, 1896).

30. Regulations for the Government of the Navy of the United States, 1900, at 75, 76-77 (Washington, 1900) and Regulations for the Government of the Navy of the United States, 1905, at 75, 76-77 (Washington, 1905).

31. Regulations for the Government of the Navy of the United States, 1909, at 85, 86-87 (Washington, 1909).

32. Regulations for the Government of the Navy of the United States (Navy Regulations), 1913, at 161R, 162R-163R (Washington, 1913), *as amended,* Change No. 7 of September 15, 1916.

33. United States Navy Regulations, 1920, at 219, 220-22 (Washington, 1920).

34. United States Navy Regulations, 1948, at 66, 73, 74 (Washington, 1948).

35. United States Navy Regulations, 1973, at 11, 28, 39 (Washington, 1973).

36. Office of the Judge Advocate General of the Navy, Memorandum from International Law Division to Administrative Law Division, JAG: 102, para. 2 (Sep. 9, 1970).

37. *Id.*

38. *Id.* at para. 8 (emphasis in original).

39. *Id.* at para. 10.

40. United States Navy Regulations, 1990, at 39-40, 71-72 (Washington, 1990).

# Conclusion

At the time of his death, Professor Lillich's manuscript was lacking only a concluding statement of the contemporary law governing the forcible protection of nationals abroad. Although we were determined to present his work without substantive alteration, we did want this volume to be as comprehensive as possible. An editorial consensus emerged that we should append a chapter as a complementary snapshot of the law as it exists today. The following article, written by a co-editor of this volume and originally published in the Dickinson Law Review in the Spring of 2000, fit the bill. It is reproduced here with the kind permission of The Dickinson Law School of The Pennsylvania State University.[†] We hope that it is an appropriate punctuation mark for Professor Lillich's research and analysis, and that it may serve as a point of departure for those scholars who will build on his impressive body of work

## Forcible Protection of Nationals Abroad

### Thomas C. Wingfield

"It was only one life. What is one life in the affairs of a state?"
—*Benito Mussolini, after running down a child in his automobile (as reported by Gen. Smedley D. Butler in address, 1931)*[1]

"This Government wants Perdicaris alive or Raisuli dead."
—*Theodore Roosevelt, committing the United States to the protection of Ion Perdicaris, kidnapped by Sherif Mulai Ahmed ibn-Muhammed er Raisuli (in State Department telegram, June 22nd, 1904)*[2]

---

[†] Thomas C. Wingfield, *Forcible Protection of Nationals Abroad*, 104 DICK. L. REV. 493 (2000). Reproduced with permission of the copyright owner, The Dickinson School of Law of The Pennsylvania State University.

## Introduction

As the two epigraphs above demonstrate, perhaps the best criterion for discriminating tyrannies from democracies is the sincere, proven emphasis placed upon the value of a single human life. The forcible protection of nationals abroad, when undertaken by a sovereign for non-pretextual reasons, is the clearest expression of that distinction in state practice. The academic challenge in evaluating such uses of force is to distinguish such protection from other legitimate uses of force, and then to distinguish these uses from other, illegitimate uses of force. Such an examination is heavily dependent upon the historical context of the threat, and of the acting state. For, as the Rev. Jesse Jackson has stated, "a text without a context is a pretext."[3]

To properly understand the "text" involved, it is important to have as clear a definition as possible. Arend and Beck define "protection of nationals" as "the use of armed force by a state to remove its nationals from another state where their lives are in actual or imminent peril."[4] Arend and Beck add four qualifications to this definition. First, consent obviates the analysis, rendering the operation something other than coercion or intervention.[5] Second, the threatened nationals need not be within the territory of the threatening state, merely within its exclusive jurisdiction. The classic example of this would be a rescue from a ship flying the threatening state's flag.[6] Third, a Chapter VII authorization would, like consent of the territorial state, obviate the analysis. Assuming the Security Council is not acting *ultra vires*, a use of force pursuant to such an authorization is almost by definition lawful.[7] Fourth, and finally, an intervention to protect the citizens of the threatening state is a humanitarian intervention, not the protection of nationals abroad. While the primary discriminator is the nationality of the victims rescued, the dimensions of the two types of intervention can vary significantly. The use of force in the protection of nationals abroad is, at its most pure, a rescue operation, lasting no longer than the evacuation itself. Humanitarian intervention, on the other hand, can involve lengthy nation-building or even government-replacement in the territorial state.[8] A lengthier, but more precise, definition would then read: "the use or threat of imminent use of armed force by a state to safeguard, and usually remove, its nationals from the territory or exclusive jurisdiction of another state, without the consent of that state or the authorization of the UN Security Council, where the lives of those nationals are in actual or imminent peril."

This article will briefly examine the historical foundation for the forcible protection of nationals abroad, recount a number of post-Charter uses of force to protect nationals, describe and evaluate alternate modern theories supporting such actions, and conclude with a description of the law today.

## Historical Development

While an exhaustive historical review of the legality of the use of force in the protection of nationals could consume several volumes, the views of three publicists provide a firm basis for the subsequent, principally post-Charter analysis.

Vattel wrote what is perhaps the seminal paragraph on the protection of nationals:

> Whoever offends the State, injures its rights, disturbs its tranquility, or does it a prejudice in any manner whatsoever, declares himself its enemy, and exposes himself to be justly punished for it. Whoever uses a citizen ill, indirectly offends the State, which is bound to protect this citizen; and the sovereign of the latter should avenge his wrongs, punish the aggressor, and, if possible, oblige him to make full reparation; since otherwise the citizen would not obtain the great end of the civil association, which is, safety.[9]

The justification for intervention in such a case is more than just a right; it becomes a duty of the sovereign. The duty, however, is tempered by a respect for the sovereignty of other nations:

> The prince . . . ought not to interfere in the causes of his subjects in foreign countries, and grant them protection, excepting in cases where justice is refused, or palpable and evident injustice done, or rules and forms openly violated, or, finally, an odious distinction made, to the prejudice of his subjects, or of foreigners in general.[10]

This duty, and this tension, has been echoed by all subsequent thoughtful commentators.

Hall, writing at the end of the 19th Century, returned to the fundamental nature of this duty: "At the root of state life lies the circumstance that the bond which exists between a state and its subjects is not severed when the latter issue from the national territory."[11] However, Hall adds with British understatement, "the clashing laws of states of European civilization still place many persons in situations that are frequently difficult and occasionally serious."[12] It is at this point that the sovereign's duty to protect his subject emerges:

> The duty of protection is correlative to the rights of a sovereign over his subjects; the maintenance of the bond between a state and its subjects while they are abroad implies that the former must watch over and protect them with in the due limit of the rights of other states. ... It enables governments to exact reparation for oppression they have suffered, or for injuries done to them otherwise than by process of law; and it gives the means of guarding them against the effect of unreasonable laws, laws totally out of harmony with the nature and degree of civilization by which a foreign power affects to be characterized, and finally of an administration of laws bad beyond a certain point. When in these directions a state grossly fails in its duties; when it is either incapable of ruling, or rules with patent injustice, the right of protection emerges in the form of diplomatic remonstrance, and in extreme cases of ulterior measures.[13]

The nature and extent of these "ulterior measures" were principally a British concern in the 19th Century, but became an American concern early in the 20th Century, as the United States Navy and Marine Corps extended America's ability to respond to "laws bad beyond a certain point."

Borchard, an American writing early in the 20th Century, addresses with textbook matter-of-factness the use of such force in the protection of nationals abroad:

> The display of force and the threat to use it . . . have frequently proved an effective means of obtaining redress . . . . This display of force usually takes the form of a national war-ship appearing before the port of the foreign country alleged to be in default. The moral influence exerted by the presence of a war vessel is great, and . . . in quarters of the world subject to frequent domestic disorder has served not only to prevent an abuse of aliens' rights, particularly of the nationals of the country to which the vessel belongs.[14]

Although such displays were frequently effective, they occasionally escalated to actual uses of force:

> The army or navy has frequently been used for the protection of citizens or their property in foreign countries in cases of emergency where the local government has failed, through inability or unwillingness, to afford adequate protection to the persons or property of the foreigners in question.[15] . . . The occasions on which troops have been landed have varied, although it has always been under circumstances where the protective faculties of the local government have been so weakened that the security of aliens, particularly nationals of the interfering state, seemed so precarious that some measure of self-help was deemed necessary.[16] . . . While the landing of troops in the cases above mentioned has

been purely protective, they have not always been able to avoid belligerent operations to effect their purpose.[17]

Vattel, Hall, and Borchard describe a legal regime which existed from the early 17th Century until the middle of the 20th Century. It was only with the entry into force of the U.N. Charter that an entirely new analytical framework was put into place, ostensibly outlawing the aggressive use of force, but preserving the "inherent" right of self-defense. Although centuries of state practice were not entirely irrelevant, future uses of force to protect nationals abroad would have to be justified within the new Charter paradigm.

The first step in understanding this new framework is to review the significant uses of force in the Charter era (post-1945), providing the factual background for testing theory and examining state practice.

## Uses of Force in the Charter Era

*United Kingdom Threatens Intervention in Iran—1946*
When rioting broke out in Iran in the summer of 1946, less than a year after the Charter had entered into force, the British government was concerned for the safety of British residents working for the Anglo-Iranian Oil Company. With the permission of the Iraqi government,[18] Britain dispatched a contingent of troops to Basra, Iraq, near the Iranian border. The U.K. also ordered two warships to anchor off Basra. They did this "in order that they may be at hand for the protection, should the circumstances demand it, of Indian, British and Arab lives, and in order to safeguard Indian and British interests in South Persia, troops are being sent from India to Basra."[19] The rioting subsided, and no entry was necessary. The Iranian government still protested the threat of force as a violation of Article 2(4) of the UN Charter and an infringement of Iranian sovereignty.[20] Britain responded that it would have intervened in case of a "grave emergency,"[21] that is, if the Iranian government had been unable or unwilling to protect the lives of British residents.

*Second Threat of Intervention in Iran by U.K.—1951*
The Iranian government precipitated another crisis when it nationalized the Anglo-Iranian Oil Company in 1951. The British government once again feared that the heightened tensions between the two countries might put British residents in Iran at risk. Accordingly, the U.K. dispatched several warships to Iraqi waters, and deployed a number of combat aircraft to British bases within Iraq.[22] British policy statements on the move were unusually clear

and to the point. Foreign Secretary Morrison stated that Britain had "every right and indeed the duty to protect British lives."[23] He went on to elaborate before the House of Commons:

> As I have repeatedly informed the House, His Majesty's government are not prepared to stand idly by if the lives of British nationals are in jeopardy. It is the responsibility of the Persian government to see to it that law and order are maintained and that all within the frontiers of Persia are protected from violence. If, however, that responsibility were not met it would equally be the right and duty of His Majesty's government to extend protection to its own nationals.[24]

Iran, on the other hand, saw the positioning of air and naval forces just outside its own borders as a threat of force unwarranted by the situation. Iran stated that the U.K. had no right to "intimidate" Iran,[25] and that Iran was "completely the master of the situation."[26] Iran took this policy position one step further, and declared before a meeting of the Sixth Committee of the UN General Assembly that even if British nationals had been mistreated, any action to intervene and protect them could not be justified as a lawful exercise of self-defense.[27]

*The Cairo Riots—1952*

A more subtle response to a more serious threat occurred in January, 1952, when large-scale rioting broke out in Cairo. This time, British property was damaged and British lives were lost.[28] In response, the U.K. developed a contingency plan to use its troops in the Suez Canal zone to move in to Cairo and Alexandria to protect endangered British residents.[29] The British government communicated its willingness to take action in a diplomatic note on January 27th, stating that it held the government of Egypt fully responsible for all damage to British property and any threat to the safety of British residents in Egypt. Further, the note warned, the U.K. reserved the right to take whatever action was required to safeguard the lives and property of its nationals.[30] The note had the desired effect, and the previously quiescent Egyptian army moved in to put down the rioters. Then-Foreign Secretary Eden explained, "the belief that we had the forces and the conviction that we were prepared to use them were powerful arguments in prodding the Egyptian army to quell the riots."[31]

## Conclusion

*Anglo-French Intervention in Egypt in 1956 (the Suez Crisis)*

Fearing that their nationals were threatened by Israeli-Egyptian war in October, 1956, Britain and France made a series of diplomatic entreaties for the belligerents to cease hostilities. When this course failed, the British and the French bombed Egyptian airstrips near the Suez Canal and, four days later, inserted a contingent of troops to occupy key points along the canal. While France emphasized other rationales, Britain relied heavily on the right to protect its own citizens abroad.[32] The British Representative to the UN, speaking before the Security Council, said:

> In Egypt there are many thousands of British and French nationals. The chain of events which began with the Israel [sic] moves into Egypt has developed into hostilities and hostilities have created a disturbed situation. In those circumstances, British and French lives must be safeguarded. I again emphasize . . . that we should certainly not want to keep any forces in the area for one moment longer than is necessary to protect our nationals.[33]

Then-Prime Minister Eden stated before the House of Commons that "there is nothing . . . in the Charter which abrogates the right of a Government to take such steps as are essential to protect the lives of their citizens."[34] He went on to explain that, when the Security Council was paralyzed by a veto (as it was in this case), that states had the right to intervene "in an emergency," to protect the lives of nationals abroad.[35] He added that this right was based on the inherent Article 51 right to self-defense,[36] and that this right could be exercised anticipatorily—that is, the injured state need not first receive the equivalent of an armed attack against its citizens before moving preemptively against the threat.[37]

Foreign Secretary Lloyd outlined three criteria for the lawful exercise of the right of protection of nationals abroad within the larger right of self-defense: first, that the nationals of the intervening state be under "an imminent threat of injury;" second, that there is a "failure or inability" by the local sovereign to protect foreign citizens; and third, that the action of the intervening state be "strictly confined to the object of protecting the nationals against injury."[38]

Finally, the Lord Chancellor, before the House of Lords, stated that "self-defence undoubtedly includes a situation in which the lives of a State's nationals abroad are threatened and it is necessary to intervene on that territory for their protection."[39]

In addition to this rationale, the British and the French also pursued the military operation to maintain international freedom of navigation through the canal, and to stop hostilities between Egypt and Israel.[40] The problem of overlapping justifications will reappear frequently in state practice.

*The Belgian Intervention in the Congo—1960*
Immediately upon declaring its independence from Belgium in July 1960, the Congo's army mutinied and touched off a week of rioting, looting, and atrocities against foreign nationals.[41] As the Congolese government was completely unable to maintain order, Belgium ordered a contingent of paratroopers already in the Congo to protect Belgian and other threatened foreign nationals.[42] Before the Security Council, the Belgian Ambassador to the UN stated that his government had "decided to intervene with the sole purpose of ensuring the safety of European and other members of the population and of protecting human lives in general."[43] This rationale mixes pure self-defense (protecting a state's own nationals), collective self-defense (protecting other foreign nationals within another state), and humanitarian intervention (protecting the citizens of the threatened state).

In Security Council debate, France argued that the Belgian troops' "mission of protecting lives and property is the direct result of the failure of the Congolese authorities and is in accord with a recognized principle of international law, namely, intervention on humanitarian grounds."[44] Argentina based its support of the Belgian intervention not on the legality of self-defense, but on the moral imperative of the situation:

> Now, we are convinced that the protection of the life and honour of individuals is a sacred duty to which all other considerations must yield. We cannot reproach the Belgian government for having assumed this duty when Belgian nationals were in danger. Any other State would have done the same thing.[45]

The United States was more guarded in its statements, and urged that Belgium should withdraw once the UN had provided military forces to stabilize the situation. In an interesting gloss on the doctrine of humanitarian intervention, Belgium actually adopted the U.S. position in a statement that is a model of concise legal advocacy: Belgium would withdraw "its intervening troops as soon as, and to the extent that, the United Nations ensures the maintenance of order and the safety of persons."[46]

*United States Intervention in the Dominican Republic—1965*
In April, 1965, the Constitutional Party forced the resignation of Dominican President Reid Cabral. Cabral's National Reconstruction Government

immediately organized to regain control of the country. By the end of the month, the situation was sufficiently out of hand that the United States felt compelled to land 400 Marines to evacuate American citizens and other foreign nationals from the country.[47] According to U.S. Ambassador to the UN Adlai Stevenson,

> In the absence of any governmental authority, Dominican law enforcement and military officials informed our Embassy that the situation was completely out of control, that the police and the Government could no longer give any guarantee concerning the safety of Americans or of any foreign nationals, and that only an immediate landing of United States forces could safeguard and protect the lives of thousands of Americans and thousands of citizens of some thirty other countries.[48]

This introduces a hybrid form of invitation—less than the pure consent rendered by an invitation from the *de jure* sovereign, but more than a simple, unilateral decision to intervene based on an external analysis of the situation. The warnings and requests of mid-to-high level officials of the defeated but arguably still lawful government fall squarely within this gray area. While this type of request does not forestall a legal analysis of the grounds for intervening (as would an invitation from the sovereign), it does add weight to the factual arguments establishing the state of chaos in a country, and therefore helps weed out instances of purely pretextual intervention.

However valid the basis for forcible protection of nationals may have been at the outset, U.S. involvement quickly escalated and policy diversified. The number of troops increased, their stay in-country was extended, and subsequent government statements announced that the United States was acting to prevent the establishment of a second communist government in the Western Hemisphere.[49] To no one's surprise, Britain supported the initial deployment, France was ambivalent, and Cuba was opposed.[50]

*The Mayaguez Incident—1975*
On May 12th, 1975, Cambodia seized an American merchant ship. Cambodia claimed the *Mayaguez* was in its territorial waters, and on a spy mission. The United States insisted that the ship had been in international waters at the time of its seizure, and that it had not been on a spy mission. On May 13th, the U.S. demanded she be released within 24 hours. Cambodia did not comply, so the United States launched an airstrike against the facility at which it was being held. The Cambodians still did not comply, so on May 14th, the U.S.

mounted a heliborne Marine infantry assault against the ship. This did achieve the desired result, and the ship and crew were freed.[51]

Between the airstrike on the 13th and the assault on the 14th, the U.S. requested the assistance of the Secretary General of the UN in securing the release of the ship. In the request, the U.S. reserved the right to take "such measures as may be necessary to protect the lives of American citizens and property, including appropriate measures of self-defense under Article 51 of the UN Charter."[52]

Cambodia condemned the assault, claiming it was "a brutal act of aggression."[53] Cambodia also stated that the attack was not militarily necessary, in that it had already begun preparations to release the ship.[54] China sided with Cambodia, labeling the assault an "act of piracy."[55] Algeria and Thailand also condemned the attack, the latter because its bases had been used as a staging area for the assault team.[56]

*The Evacuation of U.S. Citizens from Lebanon—1976*
When the long-running civil war in Lebanon reached a threshold threatening the lives of the few Americans remaining in the country, the United States evacuated a small group to a warship on June 28th, 1976, and again on July 27th.[57] Interestingly, the U.S. consulted no domestic authority before the first evacuation, but pursued a different course before the second. Instead of requesting the approval of the *de jure* Lebanese government, whose influence over events asymptotically approached irrelevance, the U.S. coordinated with those actually in control of the territory—the PLO and several other Palestinian groups.[58] While this coordination, like that with the Dominican quasi-authorities eleven years earlier—had little influence on the academic legality of the operation, it did provide an improved chance of conducting the operation with as few casualties as possible. In this case, no U.S. servicemen or Lebanese civilians were killed.[59]

*The Israeli Raid on Entebbe—1976*
On June 27th, 1976, a French airliner enroute from Tel Aviv to Paris was hijacked by four Palestinian terrorists. After a brief stop in Libya, the aircraft flew to Uganda, where it was joined by six additional terrorists. The terrorists freed all of the non-Israeli passengers, and specifically threatened the lives of those who remained. The government of Uganda was at best uncooperative in attempts to negotiate a settlement, and appeared to be providing support to the terrorists.[60]

## Conclusion

The evening of July 3rd and 4th, Israeli commandos stormed the main terminal at the Entebbe Airport in Uganda. Killed were all of the terrorists who were holding 96 Israelis hostage, along with several hostages who stood up in the middle of the melee, a number of Ugandan soldiers, and one Israeli commando. To prevent pursuit, the Israelis also destroyed the operational Ugandan fighters (approximately 10) on the tarmac.[61]

The unique aspect of this raid was that the nationals in question were taken to the foreign country against their will.[62] This suggests that the foreign nationals concerned were less responsible for weighing the risks involved in travelling to and living in the dangerous country in question. It is also more difficult for the intervening state to fashion a pretext in the rush of a terrorist event than over the course of a long-deteriorating civil situation. Finally, the actions required to rescue people in a confined hostage setting are necessarily less intrusive than to secure an area with a foreign capital against riots. These three reasons appear to make intervention in the case of a terrorist event less problematic than even traditional protection of nationals abroad.

Israel made a forceful case for its rescue mission at a meeting of the Security Council on July 9th. It claimed that it had the right "to take military action to protect its nationals in mortal danger."[63] This right, Israel claimed, was based on the inherent right of self-defense, "enshrined in international law and the Charter of the United Nations," and supported by state practice.[64] Israel stated that this exercise of self-defense met the standard of the *Caroline* case: "Necessity of self-defense, instant, overwhelming, leaving no choice of means and no moment for deliberation."[65] Finally, Israel explained that the use of force was not directed at Uganda *per se*, and employed only as much force as was necessary to secure and extract its nationals.[66]

The United States was the only country to make a clear statement supporting the legality of the Israeli raid. At the same Security Council meeting, the U.S. first stated that the intervention was "a temporary breach of the territorial integrity of Uganda."[67] While this sort of breach is normally considered a violation of the UN Charter, this case, the U.S. argued, fit within an exception. "There is a well-established right," said the U.S., "to use limited force for the protection of one's own nationals from an imminent threat of injury or death in a situation where the State in whose territory they are located is either unwilling or unable to protect them."[68] The U.S. stated that this right flows from the inherent right of self-defense and allows "necessary and appropriate" force to protect a nation's own citizens.[69] By these criteria, the U.S. concluded, the raid on Entebbe was a lawful use of force under international law. The U.S. found the force used to be proportional to the limited goal of freeing the passengers, and the use of force had ended once this goal had been achieved.[70]

France also supported the Israeli intervention, in a manner of speaking. While stating that "at first sight . . . the surprise attack by an armed force on a foreign airport for the purpose of achieving by violence an objective" appeared to violate international law, the Israeli action had not been designed to infringe the territorial integrity or political independence of Uganda, but merely to save lives.[71] The French brought up an additional legal point, that the UN General Assembly's Resolution on the Definition of Aggression listed acts which were only *prima facie* evidence of acts of aggression, and that it was up to the Security Council to determine if, "in the light of other relevant circumstances," aggression had actually been committed.[72]

*The French Threat to Intervene in the Western Sahara—1978*
On October 25th, 1978, two French technicians were captured in Mauritania by Polisario guerillas. Two days later, the French Defense Minister refused to rule out a military raid to free them. A French parachute corps was moved to Senegal, and French aircraft participated in airstrikes on Polisario military formations on December 12th, 13th, and 18th. On December 23rd, the two technicians were turned over to the UN Secretary General in Algeria.[73] Although the force was not applied in the form of a rescue mission, its indirect application had the desired result.

*The Egyptian Raid on Larnaca—1978*
The first non-Western use of force to protect nationals abroad was, at best, a learning experience for all involved. Egypt sent a planeful of commandos to Larnaca, Cyprus, on February, 19th to free Egyptian and other hostages taken the day before. Although the Egyptians received permission to land, they did not receive permission to storm the aircraft. The Cypriot authorities were successfully concluding negotiations with the terrorists, and the passengers had begun to leave the aircraft, when the Egyptians decided to attack. The Cypriot military opened fire on the Egyptians, arrested the terrorists, and helped the hostages to safety.[74]

The Egyptians defended their actions less as the protection of nationals abroad (although several of the hostages were Egyptian, and an Egyptian had been killed by the terrorists in the initial seizure of the hostages), and more as an amorphous commitment "to fight terrorism and to bring all those who use such methods to justice."[75]

# Conclusion

*The U.S. Hostage Rescue Attempt in Iran—1980*
On the evening of 24-25 April, 1980, the United States launched a commando raid into Iran to rescue 50 hostages who had been held since November 4th of the previous year. The raid ultimately failed due to weather, equipment malfunction, and bad luck.

Although the hostage incident preoccupied the United States from late 1979 to early 1981, and was responsible for an enormous amount of diplomatic maneuvering, the specific question of using force in the protection of nationals abroad was fairly straightforward. The ICJ decision in the hostages case, rendered on May 24th, characterized the actions of the "students" holding the hostages as fairly educible to the Iranian government: "[T]he approval given to these nacts by the Ayatollah Khomeini and other organs of the Iranian State, and the decision to perpetuate them, translated continuing occupation of the Embassy and detention of the hostages into acts of that State."[76] This retrospective linking of the "students" actions to the Iranian State permitted action against that state as though it had perpetrated those actions in the first place.

President Carter stated:

> I ordered this rescue mission prepared in order to safeguard American lives, to protect America's national interests, and to reduce the tensions in the world that have been caused among many nations as the crisis continued. . . . The mission . . . was a humanitarian mission. It was not directed against Iran; it was not directed against the people of Iran. It was not undertaken with any feeling of hostility toward Iran or its people.[77]

In his report to Congress, he declared: "In carrying out this operation, the United States was acting wholly within its right, in accordance with Article 51 of the United Nations Charter, to protect and rescue its citizens where the government of the territory in which they are located is unwilling or unable to protect them."[78]

While usual countries supported or condemned the raid in political terms, the Italian Foreign Minister Colombo, echoing Reisman, provided an illuminating legal comment:

> There was . . . on the part of Iran alone an extremely serious infringement of the rules of international law. The State which falls a victim to such an infringement has the power, under international law, to resort to self-help. Even the United Nations Charter recognizes this right as inherent, the exercise of which is subordinate to the powers and duties conferred on the Security Council, for restoring the rule of law. But the Charter also recognizes the right of each

permanent member of the Security Council to veto. Each permanent member must be aware of the responsibility it takes upon itself when vetoing a resolution of the Security Council, by pointing the way to self-help.[79]

*U.S. Intervention in Grenada—1983*
On October 25th, 1983, the U.S. launched Operation *Urgent Fury*, a large amphibious and air assault on the island nation of Grenada. This was in response to an increasingly anarchic situation, precipitated earlier in the month by a *coup d'etat* against the island's Marxist Prime Minister, Maurice Bishop, by hard-line members of his own government. On October 19th, Bishop and scores of others were killed in an unsuccessful attempt to regain control of the island's government. Later that same day, General Hudson Austin, head of the new "Revolutionary Military Council," announced a four-day, 24-hour, shoot-on-sight curfew. Concerned for the safety of American tourists and medical students on the island, and alarmed by the presence of a large number of armed, Cuban paramilitary construction workers on the island (completing work on an airstrip large enough to support heavy military aircraft), the United States took action.[80]

Although the Grenadian operation appeared to have the classic factual predicate for a traditional forcible protection of nationals scenario, it was not for two specific reasons. First, the operation was conducted at the request of the Governor-General of Grenada, whose constitutional authority, particularly in the absence of any other *de jure* government, was unsurpassed by any other claimant to power.[81] Second, the operation was a textbook example of collective self-defense, in that the United States' assistance was forcefully and urgently requested by the Organization of Eastern Caribbean States.[82] Despite the fact that there appear to be three independently sufficient legal justifications for the U.S./OECS intervention, 79 governments expressed some level of disapproval of the operation, and on November 2nd, the UN General Assembly voted 108 to 9 to condemn the intervention as a "violation of international law."[83] This was somewhat offset by the overwhelming support for the operation shown by the people of Grenada.[84]

*The U.S. Intervention in Panama—1989*
Six years later, another small nation in the Western Hemisphere had had its democratic election invalidated by a military strongman, and the latent threat to local citizens and foreign nationals gradually escalated to unacceptable levels. As Arend and Beck describe:

## Conclusion

On December 20, 1989, the United States launched an invasion of Panama code-named Operation 'Just Cause.' In a special press briefing given that day, Secretary of State James Baker emphasized that the 'leading objective' of the US military action had been 'to protect American lives.' [footnote omitted] Earlier on D-Day, President Bush had tersely explained the rationale for his decision to use force: 'Last Friday, [General Manuel] Noriega declared his military dictatorship to be in a state of war with the United States and publicly threatened the lives of Americans in Panama.' On Saturday, 'forces under his command shot and killed an unarmed American serviceman, wounded another, arrested and brutally beat a third American serviceman and then brutally interrogated his wife, threatening her with sexual abuse. That, said the president, 'was enough!' [footnote omitted] It was time to act.[85]

Two factors make the analysis of the intervention more difficult. First is the sheer scale of the operation: ten thousand American troops eventually seized control of the entire country, removed the *de facto* head of state to face drug trafficking charges in the U.S., and reinstalled the *de jure*, democratically-elected government.[86] Second, President Bush cited four overlapping justifications for the intervention: "to safeguard the lives of Americans, to defend democracy in Panama, to combat drug trafficking and to protect the integrity of the Panama Canal Treaty."[87] Of these, claimed Secretary of State Baker, the protection of American lives was "the leading one."[88]

Reaction to the invasion was generally negative—mildly so in Europe, and stridently so in Latin America.[89] The communist world was also condemnatory, with the Soviet Union calling the operation "a violation of the United Nations Charter and of the universally accepted norms of behavior between sovereign states."[90] China simply labeled it "a violation of internal law."[91] The United States, Britain, and France vetoed a Security Council resolution condemning the invasion.[92]

### The U.S. Intervention in Liberia—1990

On August 5th, 1990, the United States landed 255 Marines in the Liberian capital of Monrovia to evacuate U.S. and any other nationals desiring to leave the country. This was in immediate response to an announcement the day before by rebel leader Prince Johnson, who called for the arrest of all foreign nationals in the capital. Johnson apparently wished to attract international attention to his rebel faction, and provoke an international response to the seven-month-old rebellion.[93] In this, he was successful.

Without seeking or receiving permission from embattled President Samuel K. Doe or either of the rival rebel faction leaders, the Marines evacuated approximately one thousand foreign nationals from Monrovia over a two-week period.[94] On August 24th, a West African peacekeeping force arrived in Monrovia to enforce a cease-fire.[95]

Professor Lillich drew this conclusion from the international community's reaction to the evacuation:

> [T]he renewed assertion by the United States of the right of forcible protection of its nationals during the Liberian disorder, the fact that hundreds of other foreign nationals from dozens of States were evacuated with what must have been the enthusiastic (if not explicit) approval of their governments, and the near-complete absence of legal or other criticism of the rescue operation all combine to indicate that the international community, now more than ever in the post-Cold War period, is prepared to accept, endorse or, at the very least, tolerate the forcible protection of nationals abroad in appropriate cases.[96]

## Theoretical Bases for Action

The two major theories addressing the legality of the use of force in the protection of nationals abroad are the "restrictionist" theory, which views any such use of force as unlawful, and the "counter-restrictionist theory," which, as its name implies, holds the opposite view. Within the counter-restrictionist theory, there are several intermingled sub-theories supporting the general premise of allowing intervention.

*The Restrictionist Theory*
This theory, which states that there is no lawful basis for the forcible protection of nationals abroad, rests on three assumptions. First, it assumes that the sole principal goal of the United Nations is the maintenance of international peace and security. Second, it holds that the UN has a monopoly on the lawful use of force, with the narrow exception for self-defense in the case of armed attack on the territory of a state. Third, it maintains that if states were permitted to use force to protect their nationals abroad, or for any other reason beyond clear individual or collective self-defense, they would broaden this narrow mandate, using it as a pretext for any desired policy ends.[97]

Restrictionists concede that, under the pre-Charter legal regime, states did have the right to use force unilaterally in the protection of their nationals. However, they say, this right was often abused, placing weak states at the mercy of stronger ones wishing to advance national policy through violence. To end this practice, they conclude, the framers of the UN Charter specifically outlawed the unilateral use of force, except for the most obvious cases of national self-defense against armed attack, and then only to the extent that the Security Council had not yet acted. According to Ian Brownlie, "[t]he whole object of the Charter was to render unilateral use of force, even in self-defense, subject to UN control."[98]

Arend and Beck concisely summarize the textual basis for the restrictionist argument:

> For their rendition of the *jus ad bellum*, the restrictionists draw heavily upon Articles 2(4) and 51 of the UN Charter. In their view, the language of Article 2(4) clearly indicates a general prohibition on the use of force by states. [footnote omitted] No state is permitted to threaten or use force 'against the territorial integrity or political independence of any state, or in any manner inconsistent with the Purposes of the United Nations.' Article 51, which provides for 'individual and collective self-defense,' constitutes merely a narrow exception to the general prohibition of 2(4). [footnote omitted] States may defend themselves, restrictionists argue, but only after an actual 'armed attack' upon state *territory* has occurred. [footnote omitted] Typical of the restrictionist view is that described by Waldcock, himself a counter-restrictionist: '2(4) prohibits entirely any threat of use of armed force between independent States except in individual or collective self defense under Article 51 or in execution of collective measures under the Charter for maintaining or restoring peace.' [footnote omitted] The UN Charter's prohibition, the French restrictionist Viraly suggests, has the broadest range it is possible to imagine.' [footnote omitted][99]

The restrictionist theory, in its purest form, allows no use of force against any terrorist or other groups who are using force below the invasion-level of an armored column crossing a national border.

*The Counter-Restrictionist Theory*

The counter-restrictionist theory is actually a constellation of four overlapping, nonexclusive subtheories.

The first subtheory involves the survival or revival of the pre-Charter customary rule allowing forcible protection of nationals abroad. Derek Bowett argues for the survival of the customary rule. He believes that a reading of the Charter's *travaux preparatoires* shows that the framers intended to preserve the "inherent" right of self-defense, with the contours acquired from customary international law up to that point. More persuasively for Bowett, state practice since the Charter was ratified has confirmed that a significant number of states have exercised the right to protect nationals abroad, extending the customary international law norm into the present.[100]

The other version of this subtheory holds that the norm has been revived in the modern era. Arend and Beck explain:

> In their view, the UN founders mistakenly assumed that 'self-help' would no longer be necessary 'since an authoritative international organization [could now] provide the police facilities for enforcement of international rights. [footnote omitted] Unfortunately for the international system, submit Michael Reisman, Richard Lillich, and other scholars, the UN enforcement mechanisms have been confounded at virtually every turn by dissension among the Security Council's permanent membership. [footnote omitted] Article 2(4)'s prohibition on the threat or use of force, they assert, must hence be conditioned on the United Nations' capacity to respond effectively. When the UN fails to do so, customary law revives and states may intervene to protect nationals. [footnote omitted][101]

In summary, this subtheory posits that, whether it survived the entry into force of the Charter, or was extinguished by it and later revived by UN mal-, mis-, or nonfeasance, the customary norm under international law permitting the use of force in the protection of nationals abroad is alive today.[102]

The second subtheory describes the protection of nationals abroad as a permissible use of force below the Article 2(4) threshold. The article itself directs: "All Members shall refrain in their international relations from the threat or use of force against the territorial integrity or political independence of any state, or in any way inconsistent with the UN's purposes."[103] Here, the key is that Article 2(4) has two dimensions: a *quantitative* aspect regarding the *amount* of violence or coercion, and a *qualitative* aspect regarding the end to which the violence or coercion is directed. An oversimplified reading of Article 2(4) may leave the impression of a simple, and low, threshold, forbidding all uses or even threats of force not flowing from self-defense or Chapter VII authorization. The two-dimensional approach, however, keys on the language ". . . against the territorial integrity or political independence of any state . . . ." A legitimate use of force in the protection of nationals abroad does not take or hold territory, or threaten the government elected, or tolerated, by the people. Such a use of force is qualitatively different, and not the type which the framers of the Charter, with fresh memories of German and Japanese aggression, sought to circumscribe. A brief operation which, at its conclusion, has affected neither the territorial integrity nor the political independence of the threatening state would not appear to have violated the qualitative prong of the Article 2(4) prohibition.[104]

## Conclusion

The third subtheory is a complement of the second; it holds that a threat to even a single national abroad is the equivalent of an "armed attack" against the nation, allowing for a protective, and not punitive, response proportional to the injury received or threatened. That is, the forcible protection of nationals abroad is permissible self-defense under Article 51.[105] Since Article 51 appears not to create, but to simply recognize, "the *inherent* right of self-defense," counter-restrictionists believe the Charter provides "a local habitation and a name" for the customary right of the first subtheory. The problem with this subtheory appears to be that, like Article 2(4), Article 51 has both qualitative and quantitative aspects. The former fits well with the first subtheory, in that an "inherent" right could quite plausibly follow the contours of customary international law. The latter, however, suggests that there is a high threshold, "armed attack," below which the use of force is inappropriate.

The counterargument to this last point is that it is difficult to imagine that the framers of the Charter would create a legal no-man's land, wherein a rogue state would be able to inflict violent injury, but the aggrieved state would not be able to respond in self-defense.[106] The key to reconciling this apparent lacuna is proportionality: self-defense operates across the spectrum of violence, and a small "armed attack" against a national abroad may be met with a necessary and proportional nonpunitive response designed to protect the victim from further harm. To the extent that Article 51 permits reaction against less-than-overwhelming uses of force, it demands a reciprocal limitation on the scope, duration, and intensity of the protective response. The customary international legal doctrines comprising the law of armed conflict—military necessity, proportionality, and chivalry—provide these limitations even in the absence of an absolute prohibition by Article 51.

Finally, the fourth subtheory is grounded in a respect for human rights. Specifically, McDougal and Reisman reject the restrictionist premise that the UN has one overriding purpose, the maintenance of international peace and security. They argue that the UN has two such fundamental premises, each deserving equal weight: the maintenance of international peace and security, and the protection of human rights.[107]

This view is grounded in the Preamble, Articles 1, 55, and 56, and a large and growing corpus of human rights law.[108] Under this view, human rights violations are themselves threats to international peace and security. If the Security Council fails to act under Chapter VII, McDougal and Reisman argue, "the cumulative effect of articles 1, 55, and 56 [would be] to establish the legality of unilateral self-help."[109]

## Conclusion

This article defined forcible protection of nationals abroad, reviewed commentary on the concept by publicists from the late 18th Century to the end of the pre-Charter era, and then surveyed the major uses of force in the protection of nationals abroad during the Charter era.

*Lessons of State Practice*
Arend and Beck provide an outstanding structural review of state practice in the Charter era. They examine four broad areas—the nature of intervening states, the circumstances of intervention, the scope of intervention, and state justification for intervention—and explore subcriteria within each. From their analysis emerge several fascinating points about how states have protected nationals beyond their borders.[110]

The nature of the intervening states reveals two patterns: they have been almost exclusively Western, and there have been very few of them. Of the 16 episodes they describe, 13 involved the use of force by just four countries: the United States, Great Britain, France, and Belgium. Generally, these powers have been the only ones in a position to effectively project military power in a troubled region.[111]

The circumstances of the intervention have varied considerably. The number of endangered nationals has ranged from the thousands (in the Congo and the Dominican Republic) to just two (in the Western Sahara). The governmental situation has also varied, from the anarchy of no government at all (Liberia, the Dominican Republic) to a malevolent government actively threatening the nationals concerned (Uganda, Iran). The nationality has likewise varied, from the rescue of own-country nationals (Entebbe, *Mayaguez*) to the evacuation of all foreign nationals in a troubled area (the Congo, Liberia, Grenada). Interestingly, almost all such operations have occurred in areas that were, until the Charter era, under "Great Power" protection, usually as former colonies. Iran, Palestine, Egypt, Cambodia, the Congo, the Dominican Republic, Lebanon, Uganda, the Western Sahara, Grenada, Panama—all were under varying degrees of Great Power control until recently. This resulted in two situations: the turbulence which often accompanies recent independence, and a power which is both familiar with and, in a moral sense, responsible for, the former territory.[112]

The scope of the intervention ran the gamut from brief excursions measured in minutes (Entebbe, *Mayaguez*) to months-long stays (the Dominican Republic, Egypt). The longer-term operations, however, were only initially characterized as the protection of nationals abroad. Once that phase of the operation had passed, new missions with new justifications took their place. The true protective missions were extremely limited in the territorial scope, temporal duration, and military intensity of their effects.[113]

Finally, the state justifications for the interventions varied as well. Most states have relied on multiple rationales for their operations, with the protection of nationals near the top of the list in most cases. However, as operations lengthened or diversified, new justifications would be advanced once the nationals sought to be protected were secure.[114]

*A Coherent Legal Model for the Protection of Nationals Abroad*
The four subtheories advanced by the counter-restrictionists each contain helpful elements. A model which includes the most authoritative portions of all four would provide a solid legal basis for undertaking such operations in the Charter era.[115]

The first subtheory, regarding the survival or revival of the customary norm allowing protection of nationals, is perhaps best understood as a synthesis of the two. To the extent that such an understanding does not run afoul of the plain language of the Charter, it appears that a narrowly construed form of self-defense did survive the entry into force of the Charter, and that a long line of customary international law informs its use today. The second portion of this argument, however, is the more controversial. To the extent that the UN did not deliver on the security it promised in return for a limitation on the national exercise of self-defense, that inherent right must necessarily expand to meet the new threats. Without violating the plain meaning of the Charter, nations should and must protect their citizens when no another authority, national or international, is willing or able. In this sense, this additional portion of the inherent right of self-defense has been revived as the UN has often proved incapable, as an organization, of maintaining international peace and security.

The second subtheory, that such actions are below the qualitative threshold of Article 2(4), is a close call, but, in the case of a pure rescue operation, in accord with the facts. If no territory is held, and if the political structure is not materially threatened, it is difficult to argue that a rescue operation breaks the 2(4) threshold.

The third subtheory, that such operations are lawful exercises of the inherent right of self-defense, guaranteed by Article 51, is perhaps the strongest argument. By allowing the threshold of an "armed attack" to float at the level of the provocation, a militarily necessary, proportionate, and chivalrous response will guarantee compliance with international law. If a single citizen is placed in harm's way, and only that force necessary to bring her to safety is employed, then the protecting nation has gained no military advantage over the threatening nation, the *status quo* is maintained, and international peace and security are preserved. Again, it is difficult to see how such an outcome violates the object and purpose of the Charter, or the intentions of its framers.

Finally, the fourth subtheory argues for the equality of human rights with international peace and security. Since the framing of the Charter, we have learned more and more about the nature of regimes which threaten international peace and security. None of these governments have the requisite respect for the individual which is the basis for civil protections against tyranny. Far from being in tension with international peace and security, human rights are very much the foundation of international peace and security. A reading of the Charter which places these two concepts in opposition is, consciously or not, of greater service to the Benito Mussolinis of history than the Theodore Roosevelts.

## Notes

1. Benito Mussolini, *quoted by* Gen. Smedley D. Butler, *reprinted in* THE POCKET BOOK OF QUOTATIONS 379 (Henry Davidoff ed., 1952).
2. Theodore Roosevelt, *quoted in* BARBARA TUCHMAN, PRACTICING HISTORY 115 (1981).
3. Rev. Jesse Jackson, remarks on *Nightline*, December 15, 1987.
4. ANTHONY CLARK AREND AND ROBERT J. BECK, INTERNATIONAL LAW AND THE USE OF FORCE: BEYOND THE UN CHARTER PARADIGM 94 (1993).
5. *Id.* Ronzitti further restricts the scope of consent with several criteria:

> First of all, consent must come from an authority whose expression of will is ascribable to the local State. ... Secondly, the expression of will of the local State must be valid, not vitiated by the so-called 'vices de volonte.'. ... [T]he consent of the injured State must not only not be given by error, obtained by fraud, or procured by coercion but must also comply with the territorial sovereign's internal provisions regarding competence to be bound. ... Thirdly, the action by the intervening State must be strictly confined to the limits of the consent given by the local sovereign. The State whose nationals are in mortal danger, even if it is permitted to enter foreign territory, is not automatically allowed to resort to force, if it lacks authorization to do so. ... Moreover, the action of the intervening State must not infringe upon the rules by which a State is duty bound not as regards a particular subject of international law but as regards the international community as a whole. ... [T]he consent of the State cannot function as an *erga omnes* defence. ... Finally, the consent must not be contrary to a peremptory rule of international law. [footnotes omitted]

NATALINO RONZITTI, RESCUING NATIONALS ABROAD THROUGH MILITARY COERCION AND INTERVENTION ON GROUNDS OF HUMANITY 84-86 (1985). Ronzitti continues, stating that treaties are a valid vehicle of consent: "Practice shows that, by virtue of a treaty, a right to intervene in foreign territory for carrying out activities which would certainly be unlawful without the treaty so providing, is sometimes given. [footnote omitted] *Id.* at 115. For an examination of treaty-based intervention, *see* David Wippman, Treaty-Based Intervention: Who Can Say No?, 62 U. CHI. L. REV. 607 (1995).

6. AREND AND BECK, *supra* note 4, at 94. *See also* RONZITTI, *supra* note 5 at 135-148. Ronzitti also addresses the use of force against pirates and slavers. *Id.* at 137-141.

7. *Id.*

8. *Id.*

9. E. VATTEL, THE LAW OF NATIONS 161 (J. Chitty ed. 1883). *See also Louis B. Sohn, International Law and Basic Human Rights, in* RICHARD B. LILLICH AND JOHN NORTON MOORE EDS, U.S. NAVAL WAR COLLEGE INTERNATIONAL LAW STUDIES: READINGS IN INTERNATIONAL LAW FROM THE NAVAL WAR COLLEGE REVIEW 1947-1977, VOL. 62, 587, 588 (1980). Professor Sohn traces the use of force in the protection of nationals abroad back as far as the 11th Century. *Id.*

10. E. VATTEL, *supra* note 9 at 165.

11. WILLIAM EDWARD HALL, A TREATISE ON THE FOREIGN POWERS AND JURISDICTION OF THE BRITISH CROWN 2 (1894). Hall continues, describing the connection between the sovereign and the subject, and the sovereign's power over the subject:

> The legal relations by which a person is encompassed in his country of birth and residence cannot be wholly put aside when he goes abroad for a time; many of the acts which he may do outside his native state have inevitable consequences within it. He may for many purposes be temporarily under the control of another sovereign than his own, and he may be bound to yield to a foreign government a large measure of obedience; but his own state still possess a right to his allegiance; he is still an integral member of the national community. A state therefore can enact laws, enjoining or forbidding acts, and defining legal relations, which oblige its subjects abroad in common with those within its dominions. It can declare under what conditions it will regard as valid acts, done in foreign countries, which profess to have legal effect; it can visit others with penalties; it can estimate the circumstances and facts as it chooses.

*Id.*

12. *Id.* at 3.

13. *Id.* at 4.

14. EDWIN M. BORCHARD, THE DIPLOMATIC PROTECTION OF CITIZENS ABROAD 446 (1928).

15. *Id.* at 448.

16. *Id.* at 450. Borchard lists the bases for intervention:

> Among the various purposes for which troops and marines have been landed, are the following: [footnote omitted] (1) for the simple protection of American citizens in disturbed localities, the activity of the troops being in the nature of police duty; [footnote omitted] (2) for the punishment of natives for the murder or injury of American citizens in semi-civilized or backward countries; [footnote omitted] (3) for the suppression of local riots, and the restoration and preservation of order; [footnote omitted] (4) for the collection of indemnities, either with or without the delivery of a previous ultimatum; [footnote omitted] (5) for the seizure of custom-houses, as security for the payment of claims; [footnote omitted] and for purposes such as the maintenance of a stable government, the destruction of pirates infesting certain areas, and other objects.

*Id.* at 449-50.

17. *Id.* at 452.
18. AREND AND BECK, *supra* note 4, at 95.
19. RONZITTI, *supra* note 4, at 26.
20. *Id.*
21. *Id.*
22. *Id.*
23. *Id.* at 26-27.
24. *Id.* at 27.
25. *Id.*
26. *Id.*
27. *Id.*
28. *Id.* at 27-28.
29. *Id.* at 28. The troops were present in the Canal Zone pursuant to a treaty with the government of Egypt, signed on August 26, 1936. *Id.*
30. *Id.*
31. *Id.*
32. *Id.*
33. *Id.*
34. *Id.* at 29.
35. *Id.* Foreign Secretary Lloyd echoed this comment before the House of Commons, and added that the Security Council was, in any case, incapable of taking swift and decisive action. *Id.*
36. *Id.*
37. *Id.*
38. *Id.*
39. *Id.*
40. AREND AND BECK, *supra* note 4, at 96.
41. RONZITTI, *supra* note 5, at 30.
42. *Id*
43. *Id.*
44. *Id.* at 31.
45. *Id.* at 32.
46. *Id.* at 31. Two other instances in Africa, both in 1964, do not meet the criteria of protection of nationals abroad in that they were undertaken with the approval of the local sovereign. This, of course, renders the action a cooperative one between nations, and not an intervention with adversary sovereigns.

The first was the evacuation of British citizens in Zanzibar, following a *coup d'etat* against the sultan. The new government quietly invited the British, who had dispatched a warship to the area, to evacuate its own citizens. *Id.* at 32.

The second incident was a joint U.S. – Belgian operation, again in the Congo, to rescue foreign nationals from rebels. AREND AND BECK *supra* note 4, at 97. According to Professor Lillich, diplomacy and alternative measures had gotten nowhere: "[T]he United Nations got bogged down in debate upon it. They finally decided to let the Organization of African Unity attempt to do something: they tried and they were very, very unsuccessful." *Richard B. Lillich*, Forcible Self-Help Under International Law, *in* RICHARD B. LILLICH AND JOHN NORTON MOORE EDS, U.S. NAVAL WAR COLLEGE INTERNATIONAL LAW STUDIES: READINGS IN INTERNATIONAL LAW FROM THE NAVAL WAR COLLEGE REVIEW 1947-1977, VOL. 62, 587, 597 (1980) [*hereinafter* Forcible Self-Help]. The subsequent intervention was highly successful, and conducted with the permission of the Congo's government. However, this situation highlights the tenuous nature of such permission: Congolese Foreign Minister Bomboko consented to the operation, but after it had been set in motion, Prime Minister Patrice Lumumba overruled him. The practical effect of the *post hoc* withdrawal of permission was negligible, but it does serve to emphasize the role of timing in such operations. M. Akehurst, *The Use of Force to Protect Nationals Abroad*, INT'L REL. 5: 7 (1977). Professor Sohn noted that, while the scope of the mission was strictly limited to rescue of the hostages, a certain amount of force was required to effect their release: "In the process of rescuing them, the army of rebellion was more or less destroyed, but that was purely incidental." Sohn, *supra* note 9, at 597.

47. RONZITTI, *supra* note 5, at 33. Ronzitti states that " the island was, to all effects, in the throes of anarchy." *Id.*
48. AREND AND BECK, *supra* note 5, at 397-98.
49. RONZITTI, *supra* note 5, at 33.
50. AREND AND BECK, *supra* note 4, at 98.
51. RONZITTI, *supra* note 5, at 35-36.
52. *Id.* at 36.
53. AREND AND BECK, *supra* note 4, at 98.
54. RONZITTI, *supra* note 5, at 36.
55. AREND AND BECK, *supra* note 4, at 98.
56. RONZITTI, *supra* note 5, at 36.
57. AREND AND BECK, *supra* note 4, at 97-98.
58. AREND AND BECK, *supra* note 4, at 99.
59. RONZITTI, *supra* note 5, at 37.
60. *Id.*
61. AREND AND BECK, *supra* note 4, at 99.
62. *Id.*
63. RONZITTI, *supra* note 5, at 37.
64. *Id.*
65. *Id.*
66. *Id.*
67. 31 U.N. SCOR (1941st mtg.) 31, U.N. Doc. S/p.v. 1941 (1976), *quoted in* Richard B. Lillich, Introduction to Volume II: The Use of Force, Human Rights, and General International Legal Issues, *in* RICHARD B. LILLICH AND JOHN NORTON MOORE EDS, U.S. NAVAL WAR COLLEGE INTERNATIONAl LAW STUDIES: READINGS IN INTERNATIONAL LAW FROM THE NAVAL WAR COLLEGE REVIEW 1947-1977, VOL. 62, IX, XI (1980) [*hereinafter* Introduction].
68. *Id.*
69. *Id.*
70. *Id.*
71. RONZITTI, *supra* note 5, at 38.
72. *Id.*
73. *Id.* at 40.
74. *Id.* at 40-41.
75. *Id.* at 41.
76. *Id.* at 44.
77. *Id.* This Presidential Statement places an unusual emphasis on feelings. The author was present at a White House conversation, when a participant in the rescue mission was asked if he would have killed the Iranian "student" guarding the three Americans he had been assigned to recover. "Let's just say," replied the commando, "that meeting me would have been a significant emotional event in his life." Notes of conversation on file with the author.

78. *Id.* at 45. Ronzitti provides an excellent explanation:

> [Under Reisman's theory,] [t]he Charter does not abrogate a State's right to resort to self-help, including the use of armed force, which belongs to it under customary international law. The Charter simply suspends the right to resort to self-help, since it entrusts the Security Council with the task of safeguarding the rights of member States. Whenever this mechanism does not function, for example when the action of the Security Council is paralysed by veto, the States are free to resort to self-help, under the terms permitted by customary international law.

*Id.*

79. *Id.* at 46.

80. AREND AND BECK, *supra* note 4, at 101. *See generally* John Norton Moore, Grenada and the International Double Standard, 78 A. J. I. L. 145 (1984) and *Ronald M. Riggs*, The Grenada Intervention: A Legal Analysis, 109 MIL. L. REV. 1 (1985).

81. Moore, *supra* note 80, at 148 and 159-61. Moore explains:

> Constitutional niceties of internal authority are difficult to construct when the only general Constitution of a nation has been previously suspended in express violation of its provisions and a subsequent attempted coup has announced the dissolution of the Government that suspended the Constitution but was unable to consolidate effective power. It does seem clear in this setting, however, that the authority of the Governor-General to represent Grenada was stronger than that of anyone else.

*Id.* at 159.

82. *Id.* at 147-48.

83. AREND AND BECK, *supra* note 4, at 101. President Reagan reported that the condemnatory General Assembly vote had not "upset my breakfast at all." *Id.*

84. Moore, *supra* note 80, at 151-53. Moore quotes the results of a CBS News poll, conducted on November 6th: 62% felt the Americans had come "to save the lives of Americans living here," 65% said they believed the airport under construction was being built for Cuban and Soviet military purposes, 76% stated they believed Cuba wanted to take control of the Grenadian government, 81% said the American troops were "courteous and considerate," 85% stated they felt they or their family were in danger while General Austin was in power, 85% said they felt the American purpose in invading was to "free the people of Grenada from the Cubans," and 91% were "glad the Americans came to Grenada." *Id.* at 152.

85. AREND AND BECK, *supra* note 4, at 93. Professor Lillich recommended the following additional sources on the invasion of Panama:

> Compare *Abraham Sofaer*, The Legality of the United States Action in Panama, in: Columbia Journal of Transnational Law (Colum. J. Trans. L.) vol. 29, 1991, 281, with *Louis Henkin*, The Invasion of Panama Under International Law: A Gross Violation, in: Columbia Journal of Transnational Law (Colum. J. Trans. L.) vol. 29, 1991, 293. *See also* Anthony D'Amato, The Invasion of Panama Was a Lawful Response to Tyranny, in AJIL, vol. 84, 1990, 516; *Tom Farer*, Panama: Beyond the Charter Paradigm, in: AJIL, vol. 84, 1990, 503; *Ved Nanda*, The Validity of the United States Intervention in Panama Under International Law, in: AJIL, vol. 84, 1990, 494; *John Quigley*, The Legality of the United States Invasion of Panama, in: Yale JIL, vol. 15, 1990, 276; *James P. Terry*, The Panama Intervention: Law in Support of Policy, in: Naval War College Review, vol. 43, 1990, no. 4, 110; Panel, The Panama Revolution, in: American Society of International Law Proceedings (ASIL Proc.), vol. 84, 1990,

182; Recent Developments, International Intervention—The United States Invasion of Panama, in: Harvard International Law Journal (Harv. ILJ), vol. 31, 1990, 633.

*Richard B. Lillich*, Forcible Protection of Nationals Abroad: The Liberian "Incident" of 1990, 35 GERMAN YEARBOOK OF INTERNATIONAL LAW 205, 206 (1993) [hereinafter Liberia].

86. AREND AND BECK, *supra* note 4, at 102.
87. *Id.*
88. *Id.*
89. *Id.*
90. *Id.*
91. *Id.*
92. *Id.*
93. *Id.*
94. *Id.* Included in the evacuated were French, Canadian, Italian, Lebanese, and even Iraqi citizens. *Id.*
95. *Id.* at 102-103. For a more in-depth treatment of the incident, *see* Richard B. Lillich, Forcible Protection of Nationals Abroad: The Liberian "Incident" of 1990, 35 GERMAN YEARBOOK OF INTERNATIONAL LAW 205 (1993). Lillich, *supra* note 85, at 205.
96. Lillich, Liberia, *supra* note 85, at 222-23.
97. AREND AND BECK, *supra* note 4, at 105. *See also* Riggs, *supra* note 80, at 22.
98. AREND AND BECK, *supra* note 4, at 106.
99. *Id.*
100. *Id.* at 107.
101. *Id.* Reisman himself continues: "A rational and contemporary interpretation of the Charter must conclude that Article 2(4) suppresses self-help [only] insofar as the organization can assume the role of enforcer." When the UN fails in its mission "self-help prerogatives revive." [footnote omitted]. Any interpretation which fails to take this into account would merely provide "an invitation to lawbreakers who would anticipate a paralysis in the Security Council's decision dynamics." Michael Reisman, *Sanctions and Enforcement*, *in* C. Black and R. Falk (eds), THE FUTURE OF THE INTERNATIONAL LEGAL ORDER, 3: 850 (1971), *quoted in* AREND AND BECK, *supra* note 4, at 107-08.
102. Professor McDougal summarized this position eloquently:

> [T]he first important fact is that the machinery for collective police action projected by the Charter has never been implemented. We don't have the police forces for the United Nations, the collective machinery that was expected to replace self-help. In other words, there has been a failure in certain of the major provisions for implementing the Charter.
>
> If, in the light of this failure, we consider how we can implement the principal purposes of minimizing coercion, of insuring that states do not profit by coercion and violence, I submit to you that it is simply to honor lawlessness to hold that the members of one state can, with impunity, attack the nationals—individuals, ships, aircraft or other assets—of other states without any fear of response. In the absence of collective machinery to protect against attack and deprivation, I would suggest that the principle of major purpose requires an interpretation which would honor self-help against prior unlawfulness. The principle of subsequent conduct would certainly confirm this. . . .

Myers McDougal, *Authority to Use Force on the High Seas*, 20 NAVAL WAR COLLEGE REVIEW 19, 28-29 (Dec. 1967), *quoted in* Lillich, Introduction, *supra* note 67, at XI.

103. AREND AND BECK, *supra* note 4, at 108.
104. *But see* RONZITTI, *supra* note 5, at 8-9.
105. Riggs, *supra* note 80, at 24.
106. Ronzitti acknowledges the problem of assuming that an "armed attack" can involve only aggressive international war:

> [P]ractice shows that, when a State intends to wrongfully use armed coercion, it does so in one of two ways: i) by using force against the territory of another State, or ii) by exerting armed coercion within its own territory against foreign instrumentalities (e.g. embassies) or citizens (individuals or State organs, such as foreign representatives). Whereas in the former case the victim may react in self-defence, in the latter this is not possible, since it is declared that there has been no 'armed attack'.

RONZITTI, *supra* note 5, at 66. He continues:

> [I]n recent years, particularly unpleasant episodes have repeatedly occurred, such as the taking of hostages, and transnational terrorism. These events are the cause of a continual state of danger. Unless the international community acquires suitable instruments, capable of preventing and representing [sic] such criminal events, resorting to unilateral armed force is likely to continue to increase on the part of those States whose nationals become the victims of terrorist attacks, in order to fill the vacuum created by the lack of effective control mechanisms.

*Id.*

107. AREND AND BECK, *supra* note 4, at 109. *See also* Riggs, *supra* note 80, at 23.
108. AREND AND BECK, *supra* note 4, at 109. Arend and Beck summarize McDougal and Reisman's position:

> The Preamble's "repeated emphasis upon the common interests in human rights," argue Reisman and McDougal, "indicates that the use of force for the urgent protection of such rights is no less authorized than other forms of self-help," [footnote omitted] Under Article 1(3), they suggest, "promoting and encouraging respect for human rights" is set out as a fundamental purpose of the United Nations. [footnote omitted] Similarly, Article 55 of the Charter points to the UN objective of promoting "human rights" observance, while Article 56 authorizes "joint and separate action [by Members] in cooperation with the Organization for the achievement of the purposes set out in Article 55." [footnote omitted]

*Id.*

109. *Id.* AREND AND BECK, *supra* note 4, at 109. *See also* RONZITTI, *supra* note 5, at 2.
110. AREND AND BECK, *supra* note 4, at 103.
111. *Id.*
112. *Id.* at 103-04.
113. *Id.* at 104.
114. *Id.*
115. Riggs, *supra* note 80, at 25-33.

# Bibliography

Akehurst, M., *The Use of Force to Protect Nationals Abroad*, INT'L REL. 5: 7 (1977)

AREND, ANTHONY CLARK AND ROBERT J. BECK, INTERNATIONAL LAW AND THE USE OF FORCE: BEYOND THE UN CHARTER PARADIGM 94 (1993)

Borchard, Edwin M., The Diplomatic Protection of Citizens Abroad 446 (1928)

D'Amato, *Anthony*, The Invasion of Panama Was a Lawful Response to Tyranny, AJIL, vol. 84, 1990, 516

Davidoff, Henry ed., THE POCKET BOOK OF QUOTATIONS 379 (1952)

Farer, *Tom*, Panama: Beyond the Charter Paradigm, AJIL, vol. 84, 1990, 503

HALL, WILLIAM EDWARD, A TREATISE ON THE FOREIGN POWERS AND JURISDICTION OF THE BRITISH CROWN 2 (1894)

Henkin, *Louis*, The Invasion of Panama Under International Law: A Gross Violation, Columbia Journal of Transnational Law (Colum. J. Trans. L.) vol. 29, 1991, 293

Jackson, Rev. Jesse, Remarks on *Nightline*, December 15, 1987

Lillich, Richard B., Forcible Protection of Nationals Abroad: The Liberian "Incident" of 1990, 35 GERMAN YEARBOOK OF INTERNATIONAL LAW 205 (1993)

Lillich, Richard B., Introduction to Volume II: The Use of Force, Human Rights, and General International Legal Issues, *in* RICHARD B. LILLICH AND JOHN NORTON MOORE EDS, U.S. NAVAL WAR COLLEGE INTERNATIONAL LAW STUDIES: READINGS IN INTERNATIONAL LAW FROM THE NAVAL WAR COLLEGE REVIEW 1947-1977, Vol. 62, IX, XI (1980)

Lillich, Richard B., Forcible Self-Help Under International Law, *in* RICHARD B. LILLICH AND JOHN NORTON MOORE EDS, U.S. NAVAL WAR COLLEGE INTERNATIONAL LAW STUDIES: READINGS IN INTERNATIONAL LAW FROM THE NAVAL WAR COLLEGE REVIEW 1947-1977, VOL. 62, IX, XI (1980)

Moore, *John Norton*, Grenada and the International Double Standard, 78 AJIL. 145 (1984)

Nanda, *Ved,* The Validity of the United States Intervention in Panama Under International Law, AJIL, vol. 84, 1990, 494

Panel, The Panama Revolution, American Society of International Law Proceedings (ASIL Proc.), vol. 84, 1990, 182

Quigley, *John*, The Legality of the United States Invasion of Panama, Yale JIL, vol. 15, 1990, 276

Recent Developments, International Intervention—The United States Invasion of Panama, Harvard International Law Journal (Harv. ILJ), vol. 31, 1990, 633

Reisman, Michael, *Sanctions and Enforcement*, *in* C. Black and R. Falk (eds) The Future of the International Legal Order, 3: 850 (1971)

Riggs, *Ronald M.*, The Grenada Intervention: A Legal Analysis, 109 MIL. L. REV. 1 (1985)

Ronzitti, Natalino, Rescuing Nationals Abroad Through Military Coercion and Intervention on Grounds of Humanity 26 (1985)

Sofaer, *Abraham*, The Legality of the United States Action in Panama, Columbia Journal of Transnational Law (Colum. J. Trans. L.) vol. 29, 1991, 281

Sohn, *Louis B.*, International Law and Basic Human Rights, *in* Richard B. Lillich and John Norton Moore eds, U.S. Naval War College International Law Studies: Readings in International Law from the Naval War College Review 1947-1977, Vol. 62, 587, 588 (1980)

Terry, *James P.*, The Panama Intervention: Law in Support of Policy, Naval War College Review, vol. 43, 1990, no. 4, 110

Tuchman, Barbara, Practicing History 115 (1981)

Vattel, E., The Law of Nations 161 (J. Chitty ed. 1883)

*Wippman, David,* Treaty-Based Intervention: Who Can Say No?, 62 U. Chi. L. Rev. 607 (1995)

# Index

## A

*Abarenda*, USS: 154
Abéché, Chad: 105
Abyssinia: 9, 27–28
Accessory Transit Company: 120, 121–22
Accioly, H.: 19–20
Act for The Government of the Navy of the United States, An (1799): 188, 190
*Adams*, USS: 133
Adoula, Cyrille: 50
Aizpuru: 131, 132
Al-Matni, Nasib il: 44
Albania: 33–34
*Albany*, USS: 166
Alexandria, Egypt: 130, 234
Algeria: 237, 240
*Alliance*, USS: 131
Almy, Admiral: 129
Amapala, Honduras: 149–50, 168
American Cable Company: 153
American Mission compounds in China: 165–66
Ancon, Panama: 147
Anderson, Admiral: 167
Angles: 2
Anglo-Iranian Oil Company: 233
Angola: 125
Apia, Samoa: 132, 140–41
Arab League: 44
Arab nationalism: 43–44
Arend, Anthony Clark: 230, 242, 244–45, 247
Argentina: 10, 25–26, 99, 117–18, 119, 133, 236
Arias, General Desiderio: 161
Aristodemus: 2
Ariston of Tyre: 2
Army of Cuba Pacification: 148
*Asheville*, USS: 168
Asiatic Fleet: 154, 155, 170, 174–75
Asiatic Squadron: 126
Aspinwall (Colon), Panama: 128
*Atlanta*, USS: 137, 144
Atlantic Squadron: 131
Attican law: 1–2
Attwood, William: 51, 54–55
Austin, General Hudson: 241

Austria: 10
Austria-Hungary: 31

## B

Baker, James: 106, 242–43
Balmaceda: 133–34
*Baltimore*, USS: 133, 135–37
Bani-Sadr: 65
Barbary States: 4
Barnard, Philippe: 106
Basra, Iraq: 233
Bayard, Secretary of State: 14
Beck, Robert J.: 230, 242, 244–45, 247
Beirut, Lebanon: 44, 46–47, 48–49, 144
Belgium: 247
    and the Congo: 49–57, 98–99, 235–36
    and Rwanda: 104–05, 107
    and Zaire: 100–101, 105–07
Belknap, Commander: 129–30
Bell, John: 27–28
Bell, Rear Admiral: 126
Benham, Rear Admiral: 135
Bennett, W. Tapley: 60–61
Benoit, Colonel: 60
Berard, M.: 99
Bigelow, Lt. A.: 119
Bishop, Maurice: 241
Blockades: 199–200, 201, 202, 203, 205, 206, 208–09, 210–11, 212–13, 215, 219
    of Argentina: 25–26
    of Venezuela: 33
Bluefields, Nicaragua: 135, 140, 149, 174, 175
Bluntschli, J. M.: 7, 8–10, 28
Bocas del Toro, Panama: 137, 143
Bond, Karl I.: 106
Bonfils, H.: 10, 18, 26, 27, 30, 31, 33
Bonilla: 144
Borchard, Edwin: 14–15, 32, 232
Borland, Solon: 121
Bosch, Juan: 57–59, 60
*Boston*, USS: 134
Bowett, Derek: 35, 245
*Boxer*, USS: 59, 60
Boxer Protocol of 1901: 142
Boxer Rebellion: 15–16, 31–32, 141–42
*Brandywine*: 118
Brazil: 26, 134–35

# Index

*Brilliant*, HMS: 150
British Navy regulations: 188–89, 190, 191, 199
*Brooklyn*, USS: 144
Brown: 72
Brown, Admiral George: 133
Brownlie, Ian: 36–37, 244
Buenos Aires, Argentina: 25, 117–18, 119, 133
*Buffalo*, USS: 158
Bush, George: 242–43
Butler, General Smedley D.: 229
Butterfield & Swire's residence (China): 154

## C

Caamano, Francisco: 60
Cabral, Reid: 236
Cairo, Egypt: 234
Calancha: 126
Callao, Peru: 118
Camagüey, Cuba: 162–63
Cambodia: 237, 248
Cameron, Capt. C. Duncan: 27–28
Cameroon: 108
Camp Nicholson, China: 157
Canada: 107
Canton, China: 123–24, 168, 180
Cap-Haïtien, Haiti: 159, 160
Caperton, Admiral: 160
Caracas, Venezuela: 33
Carlson, Paul: 51
*Caroline* case: 14, 239
Carter, Jimmy: 64, 66, 71–72, 240–41
Carthage: 2
Cartiguenave: 161
Cave, Stephen: 30
Central African Republic: 108
Chad: 101–02, 103, 105
Chadwich, Rear Admiral French E.: 146
Chamorro, General: 174
Chamoun, Camille: 43, 44, 45–46, 47
Chang Tso-lin: 170–71
Chapei, China: 158, 177
*Charleston*, USS: 136
*Chaumont*, USS: 180
Chebab, General: 44, 46
Chemulpo, Korea: 132, 135–36
Chiang Kai-shek: 179

Chile: 133–34
Chin Kiang, China: 153, 179
China: 237, 243. *See also* particular cities
   interventions in during the Boxer Rebellion: 15–16, 31–32, 141–42
   interventions in during the Chinese Revolution of 1911: 151–55, 157, 158, 161, 163,
      165–68, 169–71, 172–73, 174–75, 176–80
   Japanese occupation of: 18–19, 35–36
   and Russia: 163
   U.S. intervention in: 120–21, 122, 124–25, 136–37, 139, 151–55, 157, 158, 161, 163,
      165–68, 169–71, 172–73, 174–75, 176–80
Chinwangtao, China: 166, 174–75
Chiujio, Higashi Kuze: 128
Cholma, Honduras: 148
Christians
   and the Barbary States: 4
   in Lebanon: 42–48
   missionaries: 14
   protection of: 13–14, 135–36, 151–52, 154, 157, 165–66, 168
   and right of forcible protection: 2
Christmas, General: 50
Christopher, W.: 70, 72
Chung King, China: 163
Ciaris Estero, Mexico: 158
Cienfuegos, Cuba: 147–48
*Cincinnati*, USS: 143, 154
Civil war or insurrection and right of protection of nationals in the affected State: 9, 11
Civil War (United States): 10, 198
Civil wars
   in China: 15, 16, 31–32, 141–42, 151–55, 157, 158, 161, 163, 165–68, 169–71, 172–73,
      174–75, 176–80
   in the Congo: 49–57
   in the Dominican Republic: 59–63
   in Guatemala: 165
   in Haiti: 159–61
   in Lebanon: 44, 46–47, 48–49, 238
   in Nicaragua: 175–76
   in Venezuela: 16, 33
Claes, Willy: 106
Clark, Commander: 131
Clark, J. Reuben: 13, 14, 29
Clark, Ramsey: 64
Cleveland, Grover: 134
*Cleveland*, USS: 164
Cold War: 43–44
Colombia: 123, 125, 126, 128, 129, 131–32, 137, 142–43, 144–45
Colombo: 241
*Colon*: 131

# Index

Colon, Panama: 128, 131–32, 142–43, 145, 149
*Columbia*, USS: 135
Concentration camps
    in Cuba: 138–39
Congo: 49–57, 98–99, 235–36, 247–48
Congo Republic (Brazzaville): 54
Constantinople, Turkey: 32, 157
Contractual claims, right to protect nationals in foreign countries regarding: 11–12
Convention of Lebanon (1861): 26–27
Coolidge, Calvin: 176
Corfu: 18–19, 33–34
Corinto, Nicaragua: 137–38, 156, 175
Cotton, Admiral: 144
Covenant of the League of Nations: 36
Creditors of foreign governments, right to protect nationals who are: 8, 10, 11–12, 15–16, 30–31, 32–33
Cromwell, Captain: 137
Cuba: 138–39, 147–48, 155–56, 162–63, 237, 241
Cumae: 2
*Cyane*, USS: 120, 121
Cyprus: 240
Czechoslovakia: 36–37, 163

## D

da Gama, Admiral: 134–35
Damascus, Syria: 34–35
David, King of the Sandwich Islands: 129–30
Dávila, Miguel: 149, 150
Davis, Rear Admiral: 127
Dawson, Thomas C.: 150
de Lesseps, Ferdinand: 29
Déby, Irdiss: 105
*Decatur*, USS: 153
Dehaene, Jean-Luc: 106
Demetrius, King: 4
*Denver*, USS: 168–69, 172
*Detroit*, USS: 135, 136, 140, 145–46
Díaz, Adolfo: 175
Dillard: 67
Dillingham, Commander: 145–46
Diplomatic personnel, protection of
    in Argentina: 119, 133
    in China: 15, 16, 31–32, 120–21, 122, 136–37, 141–42, 152, 153, 154, 161, 163, 167–68, 170, 171, 177–78, 180
    in the Dominican Republic: 161–62
    in Egypt: 130

in Guatemala: 165
  in Haiti: 159, 160
  in Hawaii: 133
  in Honduras: 168–69
  in Nicaragua: 156, 157, 166
  in Panama: 126, 137
  in Peru: 118
  in Russia: 163
  in Samoa: 140–41
  in Smyrna: 167
  in Turkey: 157
Dixon, Pierce: 98
Doe, Samuel K.: 243
Dole, Sanford B.: 134
Dominican Republic: 57–63, 70, 144, 145–46, 147, 161–62, 236–37, 248
*Don Pacifico* case: 9–10
*Dubuque*, USS: 149
Dumas, Roland: 104
Duncan, Capt.: 117
Dunn, Frederick: 18


E

Eden, Anthony: 234, 235
Egan, Patrick: 133
Egypt: 10, 11, 29–30, 43, 44, 97, 98, 130, 234–35, 240, 248
Eisenhower, Dwight D.: 45–46, 48
Eisenhower Doctrine: 43–44
El Cuero, Cuba: 155–56
*Elcano*, USS: 154, 164, 175
Elf-Aquitaine oil refinery: 103–04
Elis: 2
*Emerald*, HMS: 178–79
Emma, Dowager Queen of the Sandwich Islands: 130
Entebbe, Uganda: 41, 67, 97, 238–39, 248
*Essex*, USS: 132
Estaing, Giscard d': 101
Estrada, General Juan J.: 148, 149
European State system: 1
Evacuations of foreigners
  from the Central African Republic: 108
  from Chad: 105
  from China: 151–52, 153, 154, 176, 177, 178–79, 180
  from the Congo: 49–57, 98–99, 105–06
  from the Dominican Republic: 59–63, 236–37
  from the Falkland Islands: 117
  from Lebanon: 238

# Index

from Liberia: 243
from Mexico: 158
from Rwanda: 107
from Samoa: 141
from Zaire: 106–07

## F

Fabriga: 123
Falkland Islands: 117
*Falmouth*: 124
Fauchille, P.: 16, 27, 32, 33
Fish, Hamilton: 11–12
Flores: 127
Foochow, China: 153, 167–68
Foote, Cmdr. A. H.: 123–24
Forcible protection of nationals abroad
    Belgium in the Congo: 49–57
    collective action to provide: 16, 19, 41–42, 46, 47, 52, 107, 127, 242
    drawbacks to: 10, 31, 33
    definition of: 30
    Great Britain in China: 120–21, 123–24, 137
    Great Britain in Egypt: 234–35
    Great Britain in Iran: 233–34
    Great Britain in Nicaragua: 140
    Great Britain in Panama: 126
    *Mayaquez* incident: 237
        need for congressional authorization of: 15
    United States in Angola: 125
    United States in Argentina: 117–18
    United States in Brazil: 134–35
    United States in Chile: 133–34
    United States in China: 120–21, 122, 123–25, 136–37, 139, 141–42, 151–55, 157, 158, 161, 163, 164, 165–68, 169–71, 172–73, 174–75, 176–80
    United States in Columbia: 123, 125, 126, 128, 129, 137, 142–43
    United States in the Congo: 51–57
    United States in Cuba: 147–48, 155–56, 162–63
    United States in the Dominican Republic: 57–63, 144, 145–46, 147, 161–62, 236–37
    United States in Egypt: 130
    Unites States in Grenada: 241–42
    United States in Guatemala: 165
    United States in Haiti: 133, 159–61
    United States in Hawaii: 133, 134
    United States in Honduras: 144, 148, 149–50, 164, 168–69, 170, 172
    United States in Japan: 126–27, 128
    United States in Korea: 132, 135–36
    United States in Lebanon: 42, 45–49, 238

United States in Liberia: 243
United States in Mexico: 130, 158
United States in Morocco: 146–47
United States in Nicaragua: 120, 135, 137–38, 140, 144, 149, 156–57, 174, 175–76
United States in Panama: 123, 125, 126, 128, 129, 137, 142–43, 144–45, 147, 173, 242–43
United States in Peru: 118, 119
United States in Russia: 163–64
United States in Samoa: 132, 140–41
United States in Soviet Union: 163–64
United States in Syria: 144
United States in Turkey: 157
United States in Uruguay: 122–23, 124, 127
used as an excuse for political and/or economic intervention: 26, 35–36, 62–63, 100, 101, 237, 242–43, 248
in Zaire: 100–101, 106–07
Formosa: 16
France: 2, 36, 41, 42, 43, 99, 163, 236, 237, 239, 243, 247
action against Mexico: 10, 15–16, 26–27
and Argentina: 119
blockade of Argentina ports: 10, 25–26
and the Central African Republic: 108
and Chad: 101–02, 103, 105
and China: 31–32, 137, 169, 171, 172–73
and Egypt: 10, 11, 29–30, 234–35
and Gabon: 103–04
and Haiti: 159, 160
and Japan: 127, 128
and Mauritania: 99–100, 101, 103, 239–40
and the Ottoman Empire: 11, 34–35
and Panama: 142–43
and Portugal: 30–31
and Rwanda: 104–05, 107
and Turkey: 32–33, 157
and Zaire: 100–101, 105–07
Friedmann: 63
Frolinat (front de libération rationale du Tchad): 99–100
Fulbright, William: 62–63

## G

Gabon: 103–04, 108
*Galena*, USS: 131
Galley, Robert: 102
Garcia: 137
Garibaldi, Giuseppe: 17
Garnet, R.: 44

# Index

Gbenye, Christophe: 50, 51
*Germantown*: 122–23
Germany: 16, 31–32, 33, 36–37, 107, 130, 132, 137, 140, 149–50, 157, 159, 161
Ghotbzadeh: 65
Gilmer, Commander W. W.: 149
Godfrain, M. Jacques: 108
*Gold Star*, USS: 174–75
Gómez, José Miguel: 155
Gonaïves, Haiti: 160
Gonzalez, General: 130
Gowland, Daniel: 117
Great Britain: 36, 43, 99, 146, 237, 243, 247
    and Abyssinia; 9, 27–28
    action against Mexico: 15–16, 26–27
    and Argentina: 25, 26, 119
    and China: 31–32, 120–21, 123–24, 137, 163, 167, 169, 172–73, 174, 176, 177, 178–79
    and Corfu: 33–34
    and Egypt: 10, 11, 29–30, 97, 98, 130, 234–35
    and Honduras: 29, 149–50
    and Iran: 233–34
    and Japan: 127, 128
    and Nicaragua: 137–38, 140
    and the Ottoman Empire: 11
    and Palmerston Circular of 1848: 8
    and Panama: 125, 142–43
    reply to the King of Prussia (1753): 7
    and Russia: 163
    and Samoa: 140–41
    and the Suez Canal: 29–30, 43, 97, 98
    and Turkey: 157
    and Uruguay: 24
    and Venezuela: 16, 33
Greece
    conflicts with Turkey: 10, 167
    and Corfu: 18–19, 34
    early law: 1–2
Grenada: 241–42, 248
Grenada, Nicaragua: 175
Greytown, Nicaragua: 120, 121–22
Grotius, H.: 1–3, 4, 7, 8, 20
Grundy: 51, 55
Guantánamo Bay, Cuba: 155–56
Guardia Nacional de Nicaragua: 176
Guatemala: 165
Guatemala City, Guatemala: 165
Guiringaud, Louis de: 101, 102, 103
Gutierrez, General Lopez: 164

## H

Habré, Hissène: 105
Habyarimana: 104
Hackett Medical College: 180
Haig Reserve School: 171
Haiti: 133, 159–61
Hall, William Edward: 231–32
*Hancock*, USS: 159–60
Hankow, China: 152, 172–73, 176, 179
*Harriet*: 117
Havana, Cuba: 147–48
Hawaii: 129–30, 133, 134
Hay, John: 146–47
*Helena*, USS: 153
Henry VIII: 189
Hindmarsh, A.: 18–19, 34, 36
Hiogo, Japan: 125–26
Hobard, Earle: 177–78
Hodges, Henry: 13–14
Hollins, Commander: 121, 122
Homer: 2
Honduras: 16, 29, 144, 148, 149–50, 164, 168–69, 170, 172
Honolulu, Hawaii: 134
Hostages
   Americans held as: 50–57, 63–73, 240–41
   attempted rescues of: 65–73, 240–41
   Belgians held as: 50–57
   British subjects held as: 50–52
   Egyptians held as: 240
   French held as: 99–100, 103–04, 239–40
   Indians held as: 50–51, 52, 53
   Italians held as: 50–52
   Israelis held as: 238–39
   Pakistanis held as: 50–51, 52, 53
   rescues of: 523–57, 103–04, 238–40
   taken in the Congo: 50–57
   taken in Gabon: 103–04
   taken in Iran: 63–73, 240–41
   taken in Mauritania: 99–100, 239–40
   taken in Morocco: 146–47
Human rights violations: 247, 249
Humanitarian missions: 230, 235–36
   in the Congo: 52–53, 54–55, 57, 99
   in Iran: 66
   in Mauritania: 100
   and the Spanish-American War: 138–39

# Index

in Rwanda: 104–05
in Zaire: 106
*Huron*, USS: 166, 167, 171
Hyde, Charles Cheney: 16, 32

## I

Ichang, China: 175, 176
*Iliad*: 2
Impressment of sailors: 189
India: 158, 233
International Committee of the Red Cross: 51
International Court of Justice: 64–65, 67–68, 71, 240
International Defense Force (in China): 172
International Export Company: 161, 172
International law, principles of justifying a state's protection of nationals abroad. *See* Right of forcible protection and international law; United Nations Charter.
*Iowa*, USS: 142
Iran: 63–73, 233–34, 240–41, 248
Iraq: 45–46, 48, 233
*Iroquois*, USS: 126, 127
*Isabel*, USS: 179
Ismail: 30
Israel: 41, 67, 97, 234–35, 238–39, 248
Italy: 16, 18–19, 31, 33–34, 99, 107, 127, 128, 137, 157, 169, 241
Izmir, Turkey: 167

## J

Jackson, Jesse: 230
*Jamestown*, USS: 126
Japan: 18–19, 31, 35–36, 108, 126–27, 128, 136–37, 139, 141, 158, 163, 167, 169, 172–73, 174, 177, 178, 180
Jiménez, Juan Isidro: 161–62
*John D. Ford*, USS: 172, 179
Johnson, Lyndon B.: 52, 57–58, 60, 61–63
Johnson, Prince: 243
Johnson Administration: 58
Johnson Doctrine: 62
Joint Chiefs of Staff: 65
Jones, Lieutenant Commander Hilary P.: 147
Jouett, Admiral: 131–32
Justice, denial of, as basis for protection of citizens abroad: 1–2, 4–5, 7, 9, 11, 13–14

## K

*Kansas*, USS: 160
Kanza, Thomas: 51
Karlsbad Program: 36
Katanga: 49–50, 98–99, 100–101, 105–06
Kautz, Rear Admiral Albert: 140
*Kearsarge*, USS: 133
Kellogg-Briand Pact of 1928: 36
Kelly, Commodore: 120
Kennedy Administration: 57–58
Kentucky Island, China: 157
Kerr: 46
Khomeini, Ayatollah: 64, 70, 240
Kigali, Rwanda: 104, 107
Kindu, the Congo: 50, 51
Kinshasa, Zaire: 105, 106–07
Kisembo, Angola: 125
Kiukiang, China: 154, 164, 173, 174, 176
Kolwezi, Zaire: 100–101, 105–06
Korea: 132, 135–36, 146
Kuan, China: 167
*Kutwo*: 176

## L

La Ceiba, Honduras: 148, 150, 168, 169, 170, 172
La Curva, Honduras: 164
*Lackawanna*, USS: 130
Laguna, Honduras: 148, 164
Lakeside, China: 165
Larnaca, Cyprus: 240
Latin America, U.S. intervention in: 15. *See also* particular countries.
Law of Nations: 12
*Le Suchet*: 142–43
League of Nations: 34, 35–36, 42
Lebanon: 42–49, 108, 238, 248
Leblanc, Admiral: 25
*Legal Aspects of the Beirut Landing*, by Potter: 47–48
Leprette, M. Jacques: 100
Letters-of-marque: 2, 198, 200, 201–02
*Levant*: 123–24
Levell, Dr.: 165
*Lexington*: 117
Li Yüan-hung: 157, 166
Liao River: 136
Liberia: 243, 248

# Index

Libreville, Gabon: 103–04
Liliukalani, Queen of Hawaii: 134
Lillich, Richard B.: 229, 243, 245
Lima, Peru: 118
Lloyd, Selwyn: 98, 235
Lodge, Henry Cabot: 46
Lumumba: 99
Lynch, Cmdr. W. F.: 122–23
Lytton Commission: 35–36

## M

Machang, China: 166, 167
*Machias*, USS: 136, 142, 143
Madriz, José: 149
Malietoa Tanu: 140–41
Malik, Charles: 44–45
Managua, Nicaragua: 156, 157, 166, 174, 175
Manchu Dynasty: 151
Manchuria: 18–19, 35–36, 170–71
*Marblehead*, USS: 135
Marcy, Secretary of State: 121
*Marietta*, USS: 140, 148–50
*Marion*, USS: 125
Martens: 104
Masü Island, China: 168
Mataafa: 132, 140–41
Matachin, Panama: 131–32
Matamoros, Mexico: 130
Mauritania: 99–101, 103, 239–40, 247–48
Maximilian, Archduke Ferdinand, of Austria: 10, 27
*Maximo Jeraz*: 149
*Mayaguez*: 67, 237, 248
Mazapon, Honduras: 169
McCalla, Commanderr: 132
McClintock, Robert: 46
McCrea, Lieutenant Commander: 142, 143
McDougal, Myers: 247
McKeever, Commodore Isaac: 118, 119
McKinley, William: 138–39
Mello, Admiral: 134–35
Mena, General Luis: 156
Merchant vessels, protection of: 203, 206, 208, 210, 212, 214, 215, 217, 218, 221, 225, 237
Merewether, Col. W. L.: 28
Mervine, Commodore: 123
Methodist missions: 154
Mexico: 10, 15–16, 26–27, 130, 158

271

Miller, William: 64
Millon, Charles: 108
Missionaries
    murdered in China: 141
    murdered in the Congo: 51
    protection of: 13–14, 135–36, 151–52, 154, 165–66, 168
*Mississippi*, USS: 124–25
Mobutu: 106–07
*Monocacy*, USS: 127, 137
Monroe Doctrine: 15
Monrovia, Liberia: 243
Monte Cristi, Dominican Republic: 162
*Monterey*, USS: 154
Montevideo, Uruguay: 122–23, 124, 127
Moore, John Bassett: 12
Morocco: 146–47
Morozow, Judge: 68–69
Morrison, Herbert: 233
Mukden, China: 35
Munich agreement of 30 September 1938: 36
Murphy, Robert: 47, 48–49
Muslims in Lebanon: 42–43
Mussolini, Benito: 34, 229
Mytilini: 32–33

# N

Nagasaki, Japan: 127
Nanda: 63
Nanking, China: 152, 153, 155, 161, 172, 177–79
Nantai, China: 168
Napier, Robert: 28
Napoleon: 10
Nasser, Gamal: 43
National Command Authority: 224, 225
Nationals in foreign countries
    diplomatic protection of: 8, 9, 10, 11, 12, 14, 18, 30, 32, 33, 36, 65
    domiciliary: 8, 11, 29–30
    transient: 8, 11
Naval force, right to use to protect nationals abroad: 13, 14–15, 16, 18–19. *See also* United States Navy Regulations.
Navassa Island: 133
Navassa Phosphate Company: 133
Navy of The United Colonies of North America, Rules for the Regulation of The (1775): 190
Navy of the United States, An Act for The Government of the: 190
Nawa, Vice Admiral: 158
N'Djamena, Chad: 102, 103, 105

# Index

Nesselrode, Prince: 9–10
Nestor: 2
Netherlands: 107, 128, 177
New Orleans, Louisiana: 10
*New Orleans*, USS: 153, 164
*New York*: 146
*Neward*, USS: 142
Newchwang, China: 136
*Niagara*, USS: 165
Nicaragua: 15, 16, 120, 121–22, 135, 137–38, 140, 144, 148, 149, 156–57, 166, 174, 175–76
Nicholson, Admiral: 157
Nicholson, Lieutenant: 123
Niigata, Japan: 128
*Nimitz*, USS: 65–66
Ning-Po, China: 122
*Niobe*: 29
Nipe Bay, Cuba: 155
*Nipsic*, USS: 132
*Noa*, USS: 177–79
Noriega, Manuel: 242
North Atlantic Treaty Organization (NATO): 16
Norway: 140

## O

Obregoso: 118
Offutt, Milton: 17–18
Olivier, M.: 102
Omoa, Honduras: 29
*Oneida*, USS: 126
Operation Almandin II: 108
Operation *Just Cause*: 242–43
Operation Lamentin: 100, 101
Operation Requin: 104
Operation Tacaud: 02
Operation *Urgent Fury*: 241
Oppenheim, L.: 12, 18
*Oregon*, USS: 142
Oreste: 159
Organization of African Unity: 54–56
    Ad Hod Commission on the Congo: 51
Organization of American States (OAS): 57, 61, 62
Organization of Eastern Caribbean States: 242
Ottoman Empire: 11, 34–35, 42

## P

Pacific Mail Line: 131
Pacific Squadron: 123, 140
*Paducah*, USS: 148, 149
Pagoda, China: 168
Palestinians: 238–39, 248
Palma, Thomas Estrade: 147–48
Palmerston Circular of 1848: 8, 10
Panama: 123, 125, 126, 128, 129, 131–32, 137, 142–43, 144–45, 147, 173, 242–43, 248
Panama Canal: 145, 173
Panama City, Panama 125, 131–32, 142–43, 173
Panama Railroad: 125, 129, 131–32, 142–43, 145
*Panther*, USS: 143
Pao Ting Fu, China: 32
Patassé, Félix: 108
Paulis, the Congo: 50, 52, 56
Pearl Lagoon, Nicaragua: 175
Peking, China: 31–32, 137, 139, 141–42, 152, 154, 166, 167, 170–71
Pelew Islands: 14
Pendleton, John S.: 119
*Penobscot*, USS: 128
Perdicaris, Ion: 146–47, 229
Perry, Commodore Matthew C.: 120
Peru: 118, 119
*Petrel*, USS: 136
*Philadelphia*, USS: 140–41
Philippine Division: 152
Phillimore, R.: 7–8
Pierce, Franklin: 122
*Piscatagua*, USS: 128
Plowden, Walter: 27–28
*Plymouth*: 120
Poland: 99
*Pompey*, USS: 155
Potential injury, right of a State to protect citizens abroad against: 2, 235
Port-au-Prince, Haiti: 159, 160
Port-de-Paix, Haiti: 159
Port-Gentil, Gabon: 103
Porter, Cmdr. William D.: 125
*Portsmouth*: 123–24
Portugal and France: 30–31
Portuguese Railway Company: 30–31
Portuguese West Africa: 125
Potter: 47–48
Pradier-Fodere, F.: 11, 18, 30
Prestan: 131
*Preston*, USS: 178

# Index

Prinzapulka, Nicaragua: 175
Property rights and State's right of forcible protection: 10, 33, 138
Prussia: 127, 128
Prussia, King of: 7
Pruyn, Robert H.: 126
Puerto Cabezas, Nicaragua: 175
Puerto Cortés, Honduras: 144, 148, 150, 164, 169
Puerto Plata, Dominican Republic: 146
Puntas Arenas, Nicaragua: 120, 121

## Q

Qubain, F.: 46–47
*Quiros*, USS: 161, 165

## R

Railroads, U.S. intervention to protect in Panama: 125, 129, 131–32, 142–43, 145
*Rainbow*, USS: 157
Raisuli, Sherif Mulai: 146–47, 229
Rama, Nicaragua: 175
Rassam, Hormuzd: 28
Regulations and Instructions Relating to His Majesty's Service at Sea (1772): 188–89, 190, 191, 199
Reid Cabral, Donald: 58–59
Reisman, Michael: 241, 245, 247
Remedial measures open to a protecting State: 1–2
Rendjambe, Joseph: 103
Reprisals: 12, 19, 35, 141, 199, 202
Retortion: 12, 199
Reyes, General John P.: 140
Richardson Construction Company: 158
Right of forcible protection
    acceptable measures that may be taken: 14
    and Accioly: 19–20
    and Arend: 230, 242, 244–45, 247
    and Beck: 230, 242, 244–45, 247
    and Bluntschli: 8–9
    and Bonfils: 10
    and Borchard: 14–15
    and Clark: 13
    counter-restrictionist theory: 243–44, 245–49
    criteria for exercise of: 4–5, 7, 9, 12, 18, 98, 231–32, 235, 239, 247
    and Dunn: 18
    and Fauchille: 15–16
    Grotius and: 2–3, 4
    and Hindmarsh: 18–19

275

historical development of the concept of:1–5, 230–33
and Hodges: 13–14
and Hyde: 16
and international law: 8, 9, 13, 14–16, 17–19, 20, 28, 29, 32, 41–42, 47–49, 62–63, 67–73, 97, 98, 187–88, 232–33, 234–35, 236, 239, 241, 242,243–49
and Moore: 12
and Offutt: 17–18
and Oppenheim: 12
potential abuses of: 18–19, 36–37, 63, 70–71, 98
and Pradier-Fodere: 11
restrictionist theory: 243–45
and Stockton: 12–13
and Vattel: 3
and Winfield: 16–17
and Wolff: 3
Rio de Janeiro, Brazil: 134–35
Rio Grande Bar, Nicaragua: 175
*Rizal*, USS: 167–68
Robeson, George M.: 198
*Rochester*, USS: 170
Roman Empire: 2, 4
Ronzitti, N.: 69
Roosevelt, Franklin D.: 142, 161
Roosevelt, Theodore: 146–48, 229
*Royalist*, HMS: 140–41
Rules for the Regulation of The Navy of The United Colonies of North America (1775): 188, 190
Russia: 31, 137, 157
Russian Island: 164
Russian Revolution of 1917: 163
Russo-Japanese War: 146
Rwanda: 104–05, 107

S

Sacasa, Roberto: 135
*Sacramento*, USS: 171
Said, Mohammed: 29
*St. Lawrence*, USS: 124
St. Louis, Falkland Islands: 117
Saint-Marc, Haiti: 160
*St. Mary's*, USS: 125, 126
Salaverry, General: 118
Sam, Vilburn Guillâume: 150
*Samar*, USS: 164
Samoa: 132, 140–41
*San Francisco*, USS: 133, 144

## Index

San Isidro Air Force Base, Dominican Republic: 59, 60, 61
*San Jacinto*, USS: 124
San Juan del Norte, Nicaragua: 120, 121–22, 140
San Juan del Sue, Nicaragua: 138
San Lorenzo, Honduras: 169
San Pedro, Honduras: 148, 150
Sandwich Islands: 129–30
Santiago, Dominican Republic: 162
Santo Domingo, Dominican Republic: 58, 59, 60, 63, 144, 146, 147, 161–62
*Saratoga*, USS: 154
Saxons: 2
Schachter, O.: 69, 70–71, 72
Schwarzenberg, Prince: 9–10
*Scorpion*, USS: 147, 157
Second Expeditionary Force: 171
Secretary of the Navy: 154, 188, 193, 194, 198, 200, 203, 205, 207, 209, 211, 213, 216, 218, 219, 220, 224, 225
Senegal: 108, 239–40
Seoul, Korea: 132, 135–36, 146
Seward, William: 11–12
Seymour, Admiral: 31
Shanghai, China: 120–21, 122, 124–25, 158, 166, 169–71, 176, 177, 178, 180
Shanghai Volunteer Corps: 169
*Shark*: 119
*Shenandoah*, USS: 127
Ship transportation, U.S. protection of in Panama: 128, 129
Shu-cheng, General Pi: 177
Siciliy: 17
Sino-Japanese War: 135–37, 139
Slater, J.: 59, 60
Smyrna: 167
Solari, Admiral Emilio: 34
South Manchurian Railway: 35
Sovereign, rights of the: 2–5
Soviet Union: 43–44, 64, 99, 163–64, 243
Spain
   action against Mexico: 10, 15–16, 26–27
   and China: 137
   and the Spanish-American War: 138–39
Spanish-American Iron Works: 155
Spanish-American War: 138–39
Standard Fruit and Steamship Company 168
Standard Oil Company: 152, 177–78, 179
Stanleyville, the Congo: 50–51, 52, 53, 54, 56, 57
State responsibility to protect citizens abroad: 1–2, 3, 4, 9, 10, 11, 17–18, 20, 99, 231–32, 233
Steedman, Admiral: 129
Stein: 67–68, 71

Stevens, John H.: 134
Stevenson, Adlai: 51, 52, 55–56, 57, 236
*Stewart*, USS: 173
Stimson, Henry: 176
Stockton, Charles H.: 12–13
Stracber, General: 29
Strauss, Admiral: 167
Sudetenland: 36–37
Suez Canal: 29–30, 43, 97, 98, 234–35
Sugar plantations: 148
Sun Yat-sun: 151
*Supply*, USS: 153
Sutherland, Admiral: 156
Swatow, China: 154, 161
Sweden: 140
Swink, Captain Roy C.: 166
Syria: 34–35, 42, 43, 44, 144

# T

*Tacoma*, USS: 149–50, 159, 165
Taft, William Howard: 147–48
Taku, China: 31–32, 152, 154, 166, 180
Tamasese: 132
Tangier, Morocco: 146
Tarazi, Judge: 69
Tarquins: 2
Tegucigalpa, Honduras: 168, 169
Tehran, Iran: 63–64, 66
Tela, Honduras: 168, 170
Tellini, General Enrico: 34
Terrorist operations: 238–39, 240, 245
Thailand: 237
Théodore: 159, 160
Theodore, Emperor of Abyssinia: 27–28
Tientsin, China: 31–32, 136–37, 139, 142, 154, 167, 170–71, 173, 179–80
Tindemans: 101
Tokyo, Japan: 126
Toncontín, Honduras: 169
Torres, Colonel: 145
Trujillo, Honduras: 148
Trujillo, Rafael: 57
Tsao Kun: 169, 170
Tshisekedi: 106
Tshombe, Moise: 50, 54, 55
Tuan, Marshal: 170–71
Tungchow, China: 166, 167, 170

# Index

Tungshan, China: 168
Tunisia: 99
Turkey: 10, 14, 32, 33, 157, 167
*Tuscarora*, USS: 129–30
Tyntuke Bay, Russia: 164
Tyre: 2

## U

Uganda: 104, 238–39, 248
United Arab Republic: 44–45
United Nations: 16, 244
    Commission of Inquiry: 65
    and Dominican Republic: 62
    multinational force in Rwanda: 107
    Secretary General: 237, 240
United Nations Charter: 41, 223, 232–33, 235, 239, 243, 244, 247, 248–49
    Article 2(4): 36–37, 41–42, 48, 68, 69, 187, 233, 244, 245–46, 249
    Article 39: 64, 98
    Article 40: 98
    Article 41: 64, 98
    Article 51: 41–42, 46, 47, 48, 66–67, 68, 69, 73, 97, 98, 103, 187, 235, 237, 241, 244–45, 246–47, 249
    Chapter VII: 246, 247
United Nations General Assembly
    meetings: 234
    Resolution on the Definition of Aggression: 239
    votes: 242
United Nations Observation Group in Lebanon (UNOGIL) 45
United Nations Operation in the Congo (ONUC): 49–50, 236
United Nations Security Council
    and the Congo: 49–50, 51, 52, 53, 55–56, 98–99, 235–36
    and Egypt: 234–35
    and Entebbe: 239
    failure to act: 244, 245, 247, 248–49
    and forcible protection of nationals: 130, 239, 241, 243
    and Iran: 64, 66, 67
    and Israel: 239
    and Lebanon: 44–45, 46
    and Mauritania: 100
    and Panama: 243
    Resolution 872: 107
United Province of Rio de la Plata: 25
U.S. consulates
    guards for: 18, 119, 120–21, 122, 126, 127, 130, 132, 133–34, 135–37, 139, 140–42, 144, 146–48, 152, 153, 156, 157, 159, 161–62, 163, 165, 166, 167–68, 170, 177–78, 180

U.S. Department of the Navy: 145, 214–15, 217
U.S. Department of State
  and Cuba: 155
  and the Dominican Republic: 59
  and Haiti: 159–60
  and Lebanon: 45
  and Nicaragua: 175
  and rescue of hostages in the Congo: 52
  and right to forcibly protect nationals abroad: 13
*United States Intervention in Lebanon, The*, by Wright: 48
U.S. Naval Station, Guantánamo Bay, Cuba: 155–56, 163
United States Navy Regulations: 187, 189
  1802: 191
  1814: 192, 193
  1818: 192–93
  1821: 93–94, 196
  1841: 194
  1853: 194–95
  1858: 195
  1863: 195–96, 197
  1865: 196–97, 199
  1869: 197–200, 201–02, 204–05
  1870: 200–202, 204–05
  1876: 202, 204–05, 206
  1893: 203–06, 208, 219
  1896: 206–08, 210
  1900 and 1905: 208–10, 212
  1909: 210–12, 214, 215
  1913: 212–15, 217
  1920: 215–17, 219, 220
  1948: 204, 217–20, 221, 222, 223
  1973: 187, 188, 220–23, 225–26
  1990: 187, 188, 198–99, 223–26
*Upshur*, USS: 165
Urena, Rafael Molina: 58, 60
Uruguay: 122–23, 124, 127
Usbecks: 4

## V

Valparaiso, Chile: 133–34
Vattel, E.: 1, 3–5, 8, 11, 20, 231, 232
Venezuela: 16, 33
Vera Cruz, Mexico: 26, 27
Vernet, Louis: 117
Victor Emmanuel II: 17

# Index

Victoria, Queen of England: 28
Vladivostok, Russia: 163, 164

## W

Waldcock: 245
Waldheim, Kurt: 100
*Washington*, USS: 160
Weissman, S.: 57
Wessin, General Wessin y: 59, 60
Western Sahara: 239–40, 247–48. *See also* Mauritania.
Westlake, J.: 11–12
*Wheeling*, USS: 159
Wigny, M. Pierre: 99
Williams, J. E.: 178
Wilson, Huntington: 156
Winfield: 16–17
Wingfield, Thomas C.: 229
*Wisconsin*, USS: 143
Wolff, C.: 1, 3, 20
*Wolsey*, HMS: 178, 179
*Wolverine*, HMS: 179
Woodfred, Cuba: 155
Woolsey, Commodore M. T.: 118
Woosung, China: 124–25, 153
World War I: 33–34
Wright: 47, 48
Wuchang, China: 151–52
Wuchow, China: 165
Wuchow People's Mission Hospital: 165
Wuhu, China: 152, 153

## Y

Yangtze Valley, China: 170–71, 172
Yedo (Tokyo), Japan: 125
Yenkow, China: 136
Yingtze, China: 136
Yochow, China: 154, 165
Yokohama, Japan: 127, 128
*Yorktown*, USS: 136
Young: 50
Yu-hsiang, Feng: 171
Yüan Shinkai: 151, 157

## Z

Zaire: 49–57, 100–101, 105–07
Zamor, General: 159
Zelaya, José Santos: 135, 137–38, 140, 156
Zouérate, Mauritania: 99–100, 101